D1270248

THE ENCYCLOPEDIA OF
ENERGY MEDICINE

DATE DUE

RZ
999
.T49
2010

The Encyclopedia of
ENERGY
MEDICINE

Linnie Thomas

KVCC KALAMAZOO VALLEY
COMMUNITY COLLEGE
LIBRARY

The Encyclopedia of Energy Medicine © 2010 by Linnie Thomas. All rights reserved. No part of this publication may be used or reproduced in any manner whatsoever without written permission, except in the case of brief quotations embodied in critical articles and reviews. For further information, please contact the publisher.

Published by Fairview Press, 2450 Riverside Avenue, Minneapolis, Minnesota 55454. Fairview Press is a division of Fairview Health Services, a community-focused health system, affiliated with the University of Minnesota, providing a complete range of services, from the prevention of illness and injury to care for the most complex medical conditions. For a free current catalog of Fairview Press titles, please call toll-free 1-800-544-8207. Or visit our Web site at www.fairviewpress.org.

Library of Congress Cataloging-in-Publication Data
Thomas, Linnie, 1946-
 The encyclopedia of energy medicine / Linnie Thomas.
    p. cm.
  ISBN 978-1-57749-237-5 (alk. paper)
1. Energy medicine—Encyclopedias. I. Title.
  RZ999.T49 2010
  615.8'515--dc22

                            2010002054

Printed in the United States of America
First Printing: March 2010

14   13   12   11   10   7   6   5   4   3   2   1

Cover design by Laurie Ingram
Interior design by Ryan Scheife, Mayfly Design (www.mayflydesign.net)
Additional illustrations by Bruce A. Wilson (www.brucewilsonart.com)

Medical Disclaimer:
This publication is designed to provide accurate and authoritative information in regard to the subject matter covered. It is sold with the understanding that neither the author nor the publisher is engaged in the provision or practice of medical, nursing, or professional healthcare advice or services in any jurisdiction. If medical advice or other professional assistance is required, the services of a qualified and competent professional should be sought. Neither Fairview Press nor the author is responsible or liable, directly or indirectly, for any form of damages whatsoever resulting from the use (or misuse) of information contained in or implied by these documents.

Dedicated to

Barbara Dahl

CONTENTS

FOREWORD

The curious reader might wonder why a serious scientist, with a long-standing interest in biomedical research, would write a foreword for a book such as *The Encyclopedia of Energy Medicine*. The answers are many.

A few centuries ago energetic phenomena such as electricity and magnetism were considered "occult," a word that simply means secret, not easily understood, or concealed. We could see the effects of these energies, but we could not see the actual forces involved. They were mysterious and they elicited much confusion, debate, and even fear. Before the work of Hans Christian Oersted (1777–1851) in Denmark, Michael Faraday (1791–1867) in England, and André-Marie Ampère (1775–1836) in France, we did not know how to measure these phenomena. Rigorous scientific experiments simply had not been done. Now, thanks to the dedicated work of generations of physicists, we are comfortable with electricity and magnetism and their many everyday applications. This physics has ushered in a new age of electronic technologies that all of us use: cell phones, computers, and digital gadgets of all kinds. Key to this progress is the continuous production of new discoveries and inventions in the fields of physics and electronics.

Continuing progress in physics and biophysics is laying the foundation for a new medicine. Because of this research, therapies that have been disparagingly termed "New Age" are leading to a genuine new medicine and a new health-care system for which everyone has been longing. Biomedical research is playing a key role in establishing the validity of the therapies described in this book. The physics of Oersted, Faraday, Ampère, and their followers is providing the scientific basis for these therapies. From the perspective of the research scientist, the methods documented in this book represent new frontiers for increasing our understanding of living systems. Not only are these frontiers important, they are fascinating and exciting.

A scientific inquiry into energy medicine aims to answer two complementary questions: what does science say about biological energetics, and what does energy medicine tell us about the nature of life?

When I began my inquiry into energy medicine, some twenty-five years ago, there was only scattered interest in the subject in the world of academic medicine. The skepticism was palpable, and there were some who warned that research in this direction was inappropriate for a respectable scientist. I chose to ignore these warnings and delved into the scientific literature, taking advantage of a great resource: the library at the Marine Biological Laboratory in Woods Hole, Massachusetts. I soon discovered that there was a vast and growing volume of reliable evidence about human energetics. This knowledge had been accumulated over the previous century through painstaking work done by highly trained scientists carrying out basic research in biology, physics, and biophysics. Translating that evidence from the language of science into concepts that can be understood by health-care practitioners from all disciplines has become a rewarding career.

In recent years sources of funding have become available that have enabled biomedical researchers to explore the kinds of therapeutic phenomena described in this book. In the United States, much of this funding has come from the relatively new National Center for Complementary and Alternative Medicine and from the other divisions of the National Institutes of Health. There is now enough high-quality research, reported in leading peer-reviewed biomedical journals, to show the most committed skeptics that energy medicine is not a New Age delusion or hallucination. Some of the therapies Linnie Thomas describes here are so well researched that there is little doubt as to their effectiveness. Others await investigation and therefore represent a rich opportunity for investigators looking for an exciting and rewarding line of research.

A few examples of the research that is being done will show how far we have come in validating the therapies described in this book. This research facilitates the application of new and effective methods in hospitals and medical centers. A complete listing of this research would fill several volumes of the same size as this book, so a few examples will give a taste of this trend in biomedicine:

- One of the classic compendiums on research is *Complementary Therapies in Rehabilitation: Holistic Approaches for Prevention and Wellness* by Carol M. Davis, now in its third edition. Dr. Davis is a faculty member at the University of Miami Miller School of Medicine. Her book has opened the minds of health-care professionals worldwide to the idea of complementary therapies in rehabilitation. Her text covers evidence for the efficacy of energy medicine in therapy, prevention, and wellness. Another overview, specifically for physical therapists, is *Complementary Therapies for Physical Therapists: A Theoretical and Clinical Exploration*, edited by Robert A. Charman and published in 2000.

- An outstanding example of a therapy that has been well researched is provided by Healing Touch, which has had an exemplary research program, begun under the direction of Dr. Cynthia Hutchison and continued by Dr. Diane Wind Wardell. More than one hundred studies of Healing Touch have been completed by researchers affiliated with universities and health-care institutions around the world. The results of many of these studies have been reported in leading peer-reviewed journals and are summarized in a booklet that is now in its ninth edition (Wardell, 2008).

- The significance of the research on Healing Touch is that it supports a wide range of similar techniques that probably involve energy field interactions. Moreover, we are learning about the mechanisms involved. An important study has recently been completed under the direction of Gloria Gronowicz, a professor of surgery at the University of Connecticut Health Center. Dr. Gronowicz is a cell biologist specializing in bone cells. Her study showed that Therapeutic Touch performed by trained energy healers significantly stimulated the growth of bone and tendon cells in laboratory culture dishes. The treated cells grew significantly faster and stronger than those receiving a sham treatment, or no treatment at all. In one of the tests, Dr. Gronowicz found that cells treated with Therapeutic Touch grew at double the rate of untreated cells. The cells also absorbed more calcium, the essential mineral for growing strong bones. Dr. Gronowicz and her colleagues also looked at bone cancer cells. A treatment that stimulates growth of cancer cells would obviously be detrimental to people with cancer. But unlike healthy cells, bone cancer cells were not stimulated by Therapeutic Touch; in fact, their growth was inhibited, as documented by a decrease in differentiation and mineralization. These pioneering studies were published in two peer-reviewed research journals (Gronowicz et al., 2008; Jhaveri et al., 2008).

- Another study done in a university medical school environment showed that the application of Reiki significantly reduces noise-induced microvascular leakage in an animal model of stress (Baldwin and Schwartz, 2006). The result provided support for the use of Reiki to minimize effects of environmental stress on research animals and hospital patients. Another study at the same facility has shown that Reiki is effective in modulating heart rate in both stressed and unstressed rats, supporting its use as a stress reducer in humans (Baldwin, Wagers, and Schwartz, 2008).

- Also consider the phenomenon of BioGeometry, discussed here in Section 1. Skeptics could point to the idea of sacred geometry as pure fantasy, even though buildings and sacred sites have been constructed for millennia, with dimensions adhering to ancient geometrical ratios that are especially pleasing to the eye and that seem to have other beneficial effects. Now Dr. Gehan Ahmed Nagy of Egypt, a student of the founder of BioGeometry, Dr. Ibrahim Karim, has studied the effects of the shapes of rooms on laboratory animals. One shape stood out above all others: the hexagon. While this shape has a variety of advantages in terms of reducing heating and cooling costs and structural stability, Dr. Nagy's research indicates important additional advantages in terms of behavior and health (Nagy, 2007). This inquiry into one branch of energetics can be of value to city planners and architects designing spas, hospitals, and other healing facilities.

- Finally, there is a branch of energy medicine that is too new to be discussed in this book, even though it touches on all the therapies described here. This is the study of the physiology of a natural medicine: taking off shoes and socks and walking barefoot on the earth. Study of the physiological changes resulting from barefoot contact with the earth has revealed something profound that connects energy medicine with the very latest in biomedical research. Modern biomedicine is revealing that an energetic condition, inflammation, is the common denominator to just about every chronic disease. The reason inflammation is an energetic condition is that it is characterized by the accumulation of highly charged molecules called free radicals. While there are many diseases and disorders, a common denominator in the healing of all of them seems to be the neutralization of the free radicals with electrons. The electron is the ultimate antioxidant, and it has been suggested that many of the energy therapies have their rapid therapeutic effects by causing the movement of free or mobile electrons through the tissues to sites of inflammation that are interfering with normal structure and function. The surface of the earth is a natural source of antioxidant electrons, and they enter the barefoot person through an important acupuncture point on the ball of the foot known as Kidney 1 (Chevalier et al., 2006). Therapists who connect their patients to the earth, or who connect themselves to the earth, or both, are finding that their methods work better, faster, and easier. One of my bodywork colleagues has increased her practice from a maximum of six sessions per day, which left her exhausted, to nine or more, with plenty of energy to spare at the end of the day. Electrons from the earth are antioxidants and they impart energy to the body (Oschman, 2007).

Progress in medicine and biomedicine is entirely dependent on the development of new ideas and techniques. This is the significance of this book. Linnie Thomas has described a rich diversity of important healing approaches based on energy, each of which teaches us a piece of the puzzle of the nature of health and healing.

The therapies described here are an important part of an emerging new age of medicine and health for several reasons. First, patients are finding a great deal of satisfaction with energetic therapies that often resolve long-standing health issues that have frustrated conventional medicine. The reason: there are medical conditions that are perplexing and that even seem incurable because they are energetic in nature and are therefore unapproachable by health-care systems that leave energy out of the equations of life and health. Many physicians have observed the results of energy medicine treatments and are amazed and delighted to the point that they have begun learning energy therapies to augment their practices. For example, some eighteen hundred physicians have learned acupuncture and joined the American Academy of Medical Acupuncture.

Second, patients are also pleased with the energy practitioners themselves, who usually have more time to listen and find out exactly what their patient is experiencing. This is a major factor in the emergence of the medicine of the future. Energy medicine practitioners have turned out to be normal people with the same caring professionalism, dedication, and comprehensive training typical of anyone in the health professions. Patients are finding energetic methods to be effective, cost-effective, and noninvasive. They are finding the practitioners to be attentive, compassionate, and thorough. The book documents the extensive training and credentialing procedures now in effect for practitioners trained in the many schools of energy medicine.

Practitioners, patients, physicians, biomedical researchers, and hospital administrators are becoming comfortable with the terminology in this field. Energy is being demystified as we come to recognize what it really is. Energy refers to the various phenomena we sense with our eyes (light), ears (sound), touch (heat and vibration), and with our movement system (gravity and the energies of motion). We deal with these energies every moment of our lives. Energetic interactions enable us to sense where we are in the world and to do the things we do. Energy medicine teaches us how to be more efficient and comfortable with the forces of nature, the energies that surround and penetrate our bodies, and that our bodies radiate into the space around us.

In her introduction, the author takes up terminology that is widely used in energy medicine but that has not yet found its way into textbooks of anatomy, physiology, and medicine, even though the terms refer to phenomena that have been discussed and described by sensitive people for millennia. The reason for confusion and skepticism is obvious. There is nothing wrong with the ancient terms. It is just that modern science either has not been able to find ways of examining them or has ignored them. This situation is changing, and terms such as chakras, energy centers, meridians, and auras are gradually being demystified as we acquire more sophisticated tools for the study of human energetics.

Likewise, holism is a term whose time has come. Holism is now a politically acceptable term because of a trend in biomedicine to use the knowledge attained through the past century of reductionist research to "reassemble" the whole organism from its parts, and determine the laws that explain how the parts and systems in the body respond in a coordinated fashion to trauma and illness. The holistic energy therapist spends many hours studying the body as a whole system, and observes the principles of holism in action. Driving this inquiry is the need to appreciate whole-person healing processes that encompass all aspects of life: body, mind, emotions, and spirit.

Many of the methods described in this book rely on our growing appreciation of the clinical importance of human energy fields. These fields, which are now called biofields, have graduated from a source of skepticism and disbelief to measurable physical phenomena. For example, research into the clinical significance of biomagnetic fields produced by the human body is now being done in major medical centers around the world, as attested to by more than 200,000 web pages on biomagnetism as of this writing. The clinical electroencephalogram and electrocardiogram are being supplemented with their magnetic counterparts: the magnetoencephalogram and magnetocardiogram.

This book therefore serves a variety of important purposes. For the student looking for a rewarding career, this is the most comprehensive description of the opportunities available in a tremendously exciting and rapidly growing field. For the researcher looking for new and fertile areas for investigation, there is no better compendium of techniques and concepts waiting to be explored. For patients wondering about alternative therapies, this is an excellent place to start their search. For the hospital administrator, this is the place to find out what these practitioners are doing and how they are credentialed.

The Encyclopedia of Energy Medicine will help restore energetics to its rightful place in the world of health care.

—James L. Oschman, PhD

2008–9 President, International Society for
the Study of Subtle Energies and Energy Medicine

Author of *Energy Medicine: The Scientific Basis* and
Energy Medicine in Therapeutics and Human Performance

References

Baldwin, A. L., and Schwartz, G. E. 2006. "Personal Interaction with a Reiki Practitioner Decreases Noise-Induced Microvascular Damage in an Animal Model." *Journal of Alternative and Complementary Medicine* 12 (1): 15–22.

Baldwin, A. L., Wagers, C., and Schwartz, G. E. 2008. "Reiki Improves Heart Rate Homeostasis in Laboratory Rats. *Journal of Alternative and Complementary Medicine* 14 (4): 417–22.

Charman, R.A. 2000. *Complementary Therapies for Physical Therapists: A Theoretical and Clinical Exploration.* London: Butterworth Heinemann.

Chevalier, G., Mori, K., and Oschman, J. L. 2006. "The Effect of Earthing (Grounding) on Human Physiology." *European Biology and Bioelectromagnetics* (January 31), 600–621.

Davis, C. M., ed. 2009. *Complementary Therapies in Rehabilitation: Holistic Approaches for Prevention and Wellness.* Thorofare, NJ: Slack Incorporated.

Gronowicz, G., Jhaveri, A., Clarke, L. W., et al. 2008. "Therapeutic Touch Stimulates the Proliferation of Human Cells in Culture." *Journal of Alternative and Complementary Medicine* 14 (3): 233–39.

Jhaveri, A., Walsh, S. J., Wang, Y., McCarthy, M. B., and Gronowicz, G. 2008. "Therapeutic Touch Affects DNA Synthesis and Mineralization of Human Osteoblasts in Culture." *Journal of Orthaepedic Research* 26 (11): 1541–46.

Nagy, G. A., 2007. "Towards a Healing City." The International Federation for Housing and Planning (IFHP) 2007 Copenhagen, Futures of Cities. http://www.google.com/search?hl=en&q=gehan+ahmed+nagy+%2B+ifhp+2007+Copenhagen&btnG=Search&aq=f&oq=&aqi= (accessed July 6, 2009).

Oschman, J. L. 2007. "Can Electrons Act as Antioxidants? A Review and Commentary." *Journal of Alternative and Complementary Medicine* 13 (9): 955–67.

Wardell, D. W. 2008. *Healing Touch Research Survey.* Lakewood, CO: Healing Touch International.

ACKNOWLEDGMENTS

I wish to thank the following people:

Carrie Obry and Jill Amack, my editors, for their fine work in making this encyclopedia a far better book than I ever dreamed it could be.

Jody Stevenson, for recognizing the healer in me and making it possible for me to take my first class in Healing Touch.

Janna Moll, for mentoring me through the practitioner certification process and challenging me to move beyond my comfort zone.

Anne Day, for suggesting I teach Healing Touch.

Susan Kiley, for teaching me what it means to be a true professional.

Barbara Dahl, for mentoring me through the instructor program, for all the times she picked me up when I was down, and for her unconditional love and support while I wrote this book.

Cecil Sisk, my mother, whose belief in me never faltered.

Joyce Strahn, Tennie Bottomly, Heidi Katchia, and Elaine Jacobson, for their unending support.

Ted Brunell, for sharing useful information leading to modalities unfamiliar to me.

Tom and Jane Willhite, founders of PSI World Inc. for teaching me the concept of "to think is to create."

Jack and Norine Millay, who were there for me in my darkest hour.

Mark Walker, for help with proofreading.

All the wonderful clerks at the various state departments and government officials throughout the world, for steering me in the right direction for legal information.

Personnel at each of the offices of the modalities listed in this book, for all their patience with my unending questions and persistence.

Powell's Books, for supplying publication information needed for entries in this encyclopedia.

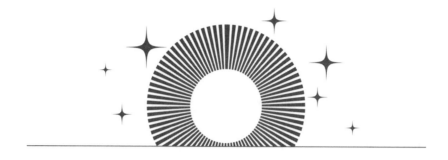

INTRODUCTION

THE FIELD OF ENERGY MEDICINE is loaded with specialized terminology such as energy medicine, holistic medicine, complementary medicine, alternative medicine, integrative medicine, and so on. How does it all fit together?

All of these terms and many more come under the umbrella of holistic medicine, which is a philosophy of caregiving that actively looks at the whole person. It forms a system of health care catering to a cooperative relationship between the physical, emotional, mental, social, psychological, environmental, lifestyle, and spiritual aspects of health and well-being. Holistic medicine includes all modalities of diagnosis and treatment, such as drugs and surgery, as well as natural and non-invasive procedures. It also emphasizes the responsibility of individuals to educate themselves and the importance of their personal efforts to maintain good health.

One of those specialized terms that has grown in popularity with the advent of holistic medicine is "modality." Where it once referred mostly to a therapeutic method or agent used (especially in physical therapy), the term now has become a buzzword that reaches across all forms of medicine. Any one of the many different complementary medicine therapies, from chiropractic to aromatherapy to Healing Touch, is called a modality. I have even heard the word applied to various traditional medicine treatments such as antibiotics. In this book the term applies to each of the individual programs within the field of energy medicine.

Energy medicine is generally understood as a subset of holistic medicine that consists of two branches. One branch focuses on the use of electrical equipment to assess or stimulate a part of the body. One of the better-known examples of this is the Transcutaneous Electrical Nerve Stimulation machine, or TENS, that encourages the body to produce pain-relieving chemicals by sending electrical impulses to the brain through a corresponding area of pain. This is a separate branch of energy medicine that we will not be pursuing. In this book, we use the term "energy medicine" to refer to the therapeutic use of a practitioner's or healer's hands to assess and balance the human energy field and enable healing and wholeness.

Energy medicine is a complementary body of work that integrates other forms of medicine. It is not intended to be a substitute for any other form of medicine, nor do energy medicine practitioners consider it an "alternative" medicine. To illustrate, I like to use the example of a person who has the unfortunate experience of breaking his leg. It is a nasty break in which the skin is torn and the bone has snapped in half. On its own, the body can heal the leg—perhaps not with full functionality restored, but in such a way that at least the person will recover from this serious injury. If a surgeon sets the bone, however, the leg will heal faster and the patient most likely will be able to walk again. If the surgeon also stitches up the wound, the leg will heal with less scarring. If the wound is sterilized, the leg will heal with less chance of infection. If the patient is given antibiotics, he will have a chance to heal without complications such as a staph infection. Similarly, energy healers believe that if they balance the disturbed field surrounding the injury, the leg will heal faster with fewer complications and less pain.

Energy Perception

While the techniques employed by various modalities throughout this encyclopedia may be similar, the way individual healers perceive the energy field changes considerably from person to person. Barbara Ann Brennan, founder of the Barbara Brennan School of Healing (page 151), and John F. Thie, founder of Touch for Health (page 127), helped set the precedent for what I call traditional Western energy medicine, which perceives the energy field as composed of seven layers penetrating and surrounding the body. This field is also called an aura, described by Donna Eden as a multilayered field that interacts with other energies in the environment, filtering out unwanted energies and drawing in others that are useful to the body. In much of ancient literature the term "aura" referred to subtle color radiances surrounding the body. *Webster's New World Dictionary* defines the aura as "a particular atmosphere or quality that seems to surround a person or thing." In energy medicine today, aura refers to an energy field that penetrates and surrounds the body.

According to John White and Stanley Krippner in their book, *Future Science: Life Energies and the Physics of Paranormal Phenomena* (New York: Anchor Books, 1977), references made to the human energy field are found in ninety-seven different cultures. Richard Gerber, in his book *Vibrational Medicine: New Choices for Healing Ourselves* (Santa Fe, NM: Bear & Company, 1988), states that the human energy field has seven layers containing the seven centers of energy known as chakras. With the exception of the crown and root chakras, the energy centers are attached in both the front and back to the hara line, sometimes called the hara column. This line extends from high above the top of the head down through the base of the spine, out of the body and into the earth. As shown in the illustration on page 5, each chakra has a specific focus and purpose. The crown connects the individual to the universal source and the root connects the person to the ground.

The early written records of the chakras occur in the *Yoga Upanishads* (circa 600 BC) and later in the *Yoga Sutras of Patanjali* (circa 200 BC). At that time, chakras were described as psychic centers of consciousness. In 1919, an Englishman named Arthur Avalon translated two texts—the *Sat-Cakra-Nirupana,* written by an Indian pundit in 1577, and the *Padaka-Pancaka,* written in the tenth century—that also list seven basic chakras existing within the energy field around the spine. Located at the top of the head, brow, throat, heart, solar plexus (just below the rib cage), sacrum (just above the pubic bone), and at the base of the spine. Each chakra spins outward both from the front and the back.

Although the seven-chakra model based on these ancient Indian texts is the most commonly accepted understanding, some modalities differ. For example, Polarity Therapy recognizes six chakras, Pranic Healing recognizes eleven, Melchizedek

Method, thirty-three, and SHEN Therapy, eight. In addition, many modalities recognize 256 smaller chakras located wherever there is a bone joint in the body.

In addition to the chakras, running within the body are also pathways of energy called "meridians." Proof of the existence of meridians was provided by a French doctor, Pierre de Vernejoul. He injected a harmless radioactive isotope into an acupressure point located on a meridian. Using a gamma-imaging camera, he traced the radioactive isotope as it traveled through the body. It followed the meridian channels documented by the Chinese over five thousand years ago. He injected the isotope into areas of the body that did not connect to the meridians and the isotope formed a random pattern. According to traditional Chinese medicine, meridians consist of fourteen specific pathways that deliver energy throughout the body. Each organ and physiological system is fed energy by a meridian. Some practitioners count twenty-four meridians, as twelve of the meridians are actually made up of pairs mirroring each other on opposite sides of the body. Our understanding of meridian pathways has not changed for thousands of years.

Some of the meridians travel up the body and others travel down the body. The first meridian is called the "central meridian" and travels from the perineum up to the middle of the lower lip. The "governing meridian," the second energy pathway, goes from the base of the spine up the back and over the head, and ends at the middle of the upper lip. Some meditations suggest putting the tip of the tongue on the roof of the mouth to connect these two meridians while meditating, allowing a continuous circuit of energy. These are the only two meridians that travel in somewhat of a straight line and thus are easy to describe. The pairs of meridians consist of the stomach, spleen, heart, small intestine, bladder, kidney, circulation sex, triple warmer, gall bladder, liver, lung, and colon (large intestine) meridians (see page 7).

Meridians are classified as either yin or yang depending on which direction they flow. Yin energy in traditional Chinese medicine is feminine and flows upward from the feet toward the head and from the shoulders toward the fingertips. Yang energy is masculine and flows from the head to the feet and from the fingertips to the shoulders. Yin meridians provide energy to nourish the body and are passive. Yang meridians are active and protective.

Energy Centers

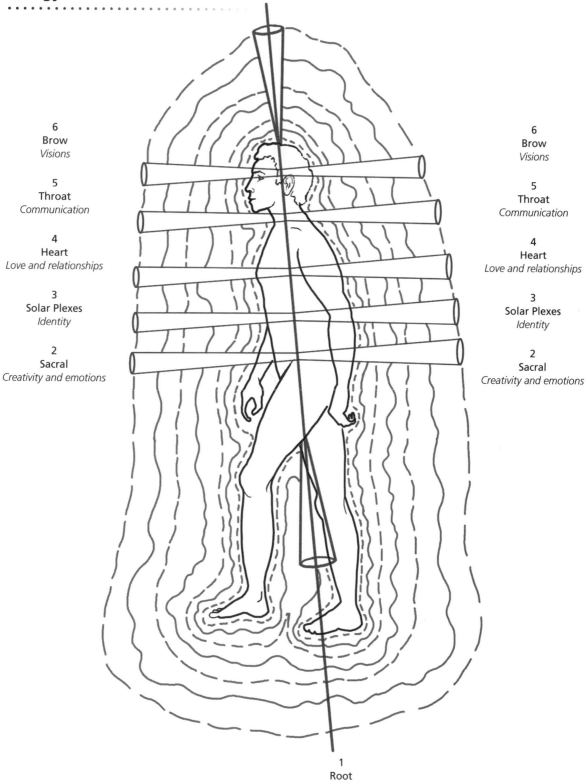

7
Crown
Spiritual connections

6
Brow
Visions

5
Throat
Communication

4
Heart
Love and relationships

3
Solar Plexes
Identity

2
Sacral
Creativity and emotions

6
Brow
Visions

5
Throat
Communication

4
Heart
Love and relationships

3
Solar Plexes
Identity

2
Sacral
Creativity and emotions

1
Root
Survival and grounding

Choice of Modalities

I have investigated over 250 different healing schools and programs. When choosing the modalities for this book, I looked for professionalism, longevity, and diversity. The modalities presented in this book have demonstrated they have staying power and the ability to reach a wide audience, but the field is constantly growing and evolving. Each of the modalities included in this encyclopedia offers something unique.

A few of the modalities planned for this book had to be deleted due to scheduling considerations. If possible, I will put them in a later edition. A number of new modalities have also come to my attention. If they meet my criteria they will also be included in the next edition.

One of the most important steps a person can take in the study of energy medicine is to discover how his or her body and mind recognize the energy field and the fluctuations within the field. Once you know how you personally recognize differences and similarities in the energy field, you can develop that ability with lots of practice. One reason there are so many energy healing models is because the founders of each modality have built a structure around their unique ability to detect differences and similarities in the field. Spend time with all of the modalities contained in this book and inquire into those that appeal to you, and remember to take care of your own physical and spiritual health. If you do not take care of yourself, you cannot take care of others.

Important Considerations

Some modalities have credentialing that provides continuing education units (CEUs) and certification. For example, several modalities issue CEUs provided by the American Holistic Nurses Association, which is accredited as an Approver of Continuing Education in Nursing by the American Nurses Credentialing Center's Commission on Accreditation. The program or school must apply for and be accepted by the organizations that provide CEUs. The program must prove its curriculum is of educational value to the student before the provider will allow the issuance of CEUs. Many states and/or nursing organizations require nurses to complete twenty hours of continuing education each year. The same is true for massage

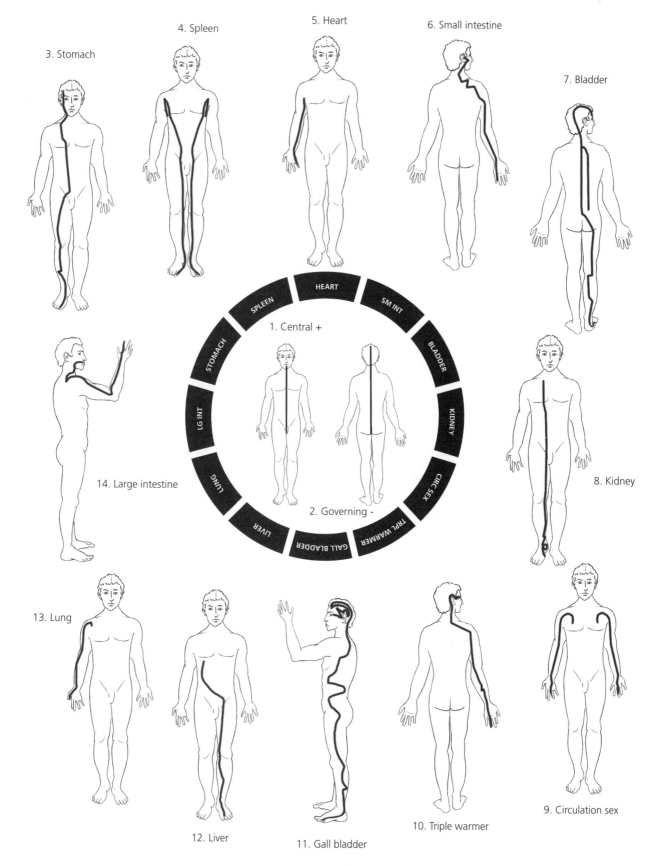

3. Stomach

4. Spleen

5. Heart

6. Small intestine

7. Bladder

14. Large intestine

1. Central +

2. Governing -

8. Kidney

13. Lung

12. Liver

11. Gall bladder

10. Triple warmer

9. Circulation sex

SPLEEN HEART SM INT BLADDER KIDNEY CIRC SEX TRPL WARMER GALL BLADDER LIVER LUNG LG INT STOMACH therapists and many other medical practices. Where possible, the providers of the continuing education units are listed in each chapter to enable the potential student to choose which one applies to his or her needs.

Achieving certification adds credibility to your work and shows you are serious enough about your practice to go the extra mile. Be aware of who supplies the certification and what credentials are associated with it. For instance, the Holistic Nurses Association endorses Healing Touch and influences the certification process. An applicant must have documented one hundred healings and have done a case study as part of the requirements for certification. As a result, certified Healing Touch practitioners are much respected in hospitals throughout the world. Remember to also monitor and be very cognizant of your own healing abilities, as being handed a certificate at the end of a workshop doesn't necessarily mean you are proficient in that healing modality.

In addition, some states require licensing of some kind before you can practice energy healing therapies. Be aware of the difference between licenses, which are issued by the government, and proficiency, which is determined by healing programs through certification. Even though some modalities say they offer licensing, they really are offering certification unless they have a government agency through which they issue a license.

Medical licenses for nursing, physical therapy, and the like will apply only if energy work is a part of your job description. As a nurse you may do energy work on a patient and log it on a patient's chart (and are covered by the nursing regulations to do so), but payment for the energy work must fall within your nursing salary and be part of your job description to obtain a medical license. If you set up a private practice on your own and accept payment directly from your clients, you must follow the massage or health regulations in your state or country for energy work regardless of whether or not you are licensed as a nurse. This is also true for ministers. In years past, energy healers could become ordained ministers and avoid massage laws. The laying on of hands was considered part of the ministerial ritual and the healer's clients became the congregation. This is no longer true. If therapeutic laying on of hands is part of a minister's job description and he or she is paid to do this by way of a salary, the massage laws do not apply. If the minister sets up a practice in which he or she is paid directly by the client, the massage laws, counseling laws, and so on must be followed. See the Legalities section of this book for more information on massage laws.

On a More Personal Note

I began this work when I was offered a scholarship to the healing school of my choice. At the time I had no knowledge of energy work, and the reams of uncultivated information on the Internet did not help very much. I had heard of the Barbara Brennan School, but even with a scholarship it was more than I could afford at the time. I looked at Reiki, but I needed something with more science behind it.

My college major was nuclear engineering and physics has always been of interest to me. Looking back, I think my interest in nuclear physics was really a search for God. Coming from a family of engineers, I needed science in order to study energy healing. Fortunately, someone I knew had taken Healing Touch. She put me in contact with the Healing Touch office and, to my delight, a class was scheduled in my neighborhood a few weeks later. I took the class and it changed my life completely. I had a lifetime of experience working with reason and logic, and I learned how to pair that with my natural intuition. Three years later, I was certified as a practitioner and two years after that I was certified as an instructor in Healing Touch. I have since taken classes in at least a third of the modalities offered in this book and have received treatments from practitioners of most of the modalities listed here (and many that are not).

My students frequently ask me what is the right form of energy healing for them to practice. I encourage them to explore their own abilities and to look for modalities that match their comfort zones. I needed science, while other students don't necessarily need this type of foundation. Some people prefer credentials, and others want to do healing work without a lot of titles and paperwork.

The entries in this book have been separated into four categories to help you find one of interest to you. The Eastern section includes modalities stemming from traditional Chinese medicine and healing techniques from other Asian countries. The Western section includes modalities with a lot of science as part of their curriculum. The Spiritual section includes techniques with a religious or spiritual foundation.

The Shamanic section includes healing programs that use some of the traditional shamanic tools such as drumming, journeying, and crystals.

Because of the rapid growth and continuing research in the field of energy medicine, information in this book is subject to change without notice.

Welcome to the exciting world of energy medicine. I hope you discover that there is something here for you.

In good health,
Linnie Thomas

EASTERN

WHEN ENCOUNTERING THE TERMS "Eastern medicine" or "Eastern philosophy," many people naturally think of traditional Chinese medicine, but the Chinese have been given credit for Eastern medicine techniques simply because they are excellent record keepers. Ancient Chinese medicine has had many outside influences. One of the biggest was traveling monks from India who shared their knowledge of Ayurveda—a form of holistic health care that is known to have been in existence five thousand years ago and is suggested to date back as much as ten thousand years—with the Chinese, Tibetans, Greeks, the Ottoman Empire, and others. Ayurveda was influenced by conquering nomadic tribes from other countries who brought with them medical practices that were incorporated into Ayurvedic medicine. In addition, Chinese trade with the Mongols, Siberians, Japanese, and Tibetans brought opportunities for sharing healing knowledge. When the popularity of Buddhism spread, Buddhist monks brought their knowledge of healing from India to China and Tibet, with many Buddhists staying in China to establish schools.

Traditional Chinese medicine maintains that everything in the universe, including human beings, is governed by the five elements in nature: wood, water, fire, earth, and metal (with some traditions substituting ether for metal). Each element is associated with a season, a body organ, one of the five senses, and a color. The chart below demonstrates the simplified relationships among each of the five elements.

Element	Wood	Fire	Earth	Metal	Water
Season	Spring	Summer	Late summer and early fall	Autumn	Winter
Organs	Liver and gall bladder	Heart and intestines	Stomach and spleen/ pancreas	Lungs and colon	Kidneys and bladder
Sense	Eye	Tongue	Touch	Nose	Ear
Color	Green	Red	Yellow	White	Blue

Another concept that forms the foundation of traditional Chinese medicine is the yin/yang theory of balanced polar opposites. Yin energy is feminine. People with slow metabolisms and chronic illnesses and who are introspective are said to have yin energy. Yang energy is masculine. People with acute illnesses and quick metabolisms and who are very outgoing are said to have yang energy. People with yin energy need to be energized, while people with yang energy need to release energy to bring them back into balance energetically. Acupuncture is one the best-known modalities in traditional Chinese medicine. Qigong and various forms of acupressure also have a Chinese heritage, along with the ancient Chinese healing wisdom involving herbs, massage, diet, and exercise.

A practitioner of the Eastern healing arts asks more questions than his or her Western counterpart. The healer will want to know the client's occupation and sources of stress on the job and at home. The intake interview will involve questions about hobbies, religion, and relaxation methods such as meditation. The Eastern medicine practitioner looks for clues as to where one or more imbalances may be found in the energy system of the client.

With the exception of BioGeometry, the modalities in this section stem from long-standing theories of traditional Chinese medicine. Some of them come by way of Japan or Tibet. BioGeometry is Egyptian in origin, and even the Egyptians were influenced by traditional Chinese medicine. Some of the BioGeometry techniques originate from the ancient Chinese way of thinking and thus belong with the other modalities in this Eastern section.

ACUPRESSURE

ACUPRESSURE MAY BE THE OLDEST known energy healing technique. The earliest known source of written text that includes acupressure is found in the *Huang Di Nei Jing Su Wen* (*The Yellow Emperor's Classic of Internal Medicine*). Compiled around 304–205 BC, this text records a dialogue between Huang Di, the Yellow Emperor, and his physician, Qi Bo, in which they discuss the whole spectrum of Chinese medicine known at that time.

Historical records of acupressure are found in India, China, Korea, and Japan. In a medical treatise from 1550 BC called *The Papyrus Ebers*, the Egyptians describe twelve meridians. The South African Bantu scratched themselves in certain places on their bodies to heal disease. A mummified man approximately five thousand years old was found in the Italian Alps with pressure points tattooed on his body. The first written recordings of *qi,* the Chinese word for energy, are found in Shang dynasty oracle bones dating somewhere between the sixteenth and eleventh centuries BC.

Like acupuncture, acupressure uses the meridian system for healing purposes. A meridian, also known as an energy tract, is a pathway in the body where energy flows. (For a description of yin/yang and the meridian system, see pages 4, 7, and 14.) Along these energy tracts are points where energy can collect, stagnate, and become blocked due to stress, trauma, or illness. By applying pressure to these points—known as acupressure points, acupuncture points, acupoints, or pressure points—the energy is released to continue its flow through the meridian system. Major acupressure points are called trigger points. These correspond with areas along the meridians where energy is most likely to congest, so practitioners often work with them first.

Traditional acupressure practitioners use their fingers, thumbs, and elbows to apply pressure firmly but gently for a few seconds and then release. This is repeated a number of times depending on the problem and the location of the pressure point. Applying pressure at these points encourages a corresponding increase in blood flow to the area along with increased flexibility of related muscles. Pressure points for various illnesses may be found near the problem area or on a distant part of the body. For example, pressure points for kidney problems are found on the soles of the feet.

A well-trained practitioner with sensitive perception skills can feel the trigger points by noticing subtle changes while moving his or her hands over the client's skin. In addition, charts are available that clearly delineate the trigger points and acupressure points along the meridians, including specialized depictions of the face, hands, feet, ears, and tongue. Old texts include 360 to 500 acupressure points, whereas contemporary charts include over 2,000 pressure points. Some practitioners specialize in certain areas, such as reflexologists, who focus on the feet, hands, and ears.

Some practitioners like to use massage along with applying pressure at the various trigger and acupressure points. Practitioners in Japan have developed a modality of acupressure called Shiatsu (page 71), which also incorporates a rocking motion, limb rotation, stretches, and meditations.

Sessions usually take about an hour, starting with a discussion of how acupressure works and an intake interview, including questions about a client's lifestyle, habits, nutrition, and symptoms. The practitioner asks questions about the client's physical, mental, emotional, and spiritual issues to see if they pertain to the specified problem. The practitioner will test for tenderness at various acupressure points, and may also check the client's pulse and feel for the temperature of a diseased or imbalanced area. Once the intake interview is complete, the practitioner performs the treatment and concludes by monitoring changes that have occurred and deciding whether further treatment is needed.

Acupressure frequently falls under massage licensing rules and laws. Even though there is no massage stroking involved, enough pressure is applied to move the skin. Many states and some countries define massage as a technique that involves the movement of the skin and, as such, require a massage license to maintain an acupressure practice.

Course Descriptions

Acupressure is taught in most massage schools, and there are very few schools that specialize in acupressure alone. The Acupressure Institute is one that is recognized by the state of California. Students who complete their basic program may practice and charge for their work in that state.

The **150-Hour Basic Program** addresses several forms of acupressure and includes nine classes: six required and three elective. During the course of the program, students learn about seventy-five acupressure points and eight styles of bodywork. Required classes include:

▶ **Fundamentals of Acupressure:** Includes 12 class hours of hands-on introduction to the main forms of acupressure, point location, self-acupressure methods, and Eastern breathing exercises.

▶ **Basic Acupressure: Extraordinary Channels and Points:** Includes 15 class hours of using and combining over forty main acupressure points, associated symptoms, and point interrelationships.

▶ **Intermediate Acupressure: Twelve Organ Meridians:** Includes 15 class hours with Basic Acupressure Class as a prerequisite. Students explore topics such as the points and direction of each organ meridian, traditional imbalances and organ associations, meridian pulse reading and traditional face reading, the body clock, including the use and location of source, entry, and exit points, and how to move and transform the energy of the body.

▶ **Advanced Acupressure:** Includes 15 class hours with basic and intermediate acupressure classes as prerequisites. Students study the correlations between the meridians, the seasons, climate, color, and the five senses in addition to various advanced acupressure techniques.

▶ **Anatomy and Physiology:** Over 18 class hours, students receive an overview of anatomical and physiological interrelationships as they pertain to acupressure, including major organs, muscles, systems, and bones and the anatomical positions of pressure points.

▶ **Business Practice and Ethics:** Over 4 class hours, students discuss ethical issues and learn important aspects of doing business, including advertising, taxes, license requirements, fees, professional associations, and insurance.

Elective classes, each one consisting of 12 hours of course instruction, are also offered as part of the 150-house basic program, including the following.

▶ **Acupressure Oil Massage:** With a prerequisite of basic acupressure, students learn basic techniques of Swedish and Esalen massage, draping and good body mechanics, and where acupressure points and meridians are incorporated into a full-body oil massage.

▶ **Acu-Yoga:** Students learn to combine acupressure points with yoga postures for self-treatment, how to work with the meridians and the chakras, deep breathing exercises, and self-care for common stress-related problems.

▶ **Ashiatsu (Barefoot Shiatsu):** Taught on floor mats with a prerequisite of Zen Shiatsu or Fundamentals of Acupressure, students learn full-body treatment in both prone and supine positions using feet and hands, how to use breath and body mechanics, and how to explore the assessment process in giving Ashiatsu.

▶ **Reflexology and Acupressure:** Students learn foot, hand, and ear reflexology points and how to explore the complementary techniques of acupressure massage and reflexology.

▶ **Touch for Health:** With a prerequisite of intermediate acupressure, students learn to use muscle testing and the main points through which to derive information about structural, emotional, and nutritional imbalances.

▶ **Tui Na I (Chinese Massage):** Taught on floor mats, students explore the fundamentals of this special type of massage.

▶ **Zen Shiatsu:** Also taught on floor mats, students learn this integrated style of Shiatsu, including how to stimulate points and release tension in the neck, shoulders, back, legs, and face and how to give a full-length body session that incorporates a wide range of motion.

The 200-Hour Program encourages students to develop a specialty for their practice. Students choose from a list of specialties and take the classes offered in that particular program. In addition, students take an apprentice training and do 10 hours of advanced clinical practice sessions. Some of the areas of study include the following.

▶ **Acupressure for Seniors:** With a prerequisite of the 150-Hour Basic Training or equivalent, students learn the following:

- Acupressure points and bodywork skills for relieving arthritic pain
- The stresses of aging, stiffness, and chronic fatigue
- Hands-on techniques for working with patients in a residential nursing home, including emotional balancing techniques and the key acupressure points for enhancing memory and concentration

▶ **Advanced Acupressure:** With a prerequisite or the 150-Hour Basic Training or equivalent, students learn advanced acupoint therapeutics and energy work skills, a deeper understanding of the different styles and theories of advanced energy work, including specific practical applications, craniosacral therapy, and guided imagery.

▶ **Sports Acupressure:** With a prerequisite of 150-Hour Basic Training or the equivalent, students learn how to:

- Apply acupressure at neuromuscular trigger points for relieving pain
- Enhance an athlete's performance while increasing muscle tone and physical endurance
- Stretches, points, and bodywork skills for warm-up and warm-down routines
- How Asian bodywork can give athletes an edge
- Specific acupressure points for relieving injuries

▶ **Stress Management:** With a prerequisite of 150-Hour Basic Training or the equivalent, students learn:

- How to give professional acupressure sessions in an office chair, on a mat, or on a massage table

- Methods for relieving stress disorders such as headaches, insomnia, chronic fatigue, and anxiety
- Thai massage in conjunction with acupressure
- Stretching for self-care
- The four aspects of stress management: point therapeutics, acupressure techniques, theory of Asian health care, and hands-on stress reduction applications

▶ **Women's Health:** With a prerequisite of 150-Hour Basic Training or the equivalent, students learn the following:

- How to work with the most appropriate acupressure points and meridians for relieving common physiological and emotional imbalances common to women
- Herbology, imagery, hypnosis, stretching, and nutrition
- Acupressure applications during pregnancy, birthing, and menopause

The 850-Hour Program prepares students to be professional acupressure therapists, with the 150-Hour Basic Training or equivalent as a prerequisite. This course prepares students to take the national exam for Asian Bodywork Therapy. Students who pass receive certification in Asian Bodywork Therapy. To finish the course students must complete the following:

- An entrance exam to establish their basic understanding of acupressure concepts and practices
- 360 hours of advanced training classes
- 105 hours of anatomy and kinesiology classes
- 30 hours of apprenticeship
- 50 hours of self-development, including 25 hours of Tai Chi
- 150 hours of project and/or teacher training
- 110 hours of documented clinical practice
- A minimum of 40 hours of advanced clinical practice sessions
- Four private 1-hour instructor consultations and 1-hour evaluation

Continuing Education Units: Yes, provided by the California Board of Registered Nurses in compliance with Title 16, Division 14, Sections 1456 and 1457, and the California Code of Regulations.

Certification: Yes, granted by the American Organization for Bodywork Therapies of Asia. Graduates of the 850-Hour Program qualify to take the Asian Bodywork Therapy exam given by the National Certification Commission for Acupuncture and Oriental Medicine. Those who pass the NCCAOM exam are certified as a Diplomat of Asian Bodywork Therapy (Dipl. ABT). Another exam option available to graduates is the Massage Therapy Exam given by the National Certification Board for Therapeutic Massage and Bodywork (NCBTMB). Those who pass the NCBTMB exam are Licensed Massage Therapists (LMT). Certification for each of the three programs is granted when a student passes a final evaluation of that program.

Participants: Students must be eighteen years of age or older. Students must also have an interview with an Acupressure Institute counselor, either in person or by phone.

Legalities: Each state has different requirements. Most require some form of licensing for acupressure. Some states and many cities ask for a thumbprint and do a background check before a license is approved. The same is true for other countries. Consult your local or national acupressure experts for more information.

Code of Ethics/Standards of Practice: Yes.

Suggested Reading

Bauer, Matthew D. *The Healing Power of Acupressure and Acupuncture.* New York: Penguin, 2005.

Gach, Michael Reed, PhD. *Acupressure for Emotional Healing: A Self-Care Guide for Trauma, Stress, and Common Emotional Imbalances.* New York: Random House, 2004.

Availability: Classes take place at the Acupressure Institute in California and on the East Coast. For a session in your area, go to www.acupressureinstitute.com.

Resources
· ·

Acupressure Institute, 1533 Sattuck Avenue, Berkeley, CA 94709, 800-442-2232, info@acupressure.com, www.acupressureinstitute.com

Bibliography
· ·

Bauer, Matthew D. *The Healing Power of Acupressure and Acupuncture.* New York: Penguin, 2005.

Gach, Michael Reed. www.acupressureinstitute.com.

Sciammarella, Joseph. *Medical Acupuncture Benefits, Side Effects, History, and Origin,* www.emedicinehealth.com/medical_acupuncture/article_em.htm.

Suvow, Scott. *History of Acupuncture in China.* www.acupuncturecare.com.

ACUPUNCTURE

ACUPUNCTURE IS THE TECHNIQUE of inserting extremely thin needles painlessly into the skin at various shallow depths along specific points on the body's meridian system to balance energy, ease pain, and help heal disease. Acupuncture is one of the fundamental techniques of traditional Chinese medicine, a holistic practice using techniques such as acupuncture, acupressure, massage, herbal medicine, Tai Chi, and Qigong to promote healing. Qi (also known as "chi"), the body's inherent life force energy, travels through the body along the pathways called meridians. When the forces of yin (low activity or energy) and yang (high activity or energy) are balanced in the body, qi flows freely; but illness, injury, or stress may cause qi to become blocked along one of the meridians. Acupuncture rebalances the energy flow, releases congested energy, and restores the body to its natural state of harmony.

Given the long history of acupuncture in numerous regions around the world, its origins are somewhat lost in antiquity. Some postulate that it was conceived after noticing that suffering soldiers felt relief when hit by arrows in certain places on their body. Another theory is that acupressure practitioners were able to put more pressure on a given spot on the body by using a small stone rather than their fingers. As a result, the technique may have progressed by experimenting with the decreasing size of the stones, until eventually needles were discovered to be effective. The earliest known text on traditional Chinese medicine, including acupuncture, is found in the *Huang Di Nei Jing Su Wen* (*The Yellow Emperor's Classic of Internal Medicine*). This landmark text, compiled around 304–205 BC, records a dialogue between Huang Di (the Yellow Emperor) and his physician (Qi Bo), in which they discuss the whole spectrum of Chinese medicine known at that time.

Going beyond traditional Chinese medicine, history shows that acupuncture and acupressure were practiced in places other than China. In a medical treatise called *The Papyrus Ebers*, the Egyptians describe the twelve meridians. The South African Bantu scratched certain areas of the body to heal disease. Arabians used hot metal probes on their ears. Eskimos employed a simple system of acupuncture using sharp stones. Native tribes in Brazil inserted darts into their bodies at specific places to cure disease. The first acupuncture instruments were made of bone or flint and were called Bian stones in China. In the search for smaller instruments, the Chinese also worked with bamboo. When the use of metals became popular, needles were made from iron, copper, bronze, silver, and gold. Modern acupuncture needles are made of stainless steel with small handles and come in numerous sizes and lengths.

In 1671, a Jesuit priest brought acupuncture to Europe and coined the name from the Latin *acus* (meaning needle) and *punctura* (meaning puncture). The first mention of acupuncture as a medical treatment in the United States was in Dr. William Osler's medical text *The Principles and Practice of Medicine* written in 1892. The 1901 edition of *Grey's Anatomy* mentions acupuncture for the relief of sciatica discomfort.

Today, acupuncture is widely recognized by allopathic and alternative practitioners around the world as an effective complementary healing practice. The efficacy of acupuncture has been well studied and documented. An example of this is the work of Zang-Hee Cho, a professor of radiological sciences and psychiatry at the University of California at Irvine. He uses functional magnetic resonance imaging (MRI) to show changes in the brain while a patient undergoes acupuncture treatment.

According to an article written by Merrily Helgesen entitled "East Meets West" for *Today@UCI*, an ezine publication for the University of California at Irvine, and published August 29, 2002, Cho, along with Dr. John Longhurst, professor of medicine, and Dr. Edward K. Wong, a neuro-ophthalmologist, worked together to set up the research. Twelve students volunteered to be the subjects.

The first half of the study involved vision. Each of the students received light stimulus to the eyes and the response in the brain activity was recorded. An acupuncture needle was inserted near the little toe of each student. According to acupuncture theory, that place on the body, known as UB67, contains an acupuncture point for eye problems. The response in brain activity from the needle insertion was identical to the stimulus by light to the eyes. Needle insertion a few centimeters from that point produced no change in brain activity.

The second half of the study concerned auditory responses. The students were subjected to audio stimulus in the form of music. A needle inserted into the hand of each student at acupoint SJ5 showed brain activity at the same place as the music stimuli. In both cases, no known physical pathway can explain the immediate brain response.

The use and acceptance of acupuncture are growing. A report of a survey written by the editorial staff of *Acupuncture Today* (January 2003, vol. 4, issue 1) stated that nearly 10 percent of the population in the United States have tried acupuncture and nearly 60 percent said they would consider it as a treatment option. Of those receiving treatment, 82 percent stated they were satisfied with their treatments. A survey published online by BioMed Central Ltd. in April 2008 stated that 9.2 percent of the Australian population used acupuncture as a form of treatment, most commonly for back pain and related issues. Over 90 percent of the Australians receiving acupuncture reported it to be helpful. The Japanese Science and Technology Agency, in a report published in 2005, cites 10,300 acupuncture clinics with 54,400 practicing acupuncturists operating in Japan.

An acupuncture session takes approximately an hour, starting with an intake interview by the acupuncturist. The first visit may take a little longer, as the acupuncturist needs to gather symptom information and ensure the client understands the procedure. With the client lying fully clothed on his or her back, the acupuncturist inserts the needles and leaves the client to relax in the room, returning approximately twenty minutes later to remove the needles and wrap up the session. The points where the needles are inserted, called acupuncture points, were traditionally conceived along three-hundred-plus acupuncture points corresponding to the body's meridian system. Today, the practice has expanded to include more than two thousand acupuncture points charted around the body, including the hands, feet, and ears, used to balance qi and promote healing. Licensed acupuncturists are trained to look at illness holistically by assessing the client's energy system, lifestyle, emotional conditions, amount of rest, nutrition, the temperature of unbalanced areas, and the effects of the environment, to name a few.

Acupuncture is an in-depth course of study that requires a license in most states and countries around the world. There are many different schools of acupuncture and Oriental medicine. Most schools require at least two years of college and many require a college degree. In addition to acupuncture, most schools include other forms of Oriental medicine, such as the use of herbs, and some traditional Western medicine classes, such as anatomy, physiology, and pathology in their curriculum. As licensed acupuncturists are not considered primary care providers, they rely on the diagnosis of a primary care physician to determine the client's condition, and usually work as partners with other medical providers.

Course Descriptions

Increasing demand for acupuncturists has created a need for more schools. As of 2009 the Accreditation Commission for Acupuncture and Oriental Medicine (ACAOM) has over sixty schools and colleges either accredited or in candidacy status. The Council of Colleges of Acupuncture and Oriental Medicine was established in 1982 to promote educational excellence in the fields of acupuncture and Chinese medicine. Members of the council must have accreditation or be candidates for accreditation with the ACAOM.

The following representative acupuncture curriculum is offered by one of the oldest Eastern medicine colleges in the United States, the Oregon College of Oriental Medicine. The school offers a master's degree in traditional Oriental medicine and a doctorate degree for licensed acupuncturists.

The **master's program** is a four-year academic program, including the following courses of study.

▶ **Qi Cultivation** is a two-year program. Students study one year of Qigong and a second year of advanced Qigong or Tai Chi. These internal development arts support personal health and creativity and provide the groundwork for direct, experiential understanding of the fundamental energetic concepts of Oriental medicine.

▶ **Oriental Therapeutic Massage:** Students study six weeks of Shiatsu, a Japanese form of acupressure, and six weeks of *tuina*, a Chinese form of massage, before determining their focus for three more quarters of study.

▶ **Traditional Chinese Medicine Theory:** Throughout the master's program, students explore theories that serve as the foundation for the practice of Chinese medicine.

▶ **Acupuncture Theory and Practice:** First-year students study the location of more than four hundred points and the basic theories and methodologies on which acupuncture is based. As they progress through the program, students master the functions of the acupuncture points, design acupuncture treatments, and learn and practice basic and advanced techniques for needling, as well as adjunctive therapies such as moxibustion, cupping, and the electrical stimulation of the points.

▶ **Chinese Herbal Medicine:** After studying more than three hundred individual herbs widely used in traditional Chinese healing, students learn how to combine these herbs into classical formulas designed to meet the needs of individual patients.

▶ **Biomedicine** includes course work in diet, nutrition, anatomy, physiology, Western pathology, clinical diagnosis, and pharmacology, plus course work in public and community health to enable students to partner with patients and their health-care providers to offer optimum care.

▶ **Professional Development:** Students develop ethical and legal awareness, case management capabilities, and marketing and practice-building skills in a series of dedicated courses, including a community outreach practicum.

▶ **Clinical Studies:** Clinical training affords students the opportunity to integrate their knowledge and skills and apply them to the treatment of patients in a carefully structured and supervised learning environment.

The **doctoral program** represents the highest formal educational credential available in the field of acupuncture and Oriental medicine in the United States. Doctoral students cultivate areas of interest and research opportunities during the program, and report greater patient confidence due to their advanced training. The program is 1,228 hours in length and consists of 536 teaching hours and 670 clinical hours.

▶ **Year I** of the three-year doctoral program introduces students to the basic theories of traditional Oriental medicine. Topics include:

- Energetic physiology
- Notions of health
- Origins of illness
- Traditional Chinese medical theory

▶ **Year II** training begins the essential techniques and clinical skills of the acupuncturist. Topics include:

- Needle insertion and manipulation
- Moxibustion
- Cupping
- Practical diagnostic skills
- Chinese herbal medicine

▶ **Year III** provides students with an opportunity to work in an acupuncture and herbal clinic. Students will be encouraged to explore areas of specialization. Topics include:

- Community health concerns
- Advanced study of traditional Chinese medicine pathology and therapeutics
- Biomedical approaches to physical and psychological assessment and treatment
- Transition from student to professional health-care provider

. . . .

Continuing Education Units: No. Inquire at the school of your choice.

Certification: The Oregon College of Oriental Medicine offers both a master's degree and a doctorate.

Participants: The Oregon College of Oriental Medicine, for example, prefers incoming students to have a college degree, but students with three years of college credit may enroll provided they complete their degree program at an accredited institution of higher learning. Students must have completed at least one college-level course in general biology, chemistry, and psychology at an accredited institution of higher learning with a grade of C or better. Students must have a master's degree or its equivalent in acupuncture and Oriental medicine to be eligible for consideration within the doctoral program.

Code of Ethics/Standards of Practice: Most acupuncture schools and schools of Oriental medicine have a code of ethics and a standards of practice. Inquire at the school of your choice.

Suggested Reading

Dechar, Lorie Eve. *Five Spirits: Alchemical Acupuncture for Psychological and Spiritual Healing.* Herndon, VA: Anthroposophic Press, 2006.

Kidson, Ruth. *Acupuncture for Everyone: What It Is, Why It Works, and How It Can Help You.* Rochester, VT: Inner Traditions, 2001.

Lian, Yu-Lin, Chun-Yang Chen, Michael G. Hammes, and Bernard C. Kolster. *The Pictorial Atlas of Acupuncture.* New York: Konemann, 2006.

Ma, Yun-tao, Mila Ma, and Zang Hee Ho. *Biomedical Acupuncture for Pain Management.* New York: Churchill Livingstone, 2005.

Availability: For a list of schools in the United States, go to www.acupunctureschools.com. To locate a licensed acupuncturist in your area, go to www.aaom.org or contact your nearest school and ask for a referral. In some states, medical insurance offers acupuncture coverage.

Resources

American Association of Acupuncture and Oriental Medicine (AAAOM), PO Box 162340, Sacramento, CA 95816, 916-443-4770, info@aaaomonline.org, www.aaaom.org

National Certification Commission for Acupuncture and Oriental Medicine (NCCAOM), 76 South Laura Street, Suite 1290, Jacksonville, FL 32202, 904-598-1005, info@nccaom.org, www.nccaom.org

Bibliography

Bauer, Matthew. *The Healing Power of Acupressure and Acupuncture.* New York: Penguin, 2005.

Sciammarella, Joseph. *Medical Acupuncture Benefits, Side Effects, History, and Origin.* www.emedicinehealth.com/medical_acupuncture/article_em.htm.

Suvow, Scott. "History of Acupuncture in China," www.acupuncturecare.com.

www.aaom.org

www.nccaom.org

www.ftp.cdc.gov/nchs

www.acupuncturedoc.com

www.ocom.edu

www.today.uci.edu

www.pubmedcentral.nih.gov

www.sciencelinks.jp

www.acupuncturetoday.com

BIOGEOMETRY™

THE SCIENCE OF BIOGEOMETRY uses a language based on its own physics of quality to induce harmony into the subtle energy between the body and the environment. As an environmental science, the effect of BioGeometry on health is not specific and not precisely predictable, but it appears to amplify and balance the energy fields of the body on all levels, thereby giving the body greater power to heal itself. The healing process resulting from a strengthening and balancing of the immune system manifests differently from one person to another.

"Sacred geometry" is a catchall term covering everything from Pythagorean and Neoplatonic geometry to religious, philosophical, and spiritual symbology. Numbers are combined with shapes to create a harmonious whole. Every part of a sacred geometry drawing or three-dimensional figure, be it a building or an object held in the hand, is fixed in size and shape. Nothing can be added or removed without disturbing the harmony of the whole composition.

Of the early temples and churches built using sacred geometry, the best known are the Parthenon in Greece and the Great Pyramids in Egypt. The Armenians built Karahundj, similar to Stonehenge, in 4200 BC, and an observatory in 2800 BC that enabled them to predict solar and lunar eclipses about a thousand years before the Egyptians. According to the founder of BioGeometry, Dr. Ibrahim Karim, in all the ancient buildings a form of BioGeometry lies at a deeper level in the heart of the design process. He says BioGeometry is founded on a new physics of quality that holds within it a practical application of the secret temple sciences.

Dr. Ibrahim Karim is an Egyptian architect and scientist who has invested thirty years of research into what he calls "a unique energy effect found in the centers of all living systems." He calls the sacred geometry patterns for healing and balancing the centers of living systems BioSignatures, which consist of precise energy patterns linked to different parts of the body. Through the uses of BioSignatures and special numerical codes, the energy balance can be specifically applied.

BioGeometry is a form of healing through environmental harmony. The detection and creation of spiritual centers in the body, the earth, and the sky, as well as their harmonious resonant interaction, are important criteria in BioGeometry.

Dr. Karim divides the energy anatomy of living things into a central or internal energy system and several peripheral energy systems superimposed on each other. The two types of systems are in constant communication with each other. The internal energy system uses the five senses and energy centers (also known as chakras) within the field around the body to interact directly with the various periphery systems and the environment.

The periphery energy systems exist both inside and outside the body. The meridian system that consists of channels of energy running throughout the body is a peripheral energy system. Dr. Karim says that the acupuncture points along the meridians—which, in traditional Chinese medicine, are places where energy can collect and block the body's proper energy flow—are also receptors where the peripheral energy system can receive information from the environment and react accordingly. The rest of the peripheral energy systems can be found superimposed upon each other within the energy field around the body. Karim specifies a vitality energy periphery, an emotional energy periphery, a mental energy periphery, and several sublevels within each.

Dr. Karim also introduces the concept of BioGeometry resonance relationships. These relationships exist on multiple levels of each of the organs of the body and are expressed as the linear energy patterns he calls BioSignatures. According to Karim, if a simple geometric shape is placed within a peripheral energy system, a resonance will form with a body part that has the same or a similar geometric configuration. This resonance amplifies the energy of the corresponding organ and can also correct the flow of energy through the organ, thus bringing it into balance energetically. He has compiled over seven hundred specific BioSignature patterns.

Relationships exist between the internal organs and other parts of the body because of the layout of the meridians. For example, a person with an elbow injury may need a BioSignature of the colon because the large intestine meridian runs through the elbow. Other relationships may exist because of similarities found between some of the shapes of parts of the bodies and the organs, such as the kidneys and ears.

BioGeometry also uses color, motion, orientation, and sound to create a vibration that balances the energy systems. Biogeometrical shapes have three primary vibrational qualities: negative green, a harmonic of ultraviolet, and a higher harmonic of gold. Negative green is at the core of energy centers in the body and power spots in nature. The higher harmonic of ultraviolet is a purifying and relaxing vibration that balances overactive organ function and has a calming effect on the nervous system. The highest harmonic of gold enhances wisdom and prosperity and balances the immune system. These three colors form a balance in each biogeometrical shape, including all life forms.

A typical BioGeometry session begins with an interview with the client and an assessment of his home and work environment to determine areas that need treatment. The practitioner checks the entire energy field for disturbances. Where there is a disturbance corresponding to the client's complaint, a drawing of a BioSignature is placed over that area or painted directly on the skin. Often, more than one BioSignature is administered due to the interrelationships within the physical and energetic body, and are sometimes given to bring out relaxation. Practitioners may recommend the client wear jewelry in the style of the appropriate BioSignature. Similar to the Chinese art of Feng Shui, the practitioner may also suggest changes concerning color, sound, and the placement of BioGeometry shapes in various rooms of the home or the workplace.

Dr. Karim insists that BioGeometry is a supportive modality and makes no medical claims as to the efficacy of the practice.

Course Descriptions

Courses are offered in Egypt and North America. Students may take the classes in three separate weekends or as one seven-day training. Due to travel constrictions, most students opt to take the classes over a seven-day foundation training session. However, students who are local to the area where classes are offered may take them in a series of three weekends, the second of which is a three-day class. An advanced training seminar is planned but not completed at the time of this writing. Students who complete the BioGeometry Foundations Training receive a Certificate of Completion from the BioGeometry Energy Systems in Cairo.

The three-part BioGeometry Foundation Training offers the basic principles and practices of BioGeometry.

▶ **Course One: Essential Concepts and Principles of BioGeometry** is a two-day class providing the background and history of BioGeometry. This class is a prerequisite for all other BioGeometry classes. Topics include:

- Ancient Egyptian methods of using spiritual energy
- Harmonics as the key to universal structure
- Creating practical effects with energy through resonance
- Vibrational foundations of human health and consciousness
- The twelve key energy qualities, including positive and negative aspects
- Effects of the sun, the earth's magnetic field, and dimensional levels on geometric energy fields
- Developing practical methods to detect and measure energy qualities
- Resonance, healing, and cleansing
- Biogeometrical design principles
- Developing BioSignatures
- Energy alchemy: transmuting toxic energies to beneficial energies

▶ **Course Two: BioGeometry Energy Balancing and Analysis** is a three-day, hands-on course that teaches fundamental practical methods used in BioGeometry, including how to detect, differentiate, and measure energy. Students practice a number of techniques to balance and enhance the energy qualities that affect the environment and human health, including methods to transmute toxic energy. Course One is a prerequisite. Topics include:

- Radiesthesia
- The principle of geometric resonance
- How to overcome detrimental resonance with other people
- How to repair ruptures and untie knots in energy patterns
- Centering

- The energetic and spiritual qualities of the higher harmonics
- Calibrating a pendulum with vibrational methods
- Using spin patterns in the human energy field to acquire information
- Balancing the energy field through polarity methods
- How to detect higher harmonics
- Cone pendulum—history, principles, and applications
- The nature of toxic energy and its effects on energy patterns and physical matter
- Safety protocols for protecting oneself from detrimental energies
- Solutions for eliminating toxic energy
- Three methods to chart detrimental earth energy grids
- Creating beneficial energy fields through color and object placement
- Practical effects of energy balancing through color and object placement
- Creating business and prosperity with BioGeometry energy balancing

▶ **Course Three: Intermediate Energy Balancing: Biosignatures and BioGeometry Design** is a two-day seminar where students learn methods to evaluate the condition of any aspect of the human energy field using anatomy charts and vibrational radiesthesia principles. Course Two is a prerequisite. Topics include:

- Central and peripheral energy systems of the body
- The history of BioSignatures, the different types developed, and how to balance energy using BioSignatures
- Using anatomy charts to analyze a partner's energy field
- Applying BioSignatures to balance a partner's energy
- Modifying BioSignatures through bionumerals
- Color balancing a person's organs, chakras, or energy system through his or her environment and physical body
- Connecting to the center
- Radiated space and enclosed space
- Interface: creating energy through combining surfaces or materials
- Transparency: energy effects from an unseen pattern defined by some of its visible parts

- The spiritual significance of perspective
- Gateway energy emissions
- The nature of the East–West energy flow
- Clearing environmental problems with BioGeometry
- The effect on energy fields of changing from day to night, and vice versa
- The geometries of the seven spiritual planes

· · · · · · · · · · · · · · · · ·

Continuing Education Units: No.

Certification: Students may earn the title of Licensed BioGeometry Practitioner.

Participants: Open to the general public. Special courses are tailored to fit the needs of professional groups such as doctors and architects.

Code of Ethics: No.

Suggested Reading

Gilbert, Robert J. *Egyptian and European Energy Work: Reclaiming the Ancient Science of Spiritual Vibration.* Book 1, *Essential Knowledge.* Available from the Vesica Institute, www.vesica.org.

———. *Egyptian and European Energy Work: Reclaiming the Ancient Science of Spiritual Vibration.* Book 2, *Methods and Tools.* Available from the Vesica Institute, www.vesica.org.

Karim, Ibrahim. *Back to a Future for Mankind: BioGeometry, Ancient Egypt, and Environment.* Cairo, Egypt: BioGeometry Consulting, 2009.

Skinner, Stephen. *Sacred Geometry: Deciphering the Code.* New York: Sterling, 2006.

Availability: Egypt, Europe, and North America. To find a session in your area, go to www.BioGeometry.com.

Resources

BioGeometry Consulting™, 17 Road 11 Maadi, Cairo, Egypt, (+202) 23784139, BioGeometryeg@hotmail.com, www.biogeometry.com/English

Vesica Institute, 1011 Tunnel Road, Suite 200, Asheville, NC 28805, 828-298-7007, info@vesica.org. www.vesica.org

Bibliography

www.vesica.org

www.luckymojo.com

www.tacentral.com

CHI NEI TSANG

C HI NEI TSANG IS A TAOIST HEALING TECHNIQUE that focuses primarily on detoxifying, regenerating, and balancing the body's vital functions by focusing on internal organs and the various systems of the body, including circulation, lymphatic, digestive, eliminative, nerve centers, tendons and muscles, and the acupuncture meridians (chi system). It is believed that these systems converge in the abdomen, which acts as their control center, and that gentle massage of the abdomen and thorax will help the body attain an optimum state. Loosely translated as "working the energy of the internal organs," Chi Nei Tsang (pronounced *chee nay song* and referred to as CNT) is also referred to as "internal organ chi massage." This healing can be given to others or can be self-administered.

Chi Nei Tsang, as an early spinoff of Qigong, came into being in the mountain ranges of Taoist China. (For a full description of Qigong, see pages 87–97.) It was used by monks in monasteries to help detoxify, strengthen, and refine their bodies to maintain the energy required to sustain their spiritual practice, often at high altitudes. Due to the Chinese Cultural Revolution and the advent of antibiotics, the practice almost became extinct. In the mid-1900s Dr. Mui Yimwattana, a Chinese refugee living in Thailand and the last of a long line of healers, took on Mantak Chia as a student after healing Chia's uncle of a shoulder problem. Dr. Mui used an early form of both Chi Nei Tsang and Thai healing massage, which Mantak Chia adapted into modern-day Chi Nei Tsang. Master Chia and his wife came to the United States in 1979 to teach Chi Nei Tsang as part of their Taoist training, later returning to Thailand. Gilles Marin, a student of Chia's, continued his work in the United States and founded the Chi Nei Tsang Institute.

According to Marin, in his book *Healing from Within with Chi Nei Tsang: Applied Chi Kung in Internal Organs Treatment*, "Chi Nei Tsang is most concerned with the origin of health problems, including psychosomatic responses, and builds the resilience of the body's defense system. This is done by working on the abdomen in a way that triggers internal 'adjustment' through what we call the client's 'insight.'" He goes on to say, "It is a connection between workings in a person that weren't previously communicating and that may have been in conflict." The four pillars of CNT are self-cultivation, chi development, a new understanding of healing, and listening touch. Like gardens, which need maintenance to grow, self-cultivation is an essential part of growth and healing. Practitioners guide clients in developing healthy habits and discarding unhealthy ones. Marin refers to this growth and refinement as internal alchemy. Practitioners are also encouraged to work on their own healing and self-cultivation. For example, a practitioner must be nonjudgmental in order to help clients work with themselves without feelings of shame.

When chi does not flow naturally through the body, symptoms of disease, pain, or discomfort begin to manifest. (See page 25 for a description of chi, also referred to as qi.) Practitioners aim to achieve a state of deep relaxation in their clients, as chi does not flow through tight muscles. A quiet setting, soft music, and gentle massaging of the abdomen bring about a state of deep relaxation, and practitioners set an example through their own deeply relaxed state. Practitioners work to make their fingers soft and fluid so the chi can flow during treatments.

When working with clients for the first time, practitioners also help clients redefine their relationship to healing. CNT practitioners use the term "cure" when addressing the physical symptoms of a disease or condition. They use the term "heal" when addressing the cause of the symptoms. They help clients, who often seek this therapy because they are experiencing pain or disease, understand that pain is considered a message, saying their physical or emotional health needs attention. Symptoms are not the cause of the disease or condition and thus are not the real issue. Practitioners work with clients physically, emotionally, mentally, and spiritually to help find the cause of the problem. If the practitioner determines that the client needs the help of an allopathic physician or another form of complementary medicine, a recommendation is made.

The fourth pillar, listening touch, is done by abdominal massage. The practitioner's goal is to train the internal organs to work more efficiently and encourage clients to feel what is going on inside their bodies. As a result, clients get in better touch with their bodies and release unprocessed emotion. The practitioner first works in areas that have no relation to any given symptoms, which helps the client relax and develop a sense of trust in the practitioner. As the treatment progresses, the practitioner talks with the client about what he or she is feeling inside, both physically and emotionally. Clients are asked to listen to their feelings without judgment, thereby getting to know themselves better and facilitating healing.

As with many Asian bodywork therapies, an analysis of breath quality as a reflection of emotional and physical health is an important part of CNT. Practitioners assess a client's breath before treatment and continue to monitor whether the client takes shallow or deep breaths while experiencing a technique. Posture is also monitored, as it affects breath circulation, which in turn affects the internal organs and the amount of oxygen they receive. All of these things supply the practitioner with information to better serve the client.

During a CNT session, the client lies faceup and fully clothed, except for the abdomen, which is exposed. The practitioner generally starts by massaging around the navel and then working outward toward the organs. He or she feels for tension in the belly, often expressed as tightness, heat, or coolness. The client is asked to breathe into the area needing work as the practitioner gently massages, and sometimes rocks, shakes, or stretches the area. As the client relaxes, the effects of the treatment increase. Once the treatment is over, the practitioner may suggest Qigong or Tai Chi exercises or demonstrate how to do effective self-massage. It frequently takes more than one treatment to complete the healing work.

Practitioners are encouraged to work on themselves for ten minutes every day and experience either a full self-treatment or receive a treatment from another practitioner at least once a week, which helps them stay in optimum health and better serve their clients.

Course Descriptions

A number of organizations offer Chi Nei Tsang classes, so the curriculum will vary. Students can become certified in CNT through institutions such as Chi Nei Tsang Institute, Healing Tao Institute, and Universal Tao. As regards to the course of the study, the Healing Tao Institute, for example, offers a 367-hour course, consisting of up to 175 hours of training in Chi Nei Tsang technique and theory, 72 hours of supervised clinical training, and 120 hours in Healing Tao Basic Training courses. The Chi Nei Tsang Institute in Oakland, California, offers four levels of practitioner certification: Beginning Practitioner is a 330-hour course of study, Intermediate Practitioner is a 580-hour course of study, Advanced Practitioner is a 695-hour course of study, and the teaching track course of study involves ongoing student teaching. (Students must complete each level to progress to the next.) Level one requirements involve two fundamentals classes, an anatomy weekend, a fusion retreat, and instruction on CNT business fundamentals and sexual energy and boundaries. Experiential classes involve 60 hours of clinical class, 50 case studies, and 10 treatments. Level two requirements involve two emotional processing retreats, a clinical class and another 60 hours of clinical class, 50 case studies, and 10 treatments. Level three requirements involve two global body attitude weekend classes and one additional anatomy weekend. The teaching track involves ongoing student teaching. According to the institute, "Classes are designed to gently awaken you to the subtle universal energies and to a better understanding of yourself." Classes at any of these organizations can be taken with the intention to become a certified CNT practitioner or simply for personal development.

The following is a sample curriculum from the Chi Nei Tsang Institute.

▶ **Chi Nei Tsang Fundamentals** is an introduction to Taoist medicine and the principles that have ruled traditional Oriental medicine for thousands of years through the use of chi exercises and the gentle manipulation of the internal organs for physical, emotional, and spiritual healing, well-being, disease prevention, and longevity. During this workshop the students will learn:

- A number of energetic exercises to promote chi circulation

- A full-body detoxifying routine, including treatment for gallstones, kidney stones, and parasites
- Manual techniques to improve, prevent, and help reverse hypoglycemia and diabetes
- How to deal with abdominal pain, including irritable bowel syndrome, menstrual cramps, endometriosis, and fibroids
- How to correct chronic back problems caused by visceral imbalance
- How to perform a one-hour Chi Nei Tsang treatment on themselves and others

▶ **Chi Nei Tsang Anatomy and Physiology Weekend** helps students understand why people get sick or fatigued during certain parts of the day or during certain seasons. Students gain a working knowledge of when internal organs and their energy pathways regenerate. In this class, the student will learn:

- The position and shape of each internal organ
- The feel of the internal organs and how to recognize their specific movements and sounds
- How to map out the acupuncture meridian system
- The basic functions (physiology) of each organ, as well as the specific mental and emotional aspects associated with each organ

▶ **Sexual Chi-Kung and Space and Boundaries Weekend** explores sexual energy as one of life's most potent energies and demonstrates how to develop appropriate personal boundaries and deliver superlative healing sessions with the utmost respect. Students will learn how to:

- Honor, cultivate, and channel sexual drive for enhanced bliss and improved health and life enjoyment
- Differentiate and harmonize male and female sexual energy
- Reduce sexual dysfunction
- Enhance creativity and improve communication skills
- Recycle ancestral emotional charges that affect intimacy and sexual expression
- Create personal boundaries and fortify any apparent weaknesses

· · · · · · · · · · · · · · · · · · ·

Continuing Education Units: Provider approved by the California Board of Registered Nursing, Provider #CEP 14793, and the California Board of Acupuncture, Provider #CEP 612.

Certification: At the Chi Nei Tsang Institute, there are four levels of certification:

1. Chi Nei Tsang Beginning Practitioner Level One Certification
2. Chi Nei Tsang Intermediate Practitioner Level Two Certification
3. Chi Nei Tsang Advanced Practitioner Level Three Certification
4. Chi Nei Tsang Institute Teacher Certification

Participants: Classes may be taken by anyone for personal growth or to lead to certification and teaching. Bodyworkers, counselors, and medical practitioners will all benefit from the courses.

Legalities: This discipline may fall under the rules of massage therapy because of the deep stroking of the abdomen. Go to the Legalities section of the book for the list of governmental agencies and contact the one in your area for specifics regarding licensing.

Suggested Reading

Marin, Gilles. *Five Elements, Six Conditions: A Taoist Approach to Emotional Healing, Psychology, and Internal Alchemy.* Berkeley, CA: North Atlantic Books, 2006.

———. *Healing from Within with Chi Nei Tsang: Applied Chi Kung in Internal Organs Treatment.* Berkeley, CA: North Atlantic Books, 1999.

Availability: Classes are available in Canada, France, Germany, Japan, New Zealand, and the United States. To locate a healing session in your area, go to www.chineitsang.com.

Resources

Chi Nei Tsang Institute, 481 36th Street, Oakland, CA 94609, 510-848-9558, cnt@chineitsang.com, classes@chineitsang.com, www.chineitsang.com

International Institute of Medical Qigong, 73-145 Guadalupe Avenue, PO Box 1435, Palm Desert, CA, 800-848-0649, info@MedicalQigong.com, www.medicalqigong.org

Bibliography

Marin, Gilles. *Healing from Within with Chi Nei Tsang: Applied Chi Kung in Internal Organs Treatment.* Berkeley, CA: North Atlantic Books, 1999.

www.chineitsang.com

www.cntcenter.com

www.healingtaoinstitute.com

EMOTIONAL FREEDOM TECHNIQUE

E MOTIONAL FREEDOM TECHNIQUE, more commonly known as EFT, is a psychoenergetic therapy using meridian theory, gentle self-administered tapping, and mind-body integration to resolve emotional issues. It is a derivation of Thought Field Therapy (see page 121) developed by Dr. Roger Callahan. Gary Craig, a Stanford engineer, studied with Dr. Callahan and created EFT in 1995 after years of simplifying and modifying Callahan's techniques. While EFT may be self-administered, clients seek practitioners for guidance in learning about the tapping sequences and in forming the most effective affirmations. Usually clients do the tapping themselves with the practitioners offering suggestions as to where to tap. The tapping sequences are frequently updated, so practitioners supply in-depth information unavailable to the casual EFT user.

EFT practitioners believe that the cause of negative emotion, such as anger, guilt, depression, fear, or stress, is a disruption in the body's energy system. By correcting the disruption on the energetic level, we can in turn heal it on an emotional level. To do so, the individual focuses on the negative emotion, repeats a series of affirming statements, and self-administers tapping movements with the fingertips on a series of places on the body that correspond to acupuncture points on the meridians. The fourteen meridians flow into, throughout, and out of the body, twelve of which are pairs that mirror each other from both sides of the body. Each meridian is connected to an organ, an emotion, or a set of emotions. (See pages 4 and 7 for more information about the meridians.) Per EFT theory, tapping the end points of the meridians creates positive change in emotional and physical health. EFT does not treat the memory of a trauma that triggers a negative emotion. Rather, it addresses the disruption in the body's energy system caused by the trauma, distressing memory, or everyday stress and fear. The energy system is balanced and a sense of calmness replaces the negative emotion.

The "Basic Recipe," as Craig calls it, consists of four steps: the setup, the sequence, the nine-gamut procedure, and the sequence. The setup is a way of preparing the energy system, which may have what Craig calls a polarity reversal that could prevent the tapping procedures from working. The technical term for this process is psychological reversal, which the individual prepares for by repeating an affirmation three times. For example, someone with a fear of public speaking might repeat the following: "Even though I have a fear of public speaking, I deeply and completely accept myself." While saying this affirmation, or something similar, the client rubs or taps on two sore spots found three inches down from the notch at the top of the sternum and three inches to each side of the sternum. Another spot that can be used for this step is called the "karate chop point" and is found on the side of the hand about one-half to three-quarters of an inch below the little finger. This point can be vigorously tapped using two fingers of the other hand. It does not matter which hand does what.

The second step is a sequence involving tapping at the end points of the major meridians. Charts detailing these points may be found in EFT books and online at www.emofree.org. Sometimes while doing the tapping the client repeats a reminder phrase, such as "fear of public speaking." The third step, the nine-gamut procedure, consists of tapping on a point on the back of the hand and performing nine separate actions. Once the nine actions are complete, step four is done by repeating the same sequence that was done in step two.

Gary Craig says the work with EFT is in the beginning stages and the program is constantly changing. As people practice it, more knowledge comes to light. The Basic Recipe has expanded into both a short version and a long version. Many practitioners have created their own basic sequence or modified it to fit specific problems. A fifth step has been added, called re-evaluation, where the client takes an inventory of the results of the treatment and either alone or with the aid of a practitioner, decides if the treatment needs to be repeated. Sometimes it takes more than one treatment to complete the work.

A good example of the effectiveness of EFT in treating phobias is shown by a study done at Curtin University in Western Australia by a team of psychologists. It shows success in treating people with a fear of spiders, snakes, and other small animals. This study was published in the *Journal of Clinical Psychology* for September 2003. Subjects taking part in the study were divided into two groups. The first group did deep breathing techniques and practiced the same protocols with the exception of the tapping sequences. The second group did the deep breathing and the EFT protocol including the tapping sequences. Subjects who did the tapping were able to walk much closer to the feared animal than those who did just the deep breathing. When retested nine months later, the subjects who included the tapping retained their ability to approach a feared animal.

EFT is readily available. Many practitioners publish the techniques on the Internet, and several books describe the techniques in detail. Hands-on experience can be found at various workshops around the United States. Gary Craig and his followers believe EFT should be available to everyone at little or no cost.

Course Descriptions

The following live workshops are from the World Center of EFT, sponsored by Gary Craig. Students may also learn EFT from videos and books found on Craig's website. The primary method of instruction is via their library of DVDs, which are available at their website, www.emofree.com. EFT certifies on three levels: the EFT Foundational Level (EFT CERT-I), the EFT Intermediate Level (EFT CERT-II), and the EFT Honors Level (EFT Cert-Honors). Students must submit to an exam at each level to receive certification at that level. EFT provides a library of DVDs for each level of training. Live workshop trainings no longer apply toward any of the certifications. However, most of the content of the live workshops is contained in the EFT Foundation library of DVDs. Students do receive a certificate of completion at the end of each workshop. This program is growing and changing. Go to the website www.emofree.com for the latest in class and certification information.

▶ **Workshop Level 1** is a 6-hour introductory course designed to give the student experience in doing EFT and a basic understanding of how it works. Topics include:

- Building bridges between EFT procedures and student beliefs
- How negative emotions can disrupt the body's energy system

- Psychological reversal
- The Basic Recipe
- Experiential learning
- What to say during the technique and when to stop it

▶ **Workshop Level 2** consists of 12 hours of instruction that brings the student to a deeper level of awareness of the effects of EFT. Level 1 or equivalency is a prerequisite. Topics include:

- Using additional tapping points
- Mastering a gentle approach
- Additional ways to zero in on core issues, including physical issues
- Testing results, working by phone, and group tapping

▶ **Workshop Level 3** is a supervised course for students who are developing their own EFT practice. Students work with a mentor until both mentor and mentee feel the student has acquired sufficient knowledge to achieve a Level 3 certificate.

. . . .

Continuing Education Units: No.

Certification: Several organizations offer certification in EFT. However, founder Gary Craig only recognizes certification provided by the World Center for EFT.

Participants: There are no restrictions to learning EFT.

Code of Ethics/Standards of Practice: No.

Suggested Reading

Craig, Gary. *The EFT Manual (EFT: Emotional Freedom Techniques)*. Fulton, CA: Energy Psychology Press, 2008.

Mountrose, Phillip, and Jane Mountrose. *The Heart and Soul of EFT and Beyond: Soulful Exploration of the Emotional Freedom Techniques and Holistic Healing*. Arroyo Grande, CA: Holistic Communications, 2006.

Availability: Workshops and a comprehensive list of practitioners are available at www.emofree.com, and online classes can be taken anywhere.

Resources

EFT, PO Box 269, Coulterville, CA 95311, www.emofree.com

Awakenings Institute, PO Box 279, Arroyo Grande, CA 93420, 805-931-0129, phil@gettingthru.org, www.gettingthru.org

Bibliography

Mountrose, Phillip, and Jane Mountrose. *The Heart and Soul of EFT and Beyond.* Arroyo Grande, CA: Holistic Communications, 2006.

www.emofree.com

JIN SHIN DO®

THE WORDS *JIN SHIN DO* come from the Japanese language. *Jin* means compassion. Students of Jin Shin Do learn to develop their own sense of compassion for themselves, family, friends, and future clients. *Shin* means spirit, and can also mean extending or creating. Japanese and Chinese philosophers believe that shin resides in the heart, influencing both the physical and emotional aspects of a person. Using meditation, acupressure techniques, and Qigong breathing and exercise techniques to clear the pathways of energy throughout the body, shin (or spirit) can more easily influence good health and a positive frame of mind.

Do (pronounced "doe") has the same meaning as the Chinese word *tao* (pronounced "dow") and means, in this case, "the way," a path leading to harmony and peace with all of nature and with each other. Taoist philosophy emphasizes harmony with nature outside and within people. Each person has a different path, but all eventually lead to the same goals: peace of mind, harmony with the environment, and knowledge of universal truth. Put together, Jin Shin Do means "the way of the compassionate spirit."

An essential element of Jin Shin Do is *ki* (in Chinese, chi, also spelled qi and in Sanskrit, prana). *Ki* is the Japanese word used to describe the life energy flowing throughout the body. Acupressure techniques help release tension, blockages, and stagnation that stop the flow of ki, enabling a person to regain physical, emotional, mental, spiritual, and energetic balance for maintaining good health and harmony.

Bodywork refers to any type of therapy that uses the hands as a method of treatment, including massage and energy healing. Asian bodywork therapy has its roots in traditional Chinese medicine. Jin Shin Do's founder, Iona Marsaa Teeguarden, a psychotherapist, began her studies in Asian bodywork therapy with macrobiotic

Shiatsu and Do-In, and by receiving Jin Shin Jyutsu treatments and taking classes from Mary Burmeister, who brought Jin Shin Jyutsu to the United States from Japan. Iona Teeguarden also studied with Korean, Chinese, and French acupuncturists and a Korean Qigong master. On a 1976 research trip to Japan, she studied with Dr. Haruki Kato, a student of Jiro Murai, the originator of Jin Shin Jyutsu (page 65).

Iona Teeguarden integrated a traditional acupressure technique used in Jin Shin Jyutsu with classic Chinese acupuncture theory, Taoist philosophy, Qigong breathing and exercise techniques, and Reichian segmental theory. About ten years later, the basic principles of Erickson psychotherapy were added to the synthesis that became Jin Shin Do Bodymind Acupressure®.

Jin Shin Jyutsu is a form of Japanese finger acupressure in which the practitioner is not considered an active participant, but merely assists in allowing universal energy to flow through him or her into the client. Jin Shin Do differs from Jin Shin Jyutsu (which uses a light touch) by using firm, direct pressure, and by emphasizing precise point location and a specific angle of pressure for each point.

Chinese acupuncture and acupressure include meridian theory and acupressure points. Meridians are channels of energy within the body. According to Iona Teeguarden, acupressure points are major places along the meridians where the flow of energy is accessible. She teaches that while most Western trigger points are acupressure points (also known as acupoints), these are a small portion of the 361 traditional acupoints. It is by holding these points that congestion blocking the flow of energy may most easily be released.

According to traditional Chinese medicine, blocked or congested energy can lead to disease. All of these topics are discussed in more detail in the chapters on acupuncture (page 25) and acupressure (page 17).

Classic Chinese acupuncture theory, including organ meridians, strange flows, and the five elements, forms the basic structure of Jin Shin Do. The twelve organ meridians and four of the eight strange flows are bilateral so that they mirror each other on both sides of the body. Meridians circulate energy, maintaining and nurturing physical, emotional, and spiritual functioning and health.

Strange flows, also known as extraordinary vessels, consist of eight pathways of energy that regulate and balance the organ meridians. The *Nan Jing*, a Chinese medical text written 1,800 years ago, describes the strange flows as rivers that allow the passage of water that can deal with storms and heavy rain. Strange flows move energy from meridians that have too much energy to those that are deficient. Jin Shin Do is the only acupressure technique to use the strange flows as the basis of its main points. The fifty-five main acupoints taught in basic Jin Shin Do occur on the strange flows. Iona Teeguarden believes using acupoints along the strange flows is a shortcut to balancing the twelve pairs of organ meridians. She says strange flow points are also points of organ meridians, as are all of the 361 traditional points.

The five elements come from traditional Chinese medicine and consist of water, wood, fire, earth, and metal. Metaphorically, they are an extension of yin/yang theory and correspond to the seasons. Water relates to the season of winter, the yin organ of the kidney, and the yang organ of the urinary bladder. Wood relates to the season of spring, the liver (yin), and the gallbladder (yang). The heart (yin) and the small intestine (yang) are represented by the season of summer and the element of fire. Late summer stems from the earth element and relates to the spleen (yin) and the stomach (yang). The fifth element in China is metal. In India it is ether. The metal element relates to autumn, the yin organs of the lungs, and the yang organ of the large intestines.

Taoism is one of two indigenous philosophies in China (the other being Confucianism). Taoists believe in going along with the natural flow of nature. While some philosophers translate Taoism into a philosophy of doing nothing, what it actually means is to do nothing that blocks, changes, reinvents, or controls the natural flow of life.

Iona Teeguarden discovered many correlations between Dr. Wilhelm Reich's segmental theories and the emotions traditionally associated with the meridians, so she integrated segmental theory with classic Chinese acupuncture theory. Dr. Reich was an Austrian psychiatrist, psychoanalyst, and scientist who talked about life energy, which he called "orgone energy." His segmental theory divides the body into seven horizontal segments, one on top of the other, each of which is composed of functionally related muscles and points. He believed that energy naturally moved vertically through the seven segments. A block, which he called muscular armor, would stop the energy from flowing into the segment above or below it. The movement of energy may be obstructed due to physical or emotional trauma, or by repressed emotions. This is because tension spreads from muscles in the front to functionally related muscles in the back, and vice versa. If tension becomes chronic, it forms what Reich called "rings of armoring." He believed muscular armoring and character armoring are the same phenomena.

Ericksonian hypnotherapy was developed by Dr. Milton Erickson, a psychiatrist and psychotherapist. By working with metaphors, telling stories, and emphasizing the positive, Dr. Erickson worked with his patients to change their negative patterns into positive ones. He used stories to induce a trance state to bypass conscious resistance and plant suggestions in the unconscious mind. Because "trance" describes the relaxed state of increased awareness experienced while receiving Jin Shin Do, Iona Teeguarden says it is important for practitioners to understand basic Ericksonian principles of trance work or hypnotherapy. These principles of communication with the unconscious mind help the practitioner to choose words that are relaxing and empowering to the individual.

A Jin Shin Do practitioner begins a session by helping the client feel fully comfortable. The client, lying faceup on a massage table, is fully clothed. The practitioner does an intake interview by asking pertinent questions to identify what needs attention. The practitioner also inquires about relevant medical history, takes energy pulses, palpates acupoints, and asks the client what the purpose is for the session. Palpating acupoints is done by pressing on a given acupressure point or pair of points to check if it is sore or tense. Generally the amount of soreness, if any, determines if work needs to be done at that point or on a line of points along the corresponding meridian. Numbness may also indicate problems.

The practitioner works with the client to identify, explore, and dissolve body-mind tension. Following Reichian segmental therapy, treatment usually starts at the shoulders and neck. Jin Shin Do practitioners hold a specific local acupressure point, a tense or armored point, with the thumb or fingers using firm pressure to release blocked or congested energy. At the same time, with the thumb or fingers of the other hand, the practitioner holds related distal (distant) points that help release the tension or blockage at the local point. The angle of approach of the finger doing the pressing is important. The client determines how much pressure the practitioner uses. Any sensation of discomfort is soon replaced by the pleasant sensation of release.

The practitioner may ask clients to focus their attention on a particular point and help with the process by breathing into it, being open to any sensations, feelings, words, or images that might come up. The practitioner works down the body, applying pressure where needed at each segment. At the end of each session, the practitioner does a Jin Shin Do neck and shoulder release to complete the healing treatment. Holding points or massaging the feet helps bring the client back into a state of awareness of his or her surroundings. Clients are then encouraged to turn onto their side, get up slowly, and, for more grounding, walk around until they feel their feet contacting the earth. There may be some discussion of what the client can do to help restore his or her own health such as diet, exercise, drinking more water, and taking longer periods of rest.

Course Descriptions

Jin Shin Do classes are offered at growth centers, health facilities, massage schools, and colleges internationally. Students wanting certification need to inquire as to whether their instructor is an authorized Jin Shin Do teacher (a trademark licensee). Classes taught by instructors who are not authorized Jin Shin Do® teachers will not count toward certification as a Registered Jin Shin Do® Acupressurist. Students are asked to follow the Jin Shin Do Foundation Code of Ethics. Jin Shin Do classes are signed off on a Jin Shin Do Foundation transcript and students can take each class with a different authorized Jin Shin Do teacher. Students are also encouraged to audit and assist with classes. The following classes are listed on the Jin Shin Do Foundation website and are taught by all authorized Jin Shin Do teachers. The first two introductory classes can also be taught by Registered Jin Shin Do Acupressurists.

Short Introductory Classes

▶ **Five-Step Neck-Shoulder Release** is a two-hour workshop in which students learn to locate key neck and shoulder points. They practice the relaxing Basic Jin Shin Do Neck Release on themselves and others, holding five key neck and shoulder acupoints bilaterally.

▶ **Fundamentals of Self-Acupressure** is an eight-hour class in which students learn to relieve the tension and discomfort of headache, backache, jaw pain, constipation, and more with the following techniques:

- The Basic Jin Shin Do Neck Release and Basic Central Release
- A simple twenty-five-point self-acupressure pattern

▶ **Jin Shin Do Acupressure Facial** is a 14-hour workshop in which students learn:

- How to work with the main neck acupoints, called "Windows of the Sky"
- Acupoints on the face and head
- The twelve-step Jin Shin Do facial, originally developed for cosmetologists, using only acupoints on the face, head, neck, arms, and head

Pass/Fail Classes

▶ **Module I** presents theories and techniques necessary for effective practice of Jin Shin Do acupressure, beginning with fifty-five main Jin Shin Do acupoints, progressing to over two hundred important acupoints and correlating acupoint location with anatomy. The class emphasizes the exact angle of acupoint stimulation. Students begin to practice by following release examples and later learn to improvise based on tension patterns and energetic assessment.

Part 1: Basic Jin Shin Do. Participants learn to:

- Locate fifty-five acupoints in relation to surrounding anatomy
- Describe how Jin Shin Do acupressure can be utilized for general relaxation and to release specific tensions
- Demonstrate acupoint combinations for common problems, including tension in the head, neck, shoulders, back, chest, abdomen, pelvis, and extremities
- Process the feelings and images that may arise from the body during acupressure release
- Perform simple movements that facilitate relaxation and structural-energetic balancing

- Identify the eight strange flows or extraordinary vessels and demonstrate their use for energy balancing

Part 2: Intermediate Jin Shin Do. Prerequisite: Basic Jin Shin Do with an authorized Jin Shin Do instructor. Participants learn to:

- Locate over a hundred additional acupoints in relation to surrounding anatomy
- Describe the twelve organ meridians, differentiating according to location and psychophysical associations
- Differentiate Western and Eastern understanding of physiology
- Identify specific acupressure point combinations for meridian release
- Demonstrate understanding of local-distal point theory
- Identify the legal and ethical role of the acupressurist, and how to build trust

Part 3: Advanced Jin Shin Do. Prerequisite: Intermediate Jin Shin Do. Participants learn to:

- Describe the Five Elements or Five Phases theory and its application to acupressure
- Locate forty additional acupoints in relation to surrounding anatomy
- Demonstrate understanding of local-distal point theory using source, luo, tonification, sedation, mu, and back shu points
- Assess energetic imbalance, identify key tension areas through pulse reading, and point palpation

Part 4: Body-Mind Processing Skills. Participants learn:

- Simple verbal skills for responsibly dealing with feelings and images that may arise during sessions
- Practice basic counseling skills such as active listening and the Body-Focusing techniques
- Describe conscious and unconscious levels of communication and the appropriate use of suggestion

▶ **Module II** provides an opportunity to review point locations and angles and to integrate the material of Module I. It includes an in-depth study of strange flows, organ meridians, segments, and five phases; and additional theories and special point groups. The body-mind focus of this class varies from teacher to teacher. Prerequisite: completion of Module I. Participants learn to:

- Demonstrate point location and assessment skills, including pulse reading and point palpation
- Describe the eight strange flows in detail and compare with the twelve organ meridians
- Demonstrate use of acupressure and Body-Focusing techniques with common tension and pain problems
- Describe special point groups: combining, entry-exit, general and group luo, and accumulation points
- Integrate segmental, strange flow, meridian, and five phases theories in designing sessions to reduce stress
- Discuss the six divisions, exogenous and endogenous causes of imbalance, the eight principles theory, and tendino-muscular meridians

▶ **Module III: 70 Hours of Clinical Experience** may be obtained as an internship (in-house work at a bodywork school) or as an externship (in a supportive professional setting with supervision).

Content:

- **Unit 1.** Clinical experience using Jin Shin Do acupressure (50 hours)
- **Unit 2.** Direct supervision and discussion of cases (20 hours)

▶ **Module IV** is 70 hours of Bodymind Acupressure with Iona M. Teeguarden.

Part 1: Bodymind Trancework. Prerequisite: Basic Jin Shin Do.

- Ericksonian techniques for working with the trance or meditative states induced by Jin Shin Do, in which there is increased receptivity to minimal cues
- Suggestive language

- Indirection
- Body focusing and place of comfort techniques
- C.A.R.E.F.O.R.S. outline of body-oriented trancework process
- Using metaphors
- Storytelling
- Exercise to develop therapeutic skills

Part 2: Bodymind Trancework and Trauma. Prerequisite: Module IV, Part 1

- Focus on healing from post-traumatic stress disorder and recovering feelings without retraumatization
- Exercises for learning safe, effective exposure and cognitive therapy techniques

Part 3: The Emotional Kaleidoscope and Abuse Issues. Prerequisite: Module IV, Part 2. Students learn to use Iona Teeguarden's Emotional Kaleidoscope theory and techniques derived from Ericksonian and Redecision therapies to help heal the wounds of abuse and nurture the core self.

. . . .

Continuing Education Units: Yes. Providers: National Certification Board for Therapeutic Massage and Bodywork, provider #026771 under category A, California Board of Registered Nursing, provider #04744, and in Illinois, Rock Valley College classes are approved for nurses. For other states, check with your instructor for nursing CEUs.

Certification: Students who complete all of the requirements (including 125 logged practice hours, 10 private JSD sessions, and a practical exam from an authorized JSD teacher) become Registered Jin Shin Do Acupressurists.

Participants: Both professional health-care providers and laypeople may attend these classes.

Code of Ethics/Standards of Practice: They have a Code of Ethics.

Suggested Reading

Teeguarden, Iona Marsaa. *Acupressure Way of Health: Jin Shin Do.* Idyllwild, CA: Jin Shin Do Foundation; Taos, NM: Redwing Book Company, 1978.

———. *A Complete Guide to Acupressure.* Idyllwild, CA: Jin Shin Do Foundation; Taos, NM: Redwing Book Company, 1996, revised 2002.

———. *The Joy of Feeling: Bodymind Acupressure.* Idyllwild, CA: Jin Shin Do Foundation; Taos, NM: Redwing Book Company, 1987.

Availability: Classes are held worldwide and frequently found at massage schools. To find a class or practitioner in your area, go to www.jinshindo.org.

Resources

American Organization for Bodywork Therapies of Asia, 1010 Haddonfield-Berlin Road, Suite 408, Voorhees, NJ 08043-3514, 856-782-1616, office@aobta.org, www.aobta.org

Jin Shin Do Foundation for Bodymind Acupressure, PO Box 416, Idyllwild, CA 92549, jinshindo@earthlink.net, www.jinshindo.org

Bibliography

Haley, Jay. *Uncommon Therapy: The Psychiatric Techniques of Milton H. Erickson, MD.* New York: W.W. Norton, 1973.

Sommers, Steve. "The 'Four Legs' of Jin Shin Do." *Acupressure News*, vol. 15, 1999.

Teeguarden, Iona Marsaa. "Extraordinary Energy Flows." *Acupressure News*, vol. 18, 2004.

———. "Jin Shin Do Acupressure: Magic or Science?" *Acupressure News*, vol. 20, 2006. Reprinted on the Jin Shin Do website, www.jinshindo.org.

www.jinshinjyutsu.com

JIN SHIN JYUTSU®

THE EARLIEST WRITTEN RECORDS of the art of Jin Shin Jyutsu are found in an ancient Japanese record called the Kojiki written in AD 712, which states that Jin Shin Jyutsu had been in use for over two thousand years. Originally passed down by word of mouth from generation to generation, Jin Shin Jyutsu almost disappeared until it was revived in the early 1900s by Master Jiro Murai. Master Murai spent over fifty years studying and experimenting with various energy techniques, recording what he felt and comparing his observations with traditional Chinese acupressure theory and the writings in the Kojiki.

Jiro Murai's student, Mary Burmeister, brought Jin Shin Jyutsu to the United States in the 1950s. Of Japanese descent, she left her home in Seattle, Washington, and traveled to Japan with the goal of gaining knowledge that would help others overcome the American prejudice against Japanese Americans. She met Jiro Murai at a social gathering and stayed in Japan for five years studying with him, and seven more years corresponding with him from the United States.

The meaning of Jin Shin Jyutsu has changed through the years, evolving into the translation "the art of the creator through the person of compassion." The essence of Jin Shin Jyutsu is a physiophilosophy using the hands to gently balance the flow of life energy in the body. It involves awakening to awareness of the complete harmony within ourselves and the universe. Burmeister called it an art and therefore a skillful creation, as opposed to a technique, which is a mechanical application. Today, Jin Shin Jyutsu in the United States can be broken down into eight core concepts. While many of these are similar to other Asian bodywork therapies, there are distinct differences.

A primary concept states that energy circulates throughout the universe and within each person. Another fundamental concept of Jin Shin Jyutsu is that this energy manifests into physical form in layers or levels known as the "depths." The seventh, eighth, and ninth depths exist on the unmanifested level (nonphysical), while depths one through six form the body.

Like most Asian bodywork therapies, the breath is considered a basic expression of life. Mary Burmeister said, "The breath is the ultimate tool. Go into the breath. Exhale and accept the gift the universe is giving you with every inhalation."

The trinity flows are pathways of energy that integrate and unify all parts of the body. The main central flow goes from the top of the head down the front, through the pubic bone, and back up to the top of the head. It is said to have a direct connection to the original source of life, recharging and revitalizing the other flows. The left and right supervisor flows complete the trinity. The two flows mirror each other and traverse up and down each side of the body, beginning at the knees. The diagonal mediator flows, while not considered a part of the trinity of flows, harmonize the supervisor flows with each other and with the main central flow. They mirror each other and start at the shoulders, going from front to back, side to side, and top to bottom, ending at the opposite knee from the starting shoulder.

Because energy moves up the front and down the back of the person in a continuous oval, there is a complementary relationship between the front and back of the body and the upper and lower parts of the body, which are distinguished by the waistline. A symptom of a problem in the upper part of the body usually finds the cause in the lower part of the body. The same holds for the front and back of the body.

Twenty-six safety energy locks, found on each side of the body, are the keys to utilizing Jin Shin Jyutsu. These are said to act as circuit breakers that close when there is a block in energy flow. A symptom of disease or pain serves as an alarm that says the energy system is out of balance.

Underlying harmony is always present, no matter what illness or emotional upset a person is experiencing. The root cause of all illness, trauma, and disharmony of any kind comes from blockages in the flow of energy. Freeing up the stagnant energy helps alleviate symptoms and remove the root cause of those systems.

A Jin Shin Jyutsu session begins with the practitioner helping the client become comfortable, usually by having the client lie faceup on a massage table. Then the practitioner begins an assessment of the client by feeling the pulse of both wrists to determine the current flow of energy, observing the body, and listening to the requests of the client. The pulse shows the practitioner the specific safety energy locks that need to be cleared to restore the flow of energy without creating any additional stress in the client's mind about the condition. The remaining treatment consists of gently placing the practitioner's fingers over one of the safety energy locks until they are cleared of congested energy. The practitioner continues to work with other safety energy locks that need to be cleared until all have been opened and the energy flow is restored. One or more depths may need work depending on the symptoms and the results of the assessment. The practitioner rechecks the client's pulse to verify that the energy is flowing freely. The practitioner may offer the client some self-help exercises to do at home.

Course Descriptions

Authorized Jin Shin Jyutsu instructors are listed on the website at www.jsjinc.net. Class materials are available in English, Spanish, German, Portuguese, Dutch, and French. The Burmeisters recommend that students take the Self-Help Class sometime during their training as Jin Shin Jyutsu practitioners. Once a student has taken the Five-Day Basic Seminar three times, he or she may use the name "Jin Shin Jyutsu" and the Japanese Kanji on their business identity. Both the name and the Kanji must bear the copyright symbol. Students who have completed three five-day basic seminars may help facilitate a self-help class. Students receive a certificate of attendance at the completion of the first five-day basic seminar and again when they have completed a third attendance. The second certificate states that they have completed 105 hours of class time.

▶ **Jin Shin Jyutsu Self-Help Class** teaches students the foundational self-sufficiency skills, which are the core of Jin Shin Jyutsu. Through self-help, Jiro Murai first proved the efficiency of these techniques. Through years of study, dedication, and direct experience, Mary Burmeister further condensed the essence of the teachings into three simple books that provide the student with dynamic tools for self-sufficiency.

▶ **The Five-Day Basic Seminar** is interspersed with lecture and ample periods of hands-on application with other participants. Each basic seminar consists of two parts. Part one, the foundation, introduces concepts such as the Safety Energy Locks, Trinity Flows, depths within the body, and the physiophilosophy of Jin Shin Jyutsu. Part two introduces the concepts of organ flows, listening to the pulse, Special Body Flows, and how to harmonize body, mind, and spirit. Part one must be taken before Part two.

▶ **Special Topic Classes** allow students to look at a specific Jin Shin Jyutsu subject in a more detailed way and provide more interaction with the instructor. Classes have a flexible format that can vary in size, number of days, and subject matter. The prerequisite is at least one five-day basic seminar.

▶ **Living the Art Seminar** explores Jin Shin Jyutsu Self-Help in depth through Mary Burmeister's three books. Students share the physiophilosophy and self-help practice with others, either privately or in a class. The prerequisite is attendance of at least one five-day basic seminar and basic knowledge of Burmeister's books.

▶ **Now Know Myself Seminar** further explores Burmeister's books with the primary objective of answering the unique concerns of student practitioners. The prerequisite is completing the five-day basic seminar three times.

· · · · · · · · · · · · · · · · ·

Continuing Education Units: Yes. Jin Shin Jyutsu is an approved provider for California Board of Registered Nursing, provider #CEP 12032; the National Certification Commission for Acupuncture and Oriental Medicine ACHB-238 for the five-day basic seminar and the living the art seminars only; and for massage therapists, approved by the National Certification Board for Therapeutic Massage and Bodywork, provider #285604-00. Check with your instructor to see if these CEUs are valid in your area.

Certification: Applicants desiring Jin Shin Jyutsu instructor certification must fill out a self-certification worksheet and a trainee application worksheet, which lists a number of tasks the applicant must accomplish. Those qualifying applicants begin a lengthy instructor candidacy program that may last from one to two years. The Jin

Shin Jyutsu Advisory Council works closely with instructor candidates and, upon approving the application, certifies the applicant as an instructor. There is no certification for practitioners. Students must take the five-day seminar at least three times before they can call themselves Jin Shin Jyutsu practitioners.

Participants: Open to anyone wanting to be more at peace with him- or herself.

Code of Ethics/Standards of Practice: No.

Suggested Reading
Burmeister, Alice. *The Touch of Healing*. New York: Bantam Books, 1997.

Availability: Classes are held in several countries all over the world can be located at www.jinshinjyutsu.com.

Resources

Jin Shin Jyutsu Inc., 8719 E. San Alberto Drive, Scottsdale, AZ 85258, 480-998-9331, info@jsjinc.net, www.jsjinc.net

Bibliography

Burmeister, Alice. *The Touch of Healing*. New York: Bantam Books, 1997.

www.jinshinjyutsu.com

www.healthandyoga.com

www.jsjinc.net

www.mysite.verizon.net/ron26/art

www.medindia.net/alternativemedicine

OHASHIATSU®

"**S**HIATSU" IS THE JAPANESE WORD for traditional Chinese acupressure. Etymologically, the word "Shiatsu" is a combination of two Japanese words. *Shimon* means "fingerprint" and *atsuryoku* means "the exertion of force or pressure." *Ohashi* means "big bridge." Together, Ohashiatsu, one of six popular styles of Shiatsu in the United States, attempts to be a "bridge" between Eastern and Western healing philosophies. The founder, Master Wataru Ohashi, who has been training practitioners and treating clients since the founding of Ohashi Institute in 1974, set the intention of bridging Eastern and Western philosophies of healing.

During the sixth century AD, a Chinese Buddhist monk named Gan Jin Osho brought Chinese medicine to Japan, and he had many pupils who spread the knowledge of Chinese medicine, including bodywork therapies. These therapies grew in popularity because family members could treat each other and their neighbors. For many centuries, Japan remained an isolated nation refusing to trade with other countries, especially the West. However, economic pressures encouraged the emperor of Japan to allow a limited number of traders access to Japan. With them came Western medicine.

In the 1800s, European influences, including in medicine, so captivated the Japanese that bodywork therapies were outlawed for some time. In 1919, Tamai Tempaku published a book on *Shiatsu Ho*, which means "finger pressure therapy." Tokujiro Namikoshi founded the Clinic of Pressure Therapy in 1925. That same year, the Shiatsu Therapists Association was formed and Shiatsu once again became a popular form of therapy.

Shiatsu stayed popular until the Allied occupation at the end of World War II, when General Douglas MacArthur outlawed body therapies and most other forms of Oriental medicine. Many people at that time who did Shiatsu and other forms of hands-on healing were blind because both the Chinese and the Japanese believed blind people had more sensitive fingers. A letter was sent to Helen Keller and she contacted President Harry Truman, who persuaded General MacArthur to make Shiatsu, acupuncture, and other Oriental healing modalities legal again.

Toshiko Phipps was the first Japanese to bring Shiatsu to the United States. He began teaching Shiatsu in the 1950s, but it wasn't until the 1970s that Shiatsu began to grow in popularity. Different styles and methods of Shiatsu have been developed since Phipps began to teach. The following five varieties, along with Ohashiatsu, comprise the six most commonly known styles of Shiatsu:

1. *Acupressure Shiatsu* follows traditional Chinese medicine in terms of clearing meridians of congested energy through the acupressure points. (For more information on meridians, see pages 4 and 7.)

2. *Five Element–Style Shiatsu* stems from the traditional Chinese medicine theories of the five elements, especially for treating emotional problems. The five elements consist of water, wood, fire, earth, and metal. Each of the five elements represents a number of different emotions and feelings, and the organ meridians are classified by elements. For example, anger is considered a wood element and connects to the liver meridian. Joy is considered a fire element and connects to the heart meridian. (For more information about five element theory, see pages 127–129.)

3. *Macrobiotic Shiatsu* uses traditional Chinese medicine meridian theory, Shiatsu performed with the bare feet, and the promotion of a harmonious way of living.

4. *Nippon-Style Shiatsu* stems from the teachings of Tokujiro Namikoshi and includes Western physiology as well as meridian theory.

5. *Zen Shiatsu*, developed by Shizuto Masunaga and gaining popularity in the United States, uses tonification and sedation principles, extended meridian channels, and Western physiology and psychology in its approach to healing. Tonification is the application of pressure on specific acupressure points to increase the rate of energy flowing through that

area. Sedation is the application of pressure on acupressure points to minimize the flow of overabundant energy.

6. Ohashiatsu focuses on continuity of movement, working from hara (center of gravity), cross-patterning, attention to "mother" and "messenger" hands, and emphasis on meridians more than on specific tsubos. Cross-patterning is what humans do when they crawl. The left hand and the right leg move together, followed by the right arm and the left leg. He has different uses for the hands. The mother hand stays in one place and senses or diagnoses the energy. The messenger hand moves and presses the appropriate places on the meridians and tsubos.

The main difference between Ohashiatsu and other forms of Eastern bodywork healing is its emphasis on communication and synergy between the practitioner and the receiver of the treatments. Energy passes between both the practitioner and the client, inspiring balance and harmony in each. Practitioners continually work on self-development and strive for physical, psychological, and spiritual harmony with their clients. To maintain this perspective, the principles of Ohashiatsu practitioners are encouraged to keep in mind are: just be there, don't press; use both hands and make a connection; be continuous; be natural; and be reverent.

As with other forms of Shiatsu, Ohashiatsu uses pressure points, called *tsubo* in Japanese. It focuses on continuity of movement, working from the hara (center of gravity), cross-patterning, attention to placement of the hands, and emphasis on meridians more than on specific tsubos. Practitioners use their hands, fingers, arms, knees, and elbows. Pressure is applied steadily with the weight of the whole body. In doing so, the practitioner manipulates the tsubos and meridians to facilitate energy flow and relieve physical pains and some of the symptoms of disease. Master Ohashi believes that Ohashiatsu is best used for maintaining good health rather than helping heal a disease, and suggests regular treatment to prevent energy blockages from forming.

During a session, an Ohashiatsu practitioner assesses the client and places him or her into one of two categories: *kyo* and *jitsu*. The kyo client presents an underfunctioning of the energy system and needs to be energized. The jitsu client presents an overfunctioning of the energy system and needs to be soothed. The session is usually done on a mat or carpeted floor with the client lying faceup. The practitioner begins working with hara in order to assess a person's health and to determine which meridians need work. There is no fixed routine. The practitioner works in a way that is appropriate to the client. The practitioner looks for stiffness, temperature fluctuation, and areas of pain, and applies pressure on the acupoints while the client exhales. For work on the back of the head, neck, and shoulders, the client is asked to lie on either side or on the stomach. The practitioner may help the client with some stretching exercises before, during, or after treatments to improve the client's flexibility and facilitate the flow of energy throughout the body.

Course Descriptions

The Ohashiatsu Institute in New York City and its affiliates follow the same curriculum, making it possible for students to study at several locations around the world. The institute's program meets a variety of goals. Some students attend courses to learn techniques for self-care, some because of an interest in Eastern culture, and some want to explore a new career or add techniques and knowledge to their current professional practice. Each course offers lecture, exercises, meditations, and hands-on training, but especially emphasizes experiential learning by students performing the techniques and concepts on themselves and others. The relaxed learning environment is one of nonjudgment, so students can find a safe place to share their experiences. The basic curriculum courses are 30 hours each and are offered in various formats throughout the year. In addition, the institute offers shorter courses that complement the course material.

▶ **Beginning I** students learn the fundamental principles of Ohashiatsu as they apply to bodywork and to every aspect of life. The benefits are felt immediately as the student becomes calmer, centered, and accepting of themselves and others. The course focuses on:

- Feeling the life force energy flow in the body
- Learning the natural movements central to Ohashiatsu
- Location of the energy meridians and some of the major acupoints
- The concept of yin and yang

- Experiencing enhanced sensitivity as well as increased body awareness and grace
- How to give a full-body session

▶ **Beginning II** emphasizes the "why" of working with specific meridians with Beginning I as a prerequisite. Topics include:

- An introduction to the five elements: fire, earth, metal, water, and wood
- How appearances, habits, emotions, and attitudes affect relationships with the five elements

▶ **Intermediate I** demonstrates why Ohashiatsu is a discipline for practitioners, with Beginning II is a prerequisite. Students learn:

- New techniques using their arms, elbows, and knees
- To increase body balance and grace
- How to make more than one connection with the client
- How to use the knees in conjunction with forearms
- Using Ohashiatsu as meditation
- An introduction to diagnostic areas of the body
- The psychological and emotional aspects of meridian energy and how they relate to the five elements

▶ **Intermediate II** introduces the Masunaga meridian extension system, with Intermediate I as a prerequisite. Dr. Masunaga, a psychologist turned Shiatsu practitioner and teacher, found that the psychological and emotional aspects of the meridians manifested themselves in other parts of the body than the traditional meridian system had shown. By learning the Masunaga meridian extensions, students will:

- Delve deeper into how physical situations can manifest in the emotions and psyche
- Learn how unbalanced emotions can result in physical pain and illness

▶ **Advanced I** further refines and broadens the techniques and concepts of Ohashiatsu. Students prepare a case study between Intermediate I and this class using knowledge from all courses. Students also learn various advanced techniques, including those involving seated positions.

▶ **Advanced II** brings students back to the basics, reminding them of the proper foundation. The course concludes with written and practical examination. Master Ohashi gives the final practical examination and tutorial. Students also learn muscle-meridian tonification, sedation, and new diagnostic approaches.

▶ **Ohashi's Oriental Diagnosis** is a 15-hour course to help students see the world from a different point of view. Students learn how to read the body for physical, mental, and spiritual conditions; how to compare Eastern and Western approaches to healing; and how to explore the precepts and paradoxes of Oriental medicine.

▶ **Anatomy I** is an 18-hour course in which students learn about the musculoskeletal anatomy, physiology, cell and tissue structure, and the nervous system.

▶ **Anatomy II** is an 18-hour course in which students learn about the endocrine, circulatory, lymphatic, immune, respiratory, digestive, urinary, reproductive, and integumentary systems; the form and function of anatomy; and the correlation of bodily systems with the five element theory.

. . . .

Continuing Education Units: Yes. The provider is the National Certification Board for Therapeutic Massage and Bodywork #450117-06.

Certification: The basic program takes about two years to complete. After graduation, students may apply to become a Certified Ohashiatsu® Instructor and join the instructor training program, which takes another year. Students not wishing to teach may apply for the title Certified Ohashiatsu® Consultant.

Participants: Courses are open to everyone of all physical capabilities and age. The modality is of interest to both experienced and inexperienced students.

Code of Ethics/Standards of Practice: Yes. The Code of Ethics is a part of the consultant contract.

Legalities: Some states and a few countries require a license for the practice of Ohashiatsu.

Suggested Reading

Ohashi, Wataru. *Beyond Shiatsu: Ohashi's Bodywork Book.* New York: Oxford University Press, 2006.

———. *Do-It-Yourself Shiatsu: How to Perform the Ancient Japanese Art of Acupressure.* New York: Penguin, 2001.

———. *Reading the Body: Ohashi's Book of Oriental Diagnosis.* New York: Penguin, 1991.

Availability: Classes are available in Austria, France, Germany, Holland, Israel, Italy, Sweden, the United Kingdom, and the United States. To find a session in your area, go to www.ohashiatsu.org.

Resources

The Ohashiatsu Institute, 147 West 25th Street, 6th Floor, New York NY 10001, 800-810-4190, info@ohashiatsu.org, www.ohashiatsu.org

Bibliography

Dubitsky, Carl. "History of Shiatsu." *ABBTA Bulletin*, Spring 1991.

Jarmey, Chris, and Gabriel Mojay. *Shiatsu: The Complete Guide.* New York: Simon & Schuster, 1991.

www.ohashi.com

www.shiatsu-co.co.uk/site/a-brief-history-of-shiatsu

www.spaanz.kiwinz.net/shiatsu-history

PRANIC HEALING®

*P*RANA IS A SANSKRIT WORD that means "vital life force" or "life force energy," which refers to the natural energy flowing through the body and keeping it alive. Pranic healing is a nontouch technique for healing emotional imbalance and physical problems by working with the individual's aura, or energetic field, where many physical and emotional problems are believed to originate. This energy field, often referred to as the etheric body, corresponds to the body's chakra system. *Chakra*, the Sanskrit word for "spinning wheels," refers to energy centers or vortexes that regulate and maintain the body's flow of energy. By working directly with this energy field, a Pranic Healer is able to determine which chakras might be unbalanced, and in turn cleanse, realign, and energize the body, mind, and spirit.

Pranic Healing, based on ancient Eastern principles, was reintroduced to the world by Grand Master Choa Kok Sui, sometimes referred to as GMCKS. A Chinese-Filipino scientist, educator, and philanthropist, Master Choa has written several practical manuals on Pranic Healing. His works are the distillation of over twenty years of studies and experimentation with topics such as yoga, chi-kung, and the Kaballah, and are published in over twenty-seven languages around the world. He primarily believes that energy healing consists of clearing out what he called "dirty," congested, or blocked energy and replacing it with "clean" healing energy.

Pranic Healing recognizes five components of energy anatomy: the chakras, the meridians, the inner aura, the outer aura, and the health aura. Master Choa Kok Sui refers to the chakras as "power centers" or "transformers," and specifies three types: major chakras, minor chakras, and mini-chakras. He believes there are eleven major chakras, which are those most often used in healing work. The minor and mini-chakras are found in the jaw, hands, feet, arms, and legs and are infrequently used in healing techniques.

According to Master Choa, chakras regulate energy and meridians are pathways where energy flows through the body. The meridians do not follow the same structure as the circulatory system or the nervous system, but have a set structure of their own. Pranic Healing identifies several large meridians and hundreds of small ones, and focuses on the two largest meridians. The front meridian, called the functional channel, goes from the top of the head, down the front of the body, and ends at the base of the spine. The governor channel runs up the back of the body from the base of the spine to the top of the head. Master Choa believes all the major chakras except the spleen are located along these two large meridians.

"Aura" comes from Latin and means "air" or "breeze." In energy medicine, it refers to the energy field that emanates from within and around the body. Master Choa specifies three dimensions of the aura. For most people the inner aura starts at the center of the body and extends out about five inches all around the body, with the outer edges closely following the contours of the body. It is composed of energy, or prana, that connects to the chakras and the meridians. The outer aura starts at the center of the body and extends out several feet from the body in the shape of an oval, forming a barrier to hold the body's energy in place. The health aura is composed of a number of two-foot-long rays that radiate outward from the pores in the skin of the body. Healthy people have straight rays while people who are ill have irregular or misshapen rays.

Prana comes from three principal sources: the Air, the Earth, and the Sun, and all three can be drawn into the body through the chakras. Sun, or solar prana, a refined energy, invigorates the whole body. Air prana, which is slightly less refined and has a lower vibration than solar prana, can be used for general healing and sweeping. Earth prana, used for increasing physical power and healing less delicate areas, has the lowest vibrational rate.

According to Master Choa, incorporating color into a Pranic Healing routine can produce a quicker, more efficient result. Each of the chakras is associated with certain colors, imbalances, and diseases. The practitioner sets an intention to focus the appropriate color on the area that needs treatment. The color is projected through the mind's eye in the form of a pastel ring with a white center, as a solid color can be too strong.

An important practice in Pranic Healing is energetic hygiene, which consists of emotional regulation, proper diet, physical exercise, maintaining a clean environment, and regulating salt in the foods we eat. According to Master Choa, salt is one of the easiest ways of clearing the aura of dirty energy. He recommends salt baths, using salt soap in the shower, or swimming in the ocean followed by a regular cleansing. A proper diet consists of foods and vitamins that are energetically clean and high in vibration. Practitioners may also recommend exercises that help cleanse the physical body of dirty energy. Clients may also be asked to cleanse their homes and work areas with Pranic Healing techniques.

Sessions begin with Pranic breathing techniques; then practitioners scan the inner aura for energetic disturbances using their hands. They clear away congestion and energy blocks by sweeping with their hands. Once the aura is clean, the practitioner replenishes or energizes weakened areas to complete the healing. The practitioner may recommend changes in diet, specific physical exercises, and the practice of one or more meditations.

The Pranic Healing system is meant as a complementary approach to orthodox medicine. Pranic Healing practitioners do not physically touch the recipient's body, diagnose disease, prescribe drugs or substances, or make any health claims or promises.

Course Descriptions

All Pranic Healing courses are experiential, which means the students learn by performing all the techniques and exercises on themselves and each other. The classes listed here are also found on the website www.pranichealing.com. All instructors teach the same material so there is little variance between a class taught in the United States and the same class taught in the Philippines.

The program has six levels of certification: Associate Pranic Healer, Certified Pranic Healer, Certified Pranic Psychotherapy, Certified Senior Pranic Healer, Certified Assistant Master Pranic Healer, and Certified Master Pranic Healer. In addition to the classes, supplementary formal sessions and teleconferences are available to discuss healing applications and experiential approaches. Applicants for each level must submit a required number of successfully healed cases.

▶ **MCKS Pranic Healing® Level I Course** is a two-day class that addresses the basics of working with the energy aura, including learning to scan, or feel, the energy, sweep away congested energy, and supplement areas in the aura that have a pranic deficiency. Students begin by learning to activate the energy centers or chakras in the centers of their hands. This enables them to become sensitive to prana and scan a person's energy field to identify blockages and then cleanse, energize, and revitalize the area with new prana. Topics covered in Pranic Healing Level 1 are as follows:

- Energetic anatomy and preventive healing
- Self-Pranic Healing
- Step-by-step techniques for specific ailments
- How to apply distant healing to those not present

Pranic Healing Level 1 is a prerequisite for all other courses.

▶ **MCKS Advanced Pranic Healing® Course is a two-day class** addressing the use of color for quicker, more effective healing results. Some of the skills taught are:

- Advanced color healing
- Advanced scanning
- Energetic methods of enhancing the body's innate healing ability
- Influencing and reprogramming the consciousness of diseased cells and organs

▶ **MCKS Pranic Psychotherapy®** is taught over a weekend or three evenings. It applies Pranic Healing techniques to healing and alleviating emotional and mental imbalances. In the Pranic Healing view, negative emotions and traumatic experiences are essentially unhealthy thought forms that become lodged in the aura and the critical energy centers. These energies are often difficult to release, requiring months or even years of traditional psychotherapy to experience improvement. In Pranic Psychotherapy, students learn advanced energetic extraction techniques on affected chakras to alleviate phobia, compulsion, and addiction. Other topics include:

- Self-healing for tension, irritability, grief, and anxiety
- Repairing damaged or cracked protective webs in the chakras to prevent future intrusion
- Purging negative programming acquired during childhood
- Healing the effects of psychic attacks
- Shielding techniques to protect the chakras, aura, and material possessions
- Extracting and disintegrating negative energies and patterns

▶ **MCKS Pranic Crystal Healing**® is a one-day or two-evening workshop in which the student learns how to harness the power of crystals and gemstones to enhance healing abilities, spirituality, and prosperity, covering topics such as:

- Increasing healing power by using special crystals
- Creating personal barriers and shields
- Activating crystals, rings, pendants, and jewelry to attract good health and prosperity
- Using crystals as protective devices to guard against emotional and psychic attack
- Learning which crystals and stones are appropriate for which purposes
- Using the colored pranic energies of color crystals

▶ **MCKS Pranic Psychic Self-Defense Course** is a one- or two-evening workshop that teaches students how to protect themselves and loved ones from psychic attack, negative intention, malicious entities, and energetic pollution. Students learn scientific ways of using pranic energy to properly protect themselves and their belongings, surroundings, and loved ones. Topics covered include:

- Closing the aura to prevent intrusion
- Understanding how psychic attack is launched and how to guard against it
- Placing a protective aura around a business to ensure prosperity
- Using holy objects for protection, empowerment, and good luck
- Practicing advanced psychic self-defense techniques, especially for healers

▶ **MCKS Higher Clairvoyance** is taught over three evenings and addresses the techniques used by high-level clairvoyants to perceive the chakras, auras, and inner worlds. This hands-on workshop reveals the hidden principles and ancient secrets to develop the "higher eyes" or "Buddha eyes" mentioned in Eastern literature. By developing sensitive vision, the student is able to quickly and safely perceive the aura, chakras, and other subtle energies.

▶ **MCKS Kriyashakti® Course** is a two-day workshop that addresses cultivating material abundance to allow freedom to pursue spiritual goals. Students learn how to properly harness the power of their thoughts, subtle energies, and auric field to create a life of prosperity and success both materially as well as spiritually, including the following:

- Inner Kriyashakti®
- Prosperity meditations
- How to harness the power of the spoken word
- Special mudras and techniques to harness the power of money and abundance

▶ **MCKS Spiritual Business Management** is a unique approach to managing both personal lives and business using spiritual and metaphysical techniques. Through the use of simple meditation techniques, students develop sharp minds, increasing their capacities for making accurate decisions within business situations. The workshop is practical and structured around the core teachings of ancient spiritual and esoteric principles in a way that is relevant to developing a modern and effective approach to corporate management, including:

- Managing stress and developing focus through proven breathing and meditation techniques
- Rapid physical and mental recharging techniques
- Creating a productive, efficient, and harmonious work environment
- Effective time management

. . . .

Continuing Education Units: No.

Certification: The program offers six levels of healer certification and one level of healer trainer certification. The Institute for Inner Studies provides the certification.

Participants: Doctors, nurses, massage therapists, acupuncturists, chiropractors, the clergy, homemakers, and engineers have all attended these classes. People from all walks of life are encouraged to attend.

Suggested Reading

Co, Stephen, Eric B. Robins, and John Merryman. *Your Hands Can Heal You.* New York: Simon & Schuster, 2004.

Sui, Choa Kok. *Miracles through Pranic Healing*, 4th edition. Makati City, Philippines: Institute for Inner Studies Publishing Foundation, 2004.

Availability: Pranic Healing is found in seventy-four countries all over the planet. For a session with an experienced practitioner, go to www.pranichealing.com.

Resources

U.S. Pranic Healing Center, The American Institute of Asian Studies, 6251 Schaefer Avenue, Suite C, Chino, CA 91710, 888-470-5656, info@ pranichealing.com, www.pranichealing.com

Bibliography

Co, Stephen, Eric B. Robins, and John Merryman. *Your Hands Can Heal You.* New York: Simon & Schuster, 2004.

www.globalpranichealing.com

www.pranichealing.com

www.yourhandscanhealyou.com

QIGONG

THE WORD *QIGONG* (pronounced *chee gong*) is a combination of two ideas: "qi" means air, breath of life, or vital energy of the body, and "gong" means the skill of working with or cultivating self-discipline and achievement. The art of Qigong consists primarily of meditation, relaxation, physical movement, mind-body integration, and breathing exercises. According to traditional Chinese medicine, of which Qigong is a part, good health is a result of a free-flowing, well-balanced energy system.

Many theories concerning the origins of Qigong abound. One theory suggests it began as a form of dancing to relieve arthritis for people who lived in damp climates. Another suggests Qigong movements began as mimicry of the movement of animals. Over time, five classic schools of Qigong took form: martial arts, Confucian, Taoist, Buddhist, and medical. Yin and yang theory forms an important part of Chinese medicine and Qigong, and each of the five Qigong divisions is classified as either yin or yang depending on whether it is active, passive, or a combination of the two. Yang can be described as the sunny side of a hill and is considered male, sun, or active. Yin is the shadow side and is considered female, earth, or passive. Still or internal (yin) forms of Qigong emphasize quiet, motionless meditation and breath regulation, and can be done while lying down, sitting, or standing motionless. Moving or external (yang) Qigong involves the movement of the body and is used to strengthen the body for health and for protection in martial arts.

During the Liang dynasty (AD 502–557), Qigong was used for martial arts purposes. Training included exercises to protect the body and develop the hands and feet as weapons against an attack. These same exercises were used by monks who meditated for extended periods of time and needed a form of movement to keep healthy. This division of Qigong is referred to as yang because it is an active exercise.

Confucian Qigong exercises calm the mind to make it more receptive to moral wisdom. Practitioners used it to attain higher moral character and intelligence. Confucian exercises are passive, and therefore yin.

Taoist Qigong uses breathing techniques, internal massage, visualization, and some physical exercise to promote a balance between the body, mind, and soul. The preservation of the physical body and a high level of virtue are the goals of practitioners of Taoist Qigong. A combination of both active and passive exercises, Taoist Qigong is said to be yin/yang.

During the Eastern Han dynasty (AD 50–60), Buddhism came to China from India and brought with it meditation and training practices. A few years later, Tibetan Buddhist monks were invited to share their practices, which influenced the practice of Qigong. These exercises, which are yin, help expand inner awareness, and practitioners use them to free the mind and cultivate virtue and wisdom, which is thought to help bring about higher levels of consciousness and enlightenment. Some Tibetan Buddhist Qigong techniques do not involve any movement of the body, but are done through visualization.

Medical Qigong exercises, also yang, are currently popular in China and are gaining in popularity in Japan. Starting in the Wei dynasty (AD 220–265), Chinese doctors began to use Qigong as a way to preserve good health and treat disease. A few hundred years later, several books on Chinese medicine contained Qigong therapies for the further treatment of disease. About this time, the Brahman Method of Indian Massage and Laozi Massage were added to Qigong exercises to promote good health.

Medical Qigong involves concentrating on breathing, mind, and movement. Practitioners who have reached a state of good health and maintain strong flow of qi can then heal others by passing qi on to a client, which can be done through hands-on touching or from a distance. By transmitting qi to another person, energy blockages can be released, allowing the energy system to be restored.

In all of its forms, Qigong emphasizes technique. Practitioners consider qi the essential element in the healing process. Because it is their aim to give qi to others, they must recharge themselves through movement and meditation, but Qigong practitioners do not do all the work. Clients are prescribed daily exercises and meditations, and healing through Qigong techniques is considered a partnership.

A session with a Qigong practitioner usually takes about an hour, perhaps with extra time allotted for the first session. The practitioner observes the physical, emotional, and energetic condition of the client and forms a treatment protocol. The client remains fully clothed while the practitioner works no more than a foot away, sometimes lightly touching the client to guide and manipulate the movement of energy. At the end of the treatment, the practitioner prescribes medical Qigong exercises and meditations tailored to meet the specific needs of the client.

Qigong has many different spellings and names. Some spell it "chi gung" or "chi kung." Other names for it have been Xingki, Daoyin, Xuangong, and Jinggon. In 1953, Liu Gui-Zheng published a paper entitled "Practice on Qigong Therapy," establishing "Qigong" as the widely accepted term.

Qigong schools are found in many countries around the world. The International Institute of Medical Qigong is fashioned after the Hai Dian University of traditional Chinese medicine in Beijing, China. The Chinese Ministry of Health honored the school for exceeding the Chinese standards for academic and clinical instruction. Their classes are samples of the many forms of Qigong practiced in both the East and the West.

Course Descriptions

The following class descriptions come from the International Institute of Medical Qigong. Their certification programs are based on curriculum from the Medical Qigong College at the Hai Dian University and are used clinically at the Xi Yuan Qigong Hospital in Beijing, China. They have four programs: medical Qigong practitioner, medical Qigong therapist, Master of medical Qigong, and Doctor of medical Qigong.

▶ **Medical Qigong Practitioner** consists of 128 hours of classwork, 72 hours of clinical work, and 8 hours for the final exam. The classwork is divided into four courses followed by a final 8-hour set of exams. Certification courses are taught both in weekly classes and intensive seminars. Classes include:

▶ **Introduction to Medical Qigong Therapy** introduces students to medical Qigong exercises that maintain good health and healing, calm the mind, and reconnect with spirit. Students also gain an understanding of the regulations of Qigong and how to develop a medical Qigong routine. Topics include:

- Basic theories of energy tonification, purgation, and regulation of the body's organs and energy channels
- Strengthening the body's protective energy field
- Respiration, posture, and mental training
- Emotional detoxification
- Healing sound therapy
- Analyzing and categorizing Qigong exercises
- Introduction to medical Qigong prescriptions
- Establishing a personal medical Qigong workout

▶ **Introduction to Medical Qigong Diagnosis and Treatments** has Introduction to Medical Qigong Therapy as a prerequisite. The class introduces the student to more theories of purgation, tonification, regulation, and cultivation. Topics include:

- A progressive series of advanced Shengong (spirit skill) meditations and exercises
- Development of advanced intuitive diagnostic skills
- Medical Qigong protocol for treating patients
- Developing energetic sensitivity and perception skills
- Energetic projection skills
- Advanced emotional detoxification therapy
- Introduction to clinical energetic diagnostic techniques
- Introduction to prescriptions and clinical treatments

▶ **Clinical Foundations of Medical Qigong Therapy** is an overview of the major principles and foundational structures that govern traditional Chinese medical Qigong. Introduction to Diagnosis and Treatments is a prerequisite. Topics include:

- Functional properties of energy
- Materializing and dematerializing energy

- Establishing a medical Qigong clinic
- Combining medical Qigong with other healing modalities
- Qi-emitting methods
- Internal organ prescriptions and healing sound therapy
- Comprehension of the body's energy matrix

▶ **The Treatment of Organ Diseases and Medical Qigong Prescription Exercises** offers students a deeper comprehension of specific organ diseases with practical clinical applications of Chinese medical Qigong therapy. Medical Qigong Diagnosis and Treatments is a prerequisite. Topics include:

- Treatment of six primary diseases: liver, heart, spleen, stomach, lung, and kidney

▶ **Clinical Theatre, Internship, and Final Examination** is a five-day seminar finishing with the final exam. Exams include written, oral, and practical examinations plus clinical competencies. Students who pass are certified as medical Qigong practitioners and are qualified to take the advanced 500-hour medical Qigong therapist training. Students receive firsthand experience with medical Qigong diagnoses and treatments. Topics include:

- Energetic dysfunction
- Symptom manifestation
- Exploring case studies
- Integrating advanced clinical modalities
- Applying advanced diagnosis and advanced energetic modulation skills

▶ **Medical Qigong Therapist** is a certification program and requires 272 hours of classroom time, 50 hours of basic traditional Chinese medicine theory, 100 hours of Western anatomy and physiology, and 132 hours of clinical experience. Medical Qigong Practitioner certification is a prerequisite. Classes include the following.

▶ **Sensory, Intuitive, and Perceptual Diagnosis** introduces the student to sensory, intuitive, and perceptual skills used in the medical Qigong clinic for the diagnosis and treatment of patients. Topics include:

- Applications of intuitive and perceptual qi diagnosis
- Diagnosis based on kinesthetic and empathic qi absorption
- Hand diagnosis based on body association
- Diagnosis based on auric fields and intention
- Long-distance medical Qigong therapy
- Faith projection
- Negative thought projections and medical Qigong therapy
- Auxiliary medical Qigong healing modalities

▶ **Medical Qigong Dao Yin Therapy and Rectifying Qi Deviations** provides students with a deeper comprehension of the body's energetic relationship to the physical structure and mental and emotional disorders and deviations of the psyche. Medical Qigong Diagnosis and Treatments is a prerequisite. Topics include:

- Postural, respiratory, and mental training
- Rectifying qi deviations occurring from improper Qigong training
- Psychic attacks using mantras for protection during encounters with spirit entities

▶ **Medical Qigong Therapy for Pediatrics, Geriatrics, Gynecology, Neurology, and Psychology** exposes students to specialized clinical treatments of physical illness and the management of the patient's emotional, mental, and spiritual states. Medical Qigong Diagnosis and Treatments is a prerequisite. Topics include:

- Early stages of child growth and development
- Prescriptions for children
- Prescriptions for senility
- Etiology and pathology of gynecological diseases
- Treatment protocols for menopause and menstrual complications
- Afflictions such as stroke, coma, facial paralysis, and multiple sclerosis
- Treating emotional anxiety, phobia, and addiction and self-treatment prescriptions for psychoemotional disorder

▶ **Introduction to Treatment of Cancer with Medical Qigong Therapy** exposes students to specialized clinical treatments of cancer and the management of the patient's emotional, mental, and spiritual state surrounding the disease. Medical Qigong Diagnosis and Treatments is a prerequisite for this course. Topics include:

- Etiology and pathology of cyst, tumor, and cancer formation
- Categorization of cysts and tumors according to traditional Chinese medicine
- Medical Qigong approach to cancer prescriptions
- Emission therapy for the treatment of brain tumors; breast cysts, tumors, and cancer; uterine tumors and cancer; cervical cancer; ovarian cysts; prostate cancer; lung cancer; and colon and rectal cancer

▶ **Clinical Theatre, Internship, and Final Examination** is a five-day seminar finishing with written, oral, and practical examinations plus clinical competencies. Students who pass are certified as Medical Qigong Therapists and are qualified to take the advanced 1,000-hour Master of Medical Qigong Training. Students will receive firsthand experience with medical Qigong diagnoses and treatments. Topics include:

- Energetic dysfunction
- Symptom manifestation
- Exploring case studies
- Integrating advanced clinical modalities
- Applying advanced diagnosis and advanced energetic modulation skills

▶ **Master of Medical Qigong** is a certification program requiring 408 classroom hours and outside class hours consisting of 32 hours of advanced traditional Chinese medicine theory; 16 hours of first aid and CPR and 32 hours of a movement style of Qigong; and 362 hours of clinical work. Medical Qigong Therapist is a prerequisite of this program. Classes include:

▶ **Introduction to Chinese Energetic Alchemy** introduces students to the study of Daoist forces and affords a deeper comprehension of the body's physical, emotional, mental, and energetic relationship to the universal and environmental energetic fields. Topics include:

- The influences of energy, food, and diet on the human body

- Prenatal and postnatal energy variations
- The spiritual aspects of the yin organs
- Advanced Shen Gong cultivation methods
- Soul projection, spirit projection, and energy projection

▶ **Energetic Anatomy and Physiology** introduces students to the five dominions of energy, energetic embryology, and traditional Chinese medicine from a medical Qigong perspective. Topics include:

- Extensive study of advanced energy manifestations and complications and how to heal them
- Understanding fetal toxins
- Fascia development and energy flow
- Yin and yang divisions
- The function of the body's energetic points
- The extraordinary yang organs
- Etiology of medical Qigong therapy
- The differentiation of syndromes and the diagnosis and treatment of patients

▶ **Treatment of Cancer with Medical Qigong Therapy** delves deeper into the study of the treatment of various types of cancers and tumor formations. Introduction to Treatment of Cancer with Medical Qigong Therapy is a prerequisite. Topics include:

- Emission therapy for the treatment of bone cancer, myeloma, leukemia, lymphoma, and skin cancer
- Radiation and chemotherapy
- Medical Qigong and surgery
- Diet and nutrition
- Social oncology

▶ **Medical Qigong Treatment of Spiritual Disorders** introduces students to Chinese spiritual dimensions and clinical interactions with the spirit world. Students will have exposure to specialized clinical treatments of spirit oppression and possession. Medical Qigong Diagnosis and Treatments is a prerequisite. Topics include:

- Sorcery and defending against psychic attack
- Dealing with benevolent and malevolent spirit entities

▶ **Clinical Theatre, Internship, and Final Examination** is a five-day seminar finishing with written, oral, and practical examinations plus clinical competencies. Students who pass are certified as Masters of Medical Qigong and are qualified to take the advanced 2,000-hour Doctor of Medical Qigong Training. Students will receive firsthand experience with medical Qigong diagnoses and treatments. Topics include:

- Energetic dysfunction
- Symptom manifestations
- Exploring case studies
- Integrating advanced clinical modalities
- Applying advanced diagnosis and advanced energetic modulation skills

▶ **Doctor of Medical Qigong** has students working toward one of three separate certification programs: oncology, independent, and gerontology. Students of the independent program may specialize in pediatrics, gynecology, neurology, psychology, and surgery. Completion of each of these programs takes about two years.

▶ **Oncology Doctor of Medical Qigong Certification Program** focuses on the treatment of various types and stages of cancer using medical Qigong treatment therapy. Students must be graduates of the Master of Medical Qigong certification program and have passed the Doctor of Medical Qigong entrance exam. The oncology program offers students:

- Medical Qigong prescription exercises and meditations used for enhancing clinical treatments
- In-depth study of each cancer's energetic etiology
- An understanding of how or why the energetic patterns within the human body can become influenced, corrupted, and create metastasis

- An understanding of the body's energetic relationship to the physical structure, including mental and emotional disorders as well as the spiritual factors of cancer formation
- Clinical protocols used for the treatment of scar tissue, organ amputation, and the treatment of side effects from radiation therapy and chemotherapy
- The study of herbal prescriptions, diet, and social oncology

▶ **Independent Doctor of Medical Qigong Certification Program** facilitates a student's desire to specialize in an area outside of oncology or gerontology. Only ten candidates at a time are accepted. Students must be graduates of the Master of Medical Qigong certification program and have passed the Doctor of Medical Qigong entrance exam, and must be self-motivated. Candidates will:

- Work closely with Dr. Bernard Shannon, executive director of the International Institute of Qigong, throughout the program
- Provide progress reports and source material summaries for review
- Write a dissertation
- Perform clinical trials

▶ **Gerontology Doctor of Medical Qigong Certification Program** focuses on geriatrics and the problems of aging. Students must be graduates of the Master of Medical Qigong certification program and have passed the Doctor of Medical Qigong entrance exam to verify academic and energetic competency. Students will work closely with Dr. Seth Lefkowitz, instructor for the gerontology program, during the course of their program, write a dissertation, and perform clinical trials

· · · · · · · · · · · · · · · · ·

Continuing Education Units: No.

Certification: Yes, presented at the completion of each course.

Participants: Open to health-care professionals, students of traditional Chinese medicine, and those interested in Chinese energetic medicine.

Code of Ethics/Standards of Practice: Yes.

Suggested Reading

Clark, Angus. *Secrets of Qigong.* London: Dorling Kindersley, 2001.

Cohen, Kenneth. *The Way of Qigong: The Art and Science of Chinese Energy Healing.* New York: Random House, 1999.

Tse, Michael. *Qigong for Health and Vitality.* New York: St. Martin's, 1996.

Availability: Classes are held almost anywhere in the world. To find a class, go to www.nqa.org. Be sure to ask which type of Qigong classes the instructor offers. For a session with a medical Qigong practitioner, go to www.qigongmedicine.com.

Resources

International Institute of Medical Qigong, 73-145 Guadalupe Avenue, PO Box 1435, Palm Desert, CA, 800-848-0649, info@MedicalQigong.com, www.medicalqigong.org

The National Qigong Association, PO Box 270065, St. Paul, MN 55127, 888-815-1893, www.nqa.org

Bibliography

www.acupuncture.com/qigng_tuina/qigonghistory

www.innerself.com/Fitness/qigong_history

www.medicalqigong.org

www.qi-energy.com/qigonghistory

REFLEXOLOGY

REFLEXOLOGY IS A COMPLEMENTARY HEALING PROCEDURE based on the idea that applying pressure at specific spots of the body, called reflex points, can stimulate a therapeutic effect in other parts of the body, including the muscular, circulatory, and lymphatic systems. Those points are located on the hands, feet, and ears (but reflexology is most commonly applied to the feet). For example, a reflex point is located at the top of the ear that is said to help regulate allergies. Another reflex point is found at the base of the heel and is said to help alleviate hemorrhoids. Reflex maps, illustrations of the reflex points and their correspondences, indicate which areas of the hands, feet, and ears can be treated to help heal various internal organs and processes of the body. These reflex points are arranged in the shape of the human body on the hands and feet. The points form the shape of a baby in the fetal position (upside down) on the ears.

The importance of feet has a long and varied history stemming from many parts of the world. The earliest known records of foot work are found in the 2330 BC Egyptian tomb of Ankhmahor ("the physician's tomb") at Saqqara. On one wall is a painting depicting a scene of physicians working on the feet and hands of their patients. Whether or not they are doing reflexology has not been determined. Reflexology references show up in histories of other cultures. Symbols are carved in 2,000-year-old stone replicas of the Buddha's feet located in India, China, and Japan. Native American record keepers tell tales of medicine men stimulating the feet as part of their healing practice. Delphi, in ancient Greece, has records of treatments on the feet similar to modern-day reflexology. Russian doctors also used pressure points on the feet to relieve stress and help ease muscle pain and tension.

Sokushindo, Japanese for reflexology, traces its origins back to India through China to about 40 BC. Buddhist monks from India traveled to China to teach Buddhism and took a form of foot massage similar to reflexology with them. Foot massage stayed popular in China until the era when the practice of binding women's feet came into vogue and touching a woman's feet was against the law. At the time, touching a man's feet was also considered impolite, and foot massage all but disappeared from China until the 1800s.

In the late 1800s, scientists began to take an interest in reflex studies, including Sir Henry Head of London, who discovered what he called "zones" on the skin, with each zone corresponding to specific organs or diseased parts of the body. Head claimed that when one of the organs was diseased, the related zone would be extrasensitive to touch. William Fitzgerald, MD, often called the father of reflexology, studied Sir Henry Head's work and that of other European and Russian scientists. In 1915, he introduced zone therapy, which postulated that there are ten zones running from each toe, up to the head, and out through the fingers, and that all parts of the body correspond to one or more of these zones. At that time, reflexology was known as zone therapy.

Joe Shelby Riley, MD, in his book *Zone Reflex* published in 1924, refers to horizontal zones as well as vertical zones throughout the body, and he also added a few pressure points to the outer ear. Up until that time, pressure points were believed to exist mainly on the feet and the hands. A physical therapist named Eunice D. Ingham developed what she called "foot reflex therapy" in the 1930s and published books on the subject. She did not limit her work to just the zones, but also took into account the anatomical model of the human body to determine the areas needing work. In 1961, physiotherapists objected to the word "therapy" in the name "zone therapy," and so "reflexology" became the accepted term.

Reflexology on the ears became popular after a French doctor, Paul Nogier, MD, documented a complete reflex map of the human body on the outer ear. He also became known as the father of auriculotherapy. The term "ear reflexology" was coined by Bill Flocco in 1982, when he founded the American Academy of Reflexology. Flocco found that some disease responds better to foot reflexology, others to hand reflexology, and still others to ear reflexology. Along with Terry Oleson, PhD, he published the first research study using reflexology in the journal *Obstetrics and*

Gynecology (December 1993, vol. 82, no. 6). The title of their study was "Randomized Controlled Study of Premenstrual Symptoms Treated with Ear, Hand, and Foot Reflexology."

A reflexology session takes about an hour, although the first visit may be longer. The practitioner does an intake interview by asking about general health issues, diet, exercise, and medical history. He or she will then look at the color, texture, and feel of the hands, feet, and ears. Treatment consists of placing pressure with the fingers, and occasionally the entire hand, at those specific sites on the feet, hands, and ears depending upon the problem that was ascertained. Sometimes the client can feel slight pain in sensitive areas of the feet, hands, or ears, but usually experiences a sense of comfort and relief.

Course Descriptions

The following classes come from the American Academy of Reflexology's Foot, Hand, Ear Reflexology Professional Certification Course. Students take both a written and a practical exam one to two months after the last day of class, each of which must be passed in order to receive certification.

▶ **Beginning Class** creates a foundation of knowledge on which the Certification Course is based. The workshop lasts four days. Students may take the first four days of class without having to continue to certification work. The first two days consist of **Foot Reflexology.** Topics include the history of the technique, its therapeutic benefits, the foot reflexology map, various foot reflexing techniques, and how to lead a session, including pressure application and a 1-hour foot reflexology routine.

Hand Reflexology is addressed on the third day. Topics include its history, a Western hand reflexology map, the similarities between the hands and feet, causes of tenderness, various techniques regarding how to hold hands for reflexing, and how to lead a session, including pressure application, contraindications, the benefits of working with the hands, and a 1-hour hand reflexology routine.

The fourth day covers **Ear Reflexology** and topics include its history and primary theories, the difference between ear reflexology and auriculotherapy, the structure of the ear, various ear reflexing techniques, and how to lead a session, including exploration of the subtle pulses of the outer ear, the advantages of the outer ear work, and a half hour ear reflexology routine.

▶ **Integration of Foot, Hand, and Ear Reflexology** is for the intermediate to advanced student intending to complete the Integrated Foot, Hand, Ear Reflexology Professional Certificate Course. It consists of four three-day weekends with time in between for students to work on their practicum hours and hone their skills. The class covers:

- Advanced foot, hand, and ear reflexology routines, including integrating all three and targeting the work for specific areas of the body
- Setting priorities when reflexing, such as determining when accessing the feet, hands, or ears is more effective
- Human anatomy from the reflexologist's point of view
- Effective use of client history forms, legal documents, the code of ethics, and licensing issues
- How to build and maintain a practice, including business and marketing skills

. . . .

Continuing Education Units: Yes. Approvers are the American Reflexology Certification Board (ARCB), the National Certification Board for Therapeutic Massage and Bodywork (NCBTMB), Associated Bodywork Massage Professionals (ABMP), and the Bureau for Private Postsecondary and Vocational Education (BPPVE).

Certification: National certification is granted by the American Reflexology Certification Board with the passage of a standardized test and completion of courses offered by an accepted school of reflexology.

Participants: Anyone interested in better health or a career in reflexology.

Code of Ethics/Standards of Practice: Yes.

Suggested Reading
Issel, Christine. 1996. *Reflexology: Art, Science, History*. United States: New Frontier Publishing.

Kolster, Bernard C., and Astrid Waskowiak. *The Reflexology Atlas*. Rochester, VT: Inner Traditions/Bear & Co., 2005.

Availability: Most classes are held at the academy. Classes are also taught in Australia, Canada, China, Germany, Holland, New Zealand, Switzerland, and across the United States.

Most massage schools have classes in reflexology. For a list of accredited reflexology schools, visit www.arcb.net. For a session with a practitioner in your area, visit www.reflexology-usa.org.

Resources

American Academy of Reflexology, 725 E. Santa Anita Avenue #B, Burbank, CA 91501, 818-841-7741, ReflexologyEdu@aol.com, www.americanacademy ofreflexology.com, www.reflexologyresearch.net

The International Institute of Reflexology, 5650 First Avenue North, PO Box 12642, St. Petersburg, FL 33733, 727-343-4811, iir@reflexology-usa.net, www .reflexology-usa.net

Bibliography

Issel, Christine. *Reflexology: Art, Science, History*. New Frontier Publishing, 1996.

www.americanacademyofreflexology.com

www.orientalstudies.biz/OrientalStudies/ChineseReflexology2.htm

www.reflexology.ie/History_of_Reflexology.562.0

www.reflexologyworld.com

www.yotsumedojo.com

REIKI

REIKI IS A SIMPLE, NATURAL METHOD of healing in which a practitioner directs energy to a client by gently laying his or her hands in various positions on a client's physical body. Reiki energy can also be self-administered or given to people, animals, objects, and the natural world through distance healing techniques.

Of the many modalities in energy healing, Reiki (pronounced *raykey*) is the most accessible and the easiest to learn. It does not include a lot of advanced techniques or specific hand movements. The practitioner simply places his or her hands on the client and lets the energy go where it will. It is not necessary for the practitioner to direct the energy.

Reiki is a lineage-based system that isn't taught in a typical sense, but rather is transferred from Reiki master to student during what is called an "attunement." Through this simple process, students become open to accessing unlimited healing energy. Each Reiki master does this somewhat differently, although the master usually opens the student's crown chakra and imprints the Reiki symbols over the student's crown and the palms of the student's hands. The Reiki symbols are sacred healing symbols that open the student to higher levels of awareness. At one time, these symbols were kept secret until the student achieved Reiki II status, but today they are freely available in books and online.

Until recently, all knowledge of the history of Reiki was passed down through a lineage tracing back to a Mrs. Hawayo Takata. She believed Reiki should be an oral tradition, so nothing was ever written down. People embellished the stories until there became almost as many versions of the history of Reiki as there are Reiki masters. Despite this, all versions of Reiki history start with Dr. Mikao Usui (b. 1865, Japan). Research into his background indicates he was never actually a doctor, but followers of Reiki continue to refer to him as Dr. Usui. His educational background varies in description by the different followers, but all agree that during a moment of enlightenment at the end of a twenty-one-day fast, Usui received the initial symbols for healing work and felt the energy flow through him. After this experience, he developed the Usui System for Natural Healing and formed an organization called the Usui Reiki Ryoho Gakkai. One of his students, Dr. Chujiro Hayashi, added hand positions and may have been the one to add the master symbols.

Some stories maintain that all of the members of the Usui Reiki Ryoho Gakkai died either naturally or by suicide to prevent Reiki from being used during World War II. The Japanese have an aversion to sharing information with Westerners and it is only recently that it has come to light that Reiki is practiced in Japan under a lineage going directly back to Mikao Usui. Dr. Usui wrote a handbook with clear instructions as to how and when to use Reiki.

Five consecutive presidents of the Usui Reiki Ryoho Gakkai have since taken on the responsibilities of running the organization. The name is often shortened to Usui Kai. Each of the five presidents created a handbook to be passed on to students. Many techniques unknown to the West are now available. Like Western Reiki, disciples of the many Reiki teachers made their own changes and several streams of Reiki exist in Japan. Western-style Reiki is gaining popularity in Japan as well. Followers of the Takata lineage believe that Takata, an American and a student of Dr. Hayashi, is the only Reiki master to have survived World War II. She took Reiki home with her to Hawaii. She is credited with forming the title of Grand Reiki Master and setting the price of Reiki classes, including the $10,000 price tag for becoming a Reiki master. Takata trained twenty-two Reiki masters, who then began spreading Reiki all over the world. Some of these Reiki masters added their own variations, such as a required waiting period between classes, new techniques, and additional steps and costs. Practitioners have adapted Reiki in various ways. Some Reiki masters offered their classes at a lower price. Others varied the program by adding symbols and teachings from Tibet, Egypt, and India. Yet another popular variation is called Karuna Reiki®, created in the 1990s by William Rand, founder of the International Center for Reiki Training (which has trademarked the term to ensure ethical standards). *Karuna*, a Sanskrit word translated as "compassionate action," suggests a heart-centered approach to healing. Many say the energy of Karuna Reiki is more focused than that of Usui Reiki and may allow practitioners to connect with spiritual guides to forge deep compassion and wisdom. Karuna Reiki Masters have added two levels of training, two attunements, four master symbols, and eight treatment symbols.

There are differences between Eastern and Western styles of Reiki. Most Western lines of Reiki involve three degrees of learning. In the first degree, the student receives an attunement, at which point he or she can perform healing on other people. The emphasis at this stage is on physical healing.

To achieve second-degree Reiki status, the student receives another attunement and the focus shifts from physical healing to include emotional, mental, and karmic healing. The student must memorize the symbols to be used with clients during a healing session. It is not until third-degree Reiki that the student learns the symbols for attuning other students. Students also learn to work with spiritual guides. After completing the course, many Reiki masters require the student to teach a Reiki I class to demonstrate that he or she is able to pass on the attunements to others. Then he or she is called a Reiki master.

While Reiki is a healing method that requires a certain amount of discipline, it is not religious in nature. The ability to perform Reiki is not dependent on the healer's intellectual capacity or spiritual development, and clients may enjoy Reiki's therapeutic benefits regardless of spiritual background or belief system. Regarding spirituality, Dr. Usui believed all students of Reiki should follow the five principles some scholars believe were written by the Japanese Meiji emperor who reigned from 1867 to 1912, known as the Gokai. These are to be contemplated in the heart twice daily, once in the morning and once in the evening. Just for today:

- Don't get angry.
- Don't worry.
- Be grateful.
- Work hard.
- Be kind to others.

Course Descriptions

The following represents a composite picture of course materials offered by many Western Reiki masters. Please consult your Reiki master before you take a class for specific information on what he or she is presenting. Beware of Reiki masters offering attunement and the title of Reiki master over the Internet. It is important to have hands-on practice in a live Reiki class with an experienced Reiki master guiding the students.

▶ **Reiki I** is usually a one-day course including lecture, discussion, and experience, but some Reiki masters offer a two- to four-day class. Most Reiki masters offer the following:

- History of Reiki
- A discussion of what it means to be a Reiki practitioner and healer, including the spiritual precepts of Reiki
- Level I attunement
- Some hand positions and an introduction to the human energy system
- Instructions for conducting a complete treatment for self and others

▶ **Reiki II** classes introduce the Reiki symbols used for healing. Other items may include:

- Specifics of using the Reiki II symbols
- Using Reiki for individual physical and spiritual conditions
- Distance healing
- Meditation that strengthens the mind and expands consciousness
- Introduction to spiritual guides

▶ **Reiki III** is usually a two-day intensive. All students give and receive attunements, and topics may include:

- Instructions for how to give Usui attunements to first- and second-degree students
- Advanced meditation to harmonize with the energy of the chakras

- The values and spiritual orientation of a true Reiki master
- Ample practice time

Most Reiki masters require a third-degree Reiki practitioner to teach a first-degree Reiki class before the student may become a master. Some masters require at least a year of practice before bestowing the title of Reiki master.

. . . .

Continuing Education Units: Some Reiki programs give out CEUs. Contact your Reiki master.

Certification: There is no official certification. Becoming a Reiki master is a close equivalent.

Participants: All individuals interested in healing work using energy-based principles can become attuned.

Code of Ethics/Standards of Practice: This is up to the individual Reiki master. If this is important to you, inquire with your teacher. For example, the Reiki Alliance requires members to agree to an extensive code of ethics.

Suggested Reading

Petter, Frank Arjava. *Reiki Fire*. Twin Lakes, WI: Lotus Press, 1997.

Rand, William Lee. *Reiki the Healing Touch: First and Second Degree Manual*. Southfield, MI: Vision Publications, 2000.

Availability: Reiki classes are available in most areas around the world. To find a class or practitioner near you, go to the International Association of Reiki Professionals at www.iarp.org.

Resources

The International Association of Reiki Professionals® (IARP), PO Box 6182, Nashua, NH 03063-6182, 603-881-8838, info@iarp.org, www.iarp.org

The International Center for Reiki Training, 21421 Hilltop Street, Unit #28, Southfield, MI 48033, 800-332-8112, center@reiki.org, www.reiki.org

The Reiki Alliance, 204 North Chestnut Street, Kellogg, ID 83837, 208-783-3535, www.reikialliance.com

Bibliography

Petter, Frank Arjava. *Reiki Fire*. Twin Lakes, WI: Lotus Press, 1997.

——, and Christine M. Grimm. *Reiki: The Legacy of Dr. Usui*. Twin Lakes, WI: Lotus Press, 1998.

Rand, William Lee. *Reiki the Healing Touch: First and Second Degree Manual*. Southfield, MI: Vision Publications, 2000.

Stein, Diane. *Essential Reiki: A Complete Guide to an Ancient Healing Art*. Berkeley, CA: Ten Speed Press, 1995.

www.aetw.org/reiki_precepts

www.newworldencyclopedia.org/entry/Emperor_Meiji

REIKI FOR ANIMALS

Reiki is a hands-on form of energy healing in which a practitioner channels healing energy through his or her hands, either directly or from a distance. (See pages 105–109 for a full description of Reiki.) Traditionally, Reiki has a long history of treating people suffering from various physical and emotional imbalances (both given to others and self-administered), and it has grown to become a widely accepted complementary healing technique. Many healers believe that the efficacy of Reiki may depend in large part on how open the recipient is to receiving the treatment. As such, many Reiki masters believe that animals, who are generally more sensitive to energy than humans, receive Reiki treatments with greater success because they do not question its healing ability.

Reiki has been shown to help maintain a healthy animal's sense of peace and balance, increase the healing power of sick animals, and help ailing animals cope with issues such as arthritis and make the transition into death. Reiki is also used for emotional healing of animals that have been abused, neglected, or injured in some way. Reiki is frequently given to domestic pets, and many zoos have incorporated practitioners into their staff to help heal their animals, including elephants and big cats. Many practitioners specialize in certain animals, such as horses, birds, farm animals, and animals found in the wild.

The way in which a Reiki treatment is given to an animal depends on its health and individual response to the practitioner. For example, an animal familiar with the practitioner might be more open to receiving the healing treatment from a close proximity. Some animals are in too much emotional or physical pain to be touched, or may not be familiar with the practitioner, in which case working from a distance may be more effective. As with all healing techniques, the recipient needs to be relaxed, open, and willing to take part in the treatment. Animals do best when treated at home or in the barn where the animal lives as they are more relaxed and comfortable in a familiar environment.

At the beginning of a treatment with an animal, the practitioner introduces him- or herself, reassures the animal of its safety, and asks for permission to perform the technique. Animals will respond in their own way, and perhaps be open to the treatment in one situation but resist it in the next. As with all healing treatments, it is important to respect the animal's right of choice. With an animal the practitioner has never met, it takes patience to build rapport, so he or she moves slowly, working at a distance comfortable to the animal. The animal determines the course of treatment and frequently will present to the healer the part of the body that needs work.

Treatment may take anywhere from a few minutes to an hour or even longer, depending on the animal, its size, and the problem it is experiencing. Many animals go into a state of complete relaxation and signal when the treatment is complete. A signal may be a yawn, turning away, or, most frequently, simply walking away. Much like people, young and senior animals often require frequent treatments of shorter duration.

The Animal Reiki Source is one example of a Reiki training center for those who would like to work with animals, and others may be found at the website of the International Association of Reiki Professionals, www.iarp.org.

Reiki should not be used as a replacement for regular veterinary care. It is intended as a complement to traditional veterinary care as an integrative approach to healing animals and maintaining their health and well-being.

Course Descriptions

The following curriculum from Kathleen Prasad, founder of Animal Reiki Source and president of the Shelter Animal Reiki Association, represents an example of the training a student on this course of study will likely pursue. Students receive a foundation of Usui Reiki Ryoho with instruction in animal approach and ethics. The program follows the traditional three degrees of Reiki common in the United States. Students receive attunements the first day of the Level 1 class. In Level 2, they are introduced to the Reiki symbols. Upon completion of Level 3, students qualify to teach Reiki and Animal Reiki and may apply for Reiki Teacher status. There is no "oversight" board for Reiki. The way it works is, if students are "certified" as Reiki III, and this is done on an individual level from teacher to student, applicants are able then to teach students.

Students who have already taken Reiki First Degree classes may enroll in the teleclasses or the correspondence classes to learn Animal Reiki. Both the teleclasses and correspondence classes consist of five lessons with the students completing homework between lessons. Upon completion of all of the homework, students receive a Certificate of Completion.

Kathleen Prasad holds classes at BrightHaven Healing Arts Center for Senior and Special Needs Animals in Santa Rosa, California, as well as special classes for shelter staff at local animal shelters such as the East Bay SPCA and the San Francisco SPCA. Prasad has also taught at sanctuaries out of state, such as Talking Horse Ranch in Arizona, the Elephant Sanctuary in Tennessee, and at the AHVMA (American Holistic Veterinary Medical Association) conference.

▶ **Reiki I and Animal Reiki Training: The Basics** is a two-day class with 6 hours of instruction and practice each day. The first day students work with people and the second day students work with animals. Students receive attunements on the first day. Topics may include:

- The origin, history, and basic principles of Reiki, including many examples of treating animals
- How to use Reiki with animals in several circumstances
- Hand positions for treating people, animals, and self
- Ample time to practice giving treatments to animals
- Receive four attunements for Level I Reiki and a Certificate of Completion of Level I Reiki
- Ongoing guidance and support by phone or e-mail

▶ **Reiki II and Animal Reiki Training: Advanced Techniques** is a two-day class that focuses on the more advanced and esoteric uses of Reiki. During the first day students are given Reiki symbols and techniques for self-treatment and spiritual development. On day two students learn techniques for the treatment of others, distant healing, and treatments for animals. The class includes the following topics:

- The three symbols used in Level II Reiki
- Learning how Level II Reiki can be used to heal animals and people
- Self-treatment
- Many examples of treatments for animals and humans
- Receiving the one attunement for Level II
- Practicing sending the different types of Level II treatments
- Receiving a Certificate of Completion for Reiki II
- Ongoing guidance and support by phone and e-mail

▶ **Reiki III and Animal Reiki Teacher Training** is a two-day class that offers second-degree Reiki practitioners the opportunity to achieve third-degree Reiki status and to become a Reiki Teacher. The class is intended for the practitioner who wants to learn to teach Reiki and animal Reiki classes. Reiki Teachers who wish to add animal Reiki to their teaching curriculum are welcome. Students receive a certificate of completion at the end of the class. This class includes:

- Discussion and practice in the traditional Japanese techniques for Levels I, II and III.
- Review of the first thee symbols and the mantra
- The fourth Reiki symbol
- Reiki III initiation/Reiju
- How to perform initiations and Reiju
- The Animal Reiki Practitioner Code of Ethics
- Lesson plans
- Teaching manuals for Levels I, II, and III

Continuing Education Units: No.

Certification: Yes.

Code of Ethics/Standards of Practice: Yes.

Suggested Reading

Fulton, Elizabeth, and Kathleen Prasad. *Animal Reiki: Using Energy to Heal the Animals in Your Life,* Berkeley, CA: Ulysses Press, 2006.

Prasad, Kathleen. *The Animal Reiki Handbook—Finding Your Way with Reiki in Your Local Shelter, Sanctuary or Rescue.* San Rafael, CA: Shelter Animal Reiki Association, 2009.

———. *Tails from the Source: The Animal Reiki Source Newsletter Collection.* Vol. 1, 2004–2005. Lulu.com, 2008.

Availability: Seminars and classes plus a practitioner directory are listed at www .animalreikisource.com.

Resources

Animal Reiki Source, 369-B Third Street, #156, San Rafael, CA 94901, 415-420-9783, info@animalreikisource.com, www.animalreikisource.com

Bibliography

Fulton, Elizabeth, and Kathleen Prasad. *Animal Reiki: Using Energy to Heal the Animals in Your Life.* Berkeley, CA: Ulysses Press, 2006.

www.animalreikisource.com

www.healingforanimals.com

TAT®—TAPAS ACUPRESSURE TECHNIQUE®

TAPAS ACUPRESSURE TECHNIQUE, more commonly known as TAT, is a psycho-energetic therapy based on traditional Chinese medicine that is said to quickly alleviate emotional and mental trauma and help promote weight loss. TAT is a simple technique in which a person lightly touches a few acupressure points located on the front of his or her head near the eyes with one hand while holding the base of the skull with the other hand (this is known as the TAT pose). The individual also directs his or her attention to the problem to be resolved, thereby stimulating the corresponding meridians in the body and encouraging information and energy to be processed and released (for more information on the meridians, see pages 4 and 7). This may be done alone or with a practitioner. A practitioner is trained to observe areas the client may have missed and gently guide the client in the right direction.

The technique was created in the 1990s by Tapas Fleming, a California-licensed acupuncturist. Events in her own life convinced her there was a need for a simple remedy to clear the effects of unpleasant or traumatic experience. While studying acupuncture, she became interested in energy psychology and eventually developed TAT by experimenting with clients who had allergies and found her technique helpful. She further developed the technique with clients who had experienced traumatic events that continued to interfere with their daily lives, and they too reported positive results from using the technique.

The following full description of the TAT pose and corresponding nine steps is from the "How to Do TAT" free download from www.tatlife.com: "With one hand, lightly touch the tip of the thumb to an area about 1/8th inch above the inner corner of the eye. With the fourth finger (ring finger) of the same hand, light touch the tip of the finger to the area one-eighth inch above the inner corner of the other eye.

Place the tip of the middle finger at the point midway between and about a half inch above the eyebrow level. Place the other hand on the back of the head so that the thumb is resting at the base of the skull just above the hairline. The palm cradles the base of the skull. No pressure is necessary."

Once the hands are in the position described above, the client puts his or her attention on nine further steps to work through the problem. In steps one and two, the problem and the opposite of the problem (in the form of an affirming resolution) are stated. Step three concerns geographical locations and general locations (such as a house, or even a group of people) where energy from the problem may be stored. The idea is to focus on healing the issues in all areas. In step four, energy is directed to healing the origins of the problem. Step five involves forgiveness and has three parts: an apology to anyone the individual may have hurt, forgiveness of anyone who hurt the individual, and forgiveness of anyone the individual has blamed for the problem. Step six covers overcoming resistance, and step seven deals with healing whatever remnants of the issue are left. Step eight consists of choosing a positive alternative outcome. In step nine, the individual fully integrates the healing into his or her body and mind.

A study funded by the National Institutes of Health concerning weight loss was done at Kaiser Permanente Medical Clinic in Portland, Oregon, and at the University of Arizona in Tucson (published in *Focus on Alternative and Complementary Therapies*, vol. 10, 38–39). The study consisted of ninety-two participants who had lost at least fifteen pounds in a weight loss program conducted at Kaiser Permanente. The study centered on maintaining the weight loss. The participants were divided into three groups. One group formed a self-directed support group, one group did Qigong, and the last group did TAT. The TAT group significantly outperformed the other two in keeping the weight off. This has led to another, much larger study funded by the National Institutes of Health, which began in May 2008.

Course Descriptions

In addition to the following workshops, DVDs and CDs are available for self-study. A full description of the nine steps is available as a free download "How to Do TAT" from www.tatlife.com. The nine-step download is available in Arabic, Chinese, Dutch, French, German, Hebrew, Indonesian, Italian, Spanish, and Swedish.

TAT has two certification levels: one for people wishing to be professional TAT practitioners and the other for trainers in TAT. Before being granted certification, the applicant's presence, understanding of TAT, skill, and ethics are taken into consideration. The program upgrades the certification requirements periodically, so be sure to check the website for any changes while working toward certification. Once a student enrolls in the certification program, the requirements are "locked in" at that point. Even if the requirements change at a later date, the student needs to fulfill only those requirements that were in place when the student registered.

▶ **Basics** is one of the workshops required to become a certified TAT professional. It is interactive and students practice with each other. The class covers:

- The basic theory of how TAT works
- Alleviating allergies, single-incident traumas, spiritual attachments, surgery issues, fears and phobias, daily stress, and bad relationships with money, to name a few
- How to work with children, groups, and animals
- How to be a good TAT practitioner

▶ **Trainer's Course** is for students who want to teach TAT and connect with others in the TAT community. The course covers important workshop topics, how to teach TAT techniques, and how to direct practice time.

▶ **Practicing Presence** allows students to develop their skills regarding one of the most important parts of practicing TAT, being present. This class helps student's professional practice in addition to encouraging an open approach to all aspects of life. Topics include a discussion of what being present really means, the obstacles that block presence and how to clear them, and how to encourage an open approach to TAT when working with groups, pairs, and individuals.

· · · · · · · · · · · · · · · ·

Continuing Education Units: Yes. Not available for all classes. Check with your instructor.

Certification: Yes. Granted by TATLife®

Participants: Open to all, including children.

Code of Ethics/Standards of Practice: Yes.

Availability: Classes are available around the world. To find a session with a practitioner in your area, go to www.tatlife.com.

Resources
. . . .

Tapas Acupressure Technique® (TAT®), PO Box 5192, Mooresville, NC 28117, 877-674-4344, 310-378-7381, CustomerService@tatlife.com, www.tatlife.com

Bibliography
. . . .

Fleming, Tapas. *How to Do TAT.* PDF available from www.TATLife.com.

———. *The TAT Professional's Manual.*

TAT®, Tapas Acupressure Technique®, and TATLife® are registered trademarks of Tapas Fleming and are being used with permission.

THOUGHT FIELD THERAPY®

D R. ROGER J. CALLAHAN had been a practicing clinical psychologist before he founded Thought Field Therapy, also known as TFT and Callahan Techniques®. To augment his practice and explore healing options beyond the traditional clinical methods, he began to explore alternative treatments such as traditional Chinese medicine and, more specifically, the meridians.

In his book *Tapping the Healer Within*, Dr. Callahan defines Thought Field Therapy as follows: "TFT is a treatment for psychological disturbances which provide a code that, when applied to a psychological problem the individual is attuned to, will eliminate perturbations in the thought field, the fundamental cause of all negative emotions. This code is elicited through TFT's causal diagnostic procedure, through which the TFT algorithms were developed." He defines algorithms as the specific sequence of actions for a particular treatment. The thought field is where critical information derived from psychological distress is located. A perturbation is a unique entity that contains active information responsible for triggering negative emotions such as grief, guilt or fear.

By tapping specific acupressure points in a particular sequence, Dr. Callahan maintains that psychological problems can be eliminated. After considerable research in various fields, he found certain eye movements were effective and added them to the healing sequence. While using TFT for many years to treat emotional problems, he discovered that it also worked for physical ailments. TFT now has algorithms for treating most of the common physical ailments and diseases people experience, as well as most psychological disorders.

A session begins with the practitioner asking the client to intentionally think about the problem or emotional distress. Dr. Callahan calls it tuning in to the perturbed thought field. Once the client is in touch with the problem, he or she will be asked to rate it on a scale of one to ten. The practitioner will write the number down. The practitioner then guides the client through a series of tapping at different places on the body. The tapping is done with two fingers, five to ten times at each spot. Tapping is to be firm but gentle. After the tapping sequence is done, the client will be asked to rate the problem again on a scale of one to ten. The practitioner will write that number down.

Once the tapping is complete, the client is asked to do what is called the nine gamut series. It consists of nine activities: six activities using the eyes, one of humming followed by counting aloud from 1 to 5 and then humming again. While all this is going on, the client taps a spot on the back of a hand called the gamut spot. When this is complete, the client is again asked to rate his or her problem on a scale of one to ten. The original tapping sequence is then repeated. At the end of a session, the client is asked to do a floor-to-ceiling eye roll while tapping the gamut spot. If the problem has not cleared, the practitioner guides the client through a sequence to eliminate the psychological reversal that may be blocking the treatment. Treatments usually take about six to eight minutes.

Course Descriptions

The following list of classes comes from the Thought Field Therapy website, www .tftrx.com/training. Instructors keep up-to-date on current trends and changes in the curriculum to ensure each level of training is the same wherever it is taught. The website also provides information for affiliated workshops and training programs not listed here.

▶ **Algorithm Level Training** provides an introduction to the practice of Thought Field Therapy and is recommended for those new to the field. Students learn the common methods or sequences that have been developed through Thought Field Therapy Causal Diagnosis. This class is a prerequisite for diagnostic level training and the trainer's training.

▶ **Basic Diagnostic Training** has two parts.

Step A is an introduction to the diagnostic level training programs using a self-study program. Students learn basic Thought Field Therapy Causal Diagnosis procedures. These methods assist in identification of a specific or individual sequence of a problem. The program also contains:

- Basic Diagnostic Self-Study Program
- The Basics to Thought Field Therapy
- The how and why of Thought Field Therapy
- A list of all the common algorithms

Step B is three days of interactive, hands-on experience and lecture. It addresses complex and recurring problems and toxins. Students learn to develop effective techniques to handle difficult clients and chronic cases. Instructors demonstrate the use of Heart Rate Variability and how to use a voltmeter for objective measurement of Thought Field Therapy efficacy.

Algorithm Level Training is a prerequisite.

▶ **Thought Field Therapy Boot Camp** is an intensive two-day training offering some of the highlights of each level of TFT trainings. Students taking this course receive a free one-year membership in the Association for Thought Field Therapy. Students also receive:

- TFT Algorithm Level Training
- Step A of the Basic Diagnostic Self-Study Program
- A self-study program concerning sensitivities, intolerances, and toxins
- Voltmeter and psychological reversal
- A downloadable algorithm wall chart
- Client success handbook

▶ **Advanced Thought Field Therapy with Heart Rate Variability and Voltmeter** provides lecture, case studies, live demonstrations, practice, and verification of findings with objective heart rate variability and voltmeter measurements. Course topics include:

- Methods based on advanced Thought Field Therapy

- The work of various specialists
- New innovations helpful to Thought Field Therapy
- Application of the specificity of Thought Field Therapy to improve other already effective techniques
- A strong focus on Heart Rate Variability measures, voltmeter measurements, and their use
- The role of toxins and sensitivities found in complex and difficult cases

▶ **Optimal Health Training** replaces the Voice Technology One on One Training. This course provides the "core secret" behind the most effective level of TFT: Voice Technology. It takes place in a small-group environment enabling students to focus on all aspects of achieving optimal mental, physical, and spiritual health. Topics include:

- Objective techniques for treating clients over the phone
- Self-help methods developed by the Callahans to support the treatment of chronic diseases
- Identifying and self-treating toxins and sensitivities

· · · · · · · · · · · · · · · · ·

Continuing Education Units: No.

Certification: After completing the TFT Algorithm and Diagnostic Level trainings, students may apply to enter the Registered, Certified Trainers Program for certification as instructors.

Participants: For health-care professionals and laypeople.

Code of Ethics/Standards of Practice: Yes.

Suggested Reading

Callahan, Roger. *Five Minute Phobia Cure: Dr. Callahan's Treatment for Fears, Phobias, and Self-Sabotage.* Wilmington, DE: Enterprise Publishing, 1989.

——, with Richard Trubo. *Tapping the Healer Within: Using Thought Field Therapy to Instantly Conquer Your Fears, Anxieties, and Emotional Distress.* New York: McGraw-Hill, 2000.

———, and Joanne Callahan. *Stop the Nightmares of Trauma*. Chapel Hill, NC: Professional Press, 2000.

Availability: Australia, Canada, China, Denmark, England, Estonia, France, Germany, Ireland, Japan, Mexico, Norway, Russia, South America, Spain, Sweden, and the United States. To locate a practitioner in your area, go to www.tftrx.com.

Resources

Association for Thought Field Therapy, PO Box 1220, La Quinta, CA 92247, 866-396-1365, chris@atft.org, www.atft.org

Bibliography

Callahan, Roger J., with Richard Trubo. *Tapping the Healer Within*. New York: McGraw-Hill, 2001.

www.tftrx.com

www.biomeridian.com/virtual-medicine

TOUCH FOR HEALTH

TOUCH FOR HEALTH, developed by John C. Thie, DC, originated in traditional Chinese medicine, chiropractics, and osteopathy, and is the forerunner of many kinesiology therapies in use today. As a way to augment his practice, Dr. Thie, a chiropractor, began working with Dr. George Goodheart in Oriental Meridian Therapy (also known as acupressure; see pages 17–24), kinesiology, the science of how the body moves, and applied kinesiology, a form of diagnosis using muscle testing as a feedback mechanism to determine how a person's body is functioning. Dr. Thie and his wife, Carrie Thie, an expert in communication and interpersonal relationships, created what was first called Health from Within and in 1973 changed the name to Touch for Health. Dr. Thie passed away in 2005 and his son, Matthew Thie, has stepped in to continue the work of educating students, developing new healing protocols, and writing articles about the technique.

Touch for Health uses muscle testing as a form of assessment to find blockages in the meridian system (for more information about meridians, see pages 4 and 7). Each meridian has a unique set of tests to check for blockages. The client extends his or her arm or leg in a position perpendicular to the body. The practitioner gently presses down on the arm or other body part. If that body part moves easily, it signifies a blockage in the particular meridian associated with that muscle test. If the body part firmly resists the pressure, the meridian is free of any blockages.

Like other types of Eastern approaches to healing, Touch for Health also uses the traditional Chinese medicine theory of the five elements that make up the material world: fire, earth, metal, water, and wood. Five element theory interprets relationships between the physiology and pathology of humans and their environment. Each of the body's organs and meridians is associated with one of the five elements with corresponding colors, sounds, flavors, and smells. Each relates to a season, with late summer/early fall making up the fifth "season." All of these associations with the five elements, including the meridians and organs, can be found on a wheel chart that shows the interrelationships between each element and its correspondences. A simpler chart is included on page 14.

The Touch for Health system incorporates seven different types of touch reflexes to facilitate and balance muscle function, energy flow, and straighten the posture. It uses approximately fifty-five neurolymphatic massage points located on the front and back torso, upper arms, and thighs. These points are closely associated with acupressure points in traditional Chinese medicine. Simply put, the lymphatic system is the garbage collector of the body by eliminating dead tissue and other waste products. It also delivers proteins, hormones, and fats to the cells, creates antibodies, and produces some of the white blood cells. Practitioners work with both the neurolymphatic points and the traditional Chinese medicine acupressure points. Acupressure points are more often held with pressure using the fingers, while neurolymphatic points are massaged by rubbing deeply at the specified points.

Located mainly on the head, neurovascular points are held to strengthen muscles and improve blood circulation to both muscles and organs. Neurovascular points are specific acupressure points corresponding to blood circulation. These points may be used to help treat hypertension as well.

In a session, which takes about an hour, the client may be sitting, standing, or lying down while fully clothed. The client and practitioner discuss the goals the client has for healing and results of the treatment. The first thing the practitioner looks at is the posture of the client. He or she then takes the pulse of the client as one way of checking for imbalances. If the client is under a lot of stress or highly agitated, the practitioner may perform an emotional stress release technique (such as holding the client's forehead with the fingers of each hand placed just above the eyes) to help the client relax.

The practitioner then performs muscle testing to check for blocked meridians. Depending on the condition of the client and the established goals, the practitioner holds neurovascular points, acupressure points, or both. The practitioner massages appropriate neurolymphatic points for approximately twenty to thirty seconds. Pressure is applied to acupressure points and neurovascular points for about a minute. If the client becomes uncomfortable, the amount of pressure is lightened or the practitioner may return to that area later.

Touch for Health practitioners are also trained in nutrition and recommendations for changes in diet may be made. The practitioner also questions the client about the intake of water and the frequency of exercise.

Many of the techniques used by Touch for Health may be self-administered. Many states and some countries require a massage license for Touch for Health practitioners. Check the Legalities section of this book to find out whom to contact in your area concerning this issue.

Course Descriptions

Even though the program was originally intended as a lay, self-care approach, many sports therapies use Touch for Health as part of their programs, and massage schools use Touch for Health as part of their training curriculum.

▶ **The Introductory Workshop** is a two-day workshop allowing the student practical, hands-on experience in the classroom, including:

- Practical skills to manage stress, reduce physical and mental pain and tension, and increase overall energy without the use of drugs
- Muscle testing
- Exercises and movements for enhanced learning and improving coordination
- Finding food sensitivities
- Techniques of applied kinesiology and acupressure massage
- History of Touch for Health

▶ **Touch for Health Level 1: Fourteen-Muscle/Meridian Balance** covers much of the same material as the introductory workshop, but in much greater depth, including:

- Muscle correction procedures
- Meridian theory
- Reflex systems for balancing muscles, posture, and energy

- Basic posture
- Biocidic foods

▶ **Touch for Health Level 2: One-Point Balancing** further expands the student's understanding and skills. The class reviews basic human anatomy and muscle movements, the basics of the Eastern health system (the five elements), and comprehensive training in massage and applied kinesiology. Prerequisites include Touch for Health Level 1 and five documented practice balancing sessions using any Level 1 techniques. The course includes numerous intermediate techniques, including pretesting and correcting, assessment of energy patterns, circuit locating, how to use a balancing wheel, and further information on the five element theory.

▶ **Touch for Health Level 3: Reactive Muscles** reviews assessment techniques and allows students time for practice, deepening and expanding students' understanding and skills. Prerequisites include Touch for Health Level 1 and 2 and five documented practice sessions using any Level 2 techniques. Topics include yin/yang theory, the pulse and pain tapping, acupressure holding point theory, and advanced content on the emotional and energetic components of the five elements.

▶ **Touch for Health Level 4** goes deeper into the students' understanding and ability to heal, with the prerequisites of Touch for Health Level 1, 2, and 3 and five documented practice balancing sessions using any Level 3 techniques. Topics include a review of all the previous levels, advance muscle testing and balancing (standing, sitting, or lying down), posture analysis and rebalancing, using sound and color to heal, nutrition as it pertains to the five elements, reactive and inhibited muscles, and neurolymphatic release.

▶ **Instructor Training Workshop** is a 60-hour course that prepares the student for certification as a Touch for Health instructor, with prerequisites of Touch for Health Level 1, 2, 3, and 4 and five documented practice balancing sessions. Topics include comprehensive training in Touch for Health techniques and teaching skills and how to run a successful Touch for Health business.

Continuing Education Units: For massage therapists: The National Certification Board for Therapeutic Massage and Bodyworkers, provider #050467-00. For RNs and LPNs: Board of Registered Nursing in California, Continuing Education Provider #CEP 13015. Nurses in Florida, Iowa, Kansas, Kentucky, Nevada, Oklahoma, Oregon, South Dakota, and Wyoming can apply directly with the appropriate state licensing agency to provide continuing education credit to nurses. Certificates are kept on file in this office for a period of no less than five years.

Certification: The North American Touch for Health Association and the International Kinesiology College certify Touch for Health instructors.

Participants: Touch for Health offers classes to seniors, massage therapists, chiropractors, acupuncturists, psychotherapists, sports coaches, and laypersons interested in the program.

Code of Ethics/Standards of Practice: Yes.

Suggested Reading

Thie, John, with Matthew Thie. *Touch for Health: A Practical Guide to Natural Health with Acupressure Touch*. Marina del Rey, CA: DeVorss & Company, 2005.

Availability: Classes are available in Australia, Bermuda, Brazil, Canada, China, Denmark, England, France, Hungary, Italy, Japan, Mexico, Norway, Netherlands, New Zealand, Poland, Puerto Rico, Russia, Scotland, Spain, South Africa, and Switzerland. For a session in your area, go to www.tfhka.org.

Resources

Touch for Health Kinesiology Association, 3225 West St. Joseph, Lansing, MI 48917, 517-327-9207 or 800-466-8342, admin@tfhka.org, www.tfhka.org

Touch for Health Education, 6162 La Gloria Drive, Malibu, CA 90265, 310-589-5269, thei@touch4health.com, www.touch4health.com

Bibliography

Thie, John, with Mary Marks. *Touch for Health*. Marina del Rey, CA: DeVorss & Company, 1973.

www.appliedkinesiology.com

www.tcmbasics.com

www.touch4health.com

www.transitiontoparenthood.com

YUEN METHOD™

THE YUEN METHOD: FULL SPECTRUM HEALING was developed by Dr. Kam Yuen, a thirty-fifth-generation Shaolin grandmaster of Tai Chi Praying Mantis Kung Fu. Yuen has degrees in chiropractics and structural engineering, extensive study in homeopathy and nutrition, and was a model and adviser for the character Caine in David Carradine's original *Kung Fu* TV series.

Dr. Yuen's view of the human body differs from traditional Chinese medicine and energetic practices. He envisions the body as a high-tech biocomputer. A computer, at its basic level, works with a series of on/off switches. Dr. Yuen sees the body functioning in the same manner, and thus the flow of energy can be gauged, tested, and corrected. In his book *Instant Pain Elimination*, he states that people have two responses to everything that happens in life: strong or weak (the switch is on or off). When we are appropriately strong to what is important to us, energy flows freely. When we are inappropriately weak, energy does not flow, and this accumulation of weaknesses can create imbalance, dysfunction, or disease.

Dr. Yuen teaches practitioners using muscle testing to find out if the client is strong or weak to a possible cause of pain, allergy, or other physical or emotional issue. (For more on muscle testing, see pages 134–135.) They then check the vertical midline of the body for a corresponding weak spot. If the client tests weak, a correction is made by mentally focusing attention at the weak spot along the spine, thus turning the "switch" back on. To be an effective practitioner, Dr. Yuen believes that the student needs no special abilities or psychic skills. He asks only to disregard limiting beliefs, keep an open mind, and remain neutral.

Healing is a part of the Shaolin tradition. The first Shaolin temple was built on the side of China's Mount Shaoshi in an area of young trees (called *lin* in Chinese), hence the name Shaolin. The land was given to an Indian Buddhist monk by the emperor Xiaowen in the late fifth century as a place to build a temple and teach Buddhism. Many people came to the temple to meditate or as a retreat and often stayed and became monks or nuns.

The long hours of meditation and little exercise became a problem for the Shaolin monks. Many fell asleep while meditating and most suffered from various diseases. In AD 526, another Indian Buddhist monk came to China and was directed to the Shaolin temple. This particular monk, called Damo by the Chinese, was the third son of an Indian prince and well versed in Yoga and Indian fighting systems. He introduced a series of exercises to the monks and called it Kung Fu, which means hard work and perfection.

Because the temple was located in a remote region, it was prone to attacks by outlaws. Damo taught the monks Indian fighting techniques to help defend the temple. In later years, more temples were built and the Kung Fu style of martial arts became well known as a defense skill. Being taught in Buddhist monasteries, the emphasis was on healing, philosophy, and learning, even though the martial arts were a serious part of the curriculum for self-defense in dangerous times.

Good health was considered imperative for the rigorous training and meditations required of a Shaolin monk. To be a priest, the student had to pass eighteen tests: six physical, six mental, and six spiritual. For four centuries, the most famous of the temples, O Mai Shan, meaning the Great White Mountain, became a library and medical university. Many of the healers were trained in healing techniques from Tibet. The library contained scrolls on healing from all over Asia. Even though war destroyed many of the temples, adept Shaolin healers became known for healing broken bones and spinal injuries. Shaolin priests, following the Buddhist and Taoist practices of nonresistance, managed to pass knowledge down from parent to child. Shaolin is now enjoying a resurgence of popularity in China, helped by the American entertainment industry.

A session begins with an interview to find out what the client would like to heal. Based on this information, the practitioner intuitively asks a series of questions about the client's physical and emotional health, and while doing so, may perform a series of muscle tests using the client's outstretched arm in relation to the energetic functioning of his or her spine. Muscle testing may be used for verification of the practitioner's intuition concerning weak points. When the weakness is located, the practitioner focuses his or her attention on that spot and with intention strengthens it. The practitioner then performs another muscle test to check whether the problem has been resolved. If the problem has not, the practitioner looks for another point of weakness and repeats the process. Yuen Method practitioners test for many levels of "influence" on the person such as physical, emotional, karmic, financial, psychological, relationships, and spiritual, making sure all levels of consciousness are congruent so that pain may be eliminated and goals attained. The monitoring for weak points along the spine continues until the initial goal set by the practitioner and the client is attained.

Course Descriptions

The following outlines form an overview of the materials covered in the three levels of Yuen Method classes. Each class is unique in itself as the classes accommodate to the energy of each group, and students may take a class multiple times. Classes do not have a formal structure. No two classes are alike, as classes follow student needs rather than structured guidelines. Dr. Yuen is currently developing a line of teleseminars as well. Go to www.yuenmethod.com for more information.

▶ **Basic Level 1:** Students learn to pinpoint issues that cause physical, mental, psychological, psychic, and spiritual problems and make corrections using the Yuen Method protocol.

- Test for energetic weakness
- Pinpoint and correct the various nonphysical levels that may be causing an illness
- Check the lymphatic system and how to properly detox using this system
- Resolve fears, phobias, and negative emotions
- Eliminate stress, anxiety, depression, grief, frustration, anger, and tension
- Eliminate side effects of medications, heavy metals, and other chemicals
- Make self-corrections and distance and remote corrections

- Utilize the many levels of energy, including macrocosmic, microcosmic, intrinsic soul cleansing, and karmic resolution

▶ **Intermediate Level 2:** Students expand their scope of influence and deepen their understanding of the origins of pain and illness. Topics include:

- Central/peripheral nervous system corrections: brain, spinal cord, cerebral spinal fluid, and meninges
- Resolving specific ailments, including indigestion, allergies and colds, asthma and respiratory ailments, chronic pain, PMS, fibromyalgia, high blood pressure and cholesterol, TMJ and jaw pain, and more
- Energetic cranial corrections
- Interactions between the digestive, respiratory, and reproductive systems
- Eliminate ear, eye, nose, and throat infection

▶ **Advanced Level 3:** Students learn a complete protocol of self-mastery. Topics include:

- Anti-aging and weight loss techniques
- Optimizing fitness, strength, endurance, flexibility, and coordination
- Resolving serious and terminal illness
- Transcending the need for attention and addiction; minimizing rejection, misunderstanding, and misinterpretation; and enhancing intuition

. . . .

Continuing Education Units: No.

Certification: Certification is offered for both practitioners and instructors. To receive practitioner certification, students must complete levels 1 though 3 at least twice. Students who plan to apply for certification must complete three internships. One of the internships must be a level 1 class, and the student must attend six classes prior to this internship. Students must also document 100 hours of practice through one-on-one time, group time, or self-corrections. Students who have completed certification have the title of Yuen Method Practitioner. Practitioners must review the class once a year to maintain their certification.

Participants: Dr. Yuen says that anyone willing to do the work may take these classes.

Code of Ethics: Dr. Yuen does not have a written Code of Ethics, but ethics are a frequent topic in all of his classes.

Suggested Reading

Yuen, Dr. Cam. 2002. *Instant Healing.* Canoga Park, CA: CEM Publishers, 2002.

———. *Instant Pain Elimination.* Canoga Park, CA: CEM Publishers, 2003.

———. *Instant Rejuvenation.* Canoga Park, CA: CEM Publishers, 2004.

Availability: Classes are available in Brazil, Canada, Europe, Hong Kong, and throughout the United States. To find a session in your area, go to www.yuenmethod .com.

Resources

Yuen Method, 22647 Ventura Blvd #379, Woodland Hills, CA 91364, 877-375-9836, contactus@yuenmethod.com, www.yuenmethod.com

Bibliography

Yuen, Cam. *Instant Pain Elimination.* Canoga Park, CA: CEM Publishers, 2003.

www.shaolin.com

www.shaolin.com.au/history

www.zhangdayong.com

WESTERN

THE SEPARATION OF THE CHURCH from the government in medieval times marks the advent of traditional Western medicine. All spiritual concepts and matters involving the soul were left to the church, while all material elements were considered part of the physical world and ruled by governments. In turn, the mind and the body came to be seen as two separate entities rather than equal components leading to a spiritual whole. René Descartes (1596–1650), often called the father of modern psychology, wrote profusely on this subject and his writings influenced both modern psychology and allopathic medicine, even today. Descartes lived during a time of considerable political upheaval. Priests, nuns, and shamans acting as healers were no longer allowed to practice their craft, and women were forbidden to practice any form of healing, be it through the therapeutic use of hands or the healing properties of herbs and plants. Medical schools and colleges were started for the education of men only, and the idea of working holistically with a patient was no longer fashionable. Medical students were more comfortable learning about the physical body, which was something that could be analyzed and monitored empirically. Because thoughts, dreams, and matters of the spirit and the soul could not be seen, they were ignored and eventually all but forgotten.

Similarly, the work of Sir Isaac Newton (1642–1727) laid the foundation for modern, rational science. Scientific study requires measurable proof before theories can be accepted by the scientific community. For more than two hundred years, Newton's three laws of physics were verified by observation and scientific experiment. His laws worked well for observable objects, including human beings. For tiny particles at very high speeds, the laws did not explain phenomena being observed by modern scientific instruments.

Albert Einstein (1879–1955) shattered the Newtonian point of view with his theory of relativity, but it wasn't until the acceptance of quantum physics and the discovery that photons and electrons could be influenced by an observer that the theory of the dualistic structure of man began to crumble. For more information about observer influence, read Lynne McTaggart's *The Field: The Quest for the Secret Force of the Universe* (New York: HarperCollins, 2002). The new rules brought about by quantum physics are showing us that forces that cannot be easily seen or touched have a real impact on the world as we know it. The idea that photons can be found in two places at once and can also travel faster than the speed of light, and that electrons communicate with each other, is helping to explain and validate the concepts of energy medicine, which are growing in popularity every day.

We have also seen that the Eastern philosophy of medicine, treating the whole person including the soul, has begun to have an impact on Western medicine, especially in the holistic branch of allopathic medicine. Ever growing in popularity, holistic medicine is being sought out by millions of patients as an alternative to the traditional paradigm of medicine that treats an individual's symptoms and ignores the deeply rooted cause of those symptoms. As we see in quantum physics, that which cannot be seen or touched is now being recognized as a legitimate force, both as a healing modality and as part of the structure of a human being.

The modalities discussed in this section have roots in Western medicine and Western philosophies, but have incorporated techniques and beliefs from the Eastern way of thinking. Many of the founders are doctors, nurses, and scientists who ventured to explore outside the box of Western medicine and found a world of healing waiting to be incorporated into the field of medicine.

ADVANCED INTEGRATIVE THERAPY
(FORMERLY SEEMORG MATRIX WORK)

ADVANCED INTEGRATIVE THERAPY (AI Therapy or AIT) is an energy psycho-therapy rather than a technique or a series of techniques. As a therapeutic modality, it consists of interrelated theory and methods taken from a number of schools of traditional psychotherapy, neurobiology, quantum physics, and energy treatments. AI Therapy requires an advanced degree so that practitioners begin with a professional level of competence. It focuses particularly on resolving more diffi-cult-to-treat psychological, psychogenic, and spiritual disorders by integrating into energy treatment useful aspects of traumatology, analytical psychology, object rela-tions, transpersonal psychology, neurobiology, and self-psychology. The goal of Ad-vanced Integrative Therapy is the client's healing, development, and individuation.

Founder Asha Clinton was inspired by the Seemorg, a bird in Persian mythol-ogy that symbolizes the transformative aspects of divine spirituality, and called her therapy Seemorg Matrix Work. It has since evolved into an integrative modality in psychoenergetic medicine that Clinton has chosen to rename Advanced Integrative Therapy.

Clinton is a psychodynamic, transpersonal therapist, in practice for over thirty years. Trained in psychology, cultural anthropology, and social work, she became disillusioned by the quality of treatment offered to persons with anxiety and per-sonality disorders and the seriously ill. Furthering her education, she studied energy psychology and eventually developed her own therapy as she could not find an effec-tive energetic therapy that dealt with these issues. As it developed, AI Therapy expanded into an integrative therapy that treats physical, spiritual, and psychological disorders and issues.

AI Therapy begins with connection, building trust and taking the client's history. Where needed, meditation, visualization, and creative expression help strengthen clients' egos and connect them to the deeper unconscious part of their psyches. Practitioners also work with clients to heal relational limitations, use coaching skills to help clients learn positive behaviors and, if desired, recommend ecumenical spiritual practices for spiritual development. Energetic protocols remove the wounded energy from the trauma being treated. Clinton defines trauma as any occurrence that, when the client thinks back to it, when it is triggered by some present event, evokes difficult emotions and/or physical sensations: gives rise to negative beliefs, desires, fantasies, compulsions, obsessions, addictions, illness, or dissociation; blocks the development of positive qualities and spiritual connection; and fractures human wholeness.

The first step in AIT therapy is to take the client's history with special emphasis on childhood experiences. The practitioner administers the Covenant Protocol, which removes the client's resistance to healing and transformation. Next the therapist analyzes the client's history in order to determine the themes that require treatment. The practitioner uses muscle testing to determine how traumatic experiences have hindered physical, psychological, and spiritual development. After muscle testing the best order of treatment is for the therapist to employ protocols to energetically remove traumatic emotions, sensations, and other symptoms. The practitioner also uses meditation, visualization, creative artistic expression, and ecumenical spiritual practice to help heal and transform the negative effects of trauma. The last step of the basic process is to help the client further develop emotionally and energetically by replacing the negative thoughts and qualities with positive ones. Energetic protocols work on thirteen specific points on the body.

Clients and therapists generally sit in chairs, although critically ill clients may recline in a bed. There are no typical sessions, but most AI Therapy tends to focus on trauma treatment. Working within a chosen theme, for example, abandonment or psychologically caused Crohn's disease, the therapist helps the client remember the relevant early childhood causes, which they then treat together. They continue to work together to energetically treat all the present symptoms, emotions, sensations, and triggers in the theme. Finally they treat the connections between the causes and the present symptoms. This three-part process is called three-step transformation. Practitioners also use other protocols, coaching, transference work, and core-belief treatments.

Course Descriptions

Completion of two Advanced Integrative Therapy Basics Seminars, AIT Basics, and Mastering AIT Practice; five sessions of group teleconsultation with each of these seminars; instructor's approval; and a master's degree or higher in a helping profession are requirements for a Certified Advanced Integrative Therapy Practitioner. An applicant without a graduate degree may be considered if he can prove he has the equivalent of two years of graduate work and two years of supervised placement in a helping profession from an accredited university. Certified practitioners must recertify every three years.

At the time of this writing, advanced practitioner and master practitioner certification is under consideration.

The following seminar descriptions represent a sample of the eighteen seminars offered by Advanced Integrative Therapy. Each of the two introductory seminars is complemented by a teleconference consultation group for which practitioners must register separately. The teleconferences last for approximately five weeks with one conference each week, depending upon the presenter's schedule.

▶ **Advanced Integrative Therapy Basics Seminar** provides students with energetic methods for treating nonpsychotic psychological imbalances. This seminar is a prerequisite for all other AIT seminars. Topics include:

- The nature of trauma and the role trauma plays in the development of psychological disorders
- Training in relevant energy psychology skills
- Two basic trauma treatment protocols
- A protocol to remove negative beliefs and instill positive beliefs
- AIT meditations
- Rapid protocols for emergency situations and for client self-treatments

- A protocol for instilling positive qualities that never developed because of trauma

▶ **Mastering AIT Practice** addresses the integration of AIT basics in to a clinical practice. Completion of this class is a requirement for certification. Course topics include:

- Case discussions, exercises, and demonstrations
- Case analysis and treatment plans
- Protocols for finding originating traumas
- Short-term protocols for clients needing brief interventions

▶ **The AIT Presence and Dissociation Seminar** focuses on repairing the ways that dissociation, repression, and disapproval diminish an individual's ability to live in the present. The seminar includes AIT treatment for allergies, boundary issues, family issues, and emotional and physical dissociation. Completion of this class is a requirement for certification. Course topics include:

- Protocols to dispel physical and emotional dissociation, repression, and disapproval
- Creating healthy ego boundaries
- Reversing the negative impact of an individual's upbringing
- Understanding and learning the need to be present

▶ **The AIT Depths Treatment Seminar** provides new methods for working with clients by focusing on the treatment of objects and their relationships and upon the transference/countertransference phenomena that often complicate and negate therapy. Topics include:

- The nature, treatment, and transformation of objects, archetypes, introjects, and alters using AIT protocols
- The energetic treatment of transference/countertransference phenomena
- Protocols that transform archetypal negativity into archetypal development

▶ **Anxiety Disorder Treatment Seminars I and II** provide treatment plans and protocols for the treatment of post-traumatic stress disorder, obsessive-compulsive disorders, panic disorders, generalized anxiety disorder, and phobias. Topics include:

- AIT theory regarding fear and anxiety in disorders and the structure of anxiety disorders
- The neurobiology of anxiety disorders
- Energetic neurobiological protocols to transform neurobiology
- A general treatment plan for anxiety disorders
- A psychological protocol for the treatment of each anxiety disorder
- A protocol that treats the physical causes of anxiety disorders
- Archetypal treatment of anxiety disorders

Continuing Education Units: Provided by the Board of Registered Nurses, provider #CEP10319, and the California Board of Behavioral Sciences, provider #PCE 2938. CEUs are provided in each state, where AIT is taught, by the National Association of Social Workers. For other areas, ask your coordinator or instructor.

Certification: Offered by the Advanced Integrative Therapy program.

Participants: All helping professionals, from beginners to advanced practitioners of energy psychology, psychiatrists, psychologists, psychotherapists, social workers, and therapeutically trained clergy. As of August 1, 2006, a master's degree or higher in a healing profession is required to become a Certified AIT Practitioner. Students are welcome to take the classes and teleconferences without the goal of certification.

Code of Ethics/Standards of Practice: They have adopted the Code of Ethics developed by the Association for Comprehensive Energy Psychology.

Suggested Reading

Clinton, Asha. "Seemorg Matrix Work: A New Transpersonal Psychotherapy," *Journal of Transpersonal Psychology,* vol. 38, no. 1, 2006.

Marohn, Stephanie, ed. *Audacious Aging*, "Creating the Freedom to Age Audaciously," chapter written by Asha Clinton. Santa Rosa, CA: Elite Books, 2009.

Availability: Classes are offered throughout Europe, Canada, Latin America, and the United States. To find a practitioner as well as a seminar schedule in your area, go to www.aitherapy.org.

Resources
. . . .

Advanced Integrative Therapy, PO Box 41, West Stockbridge, MA 01266, 413-528-1566, info@aitherapy.com, www.aitherapy.org

Bibliography
. . . .

Clinton, Asha. *The Seemorg Core Belief Matrices and Protocol*. Great Barrington, MA: AIT Press, 2006.

———. "Seemorg Matrix Work: A New Transpersonal Psychotherapy," *Journal of Transpersonal Psychology*, vol. 38, no. 1, 2006.

www.aitherapy.org

www.seemorgmatrix.org

www.feelingfree.net

ANATOMY FOR HEALERS®

I NTENDED FOR ADVANCED HEALERS from many energy medicine therapies with a practice or an intention to practice, Anatomy for Healers provides a series of classes that combine traditional anatomy (the structure of the body) and physiology (the functioning of the body) with energy healing. Students must be well versed in at least one energy medicine therapy. From cell structure to organ functioning to the body as a whole, students come away with a thorough knowledge of how the body works, both physically and energetically.

Founder Sue Hovland, a registered nurse (BSN), certified massage therapist (CMT), and Healing Touch Certified Practitioner and Instructor (HTCP/I), recognized that few energy medicine modalities include classes in anatomy and physiology. Building on her background in nursing, traditional and nontraditional anatomy classes, massage, Neuromuscular Therapy, Cranial-Sacral Therapy, human dissection, Manual Therapy, Visceral Manipulation, Manual Lymph Drainage, Zero Balancing, allergy release techniques, and several energy medicine disciplines, she created Anatomy for Healers (originally called Experiential Anatomy and Physiology for Healers) in 1996.

Hovland begin the program as an advanced class for the Healing Touch Program™. Janet Mentgen, founder of Healing Touch, supported her classes. The techniques differ from the practices of the Healing Touch Program and so Hovland maintains a separate program of her own. She does not have a certification program. Students learn about the meridian system and expand on the traditional Chinese medicine theories of the energy field and the chakra system as they relate to human anatomy. Hovland goes beyond the traditional conceptions of these theories to suggest that each organ and system has its own energy field and corresponding chakras that exchange energy between the organs and the rest of the body.

Course Descriptions

All students of Anatomy for Healers must be able to demonstrate proficiency in energy work before enrolling. Specific prerequisites include knowledge of the chakra system and the energy fields and how to assess and treat the energy system with energy therapy. Courses consist of lecture, visual aids, anatomy props, and hands-on work, to apply functional anatomy to the energy of the physical body. All instructors take a lively, interactive approach to teaching.

▶ **Anatomy for Healers Level 1: An Energetic Approach to the Healthy Body** demonstrates how the physical and energetic systems of the body are integrated, including the following topics:

- The location, structure, function, vibrational energy, and associated symbology of the organ systems of the human body (skin, muscular, skeletal, digestive, lymphatic and immune, urinary, reproductive, respiratory, cardiovascular, endocrine, and nervous)

- The application of anatomy and physiology in an energetic healing treatment

- How to locate and energetically palpate the endocrine glands and the major organs of the torso

- Interactive exercises and energetic treatments, including moving energy through the skeleton and muscles; kidney, liver, lung, and lymphatic flushes; artery chelation; limbic brain balance; pelvic relaxation; and digestive valve releases

▶ **Anatomy for Healers Level 2: An Energetic Approach to Diseases** further integrates concepts of anatomy, physiology, and pathophysiology with energy therapies. Participants are encouraged to develop their own treatments as they understand more about how the body works. Prerequisite: Anatomy for Healers Level 1. Topics include:

- A deeper understanding of the body tissues and systems, including the application of anatomy, physiology, and pathophysiology in energetic healing treatments
- Diseases and appropriate energy treatments in several corresponding systems of the body
- Experiencing an energetic connection with cells and tissues
- In-depth knowledge of several systems of the body, including skeletal (back), digestive, respiratory, cardiovascular, and endocrine, including exercises and techniques for healing disease in these systems
- Diseases and appropriate energy treatments in several corresponding systems of the body
- An energetic approach to allergies
- Developing a protocol for the energetic treatment of disease that incorporates an anatomical approach

▶ **Anatomy for Healers Level 3: The Brain and Nervous System** looks in great detail at the structure and function of various parts of the brain and nervous system and the role they play in disease. Level 3 introduces students to energy treatments for stress, trauma, and diseases not covered in the earlier classes. Participants are encouraged to synthesize their knowledge and develop their own treatments. Prerequisite: Anatomy for Healers Level 1. Topics include:

- How the heart affects the brain
- The structure, function, and subtle energy of the nervous system and many parts of the brain, including neurotransmitters
- How to "talk" to the body
- The concept of anatomy in energetic treatment protocols in the brain and nervous system
- The pathophysiology of several common diseases of the nervous system with appropriate energy treatments
- Advanced interactive exercises and energy treatments

Continuing Education Units: Hovland (as well as the other instructors of Anatomy for Healers) is a Healing Touch Certified Instructor and has been authorized to give CEUs through the Healing Touch Program.

Certification: No.

Participants: Prospective students must demonstrate proficiency in a known modality of energy medicine before enrolling in Anatomy for Healers classes. Practitioners come from many modalities.

Code of Ethics/Standards of Practice: Yes.

Suggested Reading

Kapit, Wynn, and Lawrence M. Elson. *The Anatomy Coloring Book*, 3rd edition. New York: Benjamin Cummings, 2002.

Netter, Frank. *Netter's Atlas of Human Anatomy*. New York: Barron's Educational Series Inc., Icon Learning Systems LLC, 2006.

Parker, Steve. *The Human Body Book*. New York: DK Publishing, 2007.

Availability: Workshops are taught throughout the United States and Canada and occasionally in other countries. Check www.anatomyforhealers.com for class schedules.

Resources

Anatomy for Healers, 6486 W. Long Drive, Littleton, CO 80123, 303-759-8966, suehovland@aol.com, www.anatomyforhealers.com

Bibliography

www.anatomyforhealers.com

www.powellsbooks.com

BARBARA BRENNAN SCHOOL OF HEALING®

Barbara Ann Brennan is one of the leading pioneers in Western energy medicine, and many consider her work the standard in the field. Her book *Hands of Light* is used by several modalities as part of their required reading list, and many of her techniques have been adapted by other modalities as part of their healing programs. Through her book, Brennan has defined the energy field (also known as the aura) and the energy centers (also known as chakras), and she has set the standards for other Western energetic medicine modalities.

According to Brennan, "The heart of healing is not the techniques, but the states of being out of which those techniques arise." Her school bases its work on an energy healing model where good health stems from a free flow of life energy. It is in the area of the blockage where, over time, illness is thought to occur. According to Brennan, the purpose of the healer is to clear and balance the energy field to enhance the body's natural healing process. Students of the school learn hands-on healing techniques, body psychotherapy, psychological processes, deep self-introspection, High Sense Perception, the integration of the healing arts with the healing spirit, meditation, how to commit personalized spiritual practice, and the development of professional presence. The Higher Sense Perception classes teach students how to access information using means other than the five senses, including intuition, clairaudience, clairvoyance, clairsentience, and other psychic abilities. This psychic development training is an important part of the Brennan training and healing program.

Brennan holds a bachelor's degree in physics, a master's degree in atmospheric physics, a doctorate in both theology and philosophy, and her professional experience includes working as a physicist for NASA's Goddard Space Flight Center. Curious about energy work, she trained in bioenergetic and core energetic therapy at the

Institute for Psychophysical Synthesis and at the Community of the Whole Person, and she was also in the first graduating class of what is now known as the Institute of Core Energetics. (For more information on Core Energetics, see page 183.)

Brennan began her teaching career in energy healing by establishing the Gaiabriel Foundation in New York City. In 1982, she moved to East Hampton, Long Island, and changed the name of the school to the Barbara Brennan School of Healing. In 2000, she moved the school to Boca Raton, Florida, and the state of Florida accredited the school as a specialized college in 2002. Due to an expanding student population from overseas, Brennan also set up branches of the school in Tokyo, Japan, and Neuenahr, Germany, and currently introductory workshops are held all over the world.

Students may attend the Barbara Brennan Healing School for personal transformation or to pursue a career in energy healing. The overall nature of the programs is to support the commitment of loving self-responsibility on the part of the faculty and the students. Being a healer calls a person to standards of personal excellence, and the students of the school are required to conduct their lives in and out of class with a high degree of personal integrity. Mutual respect is a keynote for both students and teachers. Throughout their interactions, instructors and staff support students in the development and practice of meticulous honesty with themselves and others. These traits are considered part of the path into the self that leads to the discovery of the most coherent forms of self-enlightenment. While many energy healing programs offer certification, the Barbara Brennan School of Healing also offers a bachelor's degree. The school is a specialized college where students may earn a bachelor of science or a professional studies diploma in Brennan Healing Science. Bachelor of science students take anatomy, physiology, and general education classes in science, math, English, humanities, and sociology or behavioral science. Anatomy and physiology is offered by the school or credits may be transferred from another accredited institution. The general education classes are provided online from the school or credits may be transferred from other accredited institutions.

A session based on the Brennan healing techniques begins with an intake interview to learn what is happening with the client. The practitioner uses both the commonly accepted five senses as well as his or her Higher Sense Perception to assess the client's true condition. Once the assessment is complete, the practitioner places hands on or above the body to begin the healing techniques. One or more techniques may be performed depending upon the client's needs. A reassessment follows the treatment and other treatments may be applied if the reassessment shows something is still out of balance. The session ends with recommendations for further treatment, if necessary, and general comments concerning overall health issues such as diet and exercise.

Course Descriptions

To receive certification as a Brennan Healing Science Practitioner, a student must complete at least 900 classroom hours (during a four-year time period), more than 100 documented client sessions, a senior thesis, an oral case presentation to the faculty, university-level anatomy and physiology courses, and a minimum of 72 sessions of personal therapy. There is also an additional two-year graduate study program for those who wish to become instructors. With the exception of Anatomy, Physiology I, and general education courses, previous education or training is not accepted as credit. Students pursuing a bachelor's degree must have proof of a high school diploma, completed GED requirements, or international equivalency. The following chart from the school catalog shows the distribution of semester credit hours needed for either a bachelor of science in Brennan Healing Science or a diploma in Brennan Healing Science Professional Studies.

Distribution of Semester Credit Hours

Area of Study	Bachelor of Science In Brennan Healing Science	Diploma in Brennan Healing Science Professional Studies
	4-year program	4-year program
Brennan Healing Science	19	19
Psych-Spiritual development	15	15
Professional practice	6	6
Integrative care	8	8

Area of Study	Bachelor of Science In Brennan Healing Science	Diploma in Brennan Healing Science Professional Studies
	4-year program	4-year program
Creative arts	8	8
Integrative Distance Learning	24	24
Senior project	4	4
General anatomy & physiology	5	5
Anatomy & physiology of the human energy field	9	-
General education	27	-

General education courses are offered online. Students may transfer up to 30 semester credit hours of general education requirements from an accredited institution.

The Professional Studies in Brennan Healing Science

Professional Studies Year 1: Journey of Personal Healing and Self-Discovery

Year 1 of the Professional Studies Program involves personal healing, self-introspection, and learning about energy and consciousness. With help from the instructor, students address and deeply explore their relationships with themselves and expand their perception of reality. Exploring their inner landscape builds the necessary foundation for the development of their healership.

▶ **Brennan Healing Science: Theory and Skills I** provides a foundation for the student's course of study with both lecture and experiential exercises. Topics include:

• Anatomy and physiology of the human energy system

- Developing high sense perception
- Basic principles of healing, including receiving guidance and healing on the first three levels of the human energy field

▶ **Psych-Spiritual Development I** investigates the self on psychological and spiritual levels, including characterology, psych-spiritual development, and group processes

▶ **Professional Practice I** explores the healer–client relationship, including professional practice development and community building.

▶ **Creative Arts I** works with the first three chakras and explores various artistic media and topics, including art as healing, art project presentation, and experiencing the body/mind/spirit through movement.

▶ **Integrative Distance Learning Modules I** weave together the core teachings of the school, including theory, procedures, techniques, exercises, and applications.

▶ **Anatomy and Physiology I** explores the human body. Topics include:

- The structure and function of the human body
- Body systems
- Assessment
- Relationships between the energy field and various systems and organs of the body

▶ **Composition I** is a basic writing course. Topics include:

- How to write an essay
- Proper language usage
- How to write a research paper

▶ **Strategies for Success I** enhances the learning experience. Topics include:

- Personal and professional success
- Managing change
- Setting and achieving goals
- Time management

Professional Studies Year 2: Journey of Relationship Healing

Year 2 deepens the experience of the previous year by holding the spiritual purpose of the fourth level of the human energy field. The focus is on being in relationship with others. Self-awareness continues to grow as the students develop healing tools that will help them create healthy relationships. They teach the principle that no one can heal another at the level of relationship unless they are actively healing their own personal relationships.

Students will begin to change their relationships with others in ever wider groups—with all species we share this Earth with and even with their guardian angels. This work is extensive as it expands through many lifetimes.

▶ **Brennan Healing Science: Theory and Skills II** teaches theory, skills, techniques, and exercises for healing on the fourth level of the Human Energy Consciousness System, which is the level of I–you relationships. Topics include:

- The physics of the fourth level
- Astral beings and objects
- Time capsule healing
- Creation of thought forms
- Healing on the fourth level of the human energy field
- Energy consciousness belief system territories

▶ **Psych-Spiritual Development II** provides a safe environment for students to explore the question "Who am I?" Topics include:

- Characterology
- Psych-spiritual development skills
- Early childhood experiences and their effect on the human energy field

▶ **Professional Practice II** explores the relational aspects of a healing practice and the responsibilities of a professional healer. Topics include:

- Ethics of a professional practice and professional practice development
- Group supervision
- Establishing and maintaining depth of contact in a therapeutic healing relationship

- Community building

▶ **Creative Arts II** facilitates the fourth level relational contact and learning time capsule healings. Topics include:

- Surrendering to the unknown
- Acquiring a sense of the resonant spectrums of energy force fields moving in waves
- Experiencing a wave as a completed cycle of expansion and contraction
- Art as healing
- Synchronizing with energy flow
- Cellular awareness

▶ **Integrative Care II** focuses on the student's relationship with others. Topics include:

- The interview and client intake process
- Comprehensive assessment and documentation
- Communication with supportive, integrative language
- Being with clients who are ill
- Discerning possible life-threatening physiological responses and personal process

▶ **Integrative Distance Learning Modules II** explores a series of seven integrated modules that assist the student in deepening the theory and application of second-year trainings. Lessons involve an in-depth investigation of:

- Theory
- Procedures
- Techniques
- Exercises
- Applications

▶ **Anatomy and Physiology II** emphasizes the physiological functioning of the body in good health and illness. This class is required for those seeking a degree and optional for diploma students. Topics include:

- The study of how gradual pollution from the environment affects the immune system
- How food and water affect the immune system
- Developing High Sense Perception
- Exploring the effects of relationships and supporting systems on health and recovery time from illness
- Integrating healing science skills with the function of the physical body
- How beliefs, thoughts, and emotions can affect the body systems
- Disease pathology, post-traumatic stress disorder, and psychoneuroimmunology

▶ **Humanities I** explores human creativity and Western cultural history. It is required for those seeking a degree and optional for diploma students. Topics include:

- Visual arts
- Literature
- History
- Architecture
- Technology

▶ **College Algebra I** is the study of real numbers and variables. It is required for those seeking a degree and optional for diploma students. Topics include:

- Operations and expression
- First- and second-degree equations
- The Cartesian coordinate system
- Radicals and exponents

▶ **Psychology I** examines the fundamentals of human psychology. It is required for those seeking a degree and optional for diploma students. Topics include:

- Biological basis of behavior
- Sensation and perception
- Motivation, learning, and memory
- Maturation and development
- Personality

- Psychological disorders
- Social psychology

Professional Studies Year 3: Journey of Spiritual Connection

The purpose of year 3 is to deepen the student's awareness and experience of the Divine by studying the spiritual levels 5, 6, and 7 of the human energy field. This sets the stage for the student to change his or her relationship to the spiritual world. Students gain an understanding of self and the Divine using greater communion. Year 3 also begins the focus of developing energetic tools that can strengthen the student's intention and surrender to Divine flow in his or her life. Instructors and staff encourage freedom of spiritual expressions and for students to become more in touch with their own spiritual and religious training.

▶ **Brennan Healing Science: Theory and Skills III** uses lecture and demonstration to help students develop an understanding of the dynamics of the human energy-conscious system and the four dimensions of being. Classes include:

- Basic field restructuring
- Restructuring organs
- Restructuring chakras
- Spiritual surgery
- Healing on levels 5–7 of the human energy field
- Healing theory and principles associated with the higher spiritual frequencies of divine energy

▶ **Psych-Spiritual Development III** centers on the question "Who am I?" in relationship with the divine. Classes include:

- Spiritual teachings providing a framework for practical application
- Experiencing the process of psych-spiritual development through meditation and group processes
- Psych-spiritual development skills
- Incarnation, child development, heritage, and the human energy field

▶ **Professional Practice III** explores uncovering unconscious expectations and limiting belief systems. Topics include:

- The development of an individual healing style
- Working with other health-care professionals
- Studying real-life situations
- How personal psychological processes affect the healer–client relationship
- Professional practice development
- Observation of case presentations

▶ **Creative Arts III** explores the relationship between healing and the healer within. Classes include:

- Art as healing
- Sacred space
- Cellular awareness
- Healing with sound
- Healing powers of movement
- Using the media of music, movement, visual art, and the spoken word

▶ **Integrative Care III** focuses on injured or extremely ill clients. Topics include:

- Interfacing with hospitals and health-care systems
- Fundamentals of working with clients who are experiencing acute or chronic illness
- Protocols for referrals
- Surgery

▶ **Integrative Distance Learning Modules III** works with integrated modules to deepen the third-year student's experience. Topics include:

- Healing science
- Psych-spiritual development
- Creative arts
- Professional practice
- Integrative care

▶ **Anatomy and Physiology III** further explores energetic and physical manifestations in a healthy body and compares them to common illnesses. It is required for those seeking a degree and optional for diploma students. Classes include:

- Pathophysiology
- Expanding High Sense Perception
- Health issues specific to men and women
- Various life stages
- Fifth-level work

▶ **Ethics** exposes students to both sides of past and present ethical dilemmas. It is required for those seeking a degree and optional for diploma students. Topics include:

- Overview of individual ethical development
- Ethical issues in business today
- The opportunity and conflict of ethical issues
- The ethical decision-making framework
- Development of an effective ethics program

▶ **Advanced Composition** emphasizes essay writing and critical analysis. It is required for those seeking a degree and optional for diploma students. Topics include:

- Complex essays
- Organization and proper usage of essays
- Completion of a research paper

▶ **Critical Thinking and Problem Solving** addresses the basic skills of logic and reasoning. It is required for those seeking a degree and optional for diploma students. Topics include:

- Problem solving
- Related argument analysis
- Providing evidence and support for asserted solutions
- Clarity, depth, precision, relevance, and fairness

Professional Studies Year 4:
Journey of Uncovering the Unique Healer within You

All the training of the previous years culminates in year 4. The student will further develop the personal, technical, and professional skills that are necessary to become a Brennan Healing Science Practitioner. As the student's unique healership emerges, it is here that the student will find autonomy. The student will learn how to integrate this work more fully into the world. Graduates of the 4-year program are certified as Brennan Healing Science Practitioners.

▶ **Brennan Healing Science: Theory and Skills IV** uses lectures, demonstrations, and experiential exercises to focus on intentionality, feeling, and manifesting life purpose, essence, and uniqueness. Classes include:

- Holding hara
- Hara healing
- Core star healing
- Long-distance and nonlocal healing
- Healing on the auric and core star dimensions

▶ **Psych-Spiritual Development IV** continues to address the question "Who am I?" Topics include:

- Integration and embodiment of the principles and skills of psych-spiritual development
- A framework for practical application
- Opportunities to directly experience the process of psych-spiritual development
- Psych-spiritual development skills

▶ **Professional Practice IV** focuses on establishing and maintaining a professional practice. Topics include:

- Legal issues
- Malpractice and general liability insurance
- Documentation and forms

- Fee setting
- Office environment
- Marketing
- The need for professional supervision
- Case presentation

▶ **Creative Arts IV** uses a combination of lectures, guided visualizations, and experiential formats. Topics include:

- Multidimensional awareness
- How artwork mirrors unconscious material in need of integration
- Using artwork to uncover the expression of essence
- Multidimensional core contact
- Experiencing body-mind-spirit through movement

▶ **Integrative Care IV** teaches basic skills in working with people who are acutely and critically ill. Topics include:

- Working with clients experiencing shock and trauma
- Crisis, the critically ill, and the healer's role
- Death and dying
- Protocol for working with specific diseases
- Identifying and working with clients with serious mental illness

▶ **Year 4 Project** provides an opportunity for students to combine Brennan work with their personal and professional interests. Its purposes are to:

- Clarify future professional development
- Explore contributions to society after graduation
- Complete a supervised project

▶ **Integrative Distance Learning Module IV** uses a series of seven integrated modules to help deepen and apply fourth-year training. Lessons involve an in-depth investigation of:

- Theory
- Procedures

- Techniques
- Exercises
- Applications

▶ **Anatomy and Physiology IV** integrates the application of skills with working with clients in a clinical setting. It is required for those seeking a degree and optional for diploma students. It is recommended, but not required, that students complete Anatomy and Physiology III prior to enrolling in this course. Classes include:

- Clinical practice sessions
- Demonstration of personal knowledge of healing science
- Client intake
- Assessment
- Accurate High Sense Perception
- Appropriate use of techniques
- Session closure
- Post-treatment recommendations

▶ **Ecology** is an introduction to environmental science. It is required for those seeking a degree and optional for diploma students. Topics include:

- Energy principles
- Relationships of organisms in ecosystems
- Human impact

. . . .

Continuing Education Units: The Continuing Education contact hours that they are able to offer for those participating in their Professional Studies program, FBHS, or IBHS workshops are obtained through the National Certification Board for Therapeutic Massage and Bodywork (NCBTMB), an approved provider.

Certification: Yes, certification as a Brennan Healing Science Practitioner is granted by the Board of Brennan Healing Science. The Professional Studies Diploma and the Bachelor of Science degree programs are licensed by the Florida Commission for Independent Education, License #2897.

Participants: Applicants must be eighteen or older and have a high school or general equivalency diploma or international equivalent.

Code of Ethics: Yes.

Principals of Practice: Yes.

Availability: The school offers introductory weekend workshops all over the world. The four-year studies programs may be taken in Boca Raton, Florida, Neuenahr, Germany, and Tokyo, Japan. Go to www.barbarabrennan.com for a complete list of introductory classes and their locations.

For a session with a practitioner go to www.barbarabrennan.com and click on the site map. Under "Welcome" click on "Find a graduate." You will find an extensive list.

Resources

Barbara Brennan School of Healing, 500 NE Spanish River Blvd., Suite 208, Boca Raton, FL 33431 USA, 561-620-9218, Japan 03-3524-7275, bbii@barbarabrennan.com, www.barbarabrennan.com

Bibliography

Brennan, Barbara Ann. *Hands of Light: A Guide to Healing through the Human Energy Field.* New York: Bantam Books, 1987.

———. *Light Emerging.* New York: Bantam Books, 1993.

Barbara Brennan School of Healing 2007–2008 School Catalog, vol. 1. Boca Raton, FL: Barbara Brennan Inc., 2007.

www.barbarabrennan.com

BE SET FREE FAST™

BE SET FREE FAST (**BSFF**) is a psychoenergetic therapy developed by psychologist Larry Phillip Nims, PhD. Dr. Nims spent seventeen years working with the techniques taught by Dr. Roger Callahan commonly known as Thought Field Therapy, or TFT. Dr. Callahan based his work on the traditional Chinese medicine theory of meridians, using a set of tapping sequences coupled with eye movements and humming to unblock trapped energy, promote healing, and eliminate emotional problems. (See pages 121–125 for more about Thought Field Therapy.) Believing that the Callahan Techniques could be simplified, Dr. Nims eventually came to the conclusion that working with the energy of our thoughts rather than the life force energy could more effectively invoke positive change. He theorizes that the subconscious is both the primary cause and the solution to our emotional and physical problems, and encourages clients to use the subconscious as an ally to eliminate stress and disharmony.

Be Set Free Fast is an acronym that stands for the following phrase: Behavioral and Emotional Symptom Elimination Training for Resolving Excess Emotion: Fear, Anger, Sadness, and Trauma. As an energy psychotherapy, BSFF focuses on the body's energy systems as the link to the individual's emotions, behavior, and psychological health. These energy systems include the electrical activity of the nervous system, acupuncture meridians, energy centers, and fields of energy within and surrounding the body. More specifically, Dr. Nims postulates that it is not the energy systems per se but the intention of the client that actually does the work. He believes emotional problems embedded in the subconscious are locked together by specific electromagnetic energy circuits, and thus recurring problems continue to show up in a person's life. Dr. Nims postulates that there are between 700 and

2,000 possible unresolved emotional root experiences that attach to a belief system or specific problem in adults. BSFF treatment sequences attempt to eliminate these roots. Through the use of a cue word, a person can replace an unwanted emotional issue with a new, more productive program. Dr. Nims strongly believes in training individuals to treat themselves, although sometimes it takes the aid of a therapist to detect and eliminate negative attitudes, judgments, and lack of forgiveness for self and others.

During the initial session, the client learns the BSFF sequence for clearing emotional issues. The client chooses a cue word as a trigger to signal an intention to the subconscious. This cue word is also used for all subsequent treatments, whether self-treated or done with the aid of a therapist. The client is asked to state a goal, for example, a desire to be confident while speaking in public. He or she speaks, thinks about, or writes down the cue word. Next, the therapist does muscle testing to determine if the client truly believes the technique will work. If the muscle test reveals the answer to be no, there is a corresponding procedure to help change that belief.

Once the client tests positive (meaning he or she believes that the treatment will work), he or she is asked to draw up a comprehensive list of all problems and symptoms related to the issue. For example, a list of problems with public speaking may contain such items as nervousness, upset stomach, or concerns over appearing foolish. The client uses the cue word to simultaneously clear all the problems connected with his or her issue, including any anger or forgiveness problems associated with other people. The client is asked to continue to do this until there is a feeling of peace and comfort in relation to the issue. Psychological reversals, where the client subconsciously sabotages him- or herself, may be resolved by using a technique called the fail-safe system. At the end of the session, there is also a closing sequence. Once the client trains his or her subconscious mind to respond to the cue word, the session can be shortened to simply concentrating on the issue at hand, setting an intention to clear it, and using the cue word to trigger the subconscious to eliminate the problem.

Course Descriptions

Prospective students must study the book *Be Set Free Fast: A Revolutionary Way to Eliminate Your Discomforts,* available as an e-book or comb-bound hard-copy version at www.besetfreefast.com, and the DVD collection before being accepted into the class. The DVD collection, titled *Personal Instruction for Everyday Freedom: The Lifetime Work of Dr. Larry Nims,* contains 8 hours of instruction, history, interviews, and demonstrations. Graduates of the BSFF Level One Training may participate in a 60-day e-mail discussion with members of their class and take part in the Buddy Session Exchange System. BSFF often refers to the Level One Training as an advanced class.

▶ **BSFF Level One Training** is a live class that works with the material presented in *Be Set Free Fast: A Revolutionary Way to Eliminate Your Discomforts* and the BSFF training DVD. Students have an opportunity to work with instructor Don Elium in seminar demonstrations. Topics include:

- New BSFF innovations by Dr. Nims
- BSFF treatment essentials and treating core issues
- BSFF self-treatment and with others
- Discovering and eliminating hidden problems
- Treating core issues
- Introductory muscle testing training with self and others
- Using BSFF without muscle testing

Continuing Education Units: California CEUs are available at no extra cost, but CEUs are not available for psychologists.

Certification: No.

Participants: For health-care professionals and laypeople.

Code of Ethics/Standards of Practice: No.

Availability: Classes are available in various locations. Go to www.besetfreefast .com for a complete list in your area.

Resources

Larry P. Nims, PhD, 3674 N. 159th Avenue, Goodyear, AZ 85395, 623-466-4112, for telephone consultations, BSFF Training, and life coaching, contact BSFF.Larry@BeSetFreeFastDVD.com, www.besetfreefast.com.

Bibliography

Nims, Larry Phillips, and Joan Sotkins. *Be Set Free Fast: A Revolutionary Way to Eliminate Your Discomforts*, 2008. Available as an e-book or comb-bound hard-copy version at www.besetfreefast.com.

www.emofree.com

www.prosperity-place.com

BI-AURA®

MAIRE CAITHLIN DENNHOFER established the Bi-Aura Foundation in 2000 after studying complementary medicine for many years. Energy therapy caught her attention and in 1995 she decided to bring it from Ireland to the United Kingdom. From there practitioners have spread to Europe and the United States.

Bi-Aura therapy builds on the premise that the human body is surrounded by a field of energy known as the aura. Within that field exist seven main energy centers called chakras that transform and conduct energy and information into and throughout the body. When working properly, the chakras interact with the aura and process energy as needed. If stress and trauma overwhelm the chakras, energy can cease to circulate properly and form unhealthy congestion in the body and the surrounding aura, perhaps leading to disease, mental illness, or emotional problems. Bi-Aura therapy initially focuses on two major energy centers: one at the top of the head called the crown chakra and another at the base of the spine called the root chakra. The crown chakra takes in cosmic energy from the Universe, and the root chakra takes in Earth energy. When all seven chakras spin in balance, energy flows freely and nourishes the body and its organs.

To begin a session, a client removes her shoes, watch, glasses, belt, or other accessories such as jewelry that may restrict the flow of energy. The practitioner scans the client's energy field using his or her hands to identify possible blockages, usually without touching the client. If it is comfortable for them to do so, the client remains standing while this is done. On completion of the opening energizing techniques, the client will be invited to sit or lie down for the detox phase and then asked to stand once more for the closing scan. Bi-Aura therapists think of their hands as magnets that pull congested energy out of the client's field and release it to the universe for recycling. Once the energy centers have been cleared, the practitioner transmits cosmic energy through his or her hands and releases it into the client. After the practitioner has cleared and energized the client in this way, he or she performs a second scan to determine whether or not further treatment is needed. Most treatments require a minimum of four sessions.

The Bi-Aura Foundation achieved charity status and now accepts donations for research and to build and maintain clinics. The foundation is a registered member of the Complementary Medical Association and the UK Healers. The Diploma in Bio-Energy Therapy has been accredited by the North East Open College Network, a self-governing arm of the National Open College Network in the United Kingdom. The diploma course is recognized as a full Level 3 qualification of 18 credits and is equivalent to the A-Level, giving graduates nationally recognized qualification in the United Kingdom.

Course Descriptions

Bi-Aura training takes place one weekend every month over the course of eight to nine months. Before going into professional practice, students must also study anatomy, physiology, and emergency first aid.

Throughout the eight- to nine-month course, students are given a thorough grounding in the philosophical theory and scientific practice of bioenergy healing. Each of the first seven weekend courses focuses on a specific major chakra, starting with the root. Students are asked to keep a journal to record their changes in energy awareness, participate in a session with a registered Bi-Aura practitioner, and develop a personal practice of qigong and meditation. The course syllabus consists of the following, divided equally between theory and practice, with specific techniques, exercises, and interactive sessions relating to each of the chakras spread across every class. Some instructors combine weekends eight and nine.

- Weekend 1: root chakra theory, the background and origin of Bi-Aura, the energy matrix and spiritual healing and integration, qigong, grounding, and exercises related to the root chakra

- Weekend 2: sacral chakra theory, the tools of Bi-Aura, cleansing internally and externally, seeing and using healing colors, the power of the focused mind

- Weekend 3: solar plexus theory, sensing subtle energy, decisions and procrastination, inner power, understanding people, medical intervention, interpreting chakra disturbances

- Weekend 4: heart chakra theory, the body's regeneration, disease and physiology, emotional detoxification, and an introduction to case studies and setting up a clinic

- Weekend 5: throat chakra theory, purity and detoxification, listening to the higher self, healing the inner self, the expression of the chakras

- Weekend 6: brow chakra theory, power points that cause change, reaching the quantum world, psychology and physiology, psychic healing, distant healing, extrasensory perception

- Weekend 7: crown chakra theory, spiritual integration, enabling or limiting beliefs, working as a therapist, legal requirements of a clinic, insurance, and clinic promotion

- Weekend 8: professional practice theory, business training program, working as a therapist, clinic setup and records, promotion, administration, accounts, legal requirements, insurance, professional therapy practice sessions, and clinical feedback and advice

- Weekend 9: an examination of the student's understanding of the purpose and application of Bi-Aura techniques and a three-hour written examination of theory followed by a debriefing and open forum

· · · · · · · · · · · · · · · · · · ·

Continuing Education Units: Talk to your instructor about the local equivalent and whether he or she offers it.

Certification: Students receive a diploma in Bio-Energy Therapy and a NOCN (National Open College Network) Level 3-A equivalent certificate upon completion of all the requirements of the course. The Bi-Aura Therapy Diploma can be used for access to a university in the United Kingdom.

Participants: The courses are constructed for beginners and for health-care professionals who want to expand their therapeutic skills.

Code of Ethics/Standards of Practice: All Bi-Aura practitioners must be registered with the Bi-Aura Foundation and adhere to a rigorous Code of Practice.

Availability: Classes are offered in England, Ireland, Northern Ireland, Scotland, and Wales. For a session in your area, go to www.bi-aura.com.

Resources

Bi-Aura Foundation, The Rookery, Newton, Northumberland, NE43 7UN, UK, +44-(0)1661-844-899, info@bi-aura.com, www.bi-aura.com

Bi-Aura Foundation, 40 The Paddock, Ashtown Gate, Navan Road, Dublin 7, Ireland, +37-(0)1-868-2516, joeconnolly2@hotmail.com, www.bi-aura.com

Bibliography

www.bi-aura.com

www.justbewell.com

BODYTALK SYSTEM™

ACCORDING TO DR. JOHN VELTHEIM, founder of the BodyTalk System, if the body and the mind are synchronized, the body will automatically heal itself. Unfortunately, the stresses and demands of illness, injury, and everyday life can compromise the effective communication naturally present in a healthy person. The objective of BodyTalk is to help the body heal itself. By using techniques such as muscle testing, tapping, and deep breathing, BodyTalk practitioners help clients re-establish a functional balance within their body, which can promote healing in relation to just about any condition, injury, or illness.

Dr. Veltheim's background in chiropractics, acupuncture, Reiki, the martial arts, Zen meditation, and applied kinesiology, plus years of experience working with clients, led him to create BodyTalk, which he is constantly expanding as he and his wife, Esther Veltheim, continue to work with clients and students. Through his experience, he concluded that the body has its own unique healing response, which can be determined and enhanced through muscle testing. By responding weak or strong to a given muscle test, the body tells the practitioner where treatment is needed and in what order. A practitioner can test for the health and well-being of organs, muscles, glands, the circulatory system, the immune system, and also the energy system.

As Veltheim says in his book *The BodyTalk System*, "The body has an innate wisdom which, when allowed, can heal the body at all levels." He adds that "no treatment is given until the body asks for it. The treatments are given in the exact sequence asked for by the body, in the exact number of treatments asked for by the body." In treatment, the practitioner places her hands over the unhealthy area of the body, then scans the rest of the body and energy system to check for missing or broken links. To restore the broken links, she taps the top of the client's head to tell the brain to repair the link, and then taps the sternum above the heart to make the changes permanent.

Lying on their back, clients remain fully clothed during a session, with the exception of taking off jewelry, shoes, and other accessories. The practitioner begins by placing one hand on the belly of the client and conducting muscle testing with the other. She then moves her hands around the body while testing for weakness and missing links, often asking the client to breathe in a certain manner to facilitate healing. Once the practitioner ascertains which areas of the body are weak and/or disconnected from other parts of the body, she places her hands on those areas to signify what the body needs to repair. The practitioner then gently taps the client's head to let the brain know what to repair and the client's heart to store the information and carry it to the rest of the body.

Course Descriptions
. . . .

Dr. Veltheim developed these courses between 1997 and 2001 to create the basic foundation of the therapy. The curriculum was designed specifically for health-care professionals, but a number of people are taking the classes to give themselves skills in energy work to help family and friends. In 2004, Dr. Veltheim began developing an advanced form of BodyTalk he calls PaRama BodyTalk. PaRama BodyTalk Unit 1 and Unit 2 are available in DVD form. The curriculum is divided into four sub-groups: the Core Curriculum, which is the foundation of BodyTalk; a simple one-day class entitled BodyTalk Access; AnimalTalk, which applies the techniques to animals; and PaRama BodyTalk, which addresses the latest findings of Dr. Veltheim.

The Core Curriculum has nine modules and several specialized courses. Modules 4 and 7 are always taught together in a single weekend seminar. Module 5 is considered a specialized class and is not included in the requirements for certification. Module 8A is for animals. Completion of Modules 1 and 2 qualifies a student to apply for certification as a Certified BodyTalk Practitioner (CBP). To achieve advanced BodyTalk certification (Advanced CBP), the student must complete modules 1, 2, 3, 4, 6, 7, and 9. Modules 1 through 9 are described here along with Unit 1. The rest of the curriculum may be found at their website, www.bodytalksystem.

com/bodytalk/overview/courses. Some classes require membership in the International BodyTalk Association in order to qualify to take the class. A few of the classes offered in DVD form have been taught live in Germany.

▶ **Module 1** consists of a comprehensive introduction to the BodyTalk System. Students learn theoretical aspects and hands-on experience with some of the techniques. Topics include:

- Breathing patterns and left/right brain and body coordination
- Energy blockages associated with birthplace and imbalances in the local environment
- Energy faults within the brain cortexes
- Health problems associated with internal and external scarring
- Balancing the twelve major body organs and eight endocrine systems
- Clearing the body of viruses, infections, parasites, food intolerances, environmental allergies, and accumulated toxins
- Clearing past and present emotional blockages, phobias, and fears

▶ **Module 2** builds on Module 1 and expands the treatment techniques to include the entire BodyTalk System. Module 1 is a prerequisite. Topics include:

- The surface energy points
- Cleansing the lymphatic system
- Working with energy blockages in the nervous and circulatory systems
- Balancing the energy systems, including the meridians and chakras
- Energy imbalances between the client and the environment
- Balancing brain function and correcting hereditary and /or environmentally influenced cell disorders

▶ **Module 3** addresses the practical foundation of the philosophy behind the BodyTalk System and how it relates to human consciousness. The course is only available to International BodyTalk Association members. Modules 1 and 2, as well as the Module 1 and 2 Advanced Procedures DVD, are prerequisites for this course. Topics include:

- Detailed review of the linking system behind BodyTalk

- Balancing the physical and subtle five senses within the BodyTalk System

- Basic consciousness, including how to address the beliefs, attitudes, and states of awareness of clients in a simple, noninvasive way that honors their own innate wisdom

- Advanced consciousness, including the understanding of space/time, guilt, individuation, masks, and habitual thinking patterns as they relate to personal and spiritual growth, enabling practitioners to balance the right/left brain complex, and helping clients recognize their natural inner harmony

▶ **Module 4** addresses the body as an energy system and is only available to International Body Talk Association members. Modules 1 and 2, as well as the Module 1 and 2 Advanced Procedures DVD, are prerequisites for this course. This module is taught in conjunction with Module 7. Topics include:

- Detailed study of the five elements

- The role of kidneys in the yin/yang balance of the body and how they relate to sexuality

- Detailed examination of Wei Qi (protective energy) and practical ways to balance its function

- The breathing cycle and its ramifications throughout the body

- The role of the diaphragm in the processing and distribution of pathological emotions and thoughts

- Study of the role of emotions within the body-mind complex and harmonization techniques

- Techniques to reorient organs, endocrines, and body parts within the body-mind complex

- Study of the emotional and psychological relationships of the major muscles and joints of the body

▶ **Module 7** focuses on sports medicine and musculoskeletal disorders. The course is only available to International Body Talk Association members. Modules 1 and 2, as well as the Module 1 and 2 Advanced Procedures DVD, are prerequisites for this course. Module 7 is taught in conjunction with Module 4. Topics include:

- Sports performance and injuries, including adhesions and improvement in range of motion
- Chronic arthritis
- Posture and spinal balancing

▶ **Module 5** has several areas of focus. The class provides a lot of time to practice hands-on work with the guidance of an experienced instructor. This class is of special value to participants with no background in bodywork. Some of the topics include:

- Information and practical skills for working in close proximity with clients
- An overview of the origins and insertions of major muscles to increase the effectiveness of rehabilitation work. Utilizing anatomical and physiological details from both Western and Oriental perspectives
- The Veltheim method of lymphatic drain

▶ **Module 6** addresses the macrocosmic view of the function of the body-mind complex. The course is only available to International Body Talk Association members. Modules 1 and 2, as well as the Module 1 and 2 Advanced Procedures DVD, are prerequisites for this course. Topics include:

- The twenty-one subchakras, the eight chakras, and the cultural, hereditary, ancestral, and planetary influences on the energy system
- Body synchronization and linking all levels of the body-mind complex using Modules 1 through 6

▶ **Module 8A** addresses issues germane to cats and dogs. It is only available to members of the International BodyTalk Association. BodyTalk Modules 1, 2, and 3 and the Modules 1 and 2 Advanced Procedures DVD are prerequisites for this class. This course may count toward continuing education hours for Certified BodyTalk Practitioners. Specific topics for this class may include:

- The principles of BodyTalk as applied to dogs and cats

- Basic classifications and characteristics of dogs and cats, including breed characteristics, basic anatomy and physiology, behavior and basic animal and group consciousness
- Creating an environment to work with animals, the safe handling of animals and the responses of animals to BodyTalk
- Working with surrogates
- Applying the basic BodyTalk balancing techniques on animals
- Dealing with emotional trauma and environmental conditions affecting animals
- Understanding the relationships between people and animals

▶ **Module 9** addresses the dissolution of the primary and secondary personality matrixes of the body-mind. These matrixes are collective personality masks that affect the health of the client. BodyTalk Modules 3 and 6 are prerequisites for this course. This course may count toward continuing education hours for Certified BodyTalk Practitioners.

▶ **PaRama BodyTalk Unit 1** is a correspondence course from Dr. Veltheim and includes the use of DVDs. This class has been taught live in Germany. International BodyTalk Association membership and BodyTalk Modules 3 and 4 are prerequisites for this course. Unit 1 may count toward continuing education hours for Certified BodyTalk Practitioners. Because this is a new part of the curriculum changes occur frequently. Some of the topics may include:

- 40 lessons of new information
- The physiology and consciousness of forty-two different brain parts
- Practical demonstrations
- A new protocol chart

Continuing Education Units: Inquire with your individual instructor.

Certification: Yes. Three levels of certification are available: Certified BodyTalk Practitioner, Advanced Certified BodyTalk Practitioner, and Certified BodyTalk Instructor.

Participants: Classes are suitable for health-care professionals as well as laypeople who want to learn to use the BodyTalk System on a nonprofessional level.

Suggested Reading

Veltheim, John. *BodyTalk Access: A New Path to Family and Community Health.* Sarasota, FL: International Body Talk Association, 2008.

———. *The BodyTalk System: The Missing Link to Optimum Health.* Sarasota, FL: PaRama Inc., 1999.

Availability: Classes are available throughout Europe and the United States as well as Japan, South Africa, and Brazil. For a session with a practitioner in your area, visit the BodyTalk website, www.bodytalksystem.com.

Resources

International BodyTalk Association, 2750 Stickney Point Road, Suite 203, Sarasota, FL 34231, 877-519-9119, International +1 941-921-7443, www .bodytalksystem.com, www.ibaglobalhealing.com, Am Anger 4B, 87487 Wiggensbach, Germany, +49 (0)8370 929421

7 Begonia Crescent, Mount Cotton, QLD 4165, Australia, +61 (07)3103 2853

Bibliography

Veltheim, John. *The BodyTalk System: The Missing Link to Optimum Health.* Sarasota, FL: PaRama Inc., 1999.

www.bodytalksystem.com

www.parama.com

CORE ENERGETICS®

ORE ENERGETICS IS A PSYCHOENERGETIC THERAPY, sometimes called a body-centered therapy for the mind and spirit. Recognizing the imperfections of the world, Core Energetics posits that the effects of the stressful or negative events, relationships, and traumas in a person's life history are held deeply in the body as emotional or energetic blocks. This therapy works with breathing, movement, and consciousness to release these blocks in the energy field caused by long-held feelings, helping clients overcome the effects of the past and release their full energy.

John Pierrakos, MD, psychiatrist and founder and creator of Core Energetics, was an early pioneer in the field of energy medicine in the United States. He studied under Wilhelm Reich, an early-twentieth-century Austrian American psychiatrist and psychoanalyst who was a student of Carl Jung's. Working with Alexander Lowen, an early proponent of mind-body psychotherapy, Pierrakos created a form of healing called bioenergetic analysis that included the will, as well as the body and emotions of a person suffering from a psychiatric disorder, as part of treatment. He eventually parted from Lowen and founded the Institute of Core Energetics. In 1989, Stuart Black took over as director of the institute.

In his book *Core Energetics: Developing the Capacity to Love and Heal*, Pierrakos shares the three main premises on which Core Energetics is based. First, the human person is a psychosomatic unit. Second, the source of all healing lies within the self. Third, all of existence forms a unity that moves toward creative evolution. Today, Core Energetics addresses the body, emotions, mind, will, and spirit and uses methods that enable energy and consciousness to work together in the healing process. Pent-up emotions stored in the body and the energy field since childhood are referred to as "frozen history."

In a session, either with groups or with individuals, a practitioner observes the client's energy flow, posture, body language, physical strength, and spiritual essence as clues forming a picture of the client's frozen history. She then asks the client to describe his or her own body and the presenting complaint, and uses all of this information to determine a course of treatment. Core Energetics employs a number of physical techniques, such as targeted breathing, hitting or kicking a mattress, specific body movements, sound, facial expressions, and holding exaggerated postures or positions. They also use softer, hands-on techniques for the energy field, many of which come from Barbara Brennan therapies (151–165). Through the use of these techniques the practitioner aids the client in releasing the energy holding old wounds in place. Using her analysis of the client, the practitioner suggests a number of techniques to help the client experience and release deeply held conflicts, restoring pleasure and a sense of fulfillment. It may take several sessions for these goals to be achieved.

Some Core Energetics practitioners ask for an autobiography ahead of time to help determine the course of treatment. Once the autobiography has been received the practitioner follows up with a phone call. At that time the practitioner sets up an appointment with the client.

Course Descriptions

The following programs come from the Institute of Core Energetics. Others are teaching Core Energetic classes that differ somewhat from this program. Many massage schools and community colleges offer courses in Core Energetics.

The program offered by the Core Energetics Institute has three divisions. The two-year Personal Transformation Program is for people who wish to pursue self-discovery. It is taught over a period of five weekends each year, with both lecture and opportunity for hands-on experience. The course provides foundations the first year and in-depth release work the second year.

The Core Practitioner Training is a four-year program designed for people from all walks of life who desire certification as a Core Energetics Practitioner. Four daylong training workshops are held five times a year in a retreat setting northwest of New York City. Room and board are included in the price. Core Energetics professional standards require the following to graduate from the program:

- Four years of attendance with five training sessions each year
- 2 hours of therapy per month during the four years with an approved Core Energetics Practitioner
- 25 hours of group supervision and 9 hours of individual supervision within the last two years
- Participation as an apprentice in two Core Energetics workshops
- A project demonstrating competence in Core Energetics
- Attendance at community meetings, case presentations, and Sunday morning spiritual integration sessions
- A year-end review each year of the student's progress

The third division, the Professional Intensive, is for licensed health-care providers only. It consists of five four-day weekends over the course of one year.

▶ **Personal Transformation Program: Living Core Energetics** addresses intimate relationships, spiritual connectedness and a sense of unity. Students will have the opportunity to leave behind childhood wounding and get on with their lives. Some of the topics include:

- Discovering and living from an innate spiritual center
- Challenging fears and reclaiming the life force they have stolen
- Intimate, fulfilling relationships
- Creating life from passion
- Achieving and sustaining balance
- Embracing and celebrating sexuality
- Learning to communicate and be in relationship from your truth

▶ **Core Practitioner Training** is a four-year course designed for students wanting certification as a Core Energetics practitioner. Students experience hands-on work, energy classes, process work, and spiritual integration sessions.

First-year topics include:

- The building blocks of Core Energetics
- Concepts of energy and consciousness
- Keys to identify client's issues, such as understanding character defense systems
- Session techniques such as observation skills, the use of appropriate touch, and energy work
- In-depth self-observation, including life tasks, core qualities, and characterology

Second-year topics include:

- Hands-on techniques developed by Dr. Pierrakos for working with the body, consciousness, and energy
- Aspects of psychosomatic unity taught by Wilhelm Reich
- Physical interventions to release blocked emotions
- Experiential understanding of breathing techniques and visualization methods

Third-year topics include:

- Integrating the spiritual aspects of working with character defense systems and Core Energetics techniques
- Penetrating the false self and reaching the core identity using the concepts of masks, the lower self, and the higher self
- Exploration of the relationship between heart energy, spirituality, love, and healing
- Supervised treatment of clients

Fourth-year topics include:

- Development of a student's individuality as a Core Energetics practitioner
- Leadership, individuality, sexuality, and ethics
- Advanced demonstration and practice sessions to help students polish their acquired skills

▶ **The Professional Intensive** is a one-year course designed specifically for licensed health-care professionals. It comprises five four-day modules.

Module 1 introduces the Core Energetics model of consciousness. Topics include:

- Masks (the pseudo personality), the lower self (destructive forces), and the higher self (real self, truth, and love)
- Pyramid model of the human being and character structures
- Energy centers and the energy field, including observation and diagnosis of the aura's pulsations
- Demonstration and exercises to help participants experience charge and discharge, expansion, grounding, contraction, flooding, leaking, and stasis
- Ethics of touch

Module 2 explores the theory and concepts for grounding. Participants pair up for experiential work. Topics include:

- Character styles of schizoid (fragmented) defense and oral (under-charged) defense
- Theory and techniques for grounding, including working with the feet, legs, eyes, and inner eyes; grounding the different character structures; grounding as the basis for a healthy ego and a healthy life; grounding as a physiological concept; grounding as a physiological indication of a person's ability to make contact with others and be in reality
- Breathing techniques such as staccato breathing and diaphragmatic breathing

Module 3 explores the character styles of the masochistic (overcharged) defense and the psychopathic (upper displacement) defense. Topics include:

- Observation and diagnosis of the physical structures of these character styles
- Working with resistance and anger in the upper body
- Core Energetics techniques for the head, neck, shoulders, arms, chest, back, and diaphragm

- The manifestation of anger in different character structures

Module 4 explores the belief systems developed in childhood concerning sexuality, gender, and identity issues. Topics include:

- Sexuality in relation to the life force, blockages to that force, and the developmental process as it affects the sexuality of each of the five character structures
- Rigid (armored) defense, Oedipal issues, and the split between the heart and the pelvis
- The principles of Core Energetics body readings
- Integrating the psychoanalytic theory of development with readings of energy, segments, blocks, chakras, and the aura
- The meaning implicit in the state of the skin, body fat, eyes, height, muscles, bone length, inhalation and exhalation, and overall personal development

Module 5 addresses the theory and meaning of each of the four stages of Core Energetics therapy. Topics include:

- Confrontation of the mask
- Contact with the lower self (concepts of evil, denial, destructiveness, and cruelty) and transforming it
- Contact with the higher self through positive intentionality, self-responsibility, and choice
- How practitioners can best work with the energy of a group
- Training in interpersonal processes and encouraging safety and trust, especially in a group
- Theories of development and research regarding the mind–body connection and understanding psychosomatics and the aura in illness and health

· · · · · · · · · · · · · · · · ·

Continuing Education Units: Ask your instructor about CEUs.

Certification: Yes. Core Energetics Institute has two certification programs. One offers certification to therapists and health-care professionals and the other offers certification as a Core Energetics Practitioner. Because there are a variety of programs offering Core Energetics, ask your instructor about certification, who offers it, and what the requirements are.

Participants: Personal Transformation Training is for people looking for personal development. Core Practitioner Training is designed to professionally train individuals with or without a background in psychology, bodywork, or energy work. The Professional Intensive is for licensed professionals.

Code of Ethics/Standards of Practice: Some organizations teaching Core Energetics have a Code of Ethics. If this is important to you, ask your instructor about it.

Legalities: Because there is some movement of the body, it would be wise to check out the legal requirements for your area. See the Legalities section starting on page 503.

Suggested Reading

Black, Stuart. 2004. *A Way of Life: Core Energetics*. iUniverse.

Gleason, Brian. 2001. *Mortal Spirit: A Theory of Spiritual-Somatic Evolution*. AuthorHouse.

Pierrakos, John C., MD. 1987. *Core Energetics: Developing the Capacity to Love and Heal*. Mendocino, CA: LifeRhythm.

Availability: Classes are offered in Australia, Brazil, Canada, Europe, Mexico, and the United States. Many massage schools also include Core Energetics as part of their curriculum. To find a practitioner in your area, go to www.coreenergetics.org.

Resources

Institute of Core Energetics, 115 East 23rd Street, Suite 12, New York, NY 10010, 800-901-1770, info@coreenergetics.org, www.coreenergetics.org

Core Energetics Evolution, PO Box 806, Mendocino, CA 95460, 707-937-1825, info@coreevolution.com, www.coreevolution.com

Bibliography

Pierrakos, John C., MD. 1987. *Core Energetics: Developing the Capacity to Love and Heal*. Mendocino, CA: LifeRhythm.

www.coreenergetics.org

www.coreevolution.com

www.energy-healing.info

www.selfgrowth.com

www.openexchange.org

www.annbradney.com

www.core-energetics-south.com

CRANIOSACRAL THERAPY

CRANIOSACRAL THERAPY (CST) is more than a simple form of bodywork. It requires the practitioner to be highly sensitive to subtle movements and misalignments within the body. The work requires a gentle touch and is mostly done on the spine and the skull and its cranial sutures, diaphragms, and fascia. It works well with other modalities such as physical therapy, chiropractic, naturopathy, osteopathy, and massage therapy. This therapy addresses the craniosacral system, which consists of the cranium, spine, and sacrum, all connected by a continuous membrane of connective tissue called the *dura mater*. The dura mater also encloses the brain and the central nervous system. Within the dura mater, cerebrospinal fluid rises and falls in what is a called the craniosacral rhythm.

The history of the modality begins in the early 1900s with Dr. William Sutherland, an osteopathic physician who referred to the inherent life force of the body as "the Breath of Life," and considered it to be the catalyst for subtle, involuntary body rhythms. His research led him to believe that the cerebrospinal fluid holds a significant role in expressing and distributing this Breath of Life, and as long as it moves freely throughout the body, a person will experience good health. He called his work cranial osteopathy. Between 1975 and 1983, Dr. John Upledger, who served as a clinical researcher and professor of biomechanics at Michigan State University, took an interest in Dr. Sutherland's work and began his own research on the subject. He supervised a team of anatomists, physiologists, biophysicists, and bioengineers in experiments testing the existence and influence of what he calls the craniosacral system. The results of those scientific studies explained the function of the craniosacral system and its use in evaluating and treating poorly understood malfunctions of the brain and spinal cord. While Dr. Sutherland's work with skull plates continued, Dr. Upledger's work concerns the craniosacral system, the dura, and the fascia.

A CranioSacral session may last from thirty to ninety minutes. The client remains fully clothed and usually lies on a massage table. The therapist gently assesses the flow of the craniosacral rhythm by lightly touching the base of the skull or the sacrum (tail bone). He or she is looking for disturbances in the rate, amplitude, symmetry, and quality of the flow of the craniosacral rhythm, and also for energy cysts that he releases for the client through a transfer of energy. The therapist then uses a variety of gentle touching techniques to balance the flow and restore the body's natural healing responses. Some techniques use a gentle rocking motion. Myofascial release is a manipulative form of bodywork that releases tension in the connective tissue of the body. Dr. Upledger also developed a technique called SomatoEmotional Release that is often used to release the effects of trauma and injury locked in the cells of the body.

Course Descriptions

CranioSacral classes are offered at massage schools, chiropractic colleges, naturopathic colleges, and by individual instructors. The following sample classes are offered by the Upledger Institute, and classes and workshops offered by other institutions may vary in content. The Upledger Institute has two forms of certification. CST Techniques Certification is for applicants who want to show expertise in CranioSacral techniques. CST Diplomate Certification is for applicants who want to show a deeper level of expertise, including the ability to integrate CranioSacral techniques with other modalities; working with health-care legislation, licensing, and insurance issues; and publishing or presenting CranioSacral information.

▶ **CranioSacral Therapy I:** The faculty recommends that a student receive a Craniosacral Therapy treatment before taking this class. In this four-day workshop, students learn gentle techniques to normalize the craniosacral system and allow the body to self-correct, including the following information and techniques:

- The scientific foundation and principles of CranioSacral Therapy and how to use it to relieve pain and dysfunction

- Finely tuned palpation skills that can be used as sensitive and intuitive health-care tools

- The subtle craniosacral rhythm and interpreting its patterns to accurately evaluate dysfunction and improvements

- Locating the source of physical problems by traveling through the fascial system, the complex web of tissue that affects all body structures and systems

- Releasing dural tube restrictions to enhance interactions between the central nervous system and the rest of the body

- Using techniques that produce dramatic health and relaxation effects

- Working with approaches to a number of common ailments such as TMJ dysfunction, head and neck pain, central nervous system disorders, and much more

- Putting a simple, effective ten-step protocol into practice right away

▶ **CranioSacral Therapy II** addresses cranial-base dysfunctions as diagnosed and treated by Dr. Sutherland. Prerequisites are CranioSacral Therapy I and a thorough working knowledge of the Ten-Step Protocol. Students will:

- Learn how to integrate Dr. Sutherland's technique for identifying lesions into the CranioSacral Therapy Ten-Step Protocol

- Enhance their abilities to conduct whole-body evaluations focusing on physiological phenomena

- Practice evaluating and treating cranial-based dysfunction

- Explore the concepts of SomatoEmotional Release and energy cysts

- Observe skilled demonstrations and participate in hands-on practice

▶ **Advanced III CranioSacral Therapy** is a five-day, in-depth experience designed especially for serious CranioSacral Therapy practitioners. Enrollment is limited to ten participants. CranioSacral Therapy II and application approval are prerequisites, and prospective students must call for an admissions application. Students will learn to:

- Participate in an in-depth study of body and mind integration using the craniosacral system as the vehicle

- Refine techniques and further develop palpation skills
- Explore the physical, mental, and emotional environment surrounding multi-therapist sessions
- Benefit from one-on-one skill evaluation
- Clear inner obstacles that may be blocking them from reaching their full potential as therapists

▶ **SomatoEmotional Release I** introduces the student to a therapeutic process to release the residual effects of trauma. Prerequisites are CranioSacral Therapy II and reading *SomatoEmotional Release* by Dr. Upledger and *Getting to Yes* by Roger Fisher et al. Course highlights include:

- Releasing repressed emotions, refining listening and comprehension skills, and acquiring advanced palpation and whole-body evaluation skills
- Acquiring other techniques and skills such as accessing and mobilizing an avenue of expression and locating and releasing energy cysts

. . . .

Continuing Education Units: The Upledger Institute and the Alliance of Healthcare Educators offer classes that satisfy CEU requirements for many different professions. Verify acceptance with your professional board.

Certification: They offer two levels of certification: CranioSacral Therapy Techniques Certification and CranioSacral Therapy Diplomate Certification.

Participants: Having a medical or massage license is a requirement for enrollment at the Upledger Institute.

Legalities: Most states and many countries require medical or massage licensing to practice CranioSacral Therapy.

Suggested Reading

Fisher, Roger, Bruce M. Patton, and William L. Ury. *Getting to Yes: Negotiating Agreement without Giving In.* New York: Penguin, 1991.

Upledger, John. *Craniosacral Therapy.* Berkeley, CA: North Atlantic Books, 2001.

———. *CranioSacral Therapy: What It Is, How It Works.* Berkeley, CA: North Atlantic Books, 2008.

———. *SomatoEmotional Release: Deciphering the Language of Life.* Berkeley, CA: North Atlantic Books, 2002.

Availability: Many massage schools offer CranioSacral Therapy classes in partnership with the Upledger Institute throughout the United States, Canada, and Italy. For a session in your area, call a massage school near you or e-mail the Upledger Institute at upledger@upledger.com and ask for a recommendation.

Resources

The Upledger Institute Inc., 11211 Prosperity Farms Road, Suite D-325, Palm Beach Gardens, FL 33410, 561-622-4334, upledger@upledger.com, www.upledger.com

Bibliography

Cohen, Don. *An Introduction to Craniosacral Therapy: Anatomy, Function, and Treatment.* Berkeley, CA: North Atlantic Books, 1995.

www.craniosacraltherapy.org

www.answers.com

EMF BALANCING TECHNIQUE®

MOST HEALING MODALITIES conceive of an energy field around and within the body and corresponding energy centers within the field called chakras. American tradition, stemming from traditional Chinese medicine, acknowledges seven major chakras radiating from the body and small energy centers at every bone joint. Except for the chakra at the top of the head and the one at the base of the spine, the remaining five major energy centers are perceived as situated within the center of the body, extending from both the front and the back of the body. (See the illustration on page 5.)

Peggy Phoenix Dubro, founder of EMF Worldwide, has added her conception of lattice work to our understanding of the human energy field, with her definition of a system in the energy anatomy that she calls the Universal Calibration Lattice®, or UCL. She conceives of twelve major energy centers (rather than seven), and from the middle of each of these centers, lines of energy in the shape of an infinity symbol extend about two feet from each side of the body at the same levels as the energy centers, connecting to lines of energy, oval in shape, that surround the body. She says that from a scientific point of view, this network of energy lines can be called an interdimensional, hyperspatial construct.

According to Dubro, as the human race evolves, the energy field grows and changes, and the Universal Calibration Lattice, discovered in 1988, is a reflection of an evolution in consciousness. After several years of observing and working with this lattice, she developed the EMF (electromagnetic energy field) Balancing technique to help keep the Universal Calibration Lattice balanced and strong. There are currently twelve phases of EMF Balancing. Each phase calibrates and balances a specific intent. For example, Phase 1 balances wisdom and emotions. Calibration is done by passing the hands in a specific pattern within specific areas of the Universal Calibration Lattice.

A session begins as practitioner and client spend some time getting to know each other, which creates a bond of trust that aids in the therapeutic process. Next, the client lies faceup on a massage table fully clothed to experience the four basic steps that make up the session. The first step is a process that gets the energy moving and flowing. The second step clears and amplifies the flow of energy in all of the energy centers and throughout the Universal Calibration Lattice. Step three balances the energy flows. The last step is a closing, where the new energy patterns resulting from the session are set according to the inner wisdom of the client. After the session, the practitioner discusses the benefits of the intents and the new energy patterns and how to apply them to daily life.

Course Descriptions

The Energy Extension Inc. was created in 1995 to handle the business and teaching ends of the EMF Balancing Technique, with the curriculum organized into two programs: the Professional Path Program for those who seek a higher level of professionalism in energy work and the Personal Growth Program for those who are simply interested in their own personal growth. The classes listed below pertain to both programs; additional classes are available for those students wishing to pursue the Professional Path Program. These are listed on the Internet and class content is provided in the Personal Growth training classes descriptions. The program is constantly growing and changing. Check the website www.emfbalancingtechnique .com/training for the latest information concerning all classes.

▶ **The Lattice Experience Workshop** is a two-day workshop that provides an experiential introduction to the Universal Calibration Lattice. Students learn how this lattice impacts their consciousness and their ability to cocreate an enlightened life. Topics include:

- The theory of the Universal Calibration Lattice—what it looks like and how it works

- An understanding of the calibration process and the new dynamics of energy as seen by Peggy Dubro
- The send symbol
- The Alternating Sweep, an exercise of clear cocreation
- Theory of the Spiral Sweep and Sacred Templates
- Learning to give and receive an introductory EMF Balancing Technique energy session
- Distance work
- Directing energy using the eyes

▶ **Personal Growth Training: Evolution of Consciousness** is a six-day workshop beginning with the Universal Calibration Lattice Workshop. Students observe demonstrations and practice on each other. They also receive training materials to help them when practicing on friends and family. Topics include:

- An overview of the Universal Calibration Lattice
- Transmitting energy over distances
- Moving energy with the eyes
- The theory of the Arc Alignment, the Infinity Express, and the Orbital Sweep Energy exercise
- Pictorial review of Phases I through IV
- Phase I: wisdom and emotions
- Phase II: self-direction and support
- Phase III: radiate core energy
- Phase IV: energetic accomplishment
- Learn how to give a session in each of the four phases

▶ **Phases V through VIII Practitioner Training "Masters in Practice"** is a six-day workshop for Personal Growth graduates, licensed certified practitioners, and accredited practitioners. Licensed certified practitioners must have completed the one-day Upgrade Internship class or Phases I-IV for noninterns. Students learn Phases V through VIII of the EMF Balancing Technique, including:

- The theory for Phases V through VIII
- Beginning the session with a client—"the client invitation"

- The selection and sequencing of the Attributes of Mastery with a client
- Template of Infinite Love Activation: Phase V
- Template of Compassion Activation: Phase VI
- Template of Infinite Presence Activation: Phase VII
- The Womb of Infinite Self: Phase VII
- Template of Infinite Wisdom Activation: Phase VIII
- The twelve Master Points of contact for each phase, including their associated patterns and alignments

▶ **Phases IX through XII Practitioner Training** is a six-day workshop with completion of Phases V through VIII as a prerequisite. Students develop their ability to use the third lattice, including the next four phases. Key learning points are:

- Using the third lattice to manifest the energy of freedom
- The dynamics of fission and fusion
- The Universal Human: Phase IX
- The Universal Parent: Phase X
- The Universal Partner: Phase XI
- The Emerging Evolutionary: Phase XII

▶ **The Lattice for Organizations** is a five-day workshop working with the corporate structure. Teachers and practitioners will learn skills to enhance private companies, government institutions, schools, hospitals, and other organizations. Topics include:

- Organizational dynamics
- Business challenges
- Leadership
- Implementing change
- The relationship between the well-being of an organization and the well-being of the individual
- The relation between the well-being of the organization and the well-being of the individual
- Calibrating and balancing human energy dynamics at both collective and individual levels within an organization

Continuing Education Units: Yes, provided by the National Certification Board for Therapeutic Massage and Bodywork. Not all teachers offer CEUs. Please ask your instructor.

Certification: The Energy Extension Inc. licenses practitioners upon completion of the Accredited Practitioner Internship for each level of training in the Professional Path Program.

Participants: The Personal Growth Program is open to all. The Professional Path Program is open to those seeking a higher level of professionalism in energy work.

Code of Ethics/Standards of Practice: They have an Accredited Practitioner Policy for each level of training and a licensing agreement for practitioners and for teachers.

Suggested Reading

Dubro, Peggy Phoenix, and David Lapierre. *Elegant Empowerment: Evolution of Consciousness.* Platinum Publishing House, 2002.

Esposito, Lina. *The Little Book on EMF: My Personal Journey through the EMF Balancing Technique.* Platinum Publishing House, 2005.

Availability: The Energy Extension Inc. offers classes throughout North and South America, Europe, Australia, and New Zealand. Practitioners may be found in over sixty countries. To locate a practitioner in your area, go to www.emfbalancingtechnique.com.

Contact Resources

The Energy Extension Inc., PO Box 4357, Sedona, AZ 86340, 928-284-3703, shana@EMFWorldwide.com, www.emfbalancingtechnique.com

Bibliography

· ·

Dubro, Peggy Phoenix, and David Lapierre. *Elegant Empowerment: Evolution of Consciousness*. Platinum Publishing House, 2002.

www.energeticarts.com

www.emfbalancingtechnique.com

ENERGY MEDICINE PARTNERSHIPS INC.

PSYCHOENERGETIC THERAPIES WORK on emotional and psychological issues. Psychospiritual healing work deals with issues of a spiritual or religious nature. Energy Medicine Partnerships Inc. offers techniques and therapies geared specifically for both psychoenergetic and psychospiritual issues as well as physical health issues. Clients do not have to relive unpleasant events in order to have them cleared. The focus is on personal transformations and the healing of the body, emotions, mind, and spirit.

Mary Jo Bulbrook, PhD, founder and director of Energy Medicine Partnerships and the Transform Your Life through Energy Medicine (TYLEM) training program, has a background as a university professor and a clinical specialist in psychiatric mental health nursing. She is a pioneer in energy medicine, beginning with teaching and practicing Therapeutic Touch (page 287) and Touch for Health (page 127) in the 1970s and moving on from there to create and teach her own material in the 1980s. She has worked with Healing Touch (page 221), Rosalyn Bruyere (page 431), South African Sangomo Credo Mutwa, aborigine elder Bob Randall, and Maori Tohuna Rose Pere. Bulbrook refers to her work as psychospiritual healing, and her techniques work with the energy field, the chakras, the meridians, the hara line, and the core star primarily combined with psychosocial, psychoenergetic, and psychospiritual approaches to health and healing.

Energy Medicine Partnerships Inc. is an international organization dedicated to providing education in energy medicine throughout the world. The original title of Bulbrook's training program was "Healing from Within and Without." The name was changed to Energetic Healing and then to its current name—Transform Your Life through Energy Medicine (TYLEM).

Students may certify as Certified Energy Medicine Practitioners or as Certified Energy Medicine Specialists. Students working toward certification as Energy Medicine Specialists must choose a specialty in the field of energy medicine, such as energy-based psychotherapy, specific physical diseases, research, publishing, and medical intuitive development. Specialists work with two mentors, one an Energy Medicine Partnerships instructor, and the other a respected authority in his or her chosen field of specialization.

A session usually takes about an hour. During the first session the practitioner will do a thorough intake interview concerning past history, health issues, and other information pertinent to the needs of the client. Subsequent sessions will include a very short intake interview to bring the practitioner up-to-date concerning the client's current issues. Often the client will be asked to do a drawing representing the client's issue to help clarify what is happening on a subconscious level.

The client reclines fully clothed on a massage table. Treatments may also be done in a chair or long distance. Once the practitioner and the client settle on a mutual goal for the healing of the issue presented by the client, the practitioner does an assessment by passing his or her hands through the client's energy field 6 or 8 inches above the body. Practitioners may also use a pendulum and/or an intuitive reading as assessment tools. At the beginning of the treatment, the client will be asked to actively participate in the process by answering questions while the practitioner works. Treatment may be done both on and off the body.

Course Descriptions

Transform Your Life through Energy Medicine (TYLEM) is the training program for Energy Medicine Partnerships. Trainings Part 1 through Part 6 may be taken in any order. An applicant may use the title Energy Medicine Practitioner upon completion of Parts 1 though 5, attending a supervised (by an approved Energy Medicine Instructor) Energy Medicine Practicum, presenting documentation of assessments and interventions from each of the five courses, and receiving approval from the Energy Medicine Partnerships program director.

Students wishing to deepen their training and go on to be Energy Medicine Specialists must take Parts 6, 7A, and 7B. Clinical skills, advanced practices, meridian work, and medical intuition make up some of the skills added to becoming an Energy Medicine Specialist. Specialist training also involves working with an Energy Medicine Instructor in a mentorship relationship for a minimum of one year. Specialists also must complete a specialty project in their chosen field of specialization, such as publishing an article or teaching a workshop. A student receives the title Energy Medicine Specialist when the Level 7B instructor recommends the student to the Energy Medicine Partnerships program director, who then awards the title. Certification is offered through Energy Medicine Partnerships International. To be recognized as a Certified Energy Medicine Practitioner or a Certified Energy Medicine Specialist, the applicant sends all of the criteria needed for certification to the certification review panel made up of certified Energy Medicine Practitioners and Specialists.

▶ **Introduction to Energy Medicine** introduces the basics of the energy system and how this applies to health and healing. The introduction is recommended for those new to energy-based healing. Topics include chakras, energy fields, and meridians.

▶ **Part 1: Clearing the Self is** a one-day workshop that addresses the theory that a person consists of the interrelated aspects of a physical body, emotions, mind, and spirit. Energetic imbalances within any of these areas can compromise health. Topics include:

- Identifying the current status of physical, emotional, mental, and spiritual health
- Energetic assessment and diagnostic tools
- Inner core balance
- Energy field draining and replenishment
- Chakra blessing

▶ **Part 2: Healing Wounds** is a one-day workshop that addresses the theory that physical, emotional, mental, and spiritual wounds stored in the energy system affect people's lives. Topics include:

- Identifying wounds and their impact on the energy system
- Theoretical background

- Assessment of the energy system, core star, and hara line, including hara line treatment and core star expansion
- Achieving a grounded sense of vitality

▶ **Part 3: Changing Limiting Beliefs** is a one-day workshop that proposes that beliefs are stored in the energy field and dramatically influence how people lead their lives. Topics include:

- Identifying beliefs, changes needed in the belief system, and how to create new beliefs
- Clearing one's eternal/soul light

▶ **Part 4: Changing Relationships Energetically** is a one-day workshop that addresses healthy relationships as essential for personal well-being. The workshop teaches students how to evaluate and influence the energy centers to change their personal relationships. Students learn to free themselves from energetic ties affecting their personal growth. Topics include:

- Identifying relationship problems and understanding how to change them energetically
- Maori Energy Vortex Healing
- Chakra clearing, balancing, and vitalizing
- Using healing heart energy

▶ **Part 5: Reshaping Family Dynamics** is a two-day workshop that explores the idea that family dynamics form lasting energy patterns. Students explore family energy patterns and address techniques to change them through energetic interventions. The student discovers new ways of connecting with family members. Topics include:

- Identifying family issues and their impact on the energy system
- Healing conception and birthing issues
- Family healing energy vortex
- Energetic reparenting
- Advanced energy field healing

▶ **Part 6: Clearing Meridians, Organs, and Body Systems** is a three-day workshop that explores meridians as an interconnected web of energy lines that nourish the internal aspects of the human body, including organs and body systems. Students learn ways to assess the meridians, alter their energy flow, and manage internal energy. A strong background in energy-based healing is required for this intensive in which students discover how meridians influence health. Topics include:

- Identifying and analyzing personal health needs
- Meridian time cycle and tracing meridians
- Energy release through the meridians
- Neurolymphatic and neurovascular points
- Meridian massage
- Touch for Health and Healing Touch techniques
- Yin/yang, energy wheel, and five element balancing
- Back flush

▶ **Parts 7A and 7B: Energy Medicine Specialist Training** builds on the background of the Energy Medicine practitioner and prepares the student for certification as either a Certified Energy Healing Practitioner or a Certified Specialist in Energy Medicine. Topics include:

- Developing medical intuition
- Treating complex energy patterns
- Connecting with spirit guides
- Advanced meridian, organ, and body system theory and practice
- Answering the call to be a healer and healing yourself
- Fulfilling an extensive mentorship process with an energy medicine instructor
- Fulfilling case study requirements
- Documenting professional leadership
- Identifying and establishing a specialty practice
- Integrating the energy medicine specialist's role into mainstream health care

· · · · · · · · · · · · · · · ·

Continuing Education Units: Energy Medicine Partnerships Inc. is an approved provider of continuing nursing education by the North Carolina Nurses Association, an accredited approver by the American Nurses Credentialing Commission on Accreditation (Approved Provider Number 076).

In March 2009, Energy Medicine Partnerships became an official provider of Continuing Education by the National Certification Board for Therapeutic Massage and Bodywork. Energy Medicine Partnerships Inc. has satisfied all of the criteria put forth by the National Certification Board for Therapeutic Massage and Bodywork and is hereby awarded the designation of Approved Provider for Continuing Education (Approved Provider Number 450986-09).

Energy Medicine Partnerships School of Energy Medicine preparing Energy Medicine Practitioners and Specialists has been added to the list of recognized programs effective August 19, 2008, through the Natural Health Practitioners of Canada Association/Association des Practicens de la Santé Naturelle du Canada, Suite 600, 10339 – 124 Street, Edmonton, AB Canada T5N 3W1. Phone 780-484-2010, toll-free 888-711-7701, www.nhpcanada.org.

Energy Medicine Partnerships is an Approved Provider of Continuing Education by the Association of Comprehensive Energy Psychology (ACEP) who certifies EMP courses for ACEP continuing education credit for recertifying as a Diplomate in Comprehensive Energy Psychology (DCEP) or Certified Energy Health Practitioner (CEHP) in order to renew their ACEP certification every two years.

Certification: Two forms of certification are offered: Certified Energy Medicine Practitioner and Certified Energy Medicine Specialist. The certification review board of Energy Medicine Partnerships Inc. is composed of Energy Medicine faculty members. Once the title of Energy Medicine Practitioner or Energy Medicine Specialist has been awarded, the student is eligible to apply to Energy Medicine Partnerships International to become certified. The application requires submitting a designated processing fee and completing a set of criteria established by Energy Medicine Partnerships International, which will be evaluated by the review board.

Participants: Energy medicine courses are resources for people interested in personal transformations and healing. Programs are intended for healers, health-care professionals, counselors, therapists, nurses, psychologists, social workers, and anyone interested in learning how to help themselves or others heal through the human energy system.

Code of Ethics/Standards of Practice: Yes.

Suggested Reading

Bulbrook, Mary Jo, PhD. *Healing Stories to Inspire, Teach, and Heal.* Carrboro, NC: Publishing Division of the North Carolina Center for Healing Touch, 2000.

Hover-Kramer, Dorothea, EdD, RN, and Karilee Halo Shames, PhD, RN. *Energetic Approaches to Emotional Healing.* Albany, NY: Delmar Publishers, 1997.

Availability: Classes are offered in Australia, Canada, Chile, Ireland, New Zealand, Peru, South Africa, and the United States. To locate a practitioner in your area, e-mail contact@energymedicinepartnerships.com.

Resources

Energy Medicine Partnerships Inc., 3211 Gibson Road, Durham, NC 27703, 919-381-4198, contact@energymedicinepartnerships.com, www.energy medicinepartnerships.com

Bibliography

Bulbrook, Mary Jo, PhD. *Energetic Healing Notebook.* Carrboro, NC: Publishing Division of the North Carolina Center for Healing Touch, 1998.

———. *Becoming a Specialist in Energy Medicine.* Carrboro, NC: Publishing Division of the North Carolina Center for Healing Touch, 2003.

———. *Energetic Healing: Clearing Meridians, Organs, and Body Systems,* Carrboro, NC: Publishing Division of the North Carolina Center for Healing Touch, 2003.

www.allgoodthings.com

www.energymedicinepartnerships.com

www.sacredcenters.com

ENERGY MEDICINE SPECIALISTS

ENERGY MEDICINE SPECIALISTS OFFERS a number of educational classes on a variety of topics in the field of energy medicine. There is no certification for these classes at the time of this writing. They are intended to broaden the student's repertoire of tools available for work in the energy field. Janna Moll is an Energy Medicine Specialist, a Healing Touch Certified Practitioner and Instructor, a certified/licensed massage therapist, and a life and business coach. Moll limits the energy medicine field to hands-on or hands-over-the-body energy therapies. Traditional Chinese medicine therapies, such as Qigong, have their own category as per the American Holistic Health Association. She is working hard to bring the field of energy medicine into professional alignment with the allopathic realm. For example, Moll offers classes to integrate energy medicine practice as part of the operating room protocol. She is a frequent speaker on energy medicine for Holistic Health Association conferences and at various workshops and seminars for doctors and other health-care professionals. She is constantly attentive to increasing and upholding high standards for energy medicine modalities and practitioners, and works for their acceptance by health professionals worldwide. She also consults on health-care accreditation to energy medicine modalities. Most of her classes augment other therapies. Sessions vary depending upon the modality of the therapist adding Moll's work to her protocols.

Course Descriptions

Energy Medicine Specialists offers beginner and advanced course work in the field of energy medicine. These courses were created by advanced practitioners and instructors and leaders in the field. These classes are intended to fill missing gaps in the education of students of energy medicine. They are growing rapidly and classes change to meet the needs of energy medicine practitioners. Check their website www.energymedicinespecialists.com for the latest updates on classes. They do not have a certification program at this time.

▶ **Advanced Chakra Diagnosis and Treatment** is a two-and-a-half-day class. Students learn how to assess the chakras and the human energy field and how to apply this information to their client treatments. Prerequisites: Students must contact Energy Medicine Specialists to see if they qualify for this class. Topics include:

- History of the chakras
- Color
- Crystals
- Sound

▶ **Advanced Hara Work for Practitioners** is a two-and-a-half-day class. This workshop is an advanced-level course for the energy medicine practitioner. Prerequisite: The class is open to energy medicine practitioners who demonstrate the appropriate background in energy medicine or with permission of Energy Medicine Specialists. Topics include:

- Trauma identification
- Diagramming and dissecting hara points and core star
- Dimensionality of the hara and its relationship to the chakras, meridians, and the matrix
- Definition and practice of distant viewing
- Hara pendulum assessment and practice
- Hara documentation
- Hara Repatterning Technique and practice
- Finding the origin of trauma
- Hara/matrix synthesis
- Hara chakra blessing

▶ **Advanced Pendulum Diagnostics and Meridians** is a two-day workshop in which students learn to quickly and accurately make detailed, complex assessments. Students learn to chart meridians and body functions and develop subtle energy assessment skills. Prerequisite: This class is for advanced practitioners only. Students must contact Energy Medicine Specialists to see if they qualify.

▶ **Communication Skills for the Energy Medicine Practitioner** is a two-day course that offers the practitioner practical skills for working with clients, such as practicing safe boundaries. Role playing is used to practice client rapport and identifying issues and problems. Prerequisite: This class is for advanced practitioners only. Applicants must contact Energy Medicine Specialists to see if they qualify.

▶ **Energy Medicine for Advanced Practitioners:** Students receive an in-depth understanding of the field of energy medicine, including its history and application within Western and complementary medicine. Participants bring case studies from their active practice to discuss with other students. Prerequisite: This class is for advanced practitioners only. Students must contact Energy Medicine Specialists to see if they qualify. Topics include:

- In-depth discussion of the energetics of disease and the integrity of a client practice
- The many aspects of assessment, intuition, and group interaction as they apply to energy diagnosis
- Understanding the factors of practitioner–client interaction and case management

▶ **Energy Medicine in Surgery** is a one-day class that includes a trip to a surgical site. Students learn how to provide integrative/holistic energy medicine treatment during surgery. Prerequisite: This class is for advanced practitioners only. Students must contact Energy Medicine Specialists to see if they qualify. Topics include:

- Suggested presurgery and postsurgery sessions with a surgical client
- Proper protocol for pre-op, the operating room, and post-op
- Interaction with surgeons, anesthesiologists, and surgical and hospital staff

▶ **Cutting the Ties That Bind Entry Level** is a six-week course designed to take students through a process of removing themselves from negativity in personal relationships and alleviating fears and negative thoughts. Through working with the subconscious mind, students are taught to eliminate old attachments and rely on their inner source of security.

. . . .

Continuing Education Units: Discuss this with the instructor.

Certification: Please go to www.energymedicinecredentialing.org for requirements.

Participants: For advanced practitioners only. All students must apply to Energy Medicine Specialists to see if they qualify for admittance.

Code of Ethics/Standards of Practice: Yes.

Suggested Reading

Andrews, Ted. *The Healer's Manual: A Beginner's Guide to Energy Therapies.* Woodbury, MN: Llewellyn Publications, 2003.

Oschman, James. *Energy Medicine: The Scientific Basis of Bioenergy Therapies.* New York: Churchill Livingstone, 2000.

Availability: Classes are offered throughout the United States. At the time of this writing, there is no compiled list of practitioners.

Resources

Energy Medicine Specialists, PO Box 262253, Highlands Ranch, CO 80163, 303-346-3809, janna@hearthealingcenter.com, www.energymedicinespecialists.com

Bibliography

Moll, Janna. "Subtle Energy, Energy Healing, and the Big Picture of Energy Medicine." American Holistic Medical Association newsletter, Winter 2006, vol. IX, no. 4.

www.energymedicinespecialists.com

ESOGETIC COLORPUNCTURE™

FOUNDED BY GERMAN ACUPUNCTURIST and naturopath Peter Mandel, Esogetic Colorpuncture is a system of aculight therapy that integrates the use of therapeutic colored light and traditional acupuncture (see page 25). (The term "esogetic" merges the two words "esoteric" and "energetic.") Both colorpuncture and acupuncture promote good health by balancing the flow of energy through the meridian system. While acupuncture uses a series of thin needles, colorpuncture uses vibrational information in the form of colored frequencies of light. A therapist uses a special wand with interchangeable tips to emit specific colors of light at strategic points of the body, including traditional acupoints and reflexology points.

Esogetic Colorpuncture operates from the premise that illness and pain come from an imbalance in the psyche and spirit, which leads to a disturbance in the physical body. When a cell's functions are no longer in balance, that cell will emit an increase of biophotons (particles of light emitted by all cells in the body) and a disturbed information flow. This increase in the emissions of biophotons can go on to further disrupt the emissions of neighboring cells and decrease the electrical receptivity of related acupuncture points.

The techniques involved in this modality are derived from a number of therapies, including Dream Zone Therapy, which uses color and esogetic herb oil to activate dreams to help release excess energy absorbed throughout the day. Mandel also uses light signals to stimulate the lymphatic system to detoxify the body, as well as pain-reducing techniques that involve infrared and colored light.

To map a client's treatment protocol, Mandel uses Kirlian photography, which exposes images to an electromagnetic field to capture a depiction of an object's energy field. A colorpuncture practitioner generally takes a Kirlian picture before and after a session in order to study the energetic imbalance that the client is presenting and suggest a course of treatment.

Throughout the session, the client remains fully clothed, except for the areas that need treatment. The practitioner focuses the frequencies of colored light using a hand-held aculight wand on various acupoints to regulate energy and information flow to different systems of the body. The fourteen colors used are red, orange, yellow, green, blue, violet, turquoise, crimson, light green, light turquoise, rose, light gray, medium gray, and dark gray, and each has a different effect on the body. The light is absorbed through the skin and transmitted along the energy meridians supporting the cellular communication, which promotes healing. Clients are asked to report their dreams, emotions, and sensations in the body, as well as observations of personal growth during the course of treatments.

Course Descriptions

The following class descriptions come from the Institute of Esogetic Colorpuncture, USA, in Grass Valley, California. It offers classes for both laypeople and health-care professionals throughout the United States and Canada. These classes follow the guidelines and requirements set by the International Mandel Institute in Switzerland. Certification is also provided by the International Mandel Institute.

▶ **Introduction to Esogetic Colorpuncture: Self-Healing with Color and Light** is a two-day seminar that teaches basic theories of color healing according to Peter Mandel as well as several self-healing treatments. Students also give and receive light treatments in class. The workshop is a prerequisite for participation in the basic certification course for professional practitioners.

▶ **Basic Practitioner Certification Course** is an eighteen-day course taught over an eight- to nine-month period in five weekends of three or four days each. This course is the foundation training for professionals who want to become certified colorpuncture practitioners. The series of workshops emphasizes practical and clinical use and allows extensive opportunities for hands-on work. Course content consists of a large body of basic therapies, including:

- Pain treatment
- Detoxification
- Brain balancing
- Meridian therapies
- Prenatal trauma
- Basic-level conflict therapy
- Gray field and soul-spirit color therapies
- Consciousness expansion

▶ **Professional Practitioner Certification Course** is a twenty-three-day course taught over a period of nine months and six long weekends. This course provides a thorough grounding in theory and hands-on practice for the serious student seeking to become a professional practitioner. Upon completion, the student receives certification from the International Mandel Institute. Topics include:

- Basic spectral colors
- Gray field and soul-spirit color therapies
- IR and UV frequencies
- Synapses tools
- Adhesive crystals
- Esogetic microdiagnostic systems for evaluating imbalances in the energy/information flow
- Iridology
- Tongue and face reading
- Body zone palpation
- Subtle levels of disease

▶ **Kirlian Energy Emission Analysis Seminars I, II, and III** address Peter Mandel's energy emission analysis system of working with Kirlian photographs. The beginning, intermediate, and advanced seminars are four days each. During these seminars, students give and receive colorpuncture treatments in conjunction with using Kirlian photographs. Completion of the introductory seminar is a prerequisite, and completion or concurrent participation in the Basic Practitioner Certification Course for Esogetic Colorpuncture is highly recommended. Topics may include:

- Identifying specific phenomena in photographs and specific colorpuncture treatments
- Reading imbalances at the level of the body, soul, and spirit
- Infrared and pain therapies

. . . .

Continuing Education Units: No.

Certification: Students may be certified as basic practitioners upon completion of the Basic Practitioner Certification Course or as professional practitioners upon completion of the Professional Practitioner Certification Course. Students may also become certified in Kirlian Energy Emission Analysis, a separate program. Certification is provided by the International Mandel Institute.

Participants: The training program is open to the general public.

Suggested Reading

Allanach, Jack. 2005. *Colour Me Healing: Colorpuncture, a New Medicine of Light.* UK: Tree Tongue Publishing.

Availability: Esogetic colorpuncture classes are offered in Brazil, Germany, Italy, Japan, Singapore, Switzerland, and the United States. To locate a practitioner in your area, go to www.colorpuncture.com.

Resources

. . . .

International Mandel Institut, Hildastrasse 8, D-76646 Bruchsal Germany, +49 07251/899155, info@colorpuncture.com, www.colorpuncture.com

Institute for Esogetic Colorpuncture, PMB 165, 101 West McKnight Way, Suite B, Grass Valley, CA 95949, 530-362-6908, manohar@colorpuncture.com, info@colorpuncture.com, www.colorpuncture.org

Akhila Rosemary Bourne, PO Box 3013, San Anselmo, CA 94979, 415-461-6641, rosemary@colorpuncture.com, www.colorpunctureusa.com

Bibliography

Allanach, Jack. *Colour Me Healing: Colorpuncture, a New Medicine of Light.* UK: Tree Tongue Publishing, 2005.

Croke, Manohar. "Esogetic Colorpuncture: A Complete Aculight Therapy System for Body, Mind, and Spirit." *Acupuncture Today* 3, no. 6, 2002.

Starwynn, Darren. "Laser and LED Treatments: Which Is Better?" *Acupuncture Today* 5, no. 6, 2004.

www.colorpuncture.org

www.acupuncturetoday.com

www.colorpuncture.com

www.answers.com/topic/kirlian-photography

HEALING TOUCH PROGRAM™

HEALING TOUCH (HT), created in 1989 by Janet Mentgen, BSN, RN, HNC, CHTP/I, is a gentle form of energy therapy in which practitioners use their hands to influence and support the human energy system. In her work, Mentgen adopted and created techniques to work with the energy field and the chakras. Mentgen taught in the Denver area through the 1980s until she was invited by the American Holistic Nurses Association (AHNA) to create a national program. It was successfully piloted in 1989. Healing Touch Program continues to be endorsed by the AHNA.

By adding other techniques from many disciplines, Mentgen expanded the program into a medically based energy therapy training program for nurses. To share her knowledge with a wider audience, including people who were not nurses, she created the Colorado Center for Healing Touch, which later became the Healing Touch Program. Because research is an integral part of the Healing Touch continuing education program, Mentgen also established the Healing Touch International Foundation Inc. as a nonprofit charitable organization in 1997 to promote humanitarian projects and research in the field of energy medicine. In 2008, the research program changed its name to the Healing Touch Worldwide Foundation. Also in 2008, the Healing Touch Professional Association was created to provide support for practitioners in the field.

Hospitals in the United States increasingly have begun offering Healing Touch, often at the request of patients asking for complements to traditional medical care. Healing Touch Program reports that more than 110,000 nurses and other health-care professionals use HT in hospitals and private practice. For example, currently Hob Osterlund, RN, of Pain Management at the Queen's Medical Center in Hawaii, uses HT as the basis for her Bosom Buddies program, in which women newly diagnosed with breast cancer pair up with a certified HT practitioner for a year. The aim of this program, which often has a waiting list of potential clients, is to offer support to patients during a time of anxiety and to encourage relaxation and well-being.

A session with a Healing Touch practitioner begins with an intake evaluation of the client to determine his or her condition. The client removes his or her shoes and reclines on a massage table fully clothed. The practitioner assesses the client's body and energy field by using a pendulum and by scanning his or her hands over the client's body. The Healing Touch interventions used by the practitioner clear the energy field and balance the energy centers. Hands are placed on or just above the body at specific points to achieve the goal of balancing the chakras and bringing them into harmony with the energy field and the physical body. Some techniques for clearing the energy field are done above the body at a distance of 6 to 8 inches. The practitioner's fingers move through the field to remove unwanted debris or congestion from the energy field.

Much of the work is done off the body, and when the practitioner touches the client, it is done lightly, approximately with about the weight of a nickel. Clients uncomfortable with being touched may request the work be done completely off the body. At the end of the session, the practitioner reassesses the client's energy field and the chakras. Closing includes grounding at the feet and some discussion as to the possibility of further treatment.

Healing Touch Courses

This multilevel program in energy-based therapy progressively moves from beginning to advanced practice. After completing Level 5, individuals are eligible to apply for certification from Healing Touch Program. The classes described here come from the Healing Touch Program.

▶ **Level 1** is a personal and experiential exploration of personal identity, beliefs, and human energy. It offers opportunities for students to learn how they perceive energy, whether by feel, sight, hearing, or intuition. Topics include:

- Twelve techniques for immediately experiencing energy, clearing block-ages, relieving pain, and calming emotions
- How to assess the energy field and the chakras
- Energy anatomy and how it interacts with the mind, body, and spirit
- The importance of the Healing Touch Standards of Practice and Code of Ethics

▶ **Level 2** addresses how to do an initial intake interview and choose the appropriate energy techniques to help a client. Level 1 is a prerequisite, and personal practice of Level 1 techniques with friends, family, or colleagues is highly encouraged. Topics include:

- Opening your own and your client's energy field to enable deeper heal-ing work
- The concept of sacred space
- How to conduct a full one-hour healing session
- Specific healing techniques for back and neck pain
- Professional documentation of sessions
- Sealing wounds and energy leaks
- How to conduct a trauma interview while giving treatment

▶ **Level 3** focuses on the development of students as healers through self-care and pre-session practices. Level 2 is a prerequisite. Topics include:

- Developing higher sense perception
- How to raise the level of personal vibration to enhance healing capabili-ties
- Advanced healing techniques, including how to work with the upper lev-els of the human energy field and the hara line, core star, soul seat, tan tien, and point of individuation
- Chelation

▶ **Level 4** prepares students for private practice and completion of the program. (It isn't necessary to advance to the level of a certified HT practitioner to take this class.) Level 3 is a prerequisite. All students partner with each other to experience and document a series of HT sessions as part of learning case management. Students explore:

- Business concepts and networking with other practitioners
- Developing a Healing Touch practice and stepping into the role of a healer
- Professional ethics and standards of practice
- The case-study process requirements for the next level and certification
- Additional advanced techniques

▶ **Level 5** focuses on completing the assignments started in Level 4. Students work with each other to critique case studies and help each other fulfill the requirements for certification. Level 4 is a prerequisite. Topics include:

- Preparation for the international certification process and its criteria (an optional step after graduating from the program)
- Evaluating personal progress and one's own level of commitment to certification
- Professional and clinical issues of private practice
- The role of research in maintaining a professional practice

▶ **Level 6** is the instructor level for the Healing Touch certified practitioner who wants to teach Healing Touch. Instructors (those who have finished Level 6) meet annually to advance their skills, network with others, and develop new activities pertinent to the work of Healing Touch. The emphasis is on group dynamics, how to set up a teaching program, the principles and methods of teaching and learning, and maintaining a Healing Touch curriculum.

· · · · · · · · · · · · · · · · · ·

Continuing Education Units: The Colorado Nurses Association approves continuing education activity for nurses. The Colorado Nurses Association is accredited as an approver of continuing education for nurses by the American Nurses Credentialing Center's Commission on Accreditation. The National Certification Board for Therapeutic Massage and Bodywork Category A. Provider Number 150780-00 approves certification for massage therapists. The Association of Professional Chaplains grants CCEs for chaplains who take Healing Touch classes.

Certification: Healing Touch Program administers certification through a separate review by the Certification Board of Reviewers using standardized criteria. Certification acknowledges learning experiences and demonstration of competence as a Healing Touch Certified Practitioner (HTCP). The American and the Canadian Holistic Nurses associations endorse Healing Touch Program (HTP).

Participants: Participants must be eighteen years of age or older. Applicants under the age of eighteen may attend if a custodial parent attends class with the applicant and has the approval of the instructor.

Code of Ethics/Standards of Practice: They have a Code of Ethics and a Scope of Practice.

Suggested Reading

Brennan, Barbara Ann. *Hands of Light: A Guide to Healing through the Human Energy Field.* New York: Bantam Books, 1987.

Hover-Kramer, Dorothea. *Healing Touch Guidebook: Practicing the Art and Science of Human Caring.* San Antonio, TX: Healing Touch Program Press, 2009.

Joy, W. Brugh. *Joy's Way: A Map for the Transformational Journey.* New York: Jeremy P. Tarcher, 1979.

Availability: Classes are offered throughout the United States, Canada, Mexico, Australia, Europe, South Africa, and South America. Go to www.healingtouchprogram.com for a list of practitioners in your area. For a class or session with Healing Touch for Babies, contact Healing Touch for Babies at healingbabies@yahoo.com, or go to www.healingtouchforbabies.com.

Resources

Healing Touch Program, 20822 Cactus Loop, San Antonio TX 78258, 210-497-5529, info@healingtouchprogram.com, www.healingtouchprogram.com, www.healingtouchresearch.com

www.energymagazineonline.com

www.HTProfessionalAssociation.com

www.HTPractitioner.com

Bibliography

Gerber, Richard. *Vibrational Medicine: New Choices for Healing Ourselves.* Santa Fe, NM: Bear & Company, 1988.

Joy, W. Brugh. *Joy's Way: A Map for the Transformational Journey.* New York: Jeremy P. Tarcher, 1979.

White, John, and Stanley Krippner. *Future Science: Life Energies and the Physics of Paranormal Phenomena.* New York: Anchor Books, 1977.

www.healingtouchprogram.com

www.sacredcenters.com

www.vxm.com

HEALING TOUCH FOR ANIMALS®:
THE KOMITOR HEALING METHOD

As a certified healing touch instructor/practitioner, certified hospital-based massage therapist, equine sports massage therapist, and certified massage therapist, Carol Komitor saw firsthand what she believed to be the extraordinary results energy medicine can have on humans. As a veterinary technician for thirteen years with a deep appreciation for animals, she felt inspired to develop energy medicine techniques specifically for animal and veterinary uses. Komitor's techniques work for all kinds of animals, from mammals to birds and even fish, and she also offers classes specifically designed for working with dogs and horses.

Using her background in Healing Touch (page 221), CranioSacral Therapy (page 191), Reiki (page 105), Light Body, aromatherapy, and sound healing (page 391), Komitor formulated her own healing techniques and founded Healing Touch for Animals in 1996. As with energy medicine disciplines that work with humans, Komitor's techniques work with the energy field and chakras of animals, both domestic and otherwise.

The mission of Healing Touch for Animals and Komitor Healing Method Inc. is to promote the health of animals through energy medicine while building a deeper connection between animals and humans. Her specific techniques introduce holistic concepts to assist with animals' healing of injury, illness, surgery, wounds, and behavioral problems. Her techniques integrate, balance, and clear the energy field and energy centers, working at the physical, emotional, mental, and spiritual level of the animal. The techniques are designed to enhance the healing process and complement traditional veterinary care.

As animals don't have the resistance that people do, they absorb healing energy relatively quickly and sessions are usually much shorter than with people. The practitioner interviews the owner of the animal as to its issues. He or she will do an energetic assessment and then apply the appropriate techniques. Practitioners talk to the animal needing treatment in a soothing voice and ask the animal for permission to do healing work. If the animal is not interested, it will walk away. It is not unusual for the animal to present the side of its body that needs the healing work to the practitioner.

Techniques vary depending on the needs of the animal. Healing work on birds can be done by placing the hands (outside of the cage) on either side of the bird or at 90 degrees from each other. The same thing can be done for fish. Birds can be held in the hands if the bird is willing to cooperate. The bird or fish receiving the healing will stay in the flow of healing energy coming from the hands and then move or swim away when the work is done.

The practitioner may do the work from a distance. Some animals are sensitive due to the nature of their problem and may not be receptive to hands-on treatment, especially if the animal has been abused and is leery of strangers. Animals in the wild are usually done from a distance.

Course Descriptions

Komitor does not offer classes for cats because they do not get along well with each other, but dogs perform well in a class setting. Students are asked not to bring dogs that behave badly or do not have good social skills. When working with horses, an experienced horse handler is always present. New students, especially those with little or no experience with horses, are never left alone with a horse.

Upon completion of both the canine and equine portions of Levels 1 through 4, a student may begin the process of certification. The student has one year from the completion of the last Level 4 class to submit a certification packet containing all required documents. Case studies, documentation of healings, and book reviews make up some of the requirements for certification.

▶ **Level 1** is a three-day experiential seminar working directly with animals to introduce the Komitor technique and philosophy of applying energy healing techniques.

The first day of this class, a prerequisite for those who have no experience with Healing Touch, gives students a foundation in energy field theory and application and prepares them to work with the animals during the remainder of the class. Topics include:

- The concept of the human and animal energy field relating to modern science and corresponding assessment skills
- Healing Touch Level 1 skills and how they can be used with holistic animal health care
- Specific benefits and techniques for animals large or small, pet or exotic, bird, mammal, reptile, or aquatic
- The benefits of the owner/pet relationship pertaining to energy-based holistic health
- Convey professionalism with the cooperative healing of traditional and holistic veterinary health care

▶ **Level 2** is a three-day workshop that includes intermediate to advanced concepts and techniques of energy-based animal healing, including an opportunity to look at the energetic perspective of difficult cases and provide a clearer understanding of holistic health care for the animal population. Level 1 is a prerequisite. Topics include:

- Fine-tuning energetic awareness and abilities
- Additional Healing Touch for Animals techniques, including personality identification, grounding, and the focus technique
- Identifying trauma and learning a Trauma Release Technique™ specific to animals
- The Vertebral Release Technique™ to relieve back injuries
- More fully addressing pet grieving and its energetic effects
- Instructions on conducting a full healing session sequence

▶ **Level 3** is a three-day workshop that includes a review of Level 2 and an introduction to essential oils. Students broaden their awareness and knowledge of energy medicine through advanced techniques. Level 2 is a prerequisite for Level 3. Topics include:

- Using essential oils in healing sessions
- Intermediate and advanced biofield energy techniques
- Encouraging cooperative veterinary interaction, focusing on accurate documentation of energy treatments
- Working with the Qi energy to accelerate healing
- Distance Healing™ work with numerous procedures
- Using the differing frequencies of various animal species to accelerate healing
- Focusing on energetic awareness through the instinctual perspective of animals

▶ **Level 4** is a three-day workshop that includes a review of Level 3 and an introduction to sound and vibrational therapy using tuning forks. Level 4 is the final level of Healing Touch for Animals before participants may be eligible for HTA certification. Level 3 is a prerequisite for Level 4. Additional topics include:

- Hara line assessment, repair, and support, including stabilization of the chakra system
- Additional advanced treatment work
- Best practices for an energy medicine for animals business
- Discussion and practice of advanced application of essential oils with animals
- Advanced biofield energy techniques

. . . .

Continuing Education Units: Offered through the Associated Bodywork and Massage Professionals.

Certification: Overseen by the Healing Touch for Animals Certification Review Board.

Participants: People interested in energy medicine who have a deep respect for animals.

Code of Ethics/Standards of Practice: Yes, plus a Practitioner Policy.

Suggested Reading

Ellenberger, W., H. Dittich, and H. Baum. *An Atlas of Animal Anatomy for Artists.* New York: Dover, 1956.

McElroy, Susan Chernak. *Animals as Teachers and Healers: True Stories and Reflections.* New York: Random House, 1996.

Schoen, Allen M., and Pam Proctor. *Love, Miracles, and Animal Healing.* New York: Fireside, 1996.

Availability: Workshops are taught throughout the United States, Canada, New Zealand, Australia, and Europe. To locate a session in your area, go to www.healing touchforanimals.com.

Resources

Healing Touch for Animals, PO Box 632171, Highlands Ranch, CO 80163, 303-470-6572, office@healingtouchforanimals.com, www.healingtouch foranimals.com

Bibliography

Komitor, Carol. *Healing Touch for Animals Level 1.* Highlands Ranch, CO: Komitor Healing Method Inc., 1996.

www.healingtouchforanimals.com

INNERSOURCE

Donna Eden is a bestselling author and popular teacher of energy medicine. Her book *Energy Medicine: Balancing Your Body's Energies for Optimal Health, Joy, and Vitality*, considered an important book in the field, was first published in 1999 and in August of 2008 was rereleased as a revised and expanded edition. Innersource is her own collection of "programs for freeing body, mind, and spirit." Following Eden's course of study leads to The Eden Energy Medicine Certification Program. Eden often collaborates with her husband, David Feinstein, PhD, a clinical psychologist and a former faculty member of The Johns Hopkins University School of Medicine.

After healing her own multiple sclerosis, Donna Eden began to more deeply explore energy healing. Along with Feinstein, she founded Innersource in 1980 to promote her teaching. In 1999, they founded the Energy Medicine Institute as a nonprofit arm to complement the work being done by Innersource and as a provider for certification.

Eden combines Chinese medicine, kinesiology, and techniques from a number of other modalities in her programs of energy healing. Her view of the body's energies goes beyond the traditional understanding of the human energy field. Eden describes nine different energy systems in and around the human body: meridians, chakras, the aura, the Celtic weave, the basic grid, the five rhythms, the triple warmer, the electrics, and the radiant circuits.

She sees the chakras as concentrated centers of swirling energy. (For a more comprehensive description of chakras, energy fields, and meridians go to pages 3–5 and 7.) According to David Feinstein in an article he wrote in 2005, "Principles of Energy Medicine," meridians delivery energy to the organs and chakras bathe the organs in energy. He also says that each chakra corresponds to an aspect of the personality and resonates with principles found in nature such as those having to do with survival, creativity, identity, love, expression, comprehension, and transcendence.

While Eden's approach involves working with the chakras and the energy field, she is more known for her work with the meridians, the Celtic weave, the basic grid, the five rhythms, the triple warmer, and the radiant circuits. The following are her definitions:

- The basic grid forms a foundation for all the other energy systems. It does not repair itself as easily as other parts of the energy system. The rest of the energy system adapts to damages or deformities within the grid. Once the grid is damaged, the rest of the system is also out of balance.

- The Celtic weave is a network of spiraling figure eights that keeps all of the energy systems functioning as a single unit. It laces through all of the other energy systems, creating a resonance between them and holding the entire energetic structure together.

- What Eden calls the five rhythms, traditional Chinese medicine calls the five elements. They are also known as the five movements or the five seasons. Traditional Chinese medicine refers to the five elements as the building blocks of the universe. Eden sees them as a rhythm directing the tone and mood of the entire energy system.

- The origin of the term triple warmer is lost in history. It is one of the fourteen meridians. However, Eden says it has the specific function of mobilizing the body's energies during a traumatic event. When a threat is perceived, the triple warmer organizes the other energy systems to activate an immune response and the fight or flight response.

- Radiant circuits, also known as strange flows, are more fluid than meridians. Meridians follow specific pathways throughout the body. Strange flows deliver energy to the body's organs and all parts of the energy system, including the meridians. They ensure the body and its energy system are functioning as a healthy, cohesive unit.

While sessions are normally performed on a massage table, they can also be done while the client is sitting or standing. Once the practitioner has noted pertinent information concerning the client's condition, he or she will begin treatment using the various interventions. Sessions usually last an hour. Treatments involve the practitioner placing his or her hands with a light touch at specific places on the body. Some work is done off the body. The practitioner also will tap at various places on a client's body and teach the client how to tap him- or herself to improve energy circulation and general good health. The practitioner's goal is to balance the energy system and bring harmony to all the different facets of the energy structure.

Course Descriptions

The classes listed below are all available as home study courses and are sometimes taught by Donna Eden in hands-on workshops. In addition, Feinstein has added his own work to the program in the form of energy psychology. He includes resources and his own list of home study classes on Innersource's website.

Students of Eden's Certification Program may follow the Eden Energy Medicine Wellness Track to practice only on themselves and family and friends, or they may follow the Eden Energy Medicine Professional Certification Track to practice Eden Energy Medicine in a professional setting. Before being listed on the website as a certified practitioner a graduate must demonstrate proficiency at several levels. To stay on the website, graduates must complete continuing education requirements that include Practitioner's conferences and advanced classes taught by Eden.

For those who do not go through the certification program, Eden's training is offered at three levels: basic, intermediate, and advanced. The basic program consists of the following four classes.

▶ **Energy Medicine Overview** introduces the underlying concepts of Energy Medicine and demonstrates how to use it for health and healing. Topics include the five basic principles of Energy Medicine and the nine energy systems of the human body. The class introduces students to various ways to approach energetic healing.

▶ **Introduction to Energy Medicine** explores the relationship between energy and the body, methods for identifying and assessing these energies, and a collection of basic energy balancing techniques to promote well-being and reprogram the body's responses to stress. Topics include:

- The relationship between the subtle energies and physical well-being
- How an energy test can assess the impact of stresses on the body
- How to distinguish between the meridians and the chakras
- Twelve basic exercises to improve flow and harmony within the subtle energy system

▶ **Basic Energy Medicine Techniques** expands on what students have already learned and provides hands-on video instruction for many of the techniques presented in *Energy Medicine*. Topics include:

- Techniques for working with the nine major energy systems: the meridians, the chakras, the aura, the Celtic weave, the basic grid, the five elements, the triple warmer, the electrics, and the radiant circuits
- Assessing the meridians using alarm points
- Assessing and balancing the chakras
- Specific techniques for relieving pain

▶ **Assessing and Addressing the Meridians** explores advanced meridian healing techniques, further study of Eden's book *Energy Medicine*, and study of John Thie's book *Touch for Health*.

Intermediate Courses

Before enrolling in the intermediate courses, students need to complete the basic courses and attend one of Innersource's Energy Medicine Five-Day Training workshops, which are held approximately twice a year. The five-day training teaches students how to become proficient in Energy Medicine and includes specific techniques to keep one's energy vital and balanced. Upon completion, students can enroll in any of the three specialized intermediate-level courses.

▶ **Becoming an Energy Tracker: Figuring Out What's Wrong and How to Fix It** teaches students how to conduct an energy healing session, including how to track and balance a client's energy. Topics include:

- Eight preliminary tests for diagnosing energy disorganization or imbalance and corresponding corrective procedures
- Specific healing techniques such as Meridian Wheel, Five-Rhythm Chart, Star Diagnostic, Chakra Balancing, and Alarm Points

▶ **The Radiant Circuits: Freeing the Spirit** offers students detailed training in strange flows, also known as radiant circuits. Topics include:

- Meeting stress with greater resilience
- Changing emotional and mental habits
- Healing past wounds
- Freeing your true inner self

▶ **The Five Elements/Five Rhythms** describes in detail the healing perspective of traditional Chinese medicine and other cultures. Topics include:

- Detailed descriptions of the energy techniques used in traditional Chinese medicine
- An understanding of the reasons why people attract disease
- Techniques for finding good health and personal fulfillment

Advanced Courses

Prerequisites are completion of the basic and intermediate courses and one of the aforementioned five-day training workshops. There are five advanced classes.

▶ **Illness, Pain, and the Difficult Case** addresses how to strategically approach specific cases when the standard methods aren't working.

▶ **Shifting Deeply Embedded Patterns** introduces an eclectic array of advanced techniques to provide deep healing and personal transformation.

▶ **Energy Medicine for Women** teaches students techniques for harmonizing the flow of hormones in a woman's body.

▶ **Color, Auras, and the Psychic Realm** attunes students to the invisible subtle realm of energy in which we all operate while developing their psychic capabilities.

▶ **The Diamond Inlay and Other Topics** covers a range of techniques for grounding and protecting yourself when working with a client's energy and includes specific advanced healing techniques.

Certification

▶ **The Eden Energy Medicine Certification Program** consists of eight four-day workshops spread over a two-year period. Prerequisites for this program are attendance at a Five-Day Basic Training and completion of Eden's book *Energy Medicine*. The curriculum and corresponding topics are as follows:

Class 1: Energy and Energy Testing, Intro to Meridians

- Energy testing and troubleshooting
- An introduction to the meridians, including the Meridian Flow Wheel and tracing and flushing meridians
- A daily energy routine and quickie energy balancer
- The Brazilian Toe Technique, and working with alarm points, magnets, and vivaxis
- Introduction to the ethics of energy healing

Class 2: Beginning Meridians

- Muscle-based energy tests for the spleen, kidney, triple warmer, gall bladder, liver, lung, and large intestine
- Testing meridians via alarm points
- Neurolymphatic and neurovascular points and their uses
- Advanced healing techniques
- Beginning substance testing protocol

Class 3: Advanced Meridians, Auric Field, and Introduction to Five Rhythms

- Muscle-based energy tests for the stomach, heart, small intestine, bladder, and more
- Pulse tests and how to work with them to relieve pain
- Testing and treating auric field and polarity issues

- Introduction to magnets and crystals
- Introduction to the five elements

Class 4: Chakras, Radiant Circuits, and Sensory Types

- Testing, cleaning, and balancing chakras
- Tracing, testing, and activating radiant circuits
- Specific advanced healing techniques

Class 5: The Five Rhythms of Energy Medicine, Advanced Substance Testing, Source Points

- Five rhythms, their meridians, and corresponding pulse tests
- Testing pulses for the purposes of working with the five rhythms
- Neurovascular element points
- The five rhythms and corresponding emotions
- Advanced substance testing and addressing possible side effects

Class 6: The Energy Medicine Session

- Conducting an Energy Medicine session, including energy tracking, choosing and making appropriate corrections, and managing expectations
- Advanced illness tracking
- Studying ethics cases

Class 7: Advanced Topics

- Working with irregular energies
- Source points and seed cells
- Vortexes
- Assemblage points
- Hormones and Energy Medicine for Women

Class 8: Eden Energy Medicine, Business Training

- The spirit of energy medicine: diagnosing hope, teaching empowerment, and spreading love

- An introduction to the nature of grid and regression
- Exploration of legal and ethical issues
- Running an Energy Medicine practice
- General business practices

. . . .

Continuing Education Units: Yes. Innersource is approved by the following national organizations: National Certification Board for Therapeutic Massage and Bodywork; American Holistic Nurses Association: National Certification Commission for Acupuncture and Oriental Medicine; and Southern Oregon University.

Certification: Yes, granted by the Eden Energy Medicine Certification Program.

Participants: The home study course and the workshops are open to anyone who would like to pursue a course of energy medicine for personal and professional use. The certification program is for the serious student who wants to set up an energy medicine practice or use the program as a complement to another healing modality.

Code of Ethics/Standards of Practice: Yes.

Suggested Reading

Eden, Donna. *Energy Medicine: Balancing Your Body's Energies for Optimal Health, Joy, and Vitality*, 2nd edition. New York: Tarcher/Penguin, 2008.

———. *Energy Medicine for Women: Aligning Your Body's Energies to Boost Your Health and Vitality.* New York: Tarcher/Penguin, 2008.

Feinstein, David. *The Promise of Energy Psychology: Revolutionary Tools for Dramatic Personal Change.* New York: Tarcher/Penguin, 2005.

———. "Energy Psychology: A Review of the Preliminary Evidence." *Psychotherapy: Theory, Review, Practice, Training* 45, 2 (2008): 199–213.

Availability: Classes are offered in Australia, Europe, New Zealand, South America, and the United States. To find a practitioner in your area, go to www.innersource .net.

Resources

Innersource, 777 East Main Street, Ashland, OR 97520, 541-482-1800, energy@innersource.net, www.innersource.net

Bibliography

Eden, Donna. *Energy Medicine: Balancing Your Body's Energies for Optimal Health, Joy, and Vitality*, 2nd edition. New York: Tarcher/Penguin, 2008.

www.innersource.net

KAIROS THERAPY

IN 2002, A GROUP OF SHEN THERAPY (page 275) instructors and practitioners formed a new school of person-centered, hands-on healing called Kairos Therapy, which built on and expanded the concept of body-centered emotion. At the heart of Kairos Therapy is the understanding that long-held stress and trauma may keep people from emotional freedom and physical health, and that each person has the potential for healing and transforming his or her own pain into health, creativity, joy, and openness.

Kairos Therapy is a specific form of hands-on emotional and physical healing that uses an external application of qi (energy) to induce a state of gentle relaxation in the client's field. Blockages and trauma held in the energy field are gently brought to the surface, where they are spontaneously released. These blockages may arise as a result of physical injury, tension or emotional pain, trauma or shock.

A session begins with the practitioner asking questions of the client regarding his or her condition. The practitioner listens for the emotional components in the fabric of the client's story. She looks for connections between emotional history and physical symptoms and then translates the information to the language of Kairos. The client is asked to lie, fully clothed, on a special table called a Kairos cradle. The practitioner places her hands on the client and moves them to areas around the body appropriate to the client's needs. The client moves into a state of relaxation and may spontaneously make connections about his life that have been unclear up to this point. He may have insights into his experience or look and feel differently about the events in his life, and his physical symptoms may resolve. Healing rarely comes quickly. Clients' emotional wounds are often too deep and require a series of healing sessions to resolve.

K iss the Earth	**T** rust returns
A ffirm Life	**H** ealing happens
I nstigate growth	**E** nergy flows
R emember, recover	**R** enaissance arrives
O pen safely	**A** ttitudes change
S hine brightly	**P** eace arises
	Y ou emerge

Course Descriptions

Kairos Therapy is undergoing a complete revision of its classes at the time of this writing. Their entry-level class is for the general public and for personal self-healing. It is a prerequisite for the certification process. Group work, classwork, and a mentored internship make up the rest of the certification program. Please go to their website for more information: www.kairostherapy.com.

Continuing Education Units: Check with your instructor.

Certification: Yes, granted by the Board of the International Association of Kairos Therapy.

Participants: All who have an interest are welcome. Students are encouraged to experience a Kairos treatment before taking a class.

Code of Ethics/Standards of Practice: They have a Code of Conduct.

Availability: Classes are offered throughout Canada, Ireland, the United Kingdom, and the United States. To locate a practitioner in your area, go to www.kairostherapy .com.

Resources

International Association for Kairos Therapy, 7 Alderbank Place, Edinburgh, Scotland EH11 1SZ, (01314) 784780, kairos@onetel.com, www.kairostherapy.com

American Kairos Therapy Association, 1285 Solano Avenue, PMB 127, Albany, CA 94706, 510-466-7751, jandeder@netwiz.net

Bibliography

www.kairostherapy.com

POLARITY THERAPY

PROPONENTS OF POLARITY THERAPY maintain there is a source of energy that flows through and around all things. This energy comes from a Universal Source that created the universe and everything in it. Movement of energy from the Source into being is the "involutionary" phase, and energy moving back to the Source is the "evolutionary" phase. The two phases become the pulsation of life. Using touch, reflex and acupressure points, positive thinking, exercise, and diet, practitioners balance and restore this natural flow of energy where it has been disturbed or blocked.

Polarity Therapy is distinct from most energy medicine disciplines in the way in which it maps out the human energy field. While many modalities refer to the numerous layers of the body's subtle energy fields (the chakras and meridians), Polarity Therapy maintains that there are three types of energy systems in the human body: long lines of current that run from north to south, transverse currents that run east to west, and spiral currents that start at the navel and expand outward. Polarity Therapy is further distinguished by its recognition of six energy centers (or chakras) rather than the more traditional seven. Dr. Randolph Stone, developer of this discipline, relied heavily on the Ayurvedic tradition of India as well as his comprehensive experience working with healing systems from around the world, including yoga, hermetics, acupuncture, reflexology, and herbology.

Much of Stone's work is based on the five elements of the Japanese interpretation of traditional Chinese medicine: earth, water, fire, and air. The fifth element in Chinese philosophy is ether. The five elements are metaphors for the energies that govern the physical, mental, emotional, psychological, and spiritual sides of a human being. For example, earth represents solidity and permanence. In the body, earth represents the bones and muscles that form the strong foundation of the body. People with strong earth tendencies resist change and are often stubborn and more conscious of their physical bodies.

In contrast, water represents fluidity and ease of movement. Blood and other bodily fluids are symbolized by water. People with strong water influences adapt to change easily and are flexible and emotional. Energy and forceful movement are symbolized by fire, which represents the metabolism and warmth of the body. Fire influence is associated with intention, desire, and motivation.

Freedom of movement and elusiveness are represented by air. Breathing is the associated bodily function. People under the influence of air have open minds and carefree attitudes. Ether, sometimes called "void," represents the unseen, such as spirit and creative energy. Thought and the ability to communicate are symbolized by ether. People with ether tendencies are creative and spontaneous.

Stone's work also uses the three principles of yin/yang theory. According to traditional Chinese philosophy, yang is said to be outgoing, positive, and expansive, whereas yin is said to be contractive, negative, and receptive. Yin/yang is neutral, a still point where energy is neither expanding nor contracting. Yin and yang represent the movement of life. Life force or the energy of life, often called chi, qi, or prana, moves through a yin/yang cycle.

Dr. Randolph Stone began a holistic medical practice using osteopathy, chiropractics, and naturopathic medicine while living in Chicago in the 1940s. Born in Engelsberg, Austria, he immigrated to the United States when he was thirteen. He learned English by reading the Bible and studied to become a Lutheran minister. However, his studies led him to other ways of thought and he joined the Theosophical Society. He felt medicine was his path, and by the age of twenty-four he had degrees in osteopathy, chiropractic, and naturopathy. He was also granted an Other Practitioners License, which allowed him to use healing methods other than the traditional drugs and surgery.

Dr. Stone traveled to India to research Ayurvedic medicine and how it combines energy, spirituality, and pathology, and he followed a yogic path for over forty years. But it wasn't just the Indian medical philosophy that influenced him. He was also a man of science. He was fascinated by the polarization of magnets and the attraction and repulsion found in the structure of an atom. He began to see how this all related to the health of the human body.

He liked to work with what he called "hopeless cases" and developed a reputation for successful energy healing work. In 1947, he wrote his first book on the subject of energy work, *The Wireless Anatomy of Man; or, A Course in Manipulative Therapy with Principles and Illustrations of the New Energy Concept of the Healing Art* (self-published in 1953) and has written several more. When he retired at eighty-four, he appointed Pierre Pannetier to carry on his work. After Stone's passing, a core group of advanced practitioners founded the American Polarity Therapy Association to continue the work and promote uniformity among practitioners.

Like other energy therapies, Polarity Therapy espouses the theory that good health is experienced when energy systems function in their natural state and energy flows smoothly without significant blockage or fixation. Unbalanced, blocked, or fixed energy due to stress or other factors leads to pain and possibly disease. Besides energy-based bodywork, Polarity Therapy includes a regimen of diet, exercise, and self-awareness to stimulate and balance the living energy field.

At the start of a session, the client removes his or her shoes and lies fully clothed on a massage table as the practitioner asks the client to breathe deeply, enabling relaxation and releasing tightness in the muscles. The practitioner assesses the energetic attributes of the client by using energetic touch and observation, and by asking questions of the client about the issue being presented. Interventions consist of hand positioning, gentle rocking of the client's body, and the manipulation of the hands or feet. Touch is done using two fingers of each hand at specified points. The depth of touch ranges from light to firm. The rocking is done by placing the hands at specified points and rocking the body gently as a mother would rock her baby. At the end of the session, the practitioner may suggest a series of exercises and changes in diet. The practitioner may also suggest ways of changing thoughts into a more positive attitude toward life or the client's problems.

Course Descriptions

Class content varies from instructor to instructor and within the various schools, programs, and academies that offer Polarity Therapy. The following class descriptions come from the Ohio Institute of Energetic Studies and Bodywork.

▶ **Theory and Basic Principles of Polarity Energy Systems:** To complete this class, the participant must demonstrate a basic understanding and working knowledge of the following Polarity principles:

- Unity and neutrality
- Duality of repulsion and attraction
- The three principles of energy flow
- The five elements
- The development of the human form as a dynamic energy system
- The basis of Ayurvedic principles

▶ **Anatomy and Physiology—Energy Model:** This class explores the relationships and functions of energy anatomy as well as the following:

- Locations
- Etheric energy pathways
- Lines of force
- Harmonic relationships

▶ **Anatomy and Physiology—Orthodox Model:** The student will demonstrate commanding knowledge of the location and functions of the major systems, including:

- Bones
- Joints
- Muscles
- Fascia
- Organs
- Fluid systems

▶ **Energetic Evaluation and Integration:** Elemental assessment is the foundation of Polarity and evaluation. To pass this class the student must demonstrate skills of:

- Client energetic assessment
- History taking
- Observation
- Interaction
- Synthesis

▶ **Polarity Energetic Bodywork:** Through energetic touch experience, the participant develops the understanding and the ability to:

- Effectively use the three types of Polarity touch: Satvic, Rajasic, and Tamasic
- Be sensitive to both verbal and nonverbal interactions with clients
- Increase clients' awareness of optimal health and other life issues through energetic protocols
- Restore energetic balance and harmony of body, mind, and spirit

▶ **Communication and Facilitation:** Through lecture, reflective listening, and guided personal directives, the participant learns:

- How personality and attitudes are influenced by life experiences, including family and sociocultural factors
- An understanding of the law of cause and effect, action and reaction
- Self-awareness and sensitivity to the needs, strengths, and unique abilities of clients

▶ **Energetics Food Awareness:** In this class, the participant explores:

- The energetic characteristics of the elements of food and Dr. Stone's Health Building Program, theoretically and experientially
- Ayurvedic concepts of the elements and the energetics of foods for maintaining a healthy balance of life energy

▶ **Business Management and Promotion:** This class concerns the business side of having a practice. Students will learn:

- How to establish a safe and viable practice that serves the community well

- The fundamentals of managing a business
- How to set up an office or suitable work space
- How to keep accurate and up-to-date client records, and accounting and tax records
- How to manage accounts payable and receivable, ordering and stocking supplies, the telephone, appointments, and employees as needed

▶ **Professional Ethics and Law:** This class covers legal issues. Students will learn:

- To understand the scope of practice permitted by law as well as the scope that is appropriate to their competence and experience
- To be aware of ethical considerations in the relationships between client and practitioner and between practitioner and other health-care professionals
- When to refer clients to appropriate medical or health-care professionals

. . . .

Continuing Education Units: It varies by the instructor or training program offering Polarity Therapy. Ask your instructor about this.

Certification: Practitioners may be certified by educational programs approved by the American Polarity Association. There are two levels of certification: Associate Polarity Practitioner (APP) and Registered Polarity Practitioner (RPP).

Participants: Applicants must be eighteen years of age or older and have a high school diploma or GED or equivalent.

Code of Ethics/Standards of Practice: Yes.

Legalities: Because Polarity Therapy uses massage in some of its techniques, check your state massage rules as to whether you need a license to practice this discipline in your area.

Suggested Reading

Seidman, Maruti. *A Guide to Polarity Therapy: The Gentle Art of Hands-On Healing,* 4th edition. Berkeley CA: North Atlantic Books, 2000.

Siegel, Alan. *Polarity Therapy: Healing with Life Energy.* Houston, TX: Masterworks International, 2006.

Availability: To find a school in your area, go to www.polarity-therapy.com. For a session with a practitioner, go to www.polaritytherapy.org.

Resources

American Polarity Therapy Association, 122 N. Elm Street, Suite 512, Greensboro, NC 27401, 336-574-1121, APTAoffices@polaritytherapy.com, www.polarity therapy.org

Bibliography

Gordon, Richard. *Your Healing Hands: The Polarity Experience.* Santa Cruz, CA: Unity Press, 1978.

Sills, Franklyn. *The Polarity Process: Energy as a Healing Art.* Rockport, MA: Element Books, 1991.

www.columbuspolarity.com

www.polaritycenter.com

www.polaritytherapy.org

FOUR BELIEFS FRAME THE ART of quantum healing. One is the belief that love is a universal vibration, the foundation of all healing, and the core essence of life. Everyone has the ability to assist in healing. It is the client who is the true healer; the practitioner merely maintains a resonance and frequency that allow the client's body to heal itself. The practitioner can amplify the energy flowing to the client through breathing and meditation techniques.

Richard Gordon, the founder of Quantum-Touch, attended the Christos School of Natural Healing in Taos, New Mexico, in the early 1970s, where he studied therapeutic massage, spiritual healing, herbal medicine, and Polarity Therapy, all of which served as the foundation for Quantum-Touch. By using various breathing and body awareness exercises, an individual can focus and amplify the energy (known as chi in Chinese and prana in Sanskrit) that runs naturally through their hands to assist in healing and balancing another person's energy. The healing capabilities of Quantum-Touch work with the principles of resonance and entrainment. By raising her own vibration, a practitioner creates a high level of energy that she can direct and apply through light physical touch to any area where there is pain, stress, inflammation, disease, or other problems. The recipient's body will entrain to the higher frequency and begin to heal itself. This innate healing power is referred to as "body intelligence."

The foundation of the Quantum-Touch healing program is based on the combined effect of Gordon's breathing and body awareness techniques, which allow the individual to control and direct the life force energy within. The practitioner begins to work with this life force energy by cupping his hands and doing a mental sweep of one side of his body by starting with one foot, sweeping to the top of the head and then down the arm and repeating this process on the other side of the body. He then inhales deeply to the count of two and exhales to the count of six. While doing the breathing patterns, the practitioner sets an intention to create an energy field suited to aid the client in the healing process. The practitioner may change the breathing patterns until he feels the buildup of energy needed to perform the healing work presented by the client.

Given the versatility of Quantum-Touch, sessions can take place in a variety of locations, and the client, who remains fully clothed, can sit, lie down, or stand. At the beginning of a healing session, the practitioner takes a few minutes to perform the breathing patterns as preparation for the healing session. Then she asks the client about the physical issue being presented and its location in the body. The practitioner places her hands gently on the area of pain, or holds her hands a few inches above the area if it is delicate, inappropriate, or the client does not want to be touched. While doing the work, the practitioner may change her breathing patterns to meet the energy needs of the client. Within the time frame of the session, which usually lasts about an hour, the practitioner works with the client until she senses that the affected areas have matched the higher frequency of the practitioner, thus allowing natural healing to occur.

Course Descriptions

Quantum-Touch offers both live workshops and interactive video workshops. The interactive videos may be watched alone, but they are designed for a group setting of three or more people, with breaks to allow them to practice what they have observed on the video. Attendance at a Basic Interactive Video Workshop qualifies a student to attend either a Supercharging or Core Transformation Workshop. Each live workshop or video counts as 4 hours toward certification. Live workshops as well as video workshops are listed on their website, www.quantumtouch.com, and are found all over the world. You do not have to know anything about Quantum-Touch to host a video workshop. Practitioner certification requirements consist of attendance at two workshops, one of which must be a live basic workshop; the other one can be a basic workshop (either live or video) or one live advanced workshop. A video workshop must have at least three people in attendance. The applicant must also complete 60 hours of healing sessions. Applicants for certification must also submit a signed copy agreeing to the Code of Ethics.

▶ **Basic Interactive Video Workshop:** This four-DVD set covers a complete live workshop experience. It comes with Richard Gordon's book *Quantum-Touch: The Power to Heal* and an information packet for conducting a video workshop at home. It is designed for a group setting enabling people to practice on each other. Topics include:

- Breathing and body awareness exercises
- Pain and inflammation
- Bones
- Back problems
- Chakras, toning, and vortexing life force energy
- The amplified resonance technique
- Working with animals

▶ **Basic Quantum-Touch Workshop:** This two-day event introduces the fundamentals of Quantum-Touch. Students learn the following techniques.

- A series of breathing and body awareness exercises to focus and amplify energy
- How to reduce pain and inflammation and eliminate back pain
- Distance healing
- The role of the chakras and how to work with their energy
- How to use toning and vortexing to increase a session's efficacy
- How to work with animals

▶ **Supercharging Quantum-Touch:** This two-day workshop of limited class size allows practitioners to take their healing skills to the next level of mastery. The instructors of this class can see their students' energy and personally direct each student to optimum effectiveness, so class size is limited to fourteen people. Students learn how to:

- Increase their efficiency and effectiveness and generate longer-lasting results from their sessions

- Raise their own or other people's energy to even greater heights for improved health, intuition, and personal transformation
- Automatically tune their vibrations to the condition they are working on
- Quantum-Touch for weight loss, emotional healing, and longevity

▶ **Core Transformation I:** This two-day workshop requires a deep level of engagement from the student. The basic workshop is a prerequisite. Students learn advanced skills to understand pain, transform physical and emotional issues, awaken inner knowing and intuition, and apply Quantum-Touch to themselves for deep personal healing.

▶ **Core Transformation II:** This two-day workshop deepens the process of opening areas that need healing. It explores blockages, paying particular attention to how they manifest as allergies, unresolved emotions, and other illnesses. Students learn techniques such as "wombing," movement, connecting with the authentic self to deepen energy flow, and identifying and clearing reactive patterns.

· · · · · · · · · · · · · · · · · ·

Continuing Education Units: Continuing Nursing Education is approved by the New Mexico Nursing Association, which is accredited by the American Nurses Credentialing Center's Commission on Accreditation. Quantum-Touch is also certified by the National Certification Board for Therapeutic Massage and Bodywork (NCBTMB) as an approved provider of continuing education.

Certification: All inquiries and submissions are subject to review and an approval process by Quantum-Touch Inc. Completion of the practitioner requirements does not guarantee or entitle certification to an applicant.

Participants: Open to all those interested in energy healing, from laypeople to alternative and traditional health-care practitioners.

Code of Ethics/Standards of Practice: Yes.

Suggested Reading

Gordon, Richard. *Quantum-Touch: The Power to Heal.* Berkeley, CA: North Atlantic Books, 1999.

Herriott, Alain. *Supercharging Quantum Touch: Advanced Techniques.* Berkeley, CA: North Atlantic Books, 2007.

Availability: Classes are offered in Australia, Austria, Belgium, Canada, Croatia, France, Germany, Greece, India, Japan, the Netherlands, New Zealand, North Vietnam, Norway, Singapore, South Africa, Spain, Sweden, Switzerland, Thailand, Trinidad, Turkey, the United Kingdom, and the United States. To locate a practitioner, go to www.quantumtouch.com.

Resources

Quantum-Touch Inc., PO Box 1240, Kapaa, HI 96746, 888-424-0041, mail@ quantumtouch.com, www.quantumtouch.com

Bibliography

Gordon, Richard. *Quantum-Touch: The Power to Heal.* Berkeley, CA: North Atlantic Books, 1999.

www.quantumtouch.com

RAPID EYE TECHNOLOGY

MANY PEOPLE BELIEVE THAT THE MIND releases stress and harmful emotions during REM sleep. Rapid Eye Technology (RET) is a psychoenergetic therapy that uses a simulation of REM (rapid eye movement that occurs when a person is dreaming) sleep to help release stress and optimize mental, emotional, physical, and spiritual health. RET uses systematic movement of the eyes and eyelids, rapid verbal communication, and special imagery to help release stressful emotions on many levels.

Ranae Johnson, PhD, founder of Rapid Eye Technology, started experimenting with alternative therapies as far back as 1966 after she discovered that her son was autistic. Not satisfied with allopathic medical treatments, she turned to alternative and complementary medicine. A major breakthrough occurred when family members reported feeling much better after doing optometric exercises along with her son, which consisted of lateral, diagonal, and vertical eye movements. Building on these exercises, she developed eye movement techniques to help with the release of emotional baggage. She formalized her studies in psychology and alternative medicine, and started training other people in RET in 1988. Today, RET uses blinking, eye movements, breathwork, imagery, and stress reduction energy work to alleviate stress by releasing energetic memories stored in the body at a cellular level.

Johnson divides the therapy into two parts: processing the pain and reframing traumatic memories. In the first half of the treatment, confined energy is accessed at the cellular level through a fast blinking technique. Once the energy is accessed, additional techniques help release the energy holding these memories locked in the cells. Once the negative emotions are cleared, the client is ready for the second half of the treatment. To facilitate the reframing of memories, Johnson uses seven principles called "skills for life": changing thought patterns to change results, altering perception to a more positive point of view, learning to be accountable for choices and accepting the freedom to choose again, understanding cause and effect, using gratitude to increase abundance in all good things, understanding health and healing, and using intuitive rhythm to create harmony with and connection to all things.

A session with a Rapid Eye technician begins with a review of the client's medical, psychological, and family history. (Johnson refers to individuals trained in RET as *technicians*.) Technicians provide a safe and nurturing environment for healing and lead the client through breathing techniques to aid in relaxation. The technician may also use energy techniques to help relieve stress as needed. The technician holds a wand in front of the client's eyes, moves the wand, and asks the client to blink; this causes the client to slip into a mental state similar to a REM sleep pattern. While the eye movement techniques occur, the technician verbally communicates with the client to link the conscious mind with the subconscious mind, releasing energy at the cellular level attached to stress or a traumatic event. The second half of the treatment involves reframing the traumatic memories. The technician introduces the seven skills for life and discusses new choices for the client to help create a happier life. Sessions may take 1 to 2 hours.

Course Descriptions

Because Rapid Eye Technology courses are taken at home, geography is not a problem. Students are supplied with books, training manuals, CDs, and DVDs to help them with their study. As a last step in the education process toward certification, a four-day live workshop is offered by the RET Institute in Salem, Oregon. Live workshops are available in other parts of the country as well.

Certified technicians, certified master technicians, and trainers are required to recertify every year to update their skills. To recertify, a technician needs to take at least 25 hours of Rapid Eye Technology classes and/or classes supporting Rapid Eye technology, such as Reiki or an Inner Child Workshop, or have documents proving he has maintained an active practice in Rapid Eye Technology or Skills for Life. A master technician needs to attend or staff a Master Rapid Eye Technology

Workshop, publish articles about Rapid Eye Technology, or have documents proving he has maintained an active practice as a master technician.

▶ **RET Technician Course:** This program is a home-study course with a four-day on-campus workshop for certification spanning a total of 100 course hours. RET certifications are offered throughout the country on a regularly scheduled basis. If a student cannot attend class on campus, certification can be completed by submitting a video recording of the student demonstrating his or her mastery of the skills. The home-study tuition includes all materials and the certification fee. The Rapid Eye Technology curriculum includes 26 hours of home-study course material, 26 hours of certification, and 48 hours of practicum. The certification topics are as follows:

- Instruction on every aspect of RET sessions
- Instruction on all eye movement techniques and processes
- How to access core issues immediately with RET
- How to do neurological integration or eye work
- Complete RET session programs with Inner Child work
- How to integrate Rapid Eye Technology processes, scripts, and tools
- Imagery scripts for releasing and reframing
- Instruction in patterning identification and resolution
- Closing processes, including built-in safeguards

The RET Institute offers additional courses as continuing education.

▶ **Immediate Release Technique (IRT) Course:** This course complements any medical, psychological, or alternative health-care practice. Students taking this course should also experience a number of sessions with a Rapid Eye technician. The class addresses the theory and hands-on experience needed to desensitize and release traumas associated with personal issues. Students learn how to handle clients confronted by challenging emotional states. This course is taught as a hands-on workshop. It is also available in a self-directed home-study format. Topics include:

- Recognizing when to assist an individual or group with emotional crisis desensitization
- Skills for life coaching

- Advanced eye movements
- Body tapping
- Imagery theory and application
- Eye patching theory and application
- Developing compassion
- Home care and self-care between full model RET sessions

▶ **Master Rapid Eye Technician (MRET) Graduate Course:** This course offers certified Rapid Eye Technicians a course of study and practice toward mastering the Rapid Eye Technology processes and techniques. Education and practice sessions provide opportunities to master skills while combining processes to maximize client experience. This course is a home-study program combined with a four-day workshop. Students must have a current RET certificate to take this course, which consists of the following:

- Document 100 hours of RET sessions with clients
- Master and understand the purpose of wand techniques and processes
- Integrate the immediate release technique and other advanced techniques in a session
- Identify a pattern and process that pattern in every session
- Learn how to use body walks as a reframing and cognitive understanding of each issue
- Learn how to use specialty manuals
- Gain experience in group demonstrations
- Learn how to market RET through workshops
- Learn how to do phone sessions

▶ **Enhanced Master Rapid Eye Technology Advanced Course:** This four-day workshop addresses tailoring sessions to clients, mixing and matching tools, and identifying archetypes or patterns. Students must have a current MRET certificate to take this course. Students will learn:

- How to process multiple issues in a group setting
- Enhanced methods for integrating the skills for life
- How to work with empathic and highly sensitive people

- How to combine energy work and RET
- How to work with specific diseases and organs
- How to work with chakra energies
- Additional advanced RET techniques

· · · · · · · · · · · · · · · · ·

Continuing Education Units: Available in some states. Ask your instructor.

Certification: Yes, granted by the Rapid Eye Institute. The Rapid Eye Institute is licensed by the Oregon Department of Education: Career School License #1792.

Participants: Must be eighteen years of age or older. Previous training in related fields is an asset, but not required.

Code of Ethics/Standards of Practice: Yes.

Suggested Reading

Johnson, Ranae. *Reclaim Your Light through the Miracle of Rapid Eye Technology.* Salem, OR: RainTree Press, 1996.

———. *Winter's Flower.* Salem, OR: RainTree Press, 1992.

Availability: Home-study courses may be taken anywhere, but most RET technicians are located in the United States. You can find technicians at www.rapideyetechnology.com.

Resources

· ·

The Rapid Eye Institute, 581 Lancaster Dr. SE #270, Salem, OR 97317, 503-399-1181, RET@rapideyetechnology.com, www.rapideyetechnology.com

Bibliography

· ·

Johnson, Ranae, with Joseph Bennette. *Rapid Eye Technology: Discovering the Perfect Self within You.* Salem, OR: RainTree Press, 1994.

www.alternativesmagazine.com

www.rapideyetechnology.com

RESONANCE REPATTERNING

RESONANCE REPATTERNING uses sound, color, light, breathing patterns, movement, essential oils, and energetic touch to form more than sixty repatterning techniques for healing both psychological and emotional issues. Founded by Chloe Faith Wordsworth in 1990 and originally called Holographic Repatterning, Wordsworth later changed the name to Resonance Repatterning.

Wordsworth attributes her lifelong interest in complementary medicine to her parents, who practiced organic gardening and complementary medicine in England. Many years of study in Polarity Therapy, the five-element system of acupuncture, edu-kinesiology, and sound healing (especially through the methods of Sharry Edward's Sound Health Alternative and Resource Center) led Wordsworth to eventually combine a number of these elements to form the Resonance Repatterning system. According to Wordsworth's book, *Quantum Change Made Easy: Breakthroughs in Personal Transformation, Self-Healing, and Achieving the Best of Who You Are*, Resonance Repatterning is structured around a set of five basic principles. The following principles and keys are taken directly from *Quantum Change Made Easy*:

1. All matter consists of pulsing frequencies of energy.
2. We are energy beings living in an ocean of vibrating frequencies—the unified field.
3. The quality of our life depends on the quality of the frequencies we resonate with.
4. When we resonate with more beneficial, coherent frequencies, we naturally change ourselves, our attitudes, and our experience of life for the better.

5. We always have a point of choice to resonate with what is noncoherent and de-energizing or to resonate with what is coherent and life-enhancing.

In addition to the five principles, practitioners work with nine keys within the Resonance Repatterning system:

1. Energy: everything is energy and energy is everything.
2. Resonance: change your resonance, change your life.
3. Kinesthetics: you are wired for coherence and self-healing.
4. Orientation: oriented, you face the direction that nurtures your soul.
5. Problems: underneath every problem is an empowering truth.
6. Intention: all great outcomes begin with intention.
7. Repatterning: bring your hidden patterns to light.
8. Modalities: modalities harmonize and balance the flow of energy—Wordsworth uses the word "modality" to refer to a healing technique.
9. Action: every coherent action leads to more coherence.

In addition, Resonance Repatterning combines six of the seven major chakras from the Indian Ayurvedic healing tradition (brow chakra, earth chakra, air chakra, water chakra, ether chakra, and fire chakra, which are described in the introductory chapter on pages 3 and 5) with these nine keys to form a mandala, which is a geometric pattern used for meditation and healing. Using the mandala as a guide, the practitioner muscle checks the client to access frequencies, unconscious beliefs, brain hemisphere integration, and subtle energy fields within the client. Each point on the mandala represents an option for positive change. The practitioner identifies an option and then checks to see if it registers positive or negative with the client. By gently applying pressure on an arm, the amount of resistance displayed by the client tells the practitioner where to direct her attention. Once the practitioner finds an option that needs attention, she fine-tunes her approach and uses a variety of interventions to bring about a coherent alignment of the body, mind, and energy systems. Interventions may involve sound, color or light, movements, breathing techniques, essential oils, or energy techniques from other modalities such as Jin Shin Jyutsu (page 65) or Polarity Therapy (page 247).

At the end of the session, the practitioner again does a muscle check to verify that the client no longer resonates with the pattern of limitation and has moved into a pattern of growth. Throughout the treatment, the client does not relive past events or traumas. The muscle checking reveals information concerning problems the client is experiencing. Most often, the client is not aware of the source of the problem. Finally, the practitioner will do a muscle check to determine if there is an action the client needs to take to complete the healing.

Course Descriptions

The Resonance Repatterning Institute offers a comprehensive curriculum through seminars, workbooks, supplies, and DVDs. Seminars, which are held around the world, can be taken individually for personal use, or a complete series may be taken as a practitioner candidate.

To certify, an applicant must complete the six basic seminars, present documentation of sessions on themselves and others, give and receive sessions with at least two Certified Resonance Repatterning practitioners, and satisfactorily demonstrate to an approved designated observer the Resonance Repatterning system, processes, and skills identified in the certification manual.

▶ **010 Empowering Yourself** is a one-day seminar that teaches the five core principles of self-empowerment and the Resonance Repatterning system of kinesiology muscle checking. This seminar is a requirement for certification. Some of the things students learn are:

- How to muscle check themselves
- The *Principle of Coherence and the Coherence Continuum* for quantum change to promote energy coherence
- The *Principle of Energy Input* for quantum change: how to work with sound, light, color, breath, movement, and energetic contacts
- The *Principle of Orientation*: how to recognize when you are disoriented and how to reestablish balance and equilibrium

- The *Principle of Problems Changing into Opportunities*, which demonstrates how internal dissonant patterns create external problems
- The *Principle of Intention for a New Possibility*: how to resonate with your optimal intention and experience quantum change

▶ **020 Fundamentals** provides the foundation upon which all subsequent seminars are built. This seminar is a requirement for certification. This is a two-day course of instruction and practice in which students learn the following:

- The basic steps of the Resonance Repatterning Mandala and how to use it in sessions
- An in-depth understanding of the Resonance Repatterning muscle indicator system
- *The Principle of Resonance*: how to muscle check the dissonant resonance holding a problem in place, identify it, and transform it for self and others
- *The Principle of Repatterning*: four initial repatterning protocols for transforming noncoherent beliefs and negative perceptions in seeing, hearing, and writing
- Additional modalities for quantum change in the fields of sound, color and light, breath, movement, and energetic contacts

▶ **030 Transforming Primary Patterns** introduces students to the idea that the human mind is the primary pattern that controls them and their lives. This seminar is a requirement for certification. Students learn the five repatterning protocols that enhance their resonance with positive thoughts:

- *Appreciation Repatterning*: expand your heart's resonant field
- *Commitment Repatterning*: transform unconscious patterns
- *Creative Expression Repatterning*: overcome blocks and experience the joy of authentic creation
- *Negative Thoughts Repatterning*: transform negative energies, such as anger, worry, fear, or jealousy, into affirmative ways of thinking
- *Self-Image Repatterning*: identify and transform negative perceptions of yourself

- Additional modalities, including the safety energy locks of Jin Shin Jyutsu, physiophilosophy, tuning forks, Katsugen, and advanced Resonance Repatterning techniques

▶ **040 Transforming Unconscious Patterns** introduces patterns dealing with family dynamics. This class is a requirement for certification. Students will learn the following:

- *Reptilian Brain Repatterning*: the unconscious fight-flight survival mechanism and how to release its hold on present situations and relationships
- *Breath Repatterning*: releases any unconscious patterns stored as the result of disrupted breathing experiences—particularly the first breath after birth
- *Earlier Experience Repatterning*: releases an individual's resonance with needs not met in the womb or in childhood that set life patterns in motion
- *Parental Repatterning*: how to resonate with the higher learning parents have for their children
- *Compensation Repatterning*: how to identify outdated behavior patterns that no longer work
- *Integration for Growth Repatterning*: how to transform your resonance with recurring negative patterns and substitute those with positive patterns

Students also learn advanced techniques such as how to use tuning forks and the Quantum Healing Codes for vibrational sound healing, the color filter torch, cranial contacts for core balance, and Hanna Somatic Movements.

▶ **050 Transforming Chakra Patterns** introduces students to the Ayurvedic chakra system and its seven major concentrated reservoirs of energy that impact the body and its emotional responses. This class is a requirement for certification. Topics include:

- *Chakra repatterning*: balancing personal resonance in tandem with chakra energy
- *Disrupted energy repatterning*: balancing the expansion and relaxation pulsation of the chakras
- *Sound frequency repatterning*: identifying generational dissonance and the effect it has on the body-mind system
- *Life Cycle Repatterning*: clearing energetic obstructions in your cycles of creative activity
- Modalities that harmonize each chakra, including the Resonance Repatterning Fusion Process, Heart Entrainment for deeper intimacy, and additional techniques to balance the chakras, including essential oils and sound healing

▶ **060 Transforming Five Element and Meridian Patterns** introduces the student to the ancient Chinese five element and meridian way of natural healing. This seminar is a requirement for certification, including the following topics:

- The attributes of each element and meridian, and how to encourage balance and strengthen the flow of qi through the body-mind system by using tuning forks, the color filter torch, gentle contact, and essential oils on powerful meridian points
- *Meridian and Five Element Repatterning*: identify and transform noncoherent patterns that disrupt the flow of qi energy in the five elements and meridians
- *Seasonal Repatterning*: identify the stress and discomfort (including allergies, depression, or a depleted immune system) that occur for people during specific seasons and their accompanying personal transitions
- *24-Hour Time Cycle Repatterning*: Qi life energy ebbs and flows in the body throughout the day; identify the time of day when your energy drops and symptoms worsen and learn how to regulate your meridian balance throughout the day
- *Mu Point Repatterning*: address patterns of fear and phobias that create energetic and behavioral blocks and learn how to release them through the meridian "mu" points

- *Decision-Making Repatterning*: encourage creative decision making by balancing the five element energy flows
- *Five Element Qualities Repatterning*: learn how to resonate with the best, most coherent qualities of who you are and transform your interactions with yourself and others
- Learn new modalities for quantum change, including sound, movement, and breathing patterns for the five elements, the meridian consonant sounds, the meridian self-massage, mu acupuncture points, and pentatonic modes

Continuing Education Units: Available in 2010.

Certification: Peer-reviewed certification is provided by the independent, incorporated, member-operated Holographic Repatterning Association.

Participants: All who have an interest in self-growth and Resonance Repatterning are welcome.

Code of Ethics/Standards of Practice: Yes.

Availability: Resonance Repatterning practitioners and clinics are located throughout the world. To find a practitioner in your area, go to the Repatterning Practitioners Association's website at www.repatterning.org and www.resonancerepatterning.net.

Resources

The Resonance Repatterning Institute, PO Box 4578, Scottsdale, AZ 85261, info@resonancerepatterning.com, www.repatterninginstitute.net

Repatterning Practitioners Association, 10645 North Tatum Blvd., PMB#134, Suite C200, Phoenix, AZ 85028-3053, 800-685-2811, www.repatterning.org

Resonance Repatterning in Mexico: institutorrmx@gmail.com

Resonance Repatterning in Spain: www.patronesderesonancia.org

Resonance Repatterning Institute UK: info@resonancerepatterninguk.net, www.resonancerepatterninguk.net

Bibliography

Wordsworth, Chloe Faith, and Gail Noble. *Quantum Change Made Easy: Breakthroughs in Personal Transformation, Self-Healing, and Achieving the Best of Who You Are.* Scottsdale, AZ: Resonance Publishing, 2007.

www.repatterninginstitute.net

SHEN THERAPY®

SHEN IS AN ACRONYM FOR Special Human Emotional Nexus. Richard Pavek, scientist and founder of SHEN Therapy, postulates that the underlying cause of physiological disorder is long-term voluntary or involuntary repression of the emotions resulting from physical and emotional trauma. He suggests that it is not the experience of an emotion but the repression of it that causes physical dysfunction to appear in one or more organs or glands, leading to a wide range of symptoms throughout the body.

Pavek calls the field around and within the body the physioemotional field or the biofield. Within this physioemotional field, he theorizes there are eight emotional centers or regions that, with the exception of the region at the navel, correspond to traditional chakra locations (see pages 3 and 5). He places these emotional centers at the regions of the crown (top of the head), forehead, throat, heart, solar plexus (just below the sternum), navel, the top of the pubic bone, and at the root or base of the spine.

With SHEN Therapy, the practitioner does not balance the energy field as in other energy medicine disciplines. Rather, the practitioner works to open up the physioemotional field to help shift unwanted emotions to where they can be dissipated or released. The therapist places her hands lightly on the body over the locations of organs, glands, or emotional centers to facilitate the release or dissipation of disruptive emotions being held at these locations. With the release of these emotions, Pavek's theory postulates the client can be free of a physical or emotional dysfunction. He believes the release of these unwanted emotions can also help heal psychosomatic and somatoform disorders, when there are symptoms of pain or discomfort of some kind but no known cause.

The first session with a SHEN therapist takes about an hour and a half. The therapist observes the client immediately upon arrival for an appointment. The therapist notes the client's body posture as well as how he looks, how he walks, how he sits, where he puts his hands, and how he breathes. The client will be asked to report sudden recent emotions, unexpected memories, or unusual dreams in the recent past and also to provide a history of emotionally painful events.

Clients remain fully clothed with the exception of shoes, which are to be removed. The client is asked to lie down on a well-padded massage table or a couch. The therapist does a hand scan of the physioemotional field by running her hands about an inch above the body and noticing changes in temperature. The therapist then performs the treatment interventions depending upon the client's needs. While lightly placing the hands at various places upon the body, the therapist directs energy into and through the client's body. Sometimes the client may be directed to breathe in specific ways. The therapist may apply gentle pressure or rocking to accelerate the release process. The client often feels a deep sense of relaxation. The client and therapist may discuss any emotions experienced by the client during the treatment. Otherwise the sessions continue in a quiet atmosphere.

At the end of the session the therapist discusses with the client how emotions relate to health. Together they outline a program for the client consisting of breathing patterns, postures, movements, and expressions that encourage a more positive emotional state.

Check the Legalities section of this book for contacts in your area concerning massage laws. Some states require a SHEN practitioner to have a massage license because of the pressure and rocking techniques.

Course Descriptions

The following course descriptions are consistent with classes taught in Ireland, New Zealand, North America, and the United Kingdom. Applicants for certification must complete an internship with a mentor listed with the International SHEN Therapy Association. If none is available the applicant is put on a waiting list. Applicants must also be members of the association. Interns may not charge a fee for SHEN Therapy until they have completed the Clinical Skills Seminar.

▶ **Level 1. The SHEN Experience Course:** This is a foundational, experiential, two-day course for those interested in finding out what SHEN is all about, and where the students will gain a basic understanding of how their emotions work. They will have an opportunity to both give and receive four of SHEN Therapy's unique relaxation techniques. Topics include:

- How and why events affect people's lives
- How experiences with painful memories can cause negative behavior patterns
- The relationship between negative feelings and physical diseases

▶ **Level 2. "Letting Go of Your Past—The Gentle Art of Emotional Unfoldment":** This is a four-day workshop. The first two days follow the same curriculum as the Level 1 class. It expands upon the Level 1 techniques and adds four more for emotional release and self-empowerment.

▶ **Level 3. Emotional Empowerment Workshop:** This is an intensive experiential seminar that empowers the participants. Students give and receive at least twenty SHEN sessions under the guidance of instructors. The seminar takes seven days and offers a variety of SHEN techniques. Participants also receive a comprehensive handbook and clear instructional charts.

This workshop is especially for those students searching for a way of letting go of deeply rooted, painful emotions that inhibit life on the physical, emotional, mental, and spiritual levels. Over the seven days, students will gain a comprehensive understanding of how emotions work and why they can be so troubling.

▶ **SHEN Clinical Skills Seminar:** This seminar comprises lectures, group practice, and the opportunity to give and receive at least twenty SHEN sessions. The seminars last eight days. Interns must take them twice, once at the beginning of the internship and again at the end of the internship. There may be a written examination during the second seminar.

A partial list of subjects follows:

- Initial and pre-session SHEN interview techniques
- Broaching delicate subjects

- Observing the client's body motion and postural clues
- Development of good session planning
- Following the client's changes on the table
- Table coaching: verbal and nonverbal coaching techniques
- Developing "intuition": becoming responsive to subtle cues
- SHEN in the external portion of the biofield, pros and cons
- Maintaining appropriate intern-client boundaries
- Intern and client expectations
- Functional conditions versus organic dysfunction
- What can and cannot be expected of SHEN
- Evaluations of chronic pain
- Starting and promoting a SHEN practice
- Interfacing with other health professionals
- Presenting SHEN to health-care institutions

. . . .

Continuing Education Units: Yes. Provider approved by the California Board of Registered Nursing, Provider No. 8484, for 60 contact hours per section. Accepted as continuing education by the American Massage Therapy Association.

Certification: Yes. Granted by the International SHEN Therapy Association via the certification committee.

Participants: Anyone may attend Levels 1–3. In order to enroll in the professional training program, students must be members of the International SHEN Therapy Association.

Code of Ethics/Standards of Practice: Yes.

Suggested Reading
Pavek, Richard R. *Handbook of SHEN*. Sausalito, CA: SHEN Therapy Institute, 1987.

Availability: Classes are available in Canada, Greece, Ireland, New Zealand, the United Kingdom, and the United States. For a session in your area go to www .SHENtherapy.net.

Resources

SHEN Therapy Institute, International SHEN Therapy Association, 20 Yellow
Ferry Harbor, Sausalito, CA 94965, 415-332-2593, SHEN_ISTA@hotmail
.com, www.SHENtherapy.info

The SHEN Center, 311 Cantrell, Calgary SW, Alberta T2W 2A3, 403-282-7888,

vaneceagreene@shaw.ca

The Heart of Ireland SHEN Centre, Edgeworthstown, Co. Longford, 043-71156,
deirdreleavy@eircom.net, shentherapy@eircom.net, www.shentherapy.ie

Kimberly House, Severnside South, Bewdley, Worcestershire DY12 2DX, (44)
1299 401407

New Zealand: PO Box 25673 St Heliers, Auckland 1740 NZ (64) 9 528 6735

Bibliography

Pavek, Richard R. *Handbook of SHEN*. Sausalito, CA: SHEN Therapy Institute,
1987.

www.holisticjunction.com

www.shentherapy.info

www.shentherapy.ie

www.shenworks.com

TELLINGTON TTOUCH™

FOUNDER LINDA TELLINGTON-JONES, PHD (Hon), developed Tellington TTouch in 1983 as a form of therapy specifically for animals. It consists of a variety of circular touching patterns to build the animal's confidence, instill cooporation, enhance the ability and willingness to learn, and promote good health. The intent of the TTouch is to activate the function of the cells and awaken cellular intelligence. As Tellington-Jones says in her book *Getting in TTouch with Your Dog*, "You can liken it to turning on the electric lights of the body." Tellington TTouch is used by animal owners, trainers, breeders, veterinarians, zoo personnel, and shelter workers to help alleviate an animal's excessive noise and chewing, leash pulling, jumping, aggressive behavior, extreme fear and shyness, resistance to grooming, excitability and nervousness, car sickness, and problems associated with aging. Much of Tellington-Jones's work comes from an extensive period of study she did with Dr. Moshe Feldenkrais. Dr. Feldenkrais's program uses movement to integrate the mind and the body in unusual ways, thus stimulating the nervous system.

Studies done at the Biofeedback Institute in Boulder, Colorado, revealed a stimulation of four different brain waves in both humans and horses as a response to one of the Tellington TTouch techniques. Normal touch or massage did not have this effect. Through extensive observations of horses, this study further concluded that TTouch had a positive effect on the animals' ability to learn.

A typical session is fifteen to twenty minutes long and takes place in a quiet setting where the animal is as comfortable and relaxed as possible. Depending on the animal and the problems the animal has, practitioners use a combination of over a dozen different TTouches and hand positions to bring body awareness to the animal. The animal can then be eased into further techniques that release pain, reduce fear, and change unwanted behavior. Several practitioners saw many positive results from this therapy and adopted it for person-to-person use, complete with three-year certification courses available in Tellington TTouch for humans in Europe. TTouch consists of circular movements of the skin, slides and lifts with the intent of activating cellular communication, and supporting the body's natural healing potential. It may be subject to the massage laws of your area. Please check the Legalities section of this book for information concerning local laws and regulations.

Course Descriptions

Courses involving horses or other large animals always have a handler for the animal present while the student is practicing techniques. Students learn not only techniques but also personality characteristics and the proper approach to an animal depending on its size and the degree of its problems. Some sessions are held at animal shelters, enabling the student to experience a wide variety of animals for practice.

After completing the first four trainings for dogs, cats, and other companion animals, students pursuing certification will be assigned a mentor and asked to keep a journal of their work to document case studies. Once the case studies are complete, the student receives a certificate as a practitioner-in-training and may begin to charge for his or her work. Upon completion of all course work, the applicant receives a Tellington TTouch Training Certificate, Practioner-1.

Applicants for certification for horses must also demonstrate a satisfactory background in dealing with horses. Practitioner-1 certification takes a minimum of two years. Practitioner-2 and Practitioner-3 certification is for applicants wishing to be instructors.

▶ **How to Become a TTouch Practitioner for Dogs, Cats, and Other Animal Companions:** This is a certification program for personal and professional use with animals. This program takes at least two years and requires a considerable investment of time and effort. It consists of six sessions (three per year) each lasting between five and seven days; these six sessions are broken down into two series, as described below. This program teaches students how to:

- Experience ways of working with dogs, cats, birds, and other companion animals
- Acquire easy-to-use skills to help with common behavior- and health-related problems
- Use techniques to help increase performance and reduce stress in show, obedience, agility, protection, and trial dogs
- Work with shelter animals to help them adapt to new environments
- Help animals recover from surgery and injury

Series 1: Four Trainings

In the first series, students learn about Tellington TTouch philosophy and techniques. Instructors demonstrate various techniques through lectures and hands-on work with dogs, cats, birds, and other small animals, with some of the sessions held at animal shelters. Students learn how to:

- Identify behavior, health, and temperament problems and learn creative solutions
- Work with cats to alleviate common issues such as aloofness, timidity, and aggression
- Use canine head collar, body wraps, and other TTouch training tools
- Use ground exercises, obstacles, and the playground of higher learning to increase the dog's learning capability
- Use TTouch for stress-free grooming

Series 1 gives the student a firm foundation in the work. Upon successful completion, students earn a certificate as a practitioner-in-training and are qualified to charge for work with individual animals and give short demonstrations.

Series 2: Two Trainings

In Series 2, students are assigned a mentor who will guide them between trainings while they keep an active journal of their work. The second series builds on the skills and tools students have learned and deepens their understanding of TTouch techniques and philosophy, including work with the individual needs of animals and satisfying the animals' owners. Students are required to:

- Attend three weeklong trainings
- Attend two weekend trainings when possible, given by TTouch practitioners or instructors
- Continue private sessions with companion animals
- Prepare case studies and learn how to market TTouch skills

Upon completion of the Series 1 and 2 course work, students receive a Tellington TTouch Training certificate that qualifies them to:

- Work privately with animals according to the agreement signed upon entry into the program
- Give one-day hands-on workshops as well as a series of hands-on trainings to groups
- Use the official TTouch logo on business cards, letterhead, and advertisements according to the terms of the agreement

In addition to the practitioner certification course, individual courses are offered to learn about horses and companion animals. Students can treat these classes as an introduction to the therapy and enroll in the certification course upon completion.

TTeam® Trainings with Horses

▶ **Hands-On Workshops:** One-day or two-day classes involving six to twenty participants and half as many horses. Students learn exercises done in-hand, Tellington TTouch techniques, and riding techniques. Participants have a hands-on opportunity to do the TTouch exercises.

▶ **One-Day Demonstration:** Using three to four horses, the practitioner demonstrates TTeam techniques. The purpose is to give an overview of what TTeam offers.

▶ **Two-Day Demonstrations:** TTeam instructors demonstrate TTouch, ground exercises, and some riding. Using four or five horses with a variety of problems and common resistances, instructors demonstrate the techniques and give the participants a chance to experience TTouch firsthand. Students also ride one or two of the horses to show how exercises can be done from the horse's back. They also demonstrate some of the equipment specific to TTeam.

▶ **Weeklong Trainings:** These consist of five to eight days with fifteen to twenty people for intensive hands-on experience in all phases of TTeam. The week usually begins with a weekend introduction for those who have never attended a TTeam training. These trainings are not competitive and foster an atmosphere of open ideas and information sharing. The procedure for becoming a practitioner is as follows:

- Attendance at a minimum of four weeklong trainings
- Completion of a formal application to the TTeam office stating a desire to be acknowledged as a TTeam practitioner, including a case history file of working with at least ten horses
- Completion of a written test available from the TTeam office

Students are then qualified to charge for their services with individuals and their horses and are encouraged to give presentations to horse clubs or 4-H groups.

· · · · · · · · · · · · · · · · ·

Continuing Education Units: No.

Certification: Yes. Offered by TTEAM and TTouch International.

Participants: Anyone with a love of animals. Some experience with horses is helpful but not required for working with horses.

Code of Ethics/Standards of Practice: No.

Suggested Reading

Tellington-Jones, Linda. *Getting in TTouch with Your Dog.* North Pomfret, VT: Trafalgar Square Publishing, 2001.

———. *The Ultimate Horse Behavior and Training Book: Enlightened and Revolutionary Solutions for the 21st Century.* North Pomfret, VT: Trafalgar Square Publishing, 2006.

Wendler, M. Cecilia, and Linda Tellington-Jones. *TTouch for Healthcare: The Health Professional's Guide to Tellington TTouch.* Santa Fe, NM: Tellington TTouch Training, 2008.

Availability: Tellington TTouch Training is available in twenty-seven countries. For a session with a practitioner in your area, go to www.ttouch.com.

Resources

· ·

Tellington TTouch Training, PO Box 3793, Santa Fe, NM 87506, 866-488-6824, info@TTouch.com, www.ttouch.com

Bibliography

· ·

Tellington-Jones, Linda. *Getting in TTouch with Your Dog*. North Pomfret, VT: Trafalgar Square Publishing, 2001.

www.ttouch.com

THERAPEUTIC TOUCH

IN THE 1970s, DOLORES KRIEGER, PHD, RN, was a professor of nursing at New York University, where she taught a course called Frontiers of Nursing to graduate nursing students. Throughout the course, she introduced a practice she called Therapeutic Touch (TT), one she had developed in 1972 with Dora Kunz, a naturally gifted healer. Therapeutic Touch is considered a scientifically based process that includes three basic assumptions: human beings consist of energy fields, illness is an imbalance in the flow of energy, and trained practitioners can intervene in an individual's energy field to assist the natural healing process. In 1979, Krieger published *The Therapeutic Touch* in which she described her work with Kunz and outlined the steps of practicing Therapeutic Touch with a larger audience.

According to Nurse Healers–Professional Associates International (NH–PAI), the official organization for Therapeutic Touch, the process of TT involves the following four phases:

1. Centering: Bringing body, mind, and emotion to a quiet, focused state of consciousness, using the breath, imagery, meditation, and/or visualizations so that the healer's full attention may be focused on the healing work.

2. Assessing: Feeling the energy field with the hands to check for imbalances and congested energy.

3. Intervention: Using techniques to balance, soothe, and clear the energy field.

4. Evaluation/Closure: Reassessing the energy field to determine the nature and duration of the treatment.

Before developing Therapeutic Touch, Krieger had studied Ayurvedic, Tibetan, and Chinese medicine; health practices such as yoga; and the techniques of Kunz and another noted healer, Oskar Estebany, who used the laying on of hands and prayer as his method of healing. Krieger and Kunz had met during a study for observing and recording the healing abilities of Estebany, a former colonel in the Hungarian cavalry who had become known during World War I for his methods of helping animals. During the war, when his own horse became ill, he knew it would be shot unless it could recover. Krieger reported in her first book that Estebany "did everything he could think of to help the horse. He massaged it, he caressed it, he talked to it, he prayed over it." Estebany kept up this work through the night and much to everyone's surprise, the horse was well in the morning. Other cavalrymen sought out Estebany when their horses were ill, and soon children of the cavalrymen brought their pets to him for healing. Although he never thought his healing abilities could extend to humans, Estebany found that they did, and he continued his healing work until he retired from the cavalry and immigrated to Canada. There, he allowed researchers and healers to examine his techniques. Krieger and Kunz were impressed with Estebany's gifts, but both believed that a healing practice didn't necessarily require a religious framework. Therapeutic Touch became their modern variation of the laying on of hands, without religious focus.

Supporters of Therapeutic Touch maintain that the practice reduces pain and anxiety, promotes relaxation, and assists in the body's natural ability to heal. Recent studies have tested the overall benefits of this holistic practice, as well as its effects on specific diseases. Barbara Denison, an Advanced Holistic Nurse, Board Certified (AHN-BC) with a master of science in nursing and clinical nurse specialty in adult health and illness, reported in the May–June 2004 issue of *Holistic Nursing Practice* on a pilot study designed to test the effectiveness of TT treatments on patients with fibromyalgia syndrome. Fibromyalgia symptoms generally include aches and pains in the neck, upper body, and hips, as well as stiffness, fatigue, and lethargy. While those receiving Therapeutic Touch, in a series of six weeks of treatments, have a statistically significant decrease in pain from before to after each individual session, there was not a large enough sample size to show more than a trend. An improvement in their quality of life was significant within the Therapeutic Touch group from before the first Therapeutic Touch treatment to after the last treatment when compared to a control group. A 2003 article in *Holistic Nursing Practice*, published by Gayle Newshan, PhD, NP, and Donna Schuller-Civitella, MPH, RN, reported the results of a large clinical study that looked specifically at the effects of TT on pain relief for a sample of 373 hospitalized patients. The patients were asked to complete a survey in which they rated their experience of pain; 12 percent of the patients who returned the survey indicated no change, but the rest of them reported some degree in pain relief. The study concluded that Therapeutic Touch, when provided in a clinical setting, may promote comfort and an increase in feelings of calm and well-being.

Currently, many health professionals, holistic practitioners, counselors, clergy, educators, and other individuals use Therapeutic Touch in their healing work. In addition, numerous universities and colleges throughout Canada and the United States offer it as part of their curriculum.

Course Descriptions

The following descriptions come from Barbara Denison, ARNP, AHN-BC, QTTC/P, an accredited Therapeutic Touch instructor by Nurse Healers–Professional Associates International. Keep in mind that class content varies depending on the instructor. At the time of this writing there is no certification program. However, NH-PAI has a peer-reviewed credentialing process to become recognized as a qualified TT practitioner and/or teacher, so that either QTTP or QTTT can be used as a designation after their name.

▶ **Basic Level Krieger and Kunz Therapeutic Touch** introduces beginning-level skills. Some of the objectives are to:

- Define Therapeutic Touch and examine its history and scientific basis
- Discuss the aspects of the Therapeutic Touch process: centering, assessment, intervention, and evaluation
- Develop a personal sense of pattern recognition of the human energy field
- Discuss beginning clinical issues affecting the integration of Therapeutic Touch into practice

- Identify three criteria to become a Therapeutic Touch practitioner as set forth by NH–PAI

▶ **Intermediate Level Krieger and Kunz Therapeutic Touch** is for students who wish to deepen their practice of Therapeutic Touch. Prerequisites include having completed at least 12 hours of content in a Basics/Beginner Therapeutic Touch program and consistent practice of Therapeutic Touch over at least a one-year period, averaging two clients per week. Students will:

- Participate in the Therapeutic Touch process by demonstrating the four aspects—centering, assessment, intervention, and evaluation—during group practice
- Discuss three theoretical frameworks supporting the process of Therapeutic Touch
- Discuss methods for integrating Therapeutic Touch into the practice setting
- Examine clinical applications of Therapeutic Touch
- Explore the use of complementary healing interventions as they relate to Therapeutic Touch

Advanced Level Krieger and Kunz Therapeutic Touch is for health-care professionals committed to TT practice and learning. Prerequisites include 12 hours of basic training, 14 hours of intermediate training, and a consistent, extended practice of Therapeutic Touch for a minimum of three to four years. Participants have the opportunity to:

- Examine the relationship of Therapeutic Touch to personal growth
- Study the relevant legal and ethical issues integral to the practice of Therapeutic Touch
- Discuss Therapeutic Touch research methods and findings of relevant and current TT research
- Critique the theoretical and philosophical base underlying Therapeutic Touch

· · · · · · · · · · · · · · · · ·

Continuing Education Units: Yes. Ask your instructor about them, as they vary in different countries and locations.

Certification: No. NH-PAI has a peer-reviewed credentialing process to become recognized as a Qualified TT practitioner and/or teacher, so that either QTTP or QTTT can be used as a designation after their name.

Participants: Therapeutic Touch is not limited to health-care providers; that's why Professional Associates International has intentionally been left in the name of Nurse Healers. Practitioners include people of all ages and from all walks of life. Qualities that could be considered prerequisites to learning Therapeutic Touch are the desire to heal, compassion, a sense of well-being, and the discipline to practice the process once it is learned.

Code of Ethics/Standards of Practice: Yes.

Suggested Reading

Krieger, Dolores. *Therapeutic Touch as Transpersonal Healing*. Englewood Cliffs, NJ: Lantern Books, 2002.

———. *Therapeutic Touch: How to Use Your Hands to Help or to Heal*. New York: Prentice Hall, 1979.

Kunz, Dora. *The Spiritual Dimension of Therapeutic Touch*. Rochester, VT: Bear & Company, 2004.

Availability: Classes can be found in Australia, Brazil, Canada, and the United States. For a session with a practitioner in your area, go to www.therapeutic-touch .org.

Resources

· ·

NH-PAI Inc., PO Box 419, Craryville, NY 12521, 518-325-1185, toll free
877-32NHPAI, nhpai@therapeutic-touch.org, www.therapeutic-touch.org

Bibliography

Krieger, Dolores, *Therapeutic Touch: How to Use Your Hands to Help or to Heal.*
    New York: Prentice Hall, 1979.

www.therapeutic-touch.org

www.bdenison.sbcusa.com

www.therapeutictouch.org

ZERO BALANCING

THE BASIC THEORY OF ZERO BALANCING (ZB) is that the body has both structure and energy. According to www.zerobalancing.com, "The structural body is what you can see and touch—bone, soft tissue, and all the body organs. The energy body is the seen and unseen movement, including muscular movements, movement of tissue fluids, cellular and molecular vibrations, movement within the body fields, and movement of the life force itself." The major source of structure in the body is the skeleton. According to John Hamwee in his book *Zero Balancing: Touching the Energy of Bone,* "The skeleton is one functional unit through which energy flows in an organized way." This approach allows practitioners to work with both the structural and energy bodies to achieve balance in their clients.

Fritz Frederick Smith, MD, founder of Zero Balancing, received a degree in zoology and chemistry and is a doctor of osteopathy and medicine. After practicing traditional allopathic medicine for seventeen years, he observed an acupuncture treatment and became intrigued with energy medicine and completed advanced degrees in acupuncture. Influenced by his father, who was a chiropractor, and his own studies as an osteopathic physician, he worked to further explain the relationship between the body's structure and how it is influenced by energy as it is conceived in traditional Chinese medicine.

In his book, *Inner Bridges: A Guide to Energy Movement and Body Structure,* Smith postulates that energy in the body has three forms. (1) The background energy field permeates and surrounds the body without inherent form. This energy field responds to the internal and external environment of the body and is directly responsive to thoughts, emotions, and physical movement. (2) Three vertical energy flows act as conduits or channels for energy passing through the body with the configurations of the body molding that energy into specific forms. The main central flow conducts currents of energy from the universe through the skull, backbone, pelvis, and legs to the earth. The second vertical flow begins at the top of each shoulder, runs down through the trunk of the body crossing at the abdomen, and joins the main central flow down the legs and into the earth. The third vertical flow begins at the collarbone and flows through the shoulders and down the arms. (3) Three internal energy flows circulate within the body along identifiable lines and patterns and enable the body to function as an individual unit. These deep-level internal energy flows consist of currents of energy moving through the bone and bone marrow. In this way, the skeleton becomes a complete functioning unit converting the deep energy flow into a figure eight. Soft tissues such as organs, muscles, and nerves contain the middle layer of internal energy flow. These pathways follow the meridians documented by traditional Chinese medicine. (For more information about meridians, read the Introduction.) The superficial layer of internal energy flows, known as *wei chi* in traditional Chinese medicine, is a coarser, denser layer of energy found just beneath the skin. Its purpose is to act as a buffer to the outside environment. It has a specific circulation path through the body and connects with the meridian layer.

Within the background energy field, there exist seven vortices of energy, commonly called chakras. Dr. Smith observed that the locations of the chakras correspond to the top and bottom of the spinal column and the major curves of the spine. The chakras connect with the background energy field, the vertical energy flows, and the internal energy flows.

Zero Balancing works with the deep level internal energy flow using a technique called the fulcrum. A fulcrum is a point where there is balance, like the center of a seesaw. By using touch, the therapist creates still points, or fulcrums, on which the body can balance. One way to create a fulcrum is by touching a bone close to the skin with a curved finger. The other way is to lightly put an area of the body into traction using the hands to gently lift and or stretch the area, creating a still point, or fulcrum, within that area. The still point allows balance to take place between the physical structure of the body and the energy flowing through it.

The desired outcome of a Zero Balancing session is to help relieve physical and mental symptoms, to improve the ability to deal with life stresses, and to organize energy fields to promote a sense of wholeness and well-being. A session generally takes thirty to forty minutes and is performed while the recipient is fully clothed, moving from a seated to a reclining position on the back. A practitioner evaluates the energy fields and energy flow in these two positions and balances the structures as needed. She may focus on body, mind, spirit, or all three, depending on where the fields are disturbed or the energy is blocked. Throughout the session, attention is given to the skeleton in particular, as it contains the deepest and strongest currents. Everything in a session is designed to promote maximum relaxation and a sense of well-being.

Course Descriptions

Applicants for the certification program must be licensed health-care professionals. Applicants must complete at least 100 hours of class time and 50 hours of practicum. The Zero Balancing Program offers two certification tracks: the intensive program and the self-paced program. Self-paced certification allows an individual to register separately for each class during the certification process. The intensive certification program is a specified course of study in which the student registers in advance for the entire program of courses. With both programs, the student is assigned a mentor to support the student during the certification process.

The Zero Balancing Health Association offers a wide variety of classes. The following three courses give an overall example of the teachings of Zero Balancing. Descriptions of the rest of the classes may be found at their website, www.zerobalancing.com.

▶ **Core Zero Balancing Program** is a 50-hour program taught in two 25-hour segments, **ZB I** and **ZB II**, separated by a period of practical experience. This core program is the foundation for all advanced ZB classes and skills.

In **Zero Balancing I**, students are encouraged to acquire significant practical experience with Zero Balancing protocol in preparation for Core ZB II. Students receive 25 continuing education units. This class is a requisite for Core ZB II and required for certification in Zero Balancing. Topics include:

- The basic Zero Balancing protocol, including theory and principles of Zero Balancing

- How to distinguish body energy and body structure through touch
- The skill involved in using energy as a working tool, including the "interface touch" used in all ZB sessions
- The energy anatomy of the skeleton
- The theory and application of fulcrums
- How to give a full Zero Balancing session

Zero Balancing II emphasizes the refined handling and controlling of energy. Students receive 25 continuing education units. This class is required for certification in Zero Balancing. Topics include:

- A review of the basic protocol with emphasis on quality touch, focus and positioning and how to deepen and expand your understanding of ZB's theory, principles, and techniques
- Advanced skills and coordination in handling energy, structure, and expanded states of consciousness
- Additional fulcrums necessary for the complete ZB protocol
- Framing a ZB session

▶ **The Art of Zero Balancing** is a four-day class that teaches students the art of putting it all together to create unique and compelling sessions for their clients. This class satisfies requirements for the certification program. Prerequisites include certification in Zero Balancing or completion of the Core ZB Program. The course teaches:

- Fulcrum art: how to craft fulcrums and sessions, including advanced fulcrums for body, mind, and spirit
- Working directly with wellness, life purpose, and mental health
- Advanced techniques such as amplifying experience by anchoring the session; "the pause" and its use, potential, and pitfalls; and the role of synchronicity in ZB

· · · · · · · · · · · · · · · · · ·

Continuing Education Units: Approved by National Certification Board for Therapeutic Massage and Bodywork, Provider #02578600; National Certification Commission for Acupuncture and Oriental Medicine, Provider #ACHB 554; California

Nurses Association, Provider #CEP 10954; Illinois Division of Professional Regulation for Physical Therapy, Provider #216-000129; Florida Board of Massage Therapy, Provider #50-4864; Maryland Board of Physical Therapy Examiners.

Certification: Requirements for the United States differ from those of the United Kingdom. Go to www.zerobalancing.com for information for your area. Certification is offered by the Zero Balancing Health Association.

Participants: Students accepted into the certification program must have a valid professional health-care license, such as massage therapist, doctor, nurse, or chiropractor in the state or country in which they practice. Both health-care providers and laypeople may take the classes.

Suggested Reading

Hamwee, John. *Zero Balancing: Touching the Energy of Bone.* Berkeley, CA: North Atlantic Books, 1999.

Smith, Fritz Frederick. *The Alchemy of Touch: Moving Towards Mastery through the Lens of Zero Balancing.* Taos, NM: Complementary Medicine Press, 2005.

———. *Inner Bridges: A Guide to Energy Movement and Body Structure.* Atlanta, GA: Humanics Publishing Group, 1986.

Availability: Classes are offered in Australia, Canada, Italy, Mexico, New Zealand, Switzerland, the United Kingdom, and the United States. To locate a Zero Balancing healing practitioner, go to www.zerobalancing.com.

Resources

· ·

Zero Balancing Health Association, Kings Contrivance Village Center, 8640 Guilford Road, Suite 240, Columbia, MD 21046, 410-381-8956, ZBHA@zerobalancing.com (USA), info@zerobalancinguk.org (UK)

ZBANZA@xtra.co.nz (New Zealand), www.zerobalancing.com

Bibliography

Hamwee, John. *Zero Balancing: Touching the Energy of Bone.* Berkeley, CA: North Atlantic Books, 1999.

Smith, Fritz Frederick. *Inner Bridges: A Guide to Energy Movement and Body Structure.* Atlanta, GA: Humanics Publishing Group, 1986.

www.zerobalancing.com

SPIRITUAL

ALL THE MODALITIES DISCUSSED IN THIS SECTION USE spirituality or religion as an important part of their healing processes. For example, Healing Touch Spiritual Ministries has ties to Christianity. While it could be argued that all forms of energetic healing are spiritual in nature, the modalities with roots in Eastern cultures concentrate on the energy flowing through and around the body while the Western modalities prefer modern science to back up their work. Sometimes it is a fine line whether a modality is spiritual in nature or shamanic, but modalities that show a tendency toward shamanic work are grouped and discussed in Section 4.

In this section, it is helpful to keep in mind the distinctions that are drawn between spirituality and religion. A religion is a specific form of worship or faith in a deity or deities adhered to by an organized group of people with the same belief patterns. Religion is usually structured with a leader who is a proponent of a specific belief system with followers who choose to commit themselves to those teachings and to the deity specified by the leader of the group. Religions have specific rituals, rules, and ceremonies that augment their belief systems.

While religion is organized, spirituality is an individualized faith that does not require a leader or a congregation coming together to worship in rituals and ceremonies. Spirituality involves a very personal experience of inner discovery, often using meditation as a tool to create a higher state of awareness of physical and nonphysical surroundings. Spirituality is the recognition that there is something beyond the five senses that influences human behavior and gives meaning to existence beyond our everyday experiences. A person can be both religious and at the same time deeply spiritual, or a person can be spiritual and not have a religious faith or be a participant in any religious activities.

Some of my students have asked me about the difference between spirituality and metaphysics. Spirituality includes a belief in a supreme being or beings and metaphysics does not. Simply put, metaphysics can be defined as "beyond the physical," and has been called a soft science in that metaphysics studies forces that cannot be touched, seen, or heard. Metaphysics studies the fundamental nature of all reality and things that transcend the natural order of existence and cannot be studied by scientific observation and experimentation.

ATTUNEMENT THERAPY

ATTUNEMENT THERAPY ORIGINATED in the work of Lloyd Arthur Meeker. After a period of personal questioning and research into spirituality, in 1932, Meeker awoke to his own spiritual commission. He began teaching, speaking, and writing under the name of Uranda and developed a healing practice using what he called the "radiant current" in a process he described as attunement.

Attunement Therapy uses a system of "gateway points," which line up with the acupuncture points along the meridians as conceived by traditional Chinese medicine. Using light touch or with hands a few inches above the body, practitioners direct energy through their hands to these gateway points, which unblocks the congested energy that can lead to disease. According to attunement theory, the endocrine glands represent a positive force of energy, and the chakra system is the naturally responsive counterpart. Endocrine glands produce and secrete hormones directly into the bloodstream to regulate growth, metabolic processes, and the activities of the organs, while the chakras help process chi. Together, they regulate the life force energy.

Each endocrine gland is said to be a "portal of radiant light energy" connecting to a level of spiritual expression. Attunement Therapy recognizes seven levels of spiritual expression. The following chart shows the relationship between the endocrine glands and seven levels of spiritual expression.

Level	Gland	Divine Spirit / Radiation	Human Expression	Opposite
Seventh	Pineal	Love	Love	Hate
Sixth	Pituitary	Truth	Wisdom	Lies / ignorance
Fifth	Thyroid	Life	Radiance	Death / tarnished
Fourth	Thymus	Purification	Assurance	Defile / insecurity
Third	Islets of Langerhans	Blessing	Realization	Cursing / spiritual
Second	Adrenals	Single eye	Tranquility	Stress / dissipation
First	Gonads	New earth	Patience	Impatience / infertile

Practitioners work with more than just the endocrine glands. The therapy has two parts. The first part focuses on techniques that do not require touch to bring balance to the various organs and systems of the body. The second half of the treatment involves the spiritual cosmology surrounding the energetic work. The practitioner helps the client focus on positive spiritual expression to more closely align with the client's personal inner God being. This keeps the healing work sacred.

A session begins with a client interview to determine what issues are at hand. The client reclines on a massage table faceup and fully clothed. The practitioner attunes to and focuses on the client's inner divinity at all times. The interventions begin with the practitioner placing one hand at the side of the client's head and the other at the base of the neck to balance the energy flow coming up the spine. The practitioner then opens the "portals of light" for each endocrine gland by placing the hands one and a half inches above the skin over each gland. The practitioner sets an intention to open a spiritual pathway at each point.

Techniques may also involve the lymphatic and immune systems, the organs, the skeletal system, the circulatory system, and other parts of the body. The practitioner uses his or her sensitivity to energetically work with the vibrational field of the client to balance the organs, body systems, and meridians.

When the client presents emotional issues or physical problems caused by emotional issues, the client is supported by means of counseling to release negative expressions and to learn to express positive attitudes of love, forgiveness, and gratitude.

A practitioner may also accompany a client to a hospital or clinic to prepare the client energetically for a surgery or other invasive treatment and to rebalance the field afterward. When the practitioner is not allowed to stay with the client, as in a surgery, the practitioner continues to work from a distance.

Course Descriptions

The International Association of Attunement Practitioners (IAAP) provides instruction and certification in Attunement Therapy. Upon completion of requirements, students may apply for certification as an Attunement Practitioner, an Advanced Attunement Practitioner, an Attunement Master, or an Attunement-Master Teacher. The following class descriptions come from the International Association of Attunement Practitioners website.

▶ **The Attunement Initiation** is a one-day workshop introducing the theory of Attunement and allowing the student to experience the process. It is a prerequisite for people who want to take the practitioner's courses. Topics include:

- The working of the One Law
- Union with the creator
- The energies of the endocrine system
- Self-attunement
- The energies of the chakra system
- The healing power of unconditional love
- Pneumaplasm: the connection between spirit and form

▶ **The Attunement Practitioner's Course** is a five-month course taught in five sequential weekends. The course addresses the entire Attunement process, the spiritual underpinnings of Attunement, and the techniques. The Attunement Initiation is a prerequisite. Topics include:

- Understanding the spirit, heart, mind, and body connection
- Heart–thymus perception versus heart–chakra perception
- Use of conscious intent and focus
- Self-attunement
- Seven endocrine glands
- Seven levels of attunement radiation
- Pneumaplasm, what it is and how it works
- Spiritual rhythms and cycles in attunement
- Spiritual control patterns and their use in attunement
- Pregnancy, birth, hospitals, doctors, surgery, dying, and death

▶ **Advanced Attunement Practitioner Training** consists of over 30 hours of training spread out over several one-day classes. The focus is on the spiritual principles in attunement, ethics, and history. The Attunement Practitioner's Course is a prerequisite. Topics include:

- Cycles of human growth and maturing
- Use of consciousness to create and discreate
- Team attunement
- Opening the seven seals
- Setting up an attunement practice
- Spiritual psychiatry and attunement
- Attunement practitioner's code and ethics

. . . .

Continuing Education Units: Some instructors offer CEUs depending on their background and location. Ask your instructor.

Certification: Yes. The International Association of Attunement Practitioners board of directors governs the instruction and certification process. Qualified students may apply for certification as an Attunement Practitioner, an Advanced Attunement Practitioner, an Attunement Master, or an Attunement-Master Teacher.

Participants: Attunement is open to everyone.

Code of Ethics/Standards of Practice: They have an Attunement Practitioner's Code.

Suggested Reading

Jorgensen, Chris. *Attunement: Love Made Visible*. Kansas City, MO: Soli Printing, 2004.

———. *A Beginner's Guide to Attunement: The Energy of Being*. Kansas City, MO: Soli Printing, 2004.

Shier, Andrew. *Attunement: A Way of Life*. Hancock, NH: Andrew Shier Publications, 1996.

Availability: Classes are offered throughout the United States. To locate a class or a session in your area, go to www.attunementpractitioners.org .

Resources

International Association of Attunement Practitioners, 1600 Genessee Street, Suite 502, Kansas City, MO 64102, chrisj@heartattune.com, www.attune mentpractitioners.org

Bibliography

www.attunementpractitioners.org

www.heartattune.com

www.geocities.com

HEALING TOUCH SPIRITUAL MINISTRY

THE CURRICULUM OF HEALING TOUCH SPIRITUAL MINISTRY (HTSM) combines the spiritual and scriptural aspects of a healing ministry for people of the Christian faith. The programs promote the art of nursing as well as the art of spiritual presence. Linda Smith, founder of Healing Touch Spiritual Ministry, comes from a background of critical care nursing, nursing education, and home health and hospice care with a specialty in compassionate care for the dying.

In 1997, Smith founded Healing Touch Spiritual Ministry, which later became the Institute of Spiritual Healing and Aromatherapy. Her vision was to bring hands-on healing back to the Christian communities. With a Christian background and a firm knowledge of the history of healing and the laying on of hands frequently mentioned in the Bible, Smith came to believe that the roots of healing can be traced back further than the history taught in Healing Touch classes. In Healing Touch, as described on pages 221–226, practitioners are taught to use a light touch of their hands to balance and clear the human energy system. The focus is on the energy field, which permeates and surrounds the body, and the energy centers, or chakras, found in the energy field, that regulate the flow of energy from the energy field to the physical body.

Beginning with the hand-laying techniques taught by the Healing Touch Program, Smith added prayer and anointing with oils to form her own healing program. Healing Touch Spiritual Ministry therapists use an essential oil for anointing purposes. An essential oil is a concentrated liquid distilled from a plant that carries a distinctive scent or essence of that plant. It is the living lifeblood of the plant and carries a vibrational frequency that can be healing for the whole person—body, mind, and spirit. The early Christians were very successful in healing people physically, emotionally, and spiritually. They innocently tapped into three forms of vibrational healing when they prayed, laid on hands, and anointed with healing oils. The essential oil is usually applied to the hands, feet, forehead, or the top of the head, depending on the technique being used by the healer.

Smith has divided the laying on of hands into four simple steps. The first step is for the practitioner to center herself by quieting the mind and putting aside personal issues. Then the practitioner sets an intention for the highest good of the client. The practitioner takes the time to breathe and reconnect to God while setting the intention.

An assessment of the energy field using the hands and/or a pendulum tells the practitioner about areas needing work. And lastly the practitioner performs the healing techniques while being open to the power of God flowing through her hands. The practitioner is an instrument of God's healing grace.

A session, as taught by Smith, begins with an intake interview to acquire the client's medical history and to discuss the client's issue or issues. The practitioner begins by placing his or her hands on the client while praying for the person to receive God's healing and by visualizing divine blessings entering the client. The practitioner will anoint the client with an essential oil, frequently on the hands or feet, and end the session with an affirmative prayer.

Course Descriptions

After a decade of offering HTSM classes, Linda Smith and her colleagues divided the growing curriculum into two distinct but complementary paths: the Healing Touch Spiritual Ministry Program (HTSM) and the Certification in Clinical Aromatherapy Program (CCA). As a way to govern both of these fields of study, they also created the Institute of Spiritual Healing and Aromatherapy (ISHA) as a governing body to meet the needs of those who want to learn how to integrate prayer, hands-on healing, and anointing with essential oils. Each program offered by ISHA has its own curriculum leading to completion or certification, ongoing continuing educational offerings, and instructor training. For more information about the aromatherapy certification program, go to their website, www.ishaaromatherapy.com.

The Basic Healing Practitioner Program

▶ **HTSM 101 Introduction to Healing Ministry** is a one-day, 8-hour class that may be taken at any time in the curriculum. Students receive hands-on experience and guided meditations. Topics include:

- The history of healing in Christianity
- Hand-laying techniques
- Roles of prayer and belief
- Developing a healing presence

▶ **HTSM 102 Introduction to Judeo-Christian Anointing** is a one-day, 8-hour class that may be taken at any time in the curriculum. Topics include:

- Anointing in the Judeo–Christian story and how it got lost in history
- Nine essential oils that have been traditionally used for anointing for spiritual and physical healing in the Bible
- Anointing combined with hand-laying techniques
- Additional simple healing techniques

▶ **HTSM 103 Using Your Hands to Heal** is a 16-hour, two-day course for those who desire to do healing work from a spiritual ministry perspective. The course incorporates a variety of healing modalities as they have emerged from the hand-laying techniques found in the Christian heritage. Topics include:

- Bioenergetic healing principles within a spiritual ministry focus
- Distance healing
- Meditation
- Working with the human energy field
- The path of the healing practitioner

▶ **HTSM 104 Forming a Healing Practice** is a 16-hour, two-day course for those students who have completed HTSM 103 and wish to deepen their healing ministry practice. The emphasis is on models of healing within present-day church and ministry settings and ways to integrate Healing Touch Spiritual Ministry into a church or parish ministry or an institutional setting such as a retreat center, hospice, or hospital. Topics include:

- Advanced intervention methods to help with specific healing needs
- Conducting intake interviews
- How to document client sessions
- Bioenergetic client assessment
- Back and neck techniques
- Conducting a 1-hour healing session

▶ **HTSM 105 The Art of Listening to Spiritual Guidance** is a three-day, 24-hour course for students who have completed HTSM 103 and 104. This in-depth course encourages students to be aware of receiving spiritual guidance as they do their healing work, including exercises to tap into divine guidance. Topics include:

- Chelation as a way to deeper spiritual healing work
- Development of Higher Sense Perception
- Understanding spirits, angelic guides, and saints
- How to do self-healings

The Advanced Healing Practitioner Program

The Advanced Healing Practitioner course is for those who hold a certificate as a healing practitioner in Healing Touch Spiritual Ministry and desire further knowledge and practice in establishing healing ministries for churches, retreat settings, institutions, and private practice. After completing this program, students receive certification and are allowed to use the title HTSM Advanced Healing Practitioner.

▶ **HTSM 201 Review Day** is an optional class for advanced students that reviews all healing techniques taught in the basic five courses in preparation for the work in the Advanced Healing Practitioner Development Course A.

▶ **HTSM 202 Advanced Healing Practitioner Development: Course A** is a 30-hour course for students who have completed the practitioner program and would like to become an Advanced Healing Practitioner in a healing ministry setting. The Basic Healing Practitioner certificate is a prerequisite. Topics include:

- Developing a vision for a Christian ministry practice of prayer
- Hands-on healing and anointing
- Case management
- Managing the mentor/apprentice relationship
- Various advanced techniques

▶ **HTSM Advanced Healing Practitioner Development: Course B** is for students who have completed Course A and a six- to twelve-month mentorship in Healing Touch Spiritual Ministry. This 30-hour course focuses on course completion and group healing work, culminating in students, presenting their vision for their own healing practice.

. . . .

Continuing Education Units: Certificates of attendance are granted to all those completing a course through the Institute of Spiritual Healing and Aromatherapy Inc. (ISHA), which is approved as a provider of continuing education in nursing by the Colorado Nurses Association, which is accredited as an approver of continuing education in nursing by the American Nurses Credentialing Center's Commission on Accreditation. The program is also approved by the California Board of Registered Nurses, providing number #13181. ISHA is also approved by the National Certification Board for Therapeutic Massage and Bodywork (NCBTMB) as a continuing education provider.

Certification: The Healing Touch Program certification board offers certification to Healing Touch Spiritual Ministries applicants. ISHA is also an approved school through the American Association of Drugless Practitioners (AADP). Students completing the Advanced Healing Practitioner Program through ISHA may apply to AADP for certification as a Certified Holistic Health Practitioner (CHHP).

Participants: Parish nurses, hospice and hospital nurses, prayer teams, chaplains, ministers, massage therapists, bodyworkers, and laypeople are all welcome to participate in this program.

Code of Ethics/Standards of Practice: Yes.

Suggested Reading

Smith, Linda. *Called into Healing: Reclaiming Our Judeo-Christian Legacy of Healing Touch*, 2nd edition. Arvada, CO: HTSM Press, 2006.

———. *Healing Oils, Healing Hands*, 2nd edition. Arvada, CO: HTSM Press, 2008.

Availability: Classes are offered throughout the United States, Europe, South Africa, and the Caribbean. For a session, e-mail staff@htspiritualministry.com and ask for a practitioner in your area.

Resources

The Institute of Spiritual Healing and Aromatherapy, PO Box 741239, Arvada, CO 80006, 303-467-7829, staff@htspiritualministry.com, www.ishahealing.com, www.htspiritualministry.com

Bibliography

Erickson, Lori. *The Healing Power of Touch*, 2006. www.beliefnet.com/Health/2006/04/The-Healing-Power-Of-Touch.aspx

Smith, Linda. *Healing Touch Spiritual Ministry—4 Simple Steps to the Laying on of Hands*, http://ezinearticles.com/?Healing-Touch-Spiritual-Ministry---4-Simple-Steps-to-the-Laying-On-Of-Hands&id=835451

www.htspiritualministry.com

www.localaccess.com

www.ishahealing.com

www.ishaaromatherapy.com

www.helpokc.com

INNER FOCUS

I NNER FOCUS SCHOOL FOR SOUL DIRECTED HEALING was founded by Dr. Alix-Sandra Parness, Doctor of Divinity, to harness the power of the soul in the process of healing. Parness calls it "Soul Directed Energy Healing" that requires both absolute presence and willingness on the part of the client and the healer. This connection activates the heart of the healer with the heart of the client and through this connection allows practitioners to direct healing energy from the level of their soul. The client often feels tingling sensations while the practitioner holds a healing intention. Both practitioner and client feel a higher sense of consciousness, which Parness refers to as "entering a stargate," a state where deep caring is understood and healing is unlimited.

According to Parness in an article written for a NaturalHealthWeb.com newsletter, one of the soul's objectives is to help solve conflicting life patterns and help us live in a state of unconditional love and light. She explains that each person has an individual soul that connects to a group soul and a planetary soul. Looking at one's relationships is a way to work through these conflicting patterns, which are present in personal relationships, group relationships, and relationships between societies. As individuals work through their own conflicting patterns, the world moves closer to a state of peace and love.

Parness is an ordained minister and Doctor of Divinity trained in many healing modalities, including Barbara Brennan and psychic surgery. She was a senior faculty member and national coordinator of the School of Energy Mastery, and founded the Inner Focus Church in 1991 and later in 1994 the Inner Focus School for Soul Directed Advanced Energy Healing. Through channeling, Parness has connected with the realms of higher energy to help create her healing work. Her goal is to provide healing and enlightened information to uplift the consciousness of individuals and societies. To that end, Dr. Parness has opened the Mystery School for Divine Mastery in Las Vegas, Nevada. The Mystery School program is designed to answer the call of this time and address the increase of Light available to everyone.

Meditation is an important part of the training process for Soul Directed Energy Healers. They are trained to discover their soul's purpose and to help their clients access their own wisdom. Healers also use interactive guided imagery to help identify energy patterns in the physical body and the energy field, and sound therapy to help release congested energy that blocks the natural flow of energy through the body and the energy field.

In an Inner Focus healing session, the healer begins by asking the client if she is willing to let go of old ways of thinking and explore a new consciousness. When the client says yes, the energy field of the healer and the client form a relationship that allows the healing work to be done. The healer holds an intention to assist the client to heal and allows energy from her heart chakra to flow through her hands to the client. It is important that the client understands that someone truly cares and is willing to help resolve the issue. While the client works through her fears and begins to believe in herself, loving energies begin to build. The client relaxes and sometimes goes into an altered state of consciousness. She may experience images of color or rediscover friends not thought of in years. The healer performs techniques to aid in the healing process while holding the client in awareness and love.

Course Descriptions

Inner Focus is a professional school organized into a three-year curriculum of one prerequisite called Basic Training and ten modules that form the core training. All classes begin at 7:00 a.m. with a 1-hour meditation developed by Hindu teacher Bagwa Shri Rajneesh. Upon graduation from the tenth module, students may use the title Advanced Energy Healer.

Inner Focus has a certification program open to graduates who wish to create a professional practice. Students may apply to enter the certification program upon the completion of Module 9. In addition to graduation, applicants must provide documentation of 100 practicums (documented sessions with a client), a case study, and a minimum of eight one-on-one sessions with a mentor and completion of all ten modules to qualify for certification. Once certified the applicant may use the title of Certified Advanced Energy Healer.

▶ **Basic Training** is a combination of teaching and experiential work. The training is focused on learning how to release and heal patterns of disease, codependency, and abuse using the student's own awareness. Students are also taught how to use these techniques for themselves and others. Topics include:

- Clairvoyant scanning
- Energetics of the chakras
- Meditation
- Soul-centered healing
- Protection and cleansing
- Living from the heart
- Power of choice
- Connecting with the higher self and the inner child
- Transmissions of light
- Grounding higher dimensions
- Transformation of core issues

▶ **Inner Focus Healing School Curriculum: Modules 1 through 9**

Module 1: Energetic Anatomy

- Healership skill: An intimate experience with the chakra system and techniques such as the Awareness Release Technique to eliminate negative aspects within the body and corresponding chakras
- Chakras one through three
- Vision skill: Clairsentience
- Development skill: Self-discovery and finding your passion

Module 2: The Ascension Process

- Healership skill: Receiving guidance and deeper work with the Awareness Release Technique

- Chakras four through eight
- Vision skill: Clairvoyant scanning and tracking
- Development skill: Higher self-communication, learning to track energy, and soul mapping
- Anatomy: The immune system

Module 3: Magnetic Healing

- Healership skill: Chelation and radiatory healing
- Chakras two and four
- Vision skill: Scanning and tracking energy
- Developmental skill: Learning to hold energy, healing the inner child, and heart-centered healing
- Anatomy: The major organs

Module 4: Dynamic Healing I

- Healership skill: Sound healing and Two-Point Healing
- Chakras one and five
- Vision skill: Clairvoyant seeing of the energy field
- Clairaudience: Tuning in to your higher self, your inner voice
- Developmental skill: Learning to listen to guidance and follow energy
- Trusting guidance: Awakening the sound of the creative spirit
- Anatomy: The bones

Module 5: Dynamic Healing II

- Healership skill: Inner physician and Chakra Reconstruction Level 1
- Conscious healing techniques
- Chakras one and five
- Vision skill: Seeing the truth and bringing it forth
- Accessing truth and healing the fear of truth
- Learning the process of disease
- Working with the hara line

Module 6: Dance of Light and Shadow I

- Healership skill: Subpersonalities and energetic dialogue
- Chakras two and four
- Vision skill: Scanning and tracking
- Developmental skill: Leaning to follow and hold energy, learning about values, releasing incomplete cycles of abuse, and understanding the disease process

Module 7: Dance of Light and Shadow II

- Healership skill: Subpersonalities and energetic dialogue
- Vision skill: Seeing from the etheric template
- Development skill: Discovering unconscious parts of the self and tracking their actions in daily life
- Anatomy: The heart

Module 8: Personal Mastery Personal Power

- Healership skill: Soul mapping, self-evaluation and appreciation, and future vision
- Vision skills: Seeing with the eyes of the soul, speaking with the voice of the higher self
- Developmental skill: Tracking the power point for healing and allowing healing to happen

Module 9: Divine Relationships

- Healership skill: Consciously working with the masters, healing angels, and Monad
- Coming into power as a healer and cutting cords of attachment
- Crystal healing
- Vision skills: Seeing with the eyes of the soul and speaking through the voice of the higher self
- Developmental skill: Understanding the male/female relationship and communication skills

- Spiritual mastery
- Review and graduation

· · · · · · · · · · · · · · · · · · · ·

Continuing Education Units: Approved by the Holistic Nurses Association, accredited as an Approver of Continuing Education in Nursing by the American Nurses Credentialing Center's Commission on Accreditation. Inner Focus is also approved by the National Certification Board for Therapeutic Massage and Bodywork as a continuing education provider under category A.

Certification: The Inner Focus Healing School offers certification, in the form of Certified Advanced Energy Healer, to graduates of the four-year program.

Participants: Inner Focus invites anyone to attend classes regardless of training or background.

Code of Ethics/Standards of Practice: No.

Availability: School programs are offered in Madison and Racine, Wisconsin; Chicago, Illinois; and Toronto. To locate a practitioner, go to www.innerfocus.org.

Resources

Inner Focus, PO Box 82280, Las Vegas, NV 89180, 702-795-3832,
www.innerfocus.org

Bibliography

www.innerfocus.org

www.energyhealers.meetup.com

www.naturalhealthweb.com

LOMILOMI

THE AUTHORITIES WHO TOOK OVER the rule of the Hawaiian Islands in the 1820s discouraged Lomilomi, the practice of early native healing. Missionaries at that time perceived Hawaiian spiritual and healing practices as the work of the devil, and legislation in 1893 outlawed all healing and spiritual practices, use of the Hawaiian language, and hula dancing in Hawaii. Elders (older tribal members), Kahunas (keepers of secrets), and Lapa'au (specialists in healing) went into hiding and became known as aunties, uncles, papas, and daddies to keep their true identities secret. Until the Religious Freedom Act of 1978 (Public Law 95-341) was passed, most Hawaiian healers remained hidden.

In 1947, the Hawaiian Board of Massage was established and included Lomilomi as a form of Hawaiian massage. Many native elders, Lapa'au, and Kahunas refused to take the tests required to become certified. It wasn't until 2001, when legislation was passed to certify native practitioners without the need for testing, that native Hawaiians were allowed to provide Lomilomi without fear of reprisals from the Board of Massage.

The first Kahuna to share the secrets of Lomilomi was Auntie Margaret Machado, who lived on the big island. In 1973, she began teaching Lomilomi to anyone who had a sincere desire to learn, whether they were of Hawaiian descent or not. She was heavily criticized by native Hawaiians for revealing what was considered by many to be sacred Hawaiian secrets. However, she was the one who brought Lomilomi to the general public and opened the doors to make it legal for natives to practice without permission from the massage board.

Lomilomi is a combination of prayer, breath and energy work, and a variety of massage strokes combined to form a unique, spiritually based form of massage.

Technically, the Hawaiian word "Lomi" means massage, and Lomilomi means "going to and from." (Hawaiians give emphasis to a word by repeating it twice.) Pukui and Elbert's *Hawaiian Dictionary* defines Lomilomi as "to rub, press, crush, massage, to work in and out, as the claws of a contented cat."

While many forms of Lomilomi have been passed down orally between generations, the two most common styles of Lomilomi are (1) temple style, also known as Hawaiian temple style, and Ke Ala Hoku (pathway to the stars), and (2) Auntie Margaret's style, which is also known as big island style.

Since Lomilomi is done with long strokes and needs exposure of the skin, the massage room is kept warm as the client reclines on the table without any clothing, but covered with a towel. Lomilomi practitioners think of the therapy as a spiritual practice, and begin each session with a prayer to make themselves conduits for healing energy. Hawaiians consider human thoughts a form of energy and strive to maintain loving and compassionate ideas as they work. As the practitioner performs the stroking maneuvers characteristic of Lomilomi, he allows healing energy to enter the client. If the client expresses issues concerning emotional grief or serious physical complaints, the practitioner may refer the client to a Ho'oponopono practitioner. (During a session, the client explains the problem he or she is experiencing. The Ho'oponopono practitioner identifies with the problem, connects with a higher power, and makes an appeal to correct the erroneous thoughts that created the problem for both himself and the client. In doing so, the healer is practicing the belief that we are all one and that by healing him- or herself, the client is also healed. Ho'oponopono healers recognize that whenever a problem appears, the healer is always present as well, and that rectifying the problem within themselves also rectifies it in their clients' lives. The practitioner maintains that spiritual connection and clears and grounds him- or herself in the process of invoking mutual love and forgiveness.)

Most states and many countries require Lomilomi practitioners to have a massage license in order to maintain a professional practice. Check the Legalities section for information regarding whom to contact concerning legislation in your area.

Course Descriptions

The classes listed here are from the Hawaiian Healing Arts College and represent the type of content one can expect to cover as a student of Lomilomi, such as:

- The true meaning of Aloha—"in the presence of the divine breath"
- The historical applications and philosophy of Lomilomi
- The spiritual aspects of Lomilomi, including Huna, the ancient tradition of Polynesia
- Body mechanics that support career longevity
- Breathing techniques to clear and restore energy
- Release techniques for specific areas of tension
- Full-body Lomilomi sessions

▶ **Introduction to Lomilomi** is an introduction to the full-body Hawaiian massage treatment. Topics include:

- Finding congested areas in the body
- The four basic Lomilomi strokes
- Integrating spiritual aspects of ancient Hawaiian Kahunas with hands-on skills

▶ **Lomilomi II** expands upon the introductory class, including topics such as:

- Specific movements to release deep-seated tension
- Recognizing the difference between emotional and physical blockage
- Balancing the pineal gland, the spiritual connector
- Introduction of the use of elbows and forearms
- Huna breathwork techniques for clearing and restoring energy
- Sciatic, hamstring, I.T. band, and neck release techniques
- Producing a sense of well-being in the body, mind, and spirit
- The gift exchange of Aloha between healer and client

▶ **Special Intensive Introduction to Lomilomi** is a weeklong course for students coming from the mainland or other countries. It covers the same material as the Introduction to Lomilomi and Lomilomi II.

. . . .

Continuing Education Units: Through the National Certification Board for Therapeutic Massage and Bodywork (NCBTMB).

Certification: Hawaiian Healing Arts provides a certificate of completion at the end of each class.

Participants: Open to anyone who has an interest in the healing arts.

Code of Ethics/Standards of Practice: No.

Suggested Reading

Jim, Harry Uhane. *Wise Secrets of Aloha: Learn and Live the Sacred Art of Lomilomi*. San Francisco: Weiser, 2007.

Availability: Lomilomi classes are taught throughout the United States, Canada, Europe, and South Africa. For a practitioner near you, go the website of the Hawaiian Lomilomi Association, www.hawaiilomolomi.com.

Resources
. . . .

Hawaiian Lomilomi Association, PO Box 2356, Kealakua, HI 96750, www .hawaiilomolomi.com

Hawaiian Healing Arts, 1400 West Grand Avenue, Suite B, Grover Beach, CA 93433, 805-489-3714 ext. 11, tamara@lomilomi.com, www.lomilomi.com

Bibliography

Jim, Harry Uhane. *Wise Secrets of Aloha: Learn and Live the Sacred Art of Lomilomi.* San Francisco: Weiser, 2007.

Lakainapali, Tracey. "Hawaiian Lomi Lomi Massage." *Aloha International,* 2002.

Mondragon, Tamara. "History of Lomi Lomi." *Massage Magazine,* July 2000.

Pukui, Mary Kawena, and Samuel H. Elbert. *Hawaiian Dictionary.* Honolulu: University of Hawaii Press, 1986.

www.harryjimlomilomi.com

www.hawaiiantemplebodywork.com

www.lomilomi.com

MELCHIZEDEK METHOD

ALTON KAMADON, FOUNDER OF THE MELCHIZEDEK METHOD, is a clairvoyant channeler and spiritual teacher. From the spiritual teachings of Hinduism, Christianity, Mayan, Hebrew, and ancient Egyptian beliefs and Vedic concepts of healing, he created the Melchizedek Method, a holographic healing modality. This therapy seeks to enhance one's healing abilities, awaken the heart, and open the practitioner to unconditional love. Kamadon encourages practitioners to take full responsibility for their own health, well-being, and harmony with the environment as well as other people.

Mentioned twice in the Bible (Genesis 14:18 and Psalms 110:4) and frequently in New Age literature, Lord Melchizedek is a popular figure in the New Age movement. He is said to oversee the ascension process and the development of all beings in this universe. He is the head of the Order of Melchizedek, the priesthood and seminary college of the Great White Brotherhood. The Great White Brotherhood is made up of ascended masters who serve as benevolent teachers (of humans still on earth) from the realm of the spirit world. Ascended masters are people who have become "enlightened" (having learned all their earthly lessons) and no longer participate in the cycle of reincarnation.

Practitioners use holographic healing and rejuvenation to help heal disease and the effects of trauma. Activation of what Kamadon calls the hologram of love serves as the basis of the therapy. Practitioners call upon "the frequency of no limitation" and are taught to establish a constant flow of love to allow individuals to be in harmony with the creator of the universe and with a greater state of receptivity conducive to healing and rejuvenation. The Melchizedek Method also teaches the skill of transporting any part of the body or thought pattern into the higher dimensions to be cleansed and healed.

The work involved in the Melchizedek Method is done off the body for physical healing and the removal of unhealthy patterns of thought. The client usually rests on a massage table faceup. At the beginning of the session, the practitioner activates the hologram of love around both him- or herself and the client, then uses guided meditations and healing techniques to address and heal whatever issues the client presents and to help strengthen the client's spiritual health and harmony.

Course Descriptions

The classes listed here can be found on several websites. Instructors all teach the same material and vary only by personal experience. Levels 1 and 2 are often taught together in one workshop.

▶ **Level 1** introduces a spherical, conscious, holographic technique incorporating thought, color, light, and energy. Topics include:

- Holographic body computer healing
- The seven outer bodies
- Healing, cleansing, and rejuvenating the physical body
- Chakras, the flow of qi, and the meridian points
- Addressing personal issues such as weight problems, abundance consciousness, origins of thought forms, and opening the heart to unconditional love

▶ **Level 2** addresses the Orbital Holographic Merkaba of Love Light Body with advanced techniques. Topics include:

- Activating the Orbital Holographic Merkaba of Love Light Body
- Working with the platinum ray and the hermetic magic therapies
- Redirecting the elements to conform to and enhance reality
- Opening dimensional doorways to time travel with teleportation
- Retrieving beneficial acts and talents from past lives on Earth and other planets

- Amplifying the 33rd degree energies of the Adam Kadmon light body with rotational light color rays
- Cosmic thought wave patterning
- Healing with frequency light/color beams and silent sound
- Opening the heart to the cosmic vibration of unconditional love

▶ **Level 3** is an initiation into the Kamadon Order of Mastery of Knowledge, Wisdom, and Unconditional Love through Unity Merkaba activation. Topics include:

- Activating the Unity Merkaba of Love and integrating it with lessons from class levels 1 and 2
- Activating the 33 chakra system
- Activating the 33rd degree of the Adam Kamadon light body
- Understanding the consciousness of live matter
- Introduction to, working with, and receiving the divine encodings of the Melchizedek Elders
- Amplifying the time–space continuum

▶ **Level 4** embraces previous concepts of love and light and introduces students to the concept of God being omnipresent, omnipotent, and omniscient. Topics include:

- Manifesting the whole Adam Kamadon 33 layered light body
- Assimilating ascension
- How the morphic resonance merkabah works
- The universal omni-merkabah of love of multiple light bodies
- Pineal gland infinite fractal waveform expansion
- Elohim lords of light and Metatron
- Merging the red and blue rays
- The 33 shiva fire rings of cellular release
- Advanced Kamadon omni healing system

▶ **Level 5** is a visual presentation of 3-D animations on screen. Students learn to expand their hearts and consciousness. Topics include:

- Activations through the Melchizedek Method
- One path vision

- Fifth dimension Metatronic powerballs of love
- Zenith light body
- Structured water
- 33-strand DNA
- Zenith Orionis healing
- Cosmic spectrum Omkabah
- Power breathwork
- Kamadon cosmic spectrum healing

. . . .

Continuing Education Units: No.

Certification: Provided by Alton Kamadom or one of his other facilitators.

Participants: For lightworkers and anyone wanting to raise his healing ability to a new level.

Code of Ethics/ Standards of Practice: No.

Suggested Reading

Melchizedek, Drunvalo. *The Ancient Secret of the Flower of Life*, volume 1. Sedona, AZ: Light Technology Publishing, 1990.

Stone, Joshua David. *Revelations of a Melchizedek Initiate*. Sedona, AZ: Light Technology Publishing, 1998.

Resources

United States Melchizedek Center, PO Box 632, 267 Main Road, Capitan, NM, 575-354-4328, melchizedekcenter@yahoo.com, www.melchizedekusa.com

The Kamadon Academy, PO Box 930, Picton NSW, Australia 2571, +61 2 4677 3605, www.kamadonacademy.com

Bibliography

Melchizedek, Drunvalo. *The Ancient Secret of the Flower of Life,* volume 1. Sedona, AZ: Light Technology Publishing, 1990.

Stone, Joshua David. *Revelations of a Melchizedek Initiate.* Sedona, AZ: Light Technology Publishing, 1998.

www.akashicinsights.com

www.altmed.blogspot.com

www.holisticwebs.com

www.lifepositive.com

www.magicoftransformation.com

www.melchizedekmethod.com

www.kamadonlove.com

www.thegreatwhitelodge.org

NOETIC FIELD THERAPY™

NOETIC FIELD THERAPY (NFT) uses practiced focus and spiritual alignment techniques to find and clear blocks in the energy field. Robert D. Waterman, EdD, founder of Noetic Field Therapy, refers to the energy field as the noetic field, which he describes as an interactive psychospiritual energy that has an intelligence of its own and surrounds and penetrates the body. He believes that each person embodies a microcosmic noetic field that can converse with the universe, which is a macrocosmic noetic field.

The word "noetic" comes from the Greek word *nous*, meaning "spiritual mind" or "intelligence." The noetic field is universal and interactive. The therapy is a psychoenergetic program that works on a spiritual level. It is also is a cooperative interchange between the practitioner and client to create physical, emotional, mental, and spiritual balance and harmony.

According to Waterman, there are seven major layers to the human noetic field:

1. The physical layer is closest to the body and reflects physical trauma and health as well as physiological beliefs and emotions.
2. The etheric layer is also close to the body and contains a blueprint for the physical body. Meridians and chakras appear in this formation and interact with the endocrine and nervous systems.
3. The emotional layer can be found within two feet of the body. It contains the feelings and emotional reactions of an individual. It is also the source of passion, power, and the ability to forgive. Waterman calls it the peacemaker.

4. The imaginal layer also extends out about two feet from the body. Intention, self-image, visual learning, healing, manifestation, and success are generated and reflected at this level.

5. The archetypal layer extends about three feet from the body and contains the map of the individual's destiny.

6. The spiritual layer exists within the same space and reflects transcendence into the psychological, social, and physical realities. Waterman says that as the noetic field comes into balance, the spiritual layer becomes more evident.

7. Also within three feet of the body is the mental layer of the noetic field. It reflects the individual's beliefs, concepts, and attitudes.

Noetic Field Therapy uses symbolic and actual contact with the energy field to create the therapeutic process. According to Waterman at www.mystery-school .com, "By extending and opening our perceptive range and sensitivities, we can: 1) determine and deconstruct the beliefs and attitudes that countermand the sensibility of our faculties, 2) do practices and activities that attune and energize the relevant faculties, 3) assume the reality of the faculty and practice refining our discernment and 4) test each new level of belief, skill and understanding through a reductive protocol."

All Noetic Field Therapy protocols begin with a prayer and alignment with the higher consciousness, universal energy, or God. The client enters the noetic field with the practitioner, which brings about a shift into an altered state of consciousness that enhances the client's ability to access appropriate information, clarity, and forgiveness.

During a session, the client lies on a massage table. The first half of the session is done in silence while the practitioner uses her hands and a pendulum to find and clear blocks in the physical and emotional layers of the noetic field without touching the client. During the second half of the session, the practitioner works with the mental and spiritual layers of the field to assist the client in identifying limiting, judgmental beliefs. The practitioner provides focused statements of self-forgiveness that allow the client to release interfering beliefs and gain the greater awareness of the client as a soul. The end of the session is done in silence to allow the client to process and respond to the experience.

Sessions usually last from 1½ to 2 hours. Three sessions, at two-week intervals, are recommended with follow-up sessions every six to twelve months. Clients are asked to refrain from alcohol and sexual activity for three days after a session to prevent any disruption of the balancing of the noetic field.

Course Descriptions

The Association of Noetic Field Therapy Practitioners is administered by the Quimby Amenti Foundation, of which Robert Waterman is president. Members of the association are required to refrain from using alcohol, tobacco products, and psychotropic or recreational drugs.

The classes described below come from the Quimby Amenti Mystery School and make up the Noetic Field Therapy Practitioner Program. Other classes are also offered and descriptions may be found at www.mystery-school.com. Students receive a certificate of completion after finishing the Noetic Field Therapy Practitioner Program and receiving a balancing from an approved practitioner.

▶ **Neogenesis: Mystery School for the New Millennium** sends students on a quest to awaken their soul and create a conscious affiliation with the spiritual realms. Students learn to:

- Clear limiting and distorting beliefs
- Dissolve archetypal implants and status quo programming
- Establish a strong center
- Access the spirit
- Extend the five senses into multidimensional awareness
- Reveal the archetype and architecture of divine nature
- Participate in the universal field of love and intelligence
- Shift from a fear-/excuse-/ego-based reality to a love-/grace-/soul-based reality

▶ **Becoming a Spiritual Scientist™: A Course for Co-Creators** teaches students how to consciously co-create with the universe. It gives students the spiritual tools to move from conditioned reality into their divinity. Students will learn to:

- Shift from story-based to intentional reality
- Deepen their awareness of their partnership with God
- Practice self-mastery skills necessary to align with spiritual energies

▶ **Spiritual Scientist II: Mastering the Shift** provides an opportunity for students to strengthen their inner foundation, including:

- Access to holiness
- Shifting beyond shame and blame
- Advanced clearing techniques
- Creating new reference points
- The quantum matrix beyond the physical body
- The noetic (spiritual) mind

▶ **Noetic Field Therapy Practitioner Program** teaches students to align and balance the Noetic Field. It provides an opportunity for the advanced student or professional to work with greater spiritual depth. Prerequisite are Neogenesis Mystery School or Spiritual Science I and II. Applicants must also have experienced a Noetic Field Balancing. Topics include:

- Aligning with higher consciousness
- Finding blocks in the energy field
- Guiding the client
- Sensing changes in the field
- Exploration of the student's own multidimensional capacity
- Relating to the client through subtle fields of reality

. . . .

Continuing Education Units: Many of the classes offer Continuing Education Units for counselors and social workers in the state of New Mexico.

Certification: Yes.

Participants: Applicants must agree to abstain from recreational drugs, tobacco use, and alcohol.

Code of Ethics/Standards of Practice: Yes/no.

Suggested Reading

Waterman, Robert D. *Foot Prints of Eternity: Ancient Wisdom Applied to Modern Psychology*. West Conshohocken, PA: Infinity Publishing, 2006.

Availability: Currently classes are offered in New Mexico, Colorado, Texas, and Germany. For a list of practitioners and classes, go to www.mystery-school.com.

Resources

Quimby Amenti Foundation, 41 Verano Loop, Santa Fe, NM 87508, info@mystery-school.com, www.mystery-school.com

Noetic Field Therapy, info@energytherapy.net, www.noetic-field-therapy.com

Bibliography

www.aurialloux.com

www.ic4u.co.nz

www.mystery-school.com

www.noetic-field-therapy.com

www.soulbodytherapies.com

www.soul-centered-healing.com

ONE LIGHT HEALING TOUCH:
ENERGY HEALING AND MYSTERY SCHOOL

ONE LIGHT HEALING TOUCH (OLHT), created by Ron Lavin, MA, is a cultivated blend of spiritual healing techniques from a variety of cultures and traditions, such as esoteric energy healing, Shamanism, and holistic, hands-on healing. These techniques include the energy field, chakra clearing, color, male–female balancing, Christ consciousness, chelation, clairvoyance, archangel assistance, distance, Chiron, kundalini, Metatron, Infinite Soul, out-of-body and past-life healing, time-line, sacred initiations into higher states of consciousness, and self-healing practices, such as meditation, visualization, sound and breath work, movement, and sacred ceremony. In an article written for the *Poughkeepsie Journal*, Lavin states: "Healing is any activity that increases communication between one's body and spirit, allowing one to move towards greater levels of self-acceptance, integration, and wholeness."

Lavin's spiritual path began with a mystical experience when he was a young boy. Much later, in 1970, while on a break between college and law school, he went on a trip to Oaxaca, Mexico, and met a Zapotec shaman, and that meeting changed his life. He was so taken with the man that he stayed and studied with the shaman for more than a year, and returned home to attend school at the Berkeley Psychic Institute and study with a thirty-third-degree Mason and Rosicrucian master, Rev. Lewis Bostwick. Wanting more, Lavin studied with a Tibetan teacher, Native American shamans, Swift Deer and Sun Bear, Dr. Brugh Joy, Richard Moss, Margo Annand, Alex Tanous, PhD, Gordon Davidson, Corinne McLaughlin, Ingo Swan,

Stylianos "Daskalos" Atteshlis, PhD, and Robert Jaffe, MD, and read many of the teachings of Alice Bailey.

Lavin's studies led him to believe that rather than working with religions per se, he could conscientiously work directly with spiritual energy and with nature's own electromagnetic forces inherent in all living things to create health and healing. He believes a healer is a vessel for light who invokes these higher levels of pure healing essence and transfers it to another by means of will, intention, and love. Lavin has brought some fifty self-healing techniques and more than fifty-five techniques for healing on others together to form the One Light Healing Touch two-year healer training schools. He currently heads fourteen OLHT schools in the United States and Germany. Along with a private practice, he has participated in distance healing studies with the California Pacific Medical Center and the National Institutes of Health (NIH).

An OLHT session begins with the client reclining comfortably while the practitioner starts a spirit-to-spirit communication with the client and moves to an energy healing modality of one or a multiplicity of types. The healer asks for permission from both the client and the client's higher self before proceeding. To begin the process, the practitioner moves her hands a little above the body while reading and scanning for blocked energy. Once found, the healer may begin to remove blockages and then opens to the energetic flow and radiates energy into one or more of the chakras, organs, or glands of the client through her hands, heart, and eyes, using one or more of fifty-five techniques to bring healing to the client and restore harmony and balance. The practitioner ends the session by discussing what changes and energy practices a client might initiate in order to remain healthy and well balanced.

Course Descriptions

Ten schools for One Light Healing Touch are in Germany, and four in the United States. Students learn esoteric, shamanic, holistic, energetic, and hands-on techniques along with meditation, visualization, sound and breath work, movement and sacred ceremony. They offer certification at each of the basic, masters, and teachers levels in the form of a certificate of completion at the end of each course.

▶ **Basic Healer Training** takes a comprehensive and grounded approach to health and healing. It employs the school's nine-point protocol. Topics include:

- Teachings on the nature of energy
- Preparing and cleansing the healer
- Clearing the energy field
- Eliminating obsolete programming
- Connecting to Source
- Tools for self-healing, including meditation, visualization, sound and breath work, movement, and sacred ceremony

▶ **Masters Training** focuses on spiritual teachings, initiations, and healing techniques. Basic Healer Training is a prerequisite. Topics include:

- Merkabah Breath
- The Kundalini and fire breath
- Out-of-body healing
- Earth grid healing
- Shamanic soul retrieval and exploration of the Akashic records
- Team healing
- Crystal healing
- Archangel initiations

▶ **Teacher Training** provides of all the information necessary to open a One Light Healing Touch school and to train students to become healers. The areas of training include:

- Presenting spiritual- and energy-based healing concepts from the esoteric, shamanic, holistic, energetic, and hands-on healing schools of thought
- Leading students in fifty healing practices and fifty-five healing techniques in the categories of meditation, visualization, sound and breath work, movement, and sacred ceremony
- Initiating students into higher states of consciousness
- Reading individual students and holding group energy

- Channeling a higher source for answers to a student's questions
- Information on student enrollment, advertising, publicity, and supplies, including training manuals, training, and homework schedules

. . . .

Continuing Education Units: Offered to nurses and massage therapists through the New York State Nurses Association (NYSNA) and the National Certification Board for Therapeutic Massage and Bodywork (NCBTMB).

Certification: Students receive a certificate of completion at the end of each course.

Participants: Professionals in holistic health and all those seeking personal growth and self-healing, including primary caregivers, massage therapists, nurses, and human resource personnel.

Availability: Classes are offered in ten schools in Germany and four in the United States. To locate a practitioner, go to www.OneLightHealingTouch.com.

Resources

One Light Healing Touch, 140 Meads Cross Road, Stormville, NY 12582, 845-878-5165, ron@onelighthealingtouch.com, www.onelighthealingtouch.com

Bibliography

Hoffman, Mala. "Health Currents." *Woodstock Times*, June 27, 2002.

Lavin, Ron, and Penny Price Lavin. "Spiritual Hands-On Healing: The Past and Future of an Ancient Practice," *Poughkeepsie Journal*: Special Millennium Section, June 7, 1999.

www.cathyfrenchhealing.com

www.helpinghands-uk.com

www.olht.de

www.onelighthealingtouch.com

THE ONENESS BLESSING®:
DEEKSHA

THE ONENESS BLESSING, also known as "Oneness Deeksha" or simply Deeksha, is a process in which spiritual energy is transferred from individual to individual through the neocortex of the brain. The therapy originated in India and offers healing and a higher sense of awareness of the physical, emotional, mental, and spiritual bodies. Most seekers of the Oneness Blessing are looking for inner peace or awakening, and while there are many definitions of awakening, in this case awakening means the recognition of the ego as an illusion. According to practitioners of the Oneness Blessing, recognizing the ego as an illusion is far more than an intellectual experience. It can be considered an alternate form of consciousness where the individual no longer perceives himself as a separate entity, but rather as one with the universe and everything contained therein.

The founders of Oneness University and the Oneness Blessing, Sri Amma and Sri Bhagavan, believe that awakening is difficult for any one individual to experience through study, meditation, or prayer. By receiving the Oneness Blessing, the seeker can speed up the process considerably. According to Kiara Windrider in his book *Deeksha: The Fire from Heaven*, when a person receives the Oneness Blessing "it sets into motion a series of neurobiological shifts within the brain. Certain areas in the frontal lobes of the brain get activated, eventually resulting in a totally different perception of reality known as the enlightened state. Additionally, the corpus callosum, which connects the two brain hemispheres, is energized, allowing the brain to synchronize and work together, further stimulating the 90 percent of the brain's functions that lie dormant in most of us." (From the book *Deeksha* © 2006 by Kiara Windrider. Reprinted with permission of New World Library, Novato, CA. www.newworldlibrary.com.)

The giver of the Oneness Blessing places her hands over the top of the head of the receiver. The giver transfers energy to the brain of the receiver to initiate neurobiological changes within the brain. According to the Oneness University in India, some sixteen centers in the brain can be either activated or deactivated to bring about the shift in perception.

The therapy may be used for healing purposes as well by working with the energy field found around the body and the chakras. By placing his or her hands at the top of the head and setting an intention, the Oneness Blessing giver removes blockages from the field and the chakras to create balance in the energy system. It is not given to pregnant women after their sixteenth week.

Course Descriptions

The Oneness Blessing training program is growing and new classes, workshops, and conferences are continually being created. However, in order to give the Oneness Blessing, all students must go for a seven-day process at one of the campuses of the Oneness University.

▶ **Doors to Oneness Level 1** is a seven-day workshop offered at several of the Oneness University campuses and is taught by the guides of the university. Students are asked to refrain from eating meat, drinking alcohol, and using tobacco before experiencing the workshop. It is also recommended that students come only when they feel they are ready for this program. There is very little talking, and no cell phones, computers, or other forms of communication outside of the intensive are allowed. While the experience is different for each person, the program focuses on helping the student awaken into Oneness. Students will:

- Learn how to understand and move through the experience of suffering
- Release conditioning and emotional charges that no longer serve them
- Discover a deeper definition of faith in their own tradition
- Learn how to make internal changes that can manifest in the outer world

- Gain empowerment to help others by learning how to transfer the Oneness Blessing
- Experience constant Oneness Blessings where unconditional love can flow

▶ **Awakening to Oneness Level 2** is a seven-day workshop offered at the Oneness University campus in Fiji. The class centers on insights from Sri Bhagavan and Sri Amma to help the student awaken into oneness. Students learn to:

- Move toward a greater experience of reality to live life in a state of connectedness and Oneness
- Find compassion and recognize the need for collective transformation of humanity
- Understand contribution and service and what they means in today's world
- See the value they provide in raising consciousness as a whole
- Move toward awakening of the intelligence that is born of total self-acceptance and love for oneself
- Experience constant Oneness Blessings where unconditional love can flow

. . . .

Continuing Education Units: No.

Certification: Yes. Students must attend Level 1 and recertify periodically.

Participants: Open to anyone seeking healing on deeper level.

Code of Ethics/Standards of Practice: No.

Suggested Reading

Ardagh, Arjuna. *Awakening to Oneness: Deeksha and the Evolution of Consciousness*. Louisville, CO: Sounds True, 2007.

Windrider, Kiara, with Grace Sears. *Deeksha: The Fire from Heaven*. Maui, HI: Inner Ocean Publishing Inc., 2006.

Availability: The seven-day intensive can only be experienced at the Oneness University campuses. Other sites for the Oneness Blessing and Deeksha events are available throughout the world. Go to www.onenessnorthamerica.org or www.onenessuniversity.org to find locations near you and for a list of available practitioners.

Resources

Oneness University World Headquarters, Campus 3, Varadaiahpalem, Chittoor District, Andhra Pradesh – 517 541, India, +91 8576 279948, webmaster@onenessuniversity.org, www.onenessuniversity.org

Info108@onenessnorthamerica.org, www.onenessnorthamerica.org

www.onenessuniversity.ru, www.onesnesscentre.org.uk, www.onenesscentre.com.au

Bibliography

Windrider, Kiara, with Grace Sears. *Deeksha: The Fire from Heaven.* Maui, HI: Inner Ocean Publishing, 2006.

www.onenessuniversity.org

www.onenessnorthamerica.org

ROHUN™

ROHUN THERAPY IS A BLEND of spiritual, psychological, and energetic healing used to release the unhealthy energies stored in the body from negative life experiences. It is a spiritual process of release and purification that clears the energy field and restores balance to the individual. Medical intuitive Patricia Hayes founded the RoHun Institute in 1983. It offers degrees and certification as a RoHun therapist, RoHun master, and RoHun doctor. The RoHun Institute at Delphi University and Spiritual Center in McCaysville, Georgia, is the original and primary RoHun training facility. Doctor RoHun is a spiritual entity that Hayes channeled in 1981 during a long series of meditations, which she transformed into a complete system of healing.

RoHun treatment is conducted in a series of purification sessions to systematically release energy blocks from each of the chakras over time. This series is usually preceded by an introductory RoHun cleanse in which an individual can begin to experience this form of healing and decide if she would like to continue to the purification sessions.

After the cleanse, the next step in the RoHun Purification Process consists of three to five consecutive sessions of RoHun Therapy averaging 2 hours per session. The therapist performs what Hayes calls thought surgery by helping the client transform negative thoughts, emotions, and habits into positive and productive ones. Therapist and client work together to identify, process, and release those blocks in the client's chakra system related to specific thoughts or emotions.

A continuation of the RoHun Purification Process is called the RoHun Skim, which takes place monthly for three months to release those energies that began to emerge in the early sessions. Therapist and client also work together to release traumatic issues that may be held deeply in the client's subconscious.

The last stage of this healing is called RoHun Shadow Purification, which calls for four to eight consecutive sessions depending on the needs of the client. The objective is to heal deep core issues relating to a client's misuse of power over time and to help reach a heightened level of awareness and love.

The primary focus of the RoHun Purification Process is psychological healing. RoHun therapies begin with a process known as the RoHun induction. With the assistance of the RoHun therapist, clients make a connection with their consciousness first before descending into the regions of the subconscious. In this manner the clients are able to see with their spiritual eyes and access their higher wisdom. Clients learn to recognize and understand the causes of mental and emotional imbalance and subsequently heal them. Once the work is complete, the client can choose advanced stages of RoHun therapy to explore the deeper connections between ego, personality, and spirituality.

Course Descriptions

The RoHun curriculum at the Delphi University of Spiritual Studies is divided into three areas of certification: RoHun Therapist Program, RoHun Masters Program, and RoHun Doctorate Program. The prerequisite is a seven-day intensive program called In-Depth Channeling.

▶ **In-Depth Channeling** trains students to use their intuitive and spiritual abilities to tune in to a person and receive a consistent flow of information, guidance, and inspiration. This class is a prerequisite for all other classes in the program. Divided into three stages, the seven-day intensive training program includes:

- Psychic sensitivity: clairvoyance, clairaudience, and clairsentience
- Channeling: learning to become a clear, reliable channel of energy and information
- Intuitive counseling: using spiritual gifts to help others
- Energy perception: perceiving, recognizing, and understanding energy

- Complementary and alternative healing: alternative methods of healing body, mind, and spirit
- Initiate training: the anatomy of consciousness
- Meditation and visualization: development of spiritual vision and the inner senses
- The human energy fields and chakras
- Past life regression: revisiting past lives to gain insight about a current life
- Sacred sound: the effects of sound, music, tone, and sacred language
- Soul readings: determining life path and purpose
- Automatic writing: allowing spirit to communicate through writing
- Spiritual art: drawing and interpreting energy
- Photograph reading: gaining information through photographs
- Psychometry: energy analysis of objects and symbols

Students who complete the course are awarded a certificate of mediumship from the Arthur Ford International Academy of Mediumship.

Upon completion of the RoHun Therapists Program, graduates receive certification as RoHun Purification Therapists, ministerial ordination in the Church of Wisdom, and eligibility to enter the master's program.

▶ **RoHun I: RoHun Cards Course** utilizes a psychotherapeutic tool, the RoHun cards, which are designed to facilitate self-healing, self-growth, and the healing of others. Topics include:

- Understanding the release/healing process that allows individuals to directly release specific blocks in the energy field
- Exploring the origin of faulty thought patterns
- Completely releasing negative and limiting energies

▶ **RoHun II: Purification Course** teaches the RoHun Healing Process of Purification. Through supervised practice, students have the opportunity to administer and receive each phase in the sequence. Attention is given to deciphering the stages of the therapeutic process, particularly the moment of healing and planning effective intervention. The student will be able to practice and perform RoHun Purification Therapy at the completion of this workshop. Topics include:

- Etheric surgery techniques for the removal of energy blocks and for resolving internal conflict and negativity
- Opening the higher chakras
- Balancing male/female energies
- Activating the inner senses and creative processes

▶ **RoHun III: Advanced Purification/Group Course** focuses on methods of extending and intensifying the basic RoHun process. Topics include:

- Introduction to Skim Sessions and advanced purification skills
- Splits in consciousness for healing specific problems
- Past life therapy
- Releasing traumatic elements of the unconscious
- The dynamics of group RoHun
- Developing a RoHun practice

▶ **RoHun IV: Shadows/Caged One Process Course** introduces techniques designed to move to increasingly greater depths of the unconsciousness. Topics include:

- Removing "caged ones" or elements of the shadow
- Lower consciousness issues and their transformation into higher states
- Creating the alternate balance and higher states of self-integration and creative functioning

RoHun Master's Program

During the course of the master's program, students earn certification in Relationship Dynamics. At completion students receive certification as RoHun Masters and are eligible for entrance to the doctorate program.

▶ **RoHun Masters I: RoHun Transformation** addresses two distinct RoHun therapeutic processes. Prerequisites are In-Depth Channeling and the RoHun Therapist Program. Topics include:

- **The Origins Process,** which explains the process of individuation and how to return to it to achieve a higher level of self-understanding.
- **The Seven Visions of Self in Transformation:** The Seven Selves are the archetypal energies residing in the seven major charkas. The goal of the Seven Selves is to guide us in attaining a collective expression of wholeness.
- Refining the seven channels of light essential to spiritualizing matter
- Power of the heart
- Creating a dynamic healing team
- Fulfilling one's purpose

▶ **RoHun Masters II: RoHun Analysis** addresses spiritual wisdom, understanding, and practice. It consists of three distinct RoHun therapeutic processes:

- The Androgynous Process
    1. Internal war between the sexes
    2. Battle of the heart and mind
    3. Using the Kundalini to heal
    4. Integrating the heart and mind
- The Divine Mother Process
    1. Mother-induced spiritual fragmentation
    2. Psychological imbalances
    3. Emotional entanglements
    4. Activating the Divine Mother
- Spirit Releasement
    1. Negative thought forms
    2. Entities
    3. Emotional attachments
    4. Higher states of consciousness

▶ **Mysteries of Male/Female Healing Course** explores the myths that deal with the complexities and healing processes of masculine and feminine energies. Students experience the special needs, actions, behavioral patterns, and requirements of each sex and take steps to heal their own male and female energies. The course includes:

- The sexual nature
- The androgynous being
- Male and female energy, integration, and healing
- The etheric body's role in healing
- Devas and the healing potency of nature

Upon completion, students receive certification as Masters of RoHun and in Male/Female Relationship Dynamics.

RoHun Doctorate Program

Each Doctor of RoHun goes through extensive training at Delphi University in metaphysical healing, intuitive and channeling skills, root causes of disease, etheric surgery, behavioral sciences, and transpersonal psychology. Prerequisites are completion of In-Depth Channeling, the RoHun Purification Therapist Program, and the RoHun Master's Program.

During the course of the Master's Program students will earn certification as Kundalini Light Energization™ Healers, certification in Advanced Kundalini Light Energization™ and Reflective Etheric Healing, and, at the end of the course, a certificate of completion. Each student receives certification as a Doctor of RoHun™ RhD upon completion of the program course and a doctoral thesis.

▶ **Spiritual Anatomy and Light Energization™ I** teaches the spiritual anatomy of the physical body with emphasis on understanding the root cause of disease, the function served by disease in spiritual awakening, and the interaction between the etheric (vital) body, the astral (emotional) body, and the physical body in attracting or repelling disease. The course also explores the physiological and cellular structure of the ego, the soul, and thought patterns. Students who complete this course receive certification as Kundalini Light Energization Healers. Topics include:

- Kundalini stimulation and consciousness expansion
- The study of vibration and the effect of fear and inherited disease

- Introduction and practice of reflective healing techniques for physical healing and regeneration
- Learning to facilitate and perform a noninvasive blood cleanse
- Learning to work in the etheric body to facilitate healing of the physical body
- Techniques for stimulating and drawing up Kundalini energy to energize the pineal and pituitary glands and enhance spiritual perception and psychic vision

▶ **Spiritual Anatomy and Light Energization II** addresses the structure and practical application of the etheric healing therapeutics for physical regeneration. Emphasis is placed on the development and expansion of the student's own abilities and forming a greater connection with spiritual forces. Students who complete this course receive certification in Advanced Kundalini Light Energization and certification as Reflective Etheric Healers. Topics include:

- Advanced healing techniques using breathing and Kundalini energy, sacred mantras and symbols, working with the elements, and employing advanced sound healing techniques
- The spiritual anatomy of the nervous system
- Accessing the healing potential of the etheric body
- The role of the ductless glands in spiritual attainment
- Beginning color and sound therapy
- Advanced energization techniques

▶ **RoHun Doctorate I: Constructs Course** explores the protective devices established by individuals during their formative years, including work with their inner child. Topics include:

- Repetitive and destructive mental constructs
- The four major fears that sabotage love and success and separate individuals from their true spiritual self
- The triggers of the external world that lead to destructive constructs

▶ **RoHun Doctorate II: Tanks and Medical Relationships** concerns the transformation and integration of the inner child into the one's everyday life. Topics include:

- The study of constructs, vaults, and tanks
- How mental constructs and fears create tanks of powerful negative emotions in the lower chakras
- How the energies of self-abuse, self-hatred, and deceit affect the physical body and often lead to disease
- Conscious and unconscious thoughts of mortality and how to transform them

. . . .

Continuing Education Units: No.

Certification: The Church of Wisdom is the certifying body of Delphi University. Upon completion of all the doctorate courses, students receive certification of the Doctorate Course Completion. Once all of the program's courses and the doctoral thesis are complete, students earn certification as Doctors of RoHun, RhD.

For students who complete the applicable metaphysician and RoHun studies, Delphi University offers a Bachelor of Science degree in metaphysical healing, a Master of Science in transpersonal psychology, and a Doctor of Science PhD in complementary and alternative medical therapies.

Participants: Anyone wanting to experience in-depth studies of metaphysics and energy healing.

Code of Ethics/Standards of Practice: Yes.

Suggested Reading

McVoy, Cullen. *Finding RoHun: Awakening through Spiritual Therapy.* Montclair, NJ: Pooka Publications, 1996.

Smith, Marshall L. *Spiritual Anatomy Book I.* McCaysville, GA: The Dimensional Brotherhood Publishers, 2007.

———. *Spiritual Anatomy Book II.* McCaysville, GA: The Dimensional Brotherhood Publishers, 2009.

Zolar. *Dancing Heart to Heart: The Story of RoHun.* McCaysville, GA: Editions Soleil, 1991.

Availability: Classes are only available at the Delphi University campus in Georgia. Practitioners may be found in twenty-two different countries. To find a practitioner for a session in your area, go to www.delphiu.com/rProfessional.htm.

Resources
. . . .

RoHun, Delphi University of Spiritual Studies, PO Box 70, 940 Old Silvermine Road, McCaysville, GA 30555, 888-335-7448, registrar@delphiu.com, www.delphiu.com

Bibliography
. . . .

McVoy, Cullen. *Finding RoHun: Awakening through Spiritual Therapy.* Montclair, NJ: Pooka Publications, 1996.

Zolar. *Dancing Heart to Heart: The Story of RoHun.* McCaysville, GA: Editions Soleil, 1991.

www.delphiu.com

www.perspectivesholistic.com

www.spirithealingbermuda.com

SPIRITUAL RESPONSE THERAPY

ACCORDING TO FOUNDER REVEREND ROBERT DETZLER, Spiritual Response Therapy is a psychic-spiritual method of researching the subconscious mind and soul records to discover and release hidden blocks to health, happiness, and spiritual growth.

As a biblical scholar, an ordained minister, and a spiritual counselor, Detzler started with the Bible in his search for healing methods. He believes that each of us has a spiritual committee composed of one or more souls, which he calls the "high self." According to Detzler's interpretation of scripture, Jesus referred to this spiritual committee as the Father within. Following Detzler's program, practitioners can access information from this spiritual committee by using charts, a pendulum, and asking yes or no questions. The pendulum moves in three directions, distinctly indicating a yes, no, or not-yet-determined answer.

Once a practitioner and client work together to identify personal life issues, they use a series of charts and a pendulum to clear negative energies or programs blocking the client's life. This healing modality accepts the premise that everyone has experienced previous existence in both spiritual and incarnational realms. Negative energy and limiting beliefs established then or now can keep an individual from realizing his or her full potential. Spiritual Response Therapy (SRT) is a meticulous process of researching the subconscious mind and soul records to discover and release hidden blocks to health, happiness, and spiritual growth. The healing method works to support clients and students to release negativity, break old destructive habits, heal emotional and physical issues, change false beliefs, perceptions, and attitudes, and attain greater clarity, balance, joy, and harmony.

In his book *Spiritual Healing*, Detzler uses other tools, including a chart of an ancient healing circle in Wales. Anyone may use a pendulum or the conscious mind to determine which "gate" indicated in the healing circle chart contains the right vibrations to break up the unwanted energy. The client places her finger over the gate and asks her higher self to program the healing energy of that gate into the body where it is needed. The practitioner also determines a color and/or a form of direct healing, such as a homeopathic remedy, to remove the negative energies stored in the client's subconscious mind. The chosen color may be applied to the client or the client may choose to wear that color for a specified period of time.

Detzler's spiritual healing method also uses a number of vector patterns or channeled healing patterns and symbols. The healing patterns are a series of lines joined together to form a specific shape. The symbols are pictures of animals or a descriptive word. Using a pendulum, the practitioner determines the appropriate pattern needed for healing. The client places his or her hand over the pattern to receive the healing vibrations from that pattern. The practitioner uses the pendulum to determine the proper duration of this energy.

A typical SRT session can be in an in-person appointment, calling in by telephone, or through written issues outlined via e-mail. Detzler contacts his spiritual committee to clear his own consciousness, then uses a pendulum and set of thirty-four charts to identify soul programs, negative energies left over from past lives or this one, and asks the client's spiritual committee to release these for more positive living. Releasing statements and affirmations may also be used.

Detzler tells or writes his research notes about the soul programs, negative energies, or past lives and makes a tape recording summarizing his findings for his long-distance clients.

Course Descriptions

Spiritual Response Therapy classes are offered in many countries and several languages. The Basic Spiritual Response Therapy class is not certified, although students receive a certificate of completion at the end of the course. Classes are informal and structured so that students have plenty of opportunity for discussion and practice. Students receive certification at the end of the Advanced Spiritual Response

SPIRITUAL RESPONSE THERAPY ✦ 359

Therapy class and are then encouraged to practice on family and friends before embarking on a professional practice. The program prefers that students take both the Basic Spiritual Response Therapy class and the advanced class before taking Spiritual Restructuring as Spiritual Response Therapy is used to clear any negative energies connected with the physical body. Students must demonstrate they have practiced Spiritual Restructuring techniques before they can earn certification for this course.

▶ **Basic Spiritual Response Therapy** is 24 to 27 hours of instruction time in which students learn to communicate with their higher selves to clear their own soul records and subconscious of negative programs and beliefs. Topics include:

- How to use a pendulum
- Soul programs
- How to identify and release negative energies that may have arisen from a past life
- Soul mates
- Cycles of disharmony
- Basic research charts

▶ **Advanced Spiritual Response Therapy.** Using Detzler's *Soul Re-Creation: Developing Your Cosmic Potential* as its textbook, this class addresses advanced teachings of spiritual response. Completion of Basic Spiritual Response Therapy is a prerequisite. Topics include:

- Researching past, present, and future lives
- Working with the high self
- Clearing blocks to greater happiness
- Releasing earthbound souls
- Recognizing soul mates and twin flames
- Interpreting dreams
- Learning the hierarchy of the light realms

▶ **Intensive SRT Skills** is a three-day concentrated review of advanced Spiritual Response Therapy techniques. This class is required every two years for serious or certified public practitioners. Those seeking certification are tested on their SRT work skills. Completion of Advanced SRT and practice are prerequisites. Topics include:

- Emphasis on staying clear with high self committee
- Accuracy and completeness of clearing work
- Latest new methods
- Requirements for certification

▶ **Spiritual Restructuring** is a six-day class that stresses the human energy system and the spiritual components of existence. Students learn to work with all systems of the body to balance the vibrations of the mental, emotional, physical, and spiritual aspects of a person. Students learn:

- Physically and spiritually adjusting the vertebrae, sacrum, hips, head, and torqued or jammed joints to improve freedom of movement
- Releasing tension in overextended muscles using gentle touch
- Touch techniques to reduce stress in muscles
- What foods to use to support the skeletal, nervous, circulatory, digestive, respiratory, and urinary systems of the body
- Working with the soul and the brain to release discordant programming, bringing harmony between the physical brain and the mind
- Clearing and balancing emotional energy
- Meditations to help identify and release suppressed emotions
- Working with spiritual energy to establish vibrational healing

▶ **Self Master I** is a two-day intensive workshop followed by three months of periodic small-group meetings. The Advanced Spiritual Response Therapy Class is a prerequisite. Topics include:

- Self-awareness through self-exploration and spiritual development
- Exploring and accomplishing a set of goals in a supportive environment
- Increasing the ability to succeed in a chosen field with ongoing support
- Mentorship in personal development and goal achievements

▶ **Self Master II** is a two-day intensive workshop followed by three months of periodic meetings. Either the Self Master I or the Spiritual Leadership I class serves as a prerequisite. Topics include mastering abundance and various advanced skills for self-growth and transformation of personal living.

. . . .

Continuing Education Units: No.

Certification: Yes, granted by the Spiritual Response Association.

Participants: Recommended for everyone, especially those with a desire for more spiritual growth and personal transformation on a Universal level of knowledge.

Code of Ethics/Standards of Practice: Yes.

Suggested Reading

Detzler, Robert. *Soul Re-Creation: Developing Your Cosmic Potential.* Redmond, WA: SRC Publishing, 1994.

———. *Spiritual Healing.* Redmond, WA: SRC Publishing, 1998.

Availability: To find a session with a certified practitioner in your area, go to www .spiritualresponse.com.

Resources

Spiritual Response Association, 2909 Pacific Avenue SE, Olympia, WA 98501, srtmail@spiritualresponse.com, www.spiritualresponse.com

Bibliography

Detzler, Robert. *Spiritual Healing.* Redmond, WA: SRC Publishing, 1998.

THETAHEALING™

VIANNA STIBAL, FOUNDER OF THETAHEALING, is a naturopath, massage therapist, and intuitive reader. In 1995, she was diagnosed with cancer in her right femur and conventional and alternative methods of healing did not help her heal. As an intuitive reader, she used some of the techniques on herself that she had used successfully with others to help heal her cancer. According to Stibal, she experienced an instantaneous healing and has had no sign of cancer since that time. Working with a physicist, Stibal concluded through electroencephalograph testing that her healing was successful in large part because she went into the theta state of brain activity.

The brain emits five levels of frequency depending upon what a person is doing. (One hertz [hz] is one complete wave cycle per second, such as a radio wave or sound wave.) The beta state has a frequency of 14 to 28 hz and is the normal activity of daily thinking, activity, and alertness. Gamma waves appear whenever the brain is involved with higher mental activity such as learning something new. The gamma state has a frequency of 26 to 70 hz. The brain slips in and out of this state as it processes information. When a person is relaxed or meditative, a frequency of 7 to 14 hz establishes the alpha state. Daydreaming and fantasizing occur at this level. Many healers enter the alpha state while they are working. The delta state has a frequency of 0 to 4 hz. This is the level of deep sleep.

The theta state, from which ThetaHealing derives its name, is a level of very deep relaxation with a frequency of 4 to 7 hz, leading to a quietness in the mind often attained by deep meditation over a long period of time. ThetaHealing practitioners achieve this state while doing healing work. It takes a bit of practice, and there is a meditation formula to follow to help the practitioner get into the theta state. The practitioner moves in and out of the theta state during the course of the treatment. It is not possible to be in the theta state and talk to a client at the same time. The length of time spent in the theta state is very short.

Stibal also builds this healing method on what she calls the four levels of beliefs, which practitioners use to determine where limiting thoughts and feelings originate. (1) The first seven years of life form *core beliefs*. Many of them have to do with survival, safety, and comfort. (2) Family history creates *genetic beliefs* on a cellular level. Many of these belief patterns show up in the form of lifestyle choices an individual makes, such as religion, career, and geographical location of residence. (3) *Historical beliefs* come from past lives, societal forces, and the collective consciousness, such as the widespread idea of scarcity in the 1930s in the United States. (4) *Soul beliefs* are those judgments people hold against themselves dealing with self-esteem and self-doubt. These deep beliefs are held on more than one level. Harboring unhealthy beliefs at any of these four levels can block an individual's path to healing. Theta-Healing practitioners help their clients pinpoint and eliminate these beliefs.

In addition, ThetaHealing delves deep into spirituality by bringing in healing energy from what practitioners refer to as the "highest plane of existence." According to Stibal, healing can take place on any of seven planes of existence. The first plane of existence consists of rocks, minerals, and all other nonorganic materials. Any organic substance, meaning that it contains at least one carbon molecule, makes up the second plane of existence. Animals and humans live in the third plane of existence. The fourth plane of existence is the realm of the spirit world. The fifth plane is divided into degrees. In the lower degrees beings with egos can still be found and dramas found in the third plane can be here also. The upper degrees contain angels, guardian angels, and guides who are only too happy to be of service to anyone who asks for help. The laws of the universe are contained in the sixth plane of existence, and the seventh plane of existence is the pure energy of Creation. ThetaHealing is done at the seventh plane of existence.

After asking the client for permission, a ThetaHealing session begins with the practitioner using muscle testing to determine if the client is properly hydrated, and then continues with muscle testing to pinpoint which of the client's deeply held beliefs are interfering with the healing process. The muscle testing is done by asking the client to form a ring with either the forefinger or the ring finger and the thumb.

As questions are asked, the practitioner pulls gently where the finger and the thumb come together. If the answer is yes, the finger and thumb stay firmly together. If the answer is no, the finger and thumb come apart easily. An important element of this work is connecting with a higher power, which practitioners refer to as the Creator. Practitioners consider themselves conduits for this healing power.

Course Descriptions

Each year the ThetaHealing Institute of Knowledge runs all of the courses back to back to save out-of-area students the trouble of flying to and from Idaho. At the end of all the courses, the student becomes a Master ThetaHealer. The Basic, Advanced, Intuitive Anatomy, and Manifesting and Abundance classes are taught throughout the United States and in several other countries. Not all of the classes are listed here. The program is growing and new classes are being offered. For a complete list, go to their website at www.thetahealing.com.

The Basic DNA class prepares the student to be a practitioner. Practitioners do not certify. Instructors certify at three levels: Basic Teachers, Advanced Teachers, and ThetaHealing Intuitive Anatomy Teachers. The Master program requires more training and is offered to certified instructors or to students who complete the entire once-a-year, back-to-back program.

▶ **Basic DNA** is a three-day intensive that introduces students to techniques to alter belief patterns and get a firm understanding of the modality. Topics include:

- The five types of brain waves
- The chakras and Kundalini
- Activating the twelve strands of DNA
- How to work with spirit guides from different realms
- An introduction to the laws of manifestation
- Doing future readings
- Balancing serotonin and noradrenaline levels
- Pulling heavy metals and radiation from the body
- Soul mates
- Planes of existence

- Protocols for healing a great variety of conditions and diseases
- How to do belief work

▶ **Advanced DNA** teaches students how to work on all of an individual's belief levels. Basic DNA is a prerequisite. Topics include:

- Working more deeply with belief structures
- The differences between channeling angels and channeling God

▶ **Intuitive Anatomy** teaches students how to read the various systems of the body on all levels with great accuracy and how to correlate beliefs with illnesses. Prerequisites are two other ThetaHealing classes and permission from the instructor. Topics include:

- Levels of beliefs and programs that hold diseases and other ailments in the body
- Major organs and the diseases associated with them
- Uncovering blocks in each of the body's systems
- Programs associated with fungus in the body

▶ **Teacher Certification** is for those students who want to become ThetaHealing instructors. Prerequisites include Basic DNA and Advanced DNA, and approval by the instructor. Topics include:

- A review of the entire collection of techniques
- A review of new teachings that increase the efficiency of healing practices
- Practice teaching and presenting core exercises
- Advanced visualizations and meditations
- Guiding students to become medical intuitives

▶ **ThetaHealing Advanced Teacher Certification** allows students to become instructors of advanced ThetaHealing seminars. Prerequisites are Basic DNA, Advanced DNA, and Teacher Certification. Topics include:

- An in-depth understanding of the seven planes of existence

- How to teach students to eliminate limiting feelings that hold them back
- Unnecessary fifth plane elements such as drama, resentment, jealousy, and anger and how to deal with them
- The inner workings of the student–teacher dynamics
- How to manage difficult students
- How to instruct in the pure spirit of cooperation

▶ **ThetaHealing Intuitive Anatomy Teacher Certification** allows ThetaHealing teachers to teach Intuitive Anatomy. Prerequisites are the completion of the Theta-Healing Basic Teachers DNA class and the Advanced ThetaHealing Teachers class. Topics are all related to advanced teaching skills.

· · · · · · · · · · · · · · · ·

Continuing Education Units: No.

Certification: Students receive a certificate at the completion of each class.

Participants: Classes are open to anyone wishing to study healing from a spiritual perspective.

Code of Ethics/Standards of Practice: Yes.

Availability: Classes are offered in Africa, Asia, Australia, Canada, Europe, India, Mexico, New Zealand, the Bahamas, and the United States. For a list of classes or practitioners in your area, go to www.thetahealing.com.

Resources

ThetaHealing Institute of Knowledge, 1615 Curlew Drive, Ammon, ID 83406, 208-524-0808 ext. 18, vianna@thetahealing.com, www.thetahealing.com, www.thetahealinginstituteofknowledge.com

Bibliography

Stibal, Vianna. *ThetaHealing, Advanced ThetaHealing, ThetaHealing Disease and Disorder.* Idaho Falls, ID: Rolling Thunder Publishing, 2006.

www.thetahealing.com

www.thetahealinginstituteofknowledge.com

SHAMANIC

THE WORD "SHAMAN" comes from the Tungus tribe in Siberia and means spiritual healer or one who sees in the dark. Shamanism in many forms has been practiced almost everywhere on the planet. Shamans can be healers, doctors, priests and priestesses, ministers, psychotherapists, counselors, mystics, and storytellers. The term "shaman" is often associated with tribes in Africa, Native Americans, and Aborigines, but shamans are also found throughout Asia and Europe. In many tribal cultures, the shaman, male or female, has the role in the tribe of healer and/ or leader of religious ceremonies.

The Druids of the ancient Celtic tribes in Western Europe, Great Britain, and Ireland are considered shamans. The Romans banned their rituals and religious ceremonies, and by the second century, the Druids had disappeared from any written history; however, since that time healers have quietly remained active.

Siberian shamans were initiated through receiving a call from a previous leader who had passed on, and they would always go through a period of intense suffering involving either a life-threatening illness, injury, or a serious psychological crisis before officially assuming the role of shaman. By surviving the crisis, the initiate proved his or her ability to perform healing work.

Among the Aborigines, older women kept the knowledge of herbs and plant medicines for the healing of nonspiritual complaints. Serious illness and death were believed to be caused by spirits or people practicing sorcery and required the help of a man or several men to perform ceremonies to remove the spirit. Often these men would go on a vision quest to find the nature of the invading spirit and discern ways to appease it.

African shamans perform spiritual work to remove evil spirits and other influences, while medicine men and women work with plants to cure diseases. Voodoo witch doctors, through ceremony, remove the offending spirit or evil influence of a patient and sometimes place it in a chicken or other small animal. Faith healing and herbal medicine dominate the voodoo healing traditions.

In Tibetan cultures, it is believed the shaman lives in two realities at the same time. The first is the inner dream time where the shaman may have spiritual encounters, and the external, or physical realm, is where the shaman performs as a healer. Tibetan religious culture centers on the practices of healing, both on a tribal level and an individual level. Buddhism has had considerable influence on the Tibetan culture. Tibetan medicine and healing techniques are taught at the College for Higher Tibetan Studies, founded by Lobsang Gyatso, in Sarah, Dharamshala, in northern India.

Students of Native American cultures use the terms "shaman" and "medicine man" or "medicine woman" interchangeably. The term "medicine man" is an English one and does not fit the true role of a Native American shaman. The medicine man for the Wasco tribe on the Warm Springs Reservation in Oregon, Ken Katchia, once told me that Native Americans are the most studied but least understood of all the peoples on the planet. North American tribes do not share much information concerning their tribal ceremonies and herbal lore for healing. The Hopi have shared a few hands-on healing techniques, but most of the herbal lore and healing work is kept secret by the Hopis and the other North American tribes. By contrast, the Peruvian natives have dwindled in numbers, and to keep their traditions known it was decided that shamanic and healing traditions needed to be shared with the white man or the traditions would be lost completely.

The term "shaman" today has changed slightly in its meaning from these ancient traditions, as healers and New Age students have connected the word to various types of contemporary healing. Many healers consider themselves shamans, and vice versa. Shamanic healers are said to have a strong connection to both Earth and the spirit realms and desire to heal each other, the communities in which they live, and the planet itself.

I once attended a conference in which shamans from several countries were part of the program. Over a thousand people came to hear them speak, and the shamans were in awe of the reception they received. To them, their work is an everyday activity that deserved no special merit, and a surprising thing came to light as they shared their stories. Although these individuals came from all over the world, often from areas that had no running water, no electricity, and no communication with the outside world, they were performing similar and often the same techniques and ceremonies in their healing work.

The modalities listed in this section have their roots in shamanic traditions and often involve techniques that differ from the other modalities listed in this book. Shamans do what is called journeying, a form of meditation in which the shaman travels via meditation or trance to the underworld, the middle world, or the upper world to perform rituals to aid in the healing of the client. Often, the shaman guides the client to join the journey.

Soul retrieval is one of the best-known techniques that is often incorporated into a shamanic journey. Shamanic healers believe that during a traumatic event in a person's life a portion of the soul may break away, and the shaman journeys to find the missing fragment of the client. Once found, the shaman reunites it with the rest of the soul through ceremony. The fragment of the soul might also adhere to the energy field of another person. When a person dies unexpectedly during a traumatic event, a fragment of his or her soul may break away before the death of the individual and attach to a similar personality or one that is receptive to its attachment. Most often, this is done without conscious awareness on the part of the recipient of the soul fragment. A shamanic healer can release these fragments and reunite them with their original owners through ceremony and healing techniques.

The modalities in this section use many shamanic tools, such as sound and light, drumming (usually used to usher a practitioner on journey into the spiritual world), stones, and crystals. Traditionally, shamans have many other functions. In this book, however, only the healing arts of shamanism are included.

DYNAMIC ENERGETIC HEALING®

DYNAMIC ENERGETIC HEALING is a psychospiritual modality that integrates a variety of spiritual resources such as energy psychology and processwork with an application of shamanic practices. Core shamanic practices include journeying, soul retrieval, divination, extraction, pyschopomp work, and healing interventions. Energy psychology applications include Emotional Freedom Technique (page 49), Tapas Acupressure Technique (page 117), and Thought Field Therapy, formerly called Callahan Techniques (page 121). Process work, also known as process-oriented psychology, was developed by a Jungian analyst, Arnold Mindell, and integrates psychology, group dynamics, spirituality, and creative expression.

Dynamic Energetic Healing was formed in 1997 through the mutual collaboration of Howard Brockman, LCSW, the modality's main founder, Mary Hammond, LPC, and Nancy Gordon, LCSW, as a synthesis of their experiences with energy psychology strategies. According to Brockman's website, Dynamic Energetic Healing "integrates and accesses universal spiritual resources in its unique application of shamanic practices historically recognized by nearly every culture." Specifically, Brockman shows his clients how to access nonordinary reality and communicate with spiritual guides, which sets his paradigm apart from many other methods of psychological change.

Principles and techniques derived from shamanism help create the foundation of this therapy. Some of the shamanic techniques include journeying, soul retrieval, drumming, and psychopomp. Journeying is a form of meditation, usually accompanied by sound, such as drumming, in which a shaman spiritually travels to other realms to accomplish various goals depending on the needs presented by the client. Practitioners in Dynamic Energetic Healing frequently vocally guide clients through a journey to determine the root or spiritual cause of an illness or psychological dysfunction.

During a traumatic event, a fragment of a person's soul or essence can break away, but soul pieces can be found and reincorporated through journey work. This form of therapy is known as soul retrieval. Clients suffering from post-traumatic stress disorder frequently have lost pieces of themselves during the time of trauma. Practitioners check victims of abuse and war veterans for lost portions of their souls.

Practitioners are also trained in psychopomp work, which helps deceased souls unable or unwilling to move on to the next world. Because Dynamic Energetic Healing addresses the body, the mind, and the spirit, pyschopomp work is an important intervention. Sometimes, a mental or emotional problem is presented by the client in which the cause is a spiritual intrusion or an attached deceased person's spirit that is affecting the client's ability to think clearly. By freeing the spirit from the client's energy field and sending it home, the client is able to function in a healthier manner. Brockman has found psychopomp work combined with past life regressions to be very helpful in relieving allergy symptoms.

Before a session begins, the client is checked for hydration through muscle testing to ensure that the session is as productive as possible. Throughout the session, the practitioner tests for various issues and responses to treatment. The client may stand for muscle testing and sit or lie down for shamanic treatments such as journey work, often aided by drums, Tibetan bowls, chimes, and rattles. The practitioner might also ask the client to perform psychoenergetic interventions such as Tapas Acupressure Technique or Emotional Freedom Technique. Throughout the treatment, the practitioner asks the client to trust in the process and offers gentle support as they work together to resolve the issues.

Course Descriptions

The following examples of classes come from Howard Brockman's website, with classes differing slightly in agenda and format between instructors. Levels I–V are each three-day classes and level VI is a two-day class. Classes must be taken in order of listing.

▶ **Dynamic Energetic Healing International™ Curriculum Level I Training** introduces the basics of Dynamic Energetic Healing, including topics such as:

- Integrating energy psychology with core shamanism and process work
- Core shamanism, dreamtime, helping spirits, the roles of the shaman, and journeying into the lower world
- Establishing energetic boundaries with aggressive and angry people
- Self-administered energy psychology interventions for anxiety, stress, and other common problems
- Manual muscle testing
- Connecting to Source
- Identifying and disempowering the inner critic
- How Dynamic Energetic Healing integrates into cognitive-based therapy orientations
- The development and history of Dynamic Energetic Healing and energy psychology
- Understanding the role of intention
- Psychoenergetic reversal and objections that block intention
- Basic interventions, including Emotional Freedom Technique, Negative Affect Erasing Method, Tapas Acupressure Technique, tapping the temporal curve, Tibetan bells, bowls, cymbals, focused prayer, and mantra
- Learning to use the chakras as an intervention

▶ **Level II Training** addresses the role of intention, trauma, and identification and establishment of spiritual resources. Topics include:

- Setting up the intention with manual muscle testing
- Categories of trauma
- Journeying into the upper world
- Limiting beliefs
- Compromised energetic boundaries
- Soul loss
- The fear or wish to die
- Collective and vicarious trauma

- Post-traumatic stress disorder symptoms
- Supernatural influences
- The Enneagram questionnaire

▶ **Level III Training** further explores post-traumatic stress disorder and complex trauma. Topics include:

- Elaboration of various types of trauma, including post-traumatic stress disorder, accidents, abandonment and neglect, illness or surgery, rejection and loss, abuse or assault, war and violence
- Complex trauma such as cumulative or threshold trauma, blocked emotions, limiting identity formulations, double binds, anger at God, and overidentification with negative archetypes
- Journeying into the middle world
- Energetic origins: the dreaming-up process and current life origins (including in utero and birth)
- Regression techniques: affect/somatic bridge, tunnel of light, Neuro-Linguistic Programming timeline
- Frontal occipital holding intervention

▶ **Level IV Training** addresses past life work. This class also explores ethical issues with an attorney as part of the curriculum. Topics include:

- Supernatural phenomena: different formulations (curses, entanglements, psychotoxic intrusions) and how to stay safe when releasing dark energy
- Clearing past life energetic origin
- Hypnotic components of Dynamic Energetic Healing
- Journeying to find spirit guides and allies
- Clearing energetic origin between lifetimes
- Three-hour ethics presentation from a visiting attorney, including risk management, scope of practice, and therapeutic right relationship
- Discussion of record keeping, informed consent, full disclosure, and advertising

▶ **Level V Training** includes review work and supervised practice, including:

- Energetic origins protocol and clearing, including current life, past life, between lifetimes, ancestral and group or collective origins
- Staying safe when dealing with supernatural phenomena
- Journeying to empower objects to enhance healing

▶ **Level VI Training** provides practice time for Dynamic Energetic Healing protocols and addresses certification requirements. Topics include:

- Comprehensive review of the Dynamic Energetic Healing protocol
- Supervised practice in pairs, including joint journeying and divination
- Releasing an earthbound spirit
- Integrating Dynamic Energetic Healing into professional practice
- Certification requirements

· · · · · · · · · · · · · · · · ·

Continuing Education Units: For licensed clinical social workers (LCSWs) in Oregon: approved by the Oregon Chapter of the National Association of Social Workers; for LCSWs and marriage and family therapists in California: approved by the Board of Behavioral Sciences provider number 4391.

Certification: National standardized certification is provided by the Association of Comprehensive Energy Psychology. Upon completion of all courses plus a number of other requirements, Howard Brockman issues a certificate stating the applicant is a Dynamic Energetic Healing certified professional.

Participants: The institute recommends this course of study to psychotherapists, social workers, counselors, marriage and family therapists, play therapists, nurses, licensed massage therapists, community leaders, energy workers, educators, intuitives, healers, and seekers.

Code of Ethics/Standards of Practice: The institute follows the energy psychology code of ethics and standards of professional practice, which may be found at www.energypsych.org.

Suggested Reading

Brockman, Howard. *Dynamic Energetic Healing: Integrating Core Shamanic Practices with Energy Psychology Applications and Processwork Principles.* Salem, OR: Columbia Press, 2006.

Availability: Classes are taught throughout the United States and occasionally in other countries. To find a session with a practitioner in your area, e-mail info@ DynamicEnergeticHealing.com.

Resources

Dynamic Energetic Healing, Pacific Northwest Center for Energetic Healing, PO Box 21646, Keizer, OR 97303, 503-585-8992, info@ DynamicEnergeticHealing.com, www.dynamicenergetichealing.com.

Bibliography

Brockman, Howard. *Dynamic Energetic Healing: Integrating Core Shamanic Practices with Energy Psychology Applications and Processwork Principles.* Salem, OR: Columbia Press, 2006.

www.dynamicenergetichealing.com

www.energyhealers.meetup.com

www.onedynamicenergetichealing.org

www.processwork.org

ESOTERIC HEALING

Esoteric comes from the Greek word *esoteriko* and means "hidden" or "deeper within," while the word "healing" means "to make whole." The origins of Esoteric Healing, as it is known today, began with Alice A. Bailey (1880–1949) in the early 1930s. Many modern healers have studied her work (much of it published after her death) as a foundation for their healing work and for training programs. Bailey defined Esoteric Healing as "the release of the soul so that its life can flow through the aggregate of organisms which constitute any particular form" (*Esoteric Healing*, vol. 4, London, England: Lucis Press, 1972).

Bailey's work has been an influential component in the development of energy healing. One group of healers in the United Kingdom in 1965, including Brenda Johnston, used Bailey's work as a foundation for their studies. Johnston found that the public was quite interested in classes of this nature and designed three introductory courses in esoteric anatomy, spirituality, and meditation. Johnston's work led to the formation of the International Health Research Network in the 1980s, which, in 1993, became the International Network of Esoteric Healing. Alan Hopking, founder of the Global Academy of Esoteric Healing (1998) and author of *Esoteric Healing: A Practical Guide Based on the Teachings of the Tibetan in the Works of Alice A. Bailey,* defines Esoteric Healing as "an art and a science calling for the use of the mind, but not the emotions, in the service of the intuition, for the purpose of transforming matter with life."

Rather than working on a physical or emotional level, Esoteric Healers believe that all permanent healing must be done by connecting to and healing at the level of the soul. It is the soul of the client that determines the outcome and allows for lasting physical, emotional, mental, and spiritual aspects of healing.

To be an Esoteric Healer, a student must exhibit the forces described as magnetism and radiation. Magnetism is the ability to invoke your own healing energy. Radiation is the ability to send healing energy to other individuals. Much of the healing work is done placing the hands at specific points on a client's body and by projecting energy through the brow chakra from the healer's soul to the client.

Sessions begin with a brief intake of the client's medical history. Treatments may be done on a massage table or while the client is sitting in a chair. Most sessions take from thirty to forty-five minutes. The client is asked to remain relaxed and comfortable. The first task of a healer is to align his or her soul with that of the client and with a spiritual source. Through meditation, the healer uses triangles of etheric energy between the chakras and the endocrine glands in order to release blockages to the flow of soul energy. Most work is done off the body. At the end of the treatment, the client is given time to reflect on any thoughts, feelings, and memories that may have come to the surface during treatment.

Course Descriptions

The International Network of Esoteric Healing (INEH) was founded by Brenda Johnston in 1982 and is dedicated to the practice and study of Esoteric Healing. Their courses are held worldwide, teaching techniques that form a basis for the science of healing using the energy field. All INEH instructors must have at least three years of practical experience followed by two to three years of a teacher training program.

▶ **The INEH Esoteric Healing Course** consists of four parts, each requiring a seminar intensive of four to five days. Sessions are grouped together with lectures, discussions, practical instruction, and group meditation. Throughout the course, emphasis is placed on training the higher intuition as it links to the conscious mind. Course highlights include:

- In-depth study of the etheric body and chakra system
- Working with the formula, which connects the soul of the healer with the soul of the individual
- Understanding the ten laws and the six rules of Esoteric Healing

- Practical techniques for balancing the chakras and restoring the energy triangles between major and minor chakras
- The esoteric cause of disease
- Teaching on meditation and the building of the antahkarana
- The seven rays and their conditioning effect on health and disease
- Overview of esoteric astrology in relation to health and disease
- Overview of cosmology as per the teachings or Djwhal Khul and Alice Bailey

Course objectives include:

- Invoking the soul as the healer and discovering what prevents the healing process
- Exploring techniques for transmitting energy to all parts of the personality: physical and etheric, emotional, and mental
- Self-awareness and self-healing
- Understanding the subjective causes of disease
- Understanding the seven principles and vehicles for consciousness and the related charkas
- Learning the function and purpose of energy triangles
- Learning the value of group consciousness
- The uses of esoteric healing in everyday life
- How to apply esoteric healing as a complementary health technique within a clinical situation, be it in surgery, consultation, hospital, or home

. . . .

Continuing Education Units: Ask your instructor.

Certification: No.

Participants: Courses are available worldwide to medical and nonmedical practitioners who seek a deeper understanding of health and disease.

Suggested Reading

Bailey, Alice. *Esoteric Healing*, vol. I. London: Lucis Publishing, 1972.

———. *The Unfinished Autobiography of Alice A. Bailey*. New York: Lucis Publishing, 1951.

Hopking, Alan. *Esoteric Healing: A Practical Guide Based on the Teachings of the Tibetan in the Works of Alice A. Bailey*. Nevada City, CA: Blue Dolphin, 2004.

Availability: The International Network of Esoteric Healing offers courses in Australia, Bulgaria, Czech Republic, Denmark, Germany, Greece, Hong Kong, Italy, Japan, the Netherlands, New Zealand, Poland, Spain, South Africa, Sweden, the United Kingdom, the United States, and Zimbabwe.

For a session with a practitioner in your area, e-mail info@ineh.org.

Resources
. . . .

The International Network of Esoteric Healing, The Barn, Whichers Gate Road, Rowlands Castle, Hampshire, P09 6BB UK, 0705-412499 (UK), 612-825-8324 (USA), info@ineh.org, www.ineh.org

Bibliography
. . . .

Hopking, Alan. *Esoteric Healing: A Practical Guide Based on the Teachings of the Tibetan in the Works of Alice A. Bailey*. Nevada City, CA: Blue Dolphin, 2004.

www.bluedolphinpublishing.com/Hopking

www.esoterichealing.com

www.ineh.org

www.lucistrust.org

www.sevenraystoday.com

www.theesotericbloom.com

THE FOUR WINDS

IN ANCIENT TIMES, THE SHAMAN was known as the wise man or woman who served as the tribe's counselor and healer, and often as the adviser to the village chief or tribal leader. Shamans frequently kept the oral history of their people, passing this knowledge on to an apprentice as they aged. When serving as healers, shamans used herbs, energy medicine, counseling, and prayer to help the people under their care. Currently, shamans of indigenous tribes continue to use a mix of herbal medicine, energy healing, and spiritual counsel to aid and support those in need.

Alberto Villoldo, PhD, is one of the better-known shamans in the world today. He began his professional life as a psychologist and clinical professor at San Francisco State University, directing the Biological Self-Regulation Lab. During this time, Villoldo began to investigate how energy medicine and visualization might change the chemistry of the brain. He also studied psychoneuroimmunology, which concerns how moods, thoughts, and emotions influence human health.

By his own account, Villoldo's investigations in the lab revealed that energy healing increased the production of endorphins (chemicals responsible for reducing pain) by half. Villoldo sought further answers, believing "the microscope was the wrong instrument to answer the questions I was asking" and that his greater desire was "to find a system larger than the neural networks of the brain" (www.thefour winds.com/about-alberto-villoldo.php). He soon resigned from his position at the university and began his own journey of inquiry and healing. Villoldo went to the Amazon, seeking the ancient knowledge of Inca sages, medicine men and women, sorcerers, and shamans. For many years, he has traveled to remote villages, learning energy medicine, herbal medicine, and sacred methods used to transform the body and heal the soul. In his words, "My own journey into shamanism was guided by my desire to become whole. In healing my own soul wounds, I walked the path of the wounded healer and learned to transform the pain, grief, anger, and shame that lived within me into sources of strength and compassion" (www.thefourwinds .com/about-alberto-villoldo.php). Wanting to share what he had learned, Villoldo founded the Four Winds Society in 1984, which sponsors a number of energy medicine training programs, including the Healing the Light Body School. Since that time, Villoldo has continued to travel, learning and teaching the ways of a five-thousand-year-old energy medicine practice that heals through spirit and light.

The Four Winds Society was established as an international research and training program in which students may achieve personal healing while learning the ancient art of energy medicine. According to Villoldo, the crux of all shamanic healing is the human spirit. Because his philosophy emphasizes the treatment of illness before it manifests physically, work is done in what he refers to as the Luminous Energy Field surrounding the body, with a goal of helping people achieve "a place of extraordinary health." Villoldo's aim is to change the world by training healers. He believes human beings are caretakers of the Earth and that planetary healing is possible with a change of vision and consciousness. His programs place an emphasis on ethics and integrity. Sacred space is created for students to learn the healing arts in a safe and protected environment.

The Sanctuary Project, also founded by Villoldo, provides support and shelter to indigenous master healers as they descend from the Andes to live in Peruvian cities. Since 2002, the Sanctuary Project has worked to preserve and document the wisdom, stories, and ceremonies of these aging teachers who can help others learn the ways of the healer before, in the words of the Sanctuary's mission, "the path vanishes."

While practitioners frequently do hands-on work as part of the healing protocol, sessions vary from practitioner to practitioner. There is no strict set of rules as to hand placement or whether work is done on or off the body. Shamans often use tools, such as rattles, drums, chimes, feathers, Tibetan bowls, and herbs for smudging. Sage is a common herb for this purpose. The sage is set on fire and the smoke from the burning sage is wafted over the client to help clear the energy field.

The Four Winds Training Programs

Since 1982, the Healing the Light Body School has aimed to teach mastery in the healing arts. In this professional training program, practitioners are given a protected space in which to heal themselves and learn to bring balance to the body, the soul, and the Earth. The curriculum introduces rituals and rites associated with shamanic traditions. Students are also offered the opportunity to take a two-week expedition to Peru to connect with local shamans and experience the energy of sacred places. The Healing the Light Body School takes two years to complete, and students attend classes twice a year with time for practice and assimilation between sessions. Upon completion of this course and three mastery classes, students may apply for certification in luminous healing and energy medicine.

Classes and their content are subject to frequent changes. Go to www.thefour winds.com for up-to-date curriculum.

▶ The Healing the Light Body School is composed of four sessions beginning with **Illumination**. In this course, students learn:

- The Illumination Process to clear energy loops
- Erasing imprints of disease in the Luminous Energy Field
- The beginnings of the mystery teachings, using the Path of the Serpent of the South to start transforming wounds into sources of power and compassion

In the **Extraction** session, students are introduced to:

- Fear, envy, and anger as energies that may penetrate the Luminous Energy Field
- Crystallized energies and intrusive energies
- Entities in the Luminous Energy Field
- The Path of the Jaguar of the West as a way of the peaceful warrior

The **Soul Retrieval** session focuses on:

- How to journey
- The Essential Self

- The Path of the Hummingbird of the North to learn more of the mystery teachings

The session on **Great Rites** teaches students:

- How to assist someone on his or her final journey
- Maps of the afterlife
- How energy and vision can create reality
- The Path of the Eagle of the East to learn to dream the world into being

▶ The **Medicine Wheel** is a separate program for personal transformation using the Inca Medicine Wheel. Throughout the program, students receive rites of passage and initiation into the mystery teachings of the shaman's way.

- The Path of the Serpent of the South: a shamanic way of personal healing
- The Path of the Jaguar of the West: to move beyond fear and walk a path of peace
- The Path of the Hummingbird of the North: the practice of invisibility and how to step outside time
- The Path of the Eagle of the East: the gift of vision

Masters Courses are for serious students who have completed the Healing the Light Body and Medicine Wheel programs. Not all the Masters classes are mentioned here. The classes listed below offer healing techniques and ceremonies. For other classes, see their website, www.thefourwinds.com.

▶ **Advanced Soul Retrieval** is a mastery-level training that offers certification upon completion. It offers advanced journeying techniques for personal healing and planetary healing. Students will learn:

- Soul retrieval
- Working with the sacred
- Advanced divination and seeing
- Advanced soul retrieval

▶ In **Walking with Protection in the World,** students learn how to take care of themselves while doing their healing work. The curriculum includes the following:

- Using protection and light
- Unwinding harmful energies
- Removing negative energies

▶ **Working with the Sacred** introduces archetypes as ancient structures of the psyche. Students will learn:

- How the archetypes, the gods of old, still inform and guide all human activity
- To design mythic maps that shape and guide people's lives
- How to create ceremony to bring deep undercurrents into balance
- Archetypal analysis for personal transformation and client work

▶ **Beyond Soul Retrieval** covers the ancient art of recovering the essential self and the rewriting of outdated soul contracts. Students will learn:

- Journeying to the four chambers of the soul
- Discovering the source of original wounding
- Soul contracts and how to rewrite them

· · · · · · · · · · · · · · · · ·

Continuing Education Units: Offered by a Board of Registered Nurses licensed as a continuing education provider in the state of California.

Certification: Yes.

Participants: Open to anyone with an interest in healing themselves and the planet.

Code of Ethics/Standards of Practice: Yes.

Suggested Reading
Villoldo, Alberto. *Mending the Past and Healing the Future with Soul Retrieval.* Carlsbad, CA: Hay House, 2006.

———. *Shaman, Healer, Sage.* New York: Harmony Books, 2000.

Availability: Classes are taught in California, Utah, New England, the Netherlands, Ireland, Sweden, and the United Kingdom. To find out more about classes, go to www.thefourwinds.com.

Resources

The Four Winds Society, PO Box 680675, Park City, UT 84068-0675,

USA: 435-647-5988 or 888-437-4077; England: 0800-081-1523; Europe: 0044-800-081-1523; Australia: 1800-676-212; other countries: 001-435-647-5988; fourwinds@thefourwinds.com, www.thefourwinds.com

Bibliography

Villoldo, Alberto. S*haman, Healer, Sage.* New York: Harmony Books, 2000.

www.thefourwinds.com

HEALING SOUNDS

According to Jonathan Goldman, founder of the Sound Healers Association and author of *Healing Sounds: The Power of Harmonics*, "Healing Sounds focuses on the ability of harmonics to create vibrational changes. Those vibrational changes can promote positive shifting and rebalancing within a person's energy field, physical body, and mental and emotional outlook."

Sound Healing is based on three principles from quantum physics:

1. Everything in the universe is in a state of vibration.
2. When the body is in a state of good health, everything in the body vibrates in resonance or harmony. When disease is present, the body no longer vibrates in resonance or harmony.
3. Sound is an energy that can change the vibrational rate of objects.

Harmonics are multiples of simple sounds or notes. Sound vibrates in the form of waves, which are measured in hertz. One hertz is the equivalent of one cycle of a wave per second. The number of hertz (hz) determines the frequency of the sound. Musicians refer to the frequency of a musical note as the pitch. The note on a piano known as middle C vibrates at approximately 256 hz. The C above middle C is a harmonic of that note and vibrates at 512 hz. Middle C is the first harmonic, also called as the fundamental note, and the C above middle C is the second harmonic of that note.

When the middle C key is struck on the piano, a hammer strikes a wire string, causing it to vibrate at 256 hz. Resonance is the frequency at which a body of mass most naturally vibrates. The middle C string resonates at 256 hz. Other wires on the piano can also resonate with the wire that was struck even though you may not be able to hear them. The wood that makes up the piano also resonates with the C string. Every part of the piano resonates at its own natural frequency when the middle C string is struck. The individual frequencies of all the parts of the piano that are resonating with the middle C string are called overtones. This is why middle C played on a violin or a trumpet sounds different from one played on a piano. If the overtones were electronically removed, all three instruments would sound alike.

Even though tables, chairs, and fingernails may seem to be solid they all vibrate at a resonant frequency for each one. Bones, organs, skin, and other parts of the body have their own resonant frequencies and blend together to make a composite frequency. Each person has a unique composite frequency. Disease or injury can cause a part of the body to vibrate out of resonance with the rest of the body. Goldman originally became interested in the harmonics of sound in 1981 after talking to Pir Vilayat Khan, spiritual head of the Sufi Order of the West and speaker at a conference sponsored by the Sufi Healing Order. They discussed the possibility of a relationship between specific notes and the chakras, and Khan introduced Goldman to his understanding of the healing power of sound and harmonics. From there, he began experimenting with the harmonics of human voices and eventually began to vocalize harmonics, which sounded good and produced pleasant sensations in the body at the same time.

In time, Goldman began teaching toning in workshops. Toning is the process of sounding a note with the voice and holding that note for long periods of time. Choirs can hold a note for a very long time simply by having individuals in the choir breathe at different times. The note sounds continuous even though when individually sung it is not.

Goldman noticed he could hear harmonics when a healer scanned another person using sound. Scanning using a musical tone is done with a tuning fork, the human voice, or another sound tool. For example, the healer will move a tuning fork up and down the body, noting any changes as it moves over the chakras. Frustrated by the lack of written material on this subject, Goldman began to study physics as it related to sound, and he continues to study with masters of sound in both scientific and spiritual traditions in order to bring these two fields together. He learned many sounds and sound techniques from the music of Steven Halpern and John Beaulieu and toning exercises from Sarah Benson and students of toning pioneer Elizabeth

Laurel Keyes. He has worked with the Dalai Lama's chanting Gyuto and Gyume monks and now teaches Tibetan overtone chanting.

He also teaches many other aspects of sound healing, including various techniques of vocal toning to resonate the physical body, brain, and the chakras; the use of specific chants and mantras for conscious enhancement; how to understand and work with specific binaural beat frequencies to create brain wave synchronization; and the utilization of Pythagorean tuning forks to balance and align the neuromuscular system.

From his experimentation and what he learned from others, Goldman theorized that the true healing power of sound is through harmonics. He created a system he calls the "seven sacred vowel sounds," which are used to resonate with and align each of the individual chakras. While an instrument can create sound and project it at the body, Goldman prefers using the human voice.

During a sound healing session, the client is asked to lie down on a bed, couch, or massage table. The healer uses his or her own voice to project the correct frequency into the body, chakra, or energy field to restore resonance to a disturbed area of the energy field. The energy the practitioner puts into the sound is as important as the sound itself. The practitioner begins at the feet and sings a low tone. Moving up the body, the practitioner continuously changes the tone to a higher frequency, ending at the head. Experienced practitioners can determine changes in the sound when there is a place of imbalance in the energy field. The frequency of the note changes slightly when there is an imbalance. At a place of imbalance, the practitioner projects a specific harmonic into that area until the sound of the harmonic rings true.

Sound healers use other tools than just the voice. Music therapy in the form of songs and music helps the client to relax at the beginning of a session. The healer may have the client listen to specific music using imagery. Specific frequencies via an electronic medium may be used for correcting an imbalance. Many sound healers use tuning forks to hold a specific note. The sound healer may have the client chant a mantra to help the client relax and hold the balance of a newly corrected part of the energy field. Also available to the sound healer as tools are vibro-acoustic beds and chairs that project music or tones into the body of the client.

Course Descriptions

Several schools in sound healing are available to the student. The following classes are offered or endorsed by the Sound Healers Association of which Jonathon Goldman is a director. Students are given a certificate of completion at the end of each course. The Sound Healers Association is an inclusive organization with no restrictions on who may join.

▶ **Healing Sounds Correspondence Course** is a sixteen-week program that allows the individual study of sound healing and frequency shifting in the privacy of one's own home. Students explore the world of sound healing through the experience of using their own voices as instruments of self-healing and transformation. The course has a step-by-step process for learning to use sound for vibrational repatterning and alignment. No prior musical ability is necessary.

Audio content and reading material are included, with topics covering:

- Learning to create vocal harmonics
- Vowels as mantras
- Self-healing techniques using sound
- Breathwork
- Toning
- Three Healing Sounds Correspondence Course telephone consultations

▶ **Healing Sounds Seminar** is a weekend class in which students learn the scientific and spiritual basis of using sound for healing and transformation. Topics include:

- Energizing and balancing the brain
- Vocal harmonics: how to produce two or more notes at the same time with one's own voice
- Energizing the physical body and the chakras
- Improving the quality of the voice
- Pythagorean tuning forks
- The angel chakra
- Mantras, initiatory chants, and overtoning of vocal harmonics

- Invoking divine energies
- Initiating transdimensional frequency shifts

▶ **International Healing Sounds Intensive** is a nine-day experience of learning to use sound for vibrational patterning and alignment. The intensive covers the latest in scientific material on sonics and the sacred sounds from different traditions. Topics include:

- Principles of Sound Healing
- Psychoacoustics and the brain
- Vowels as mantras
- Music improvisation
- Breath and the Merkabah
- Overtoning: vocal harmonics for healing
- Sonic shamanism
- Therapeutic uses of music
- Color, light, and sound
- Peruvian whistling vessels, Rhi ratio tuning forks, and Tibetan bowls
- Bija mantras and sacred chants
- Use of sound for self-transformation and healing

▶ **Frequencies of Healing** is a weekend class that explores the healing and transformational nature of sound. Topics include:

- The scientific and spiritual basis of sound healing
- Vocal toning the chakras
- Breath and toning exercises
- Names as mantras
- Pythagorean tuning forks
- Fundamentals of vocal harmonics
- Angel chakra activation
- Sonic compassion initiation
- Self-created sounds to enhance personal health and wellness
- Energizing and balancing the brain

· · · · · · · · · · · · · · · · · ·

Continuing Education Units: No.

Certification: Students receive a certificate stating that they have completed the course from the Sound Healers Association.

Participants: The Sound Healers Association recommends its course of study to anyone who wishes to use sound as a means to access deeper levels of consciousness and self-transformation.

Code of Ethics/Standards of Practice: They have a statement of purpose.

Suggested Reading

Goldman, Jonathan. *Healing Sounds: The Power of Harmonics.* Rochester, VT: Healing Arts Press, 2002.

——. *The Seven Secrets of Sound Healing.* Carlsbad, CA: Hay House, 2008.

Resources

· ·

Sound Healers Association, PO Box 2240, Boulder, CO 80306, 800-246-9764, 303-443-8181, info@soundhealersassociation.org, www.soundhealersassociation.org

Bibliography

· ·

Goldman, Jonathan. *Healing Sounds: The Power of Harmonics.* Rochester, VT: Healing Arts Press, 2002.

www.consciousmedianetwork.com

www.furious.com

www.healingsounds.com

www.soundhealersassociation.org

HEART AND SOUL HEALING

HEART AND SOUL HEALING was developed by Ken Page and his wife, Nancy Nester, as a method of deeply healing all aspects of a person on both a cellular and a multidimensional level. Their healing techniques promote positive vibrational changes within our bodies in order to break down and release old cellular energy patterns. Their philosophy of healing, tied closely to this cellular transformation, is about "addressing issues on every level and dimension of existence. Since all things are interconnected holographically, everything is happening right now, on all realities, simultaneously" (taken from www.kenpage.com).

Heart and Soul Healing emphasizes finding old or distorted thought and energy patterns to which the subconscious is still giving energy. These patterns are released or altered to the benefit of the client. Page has also developed techniques for finding and reintegrating lost pieces of the soul to restore balance, removing energetic attachments to other people and dark energy, and resolving and releasing negative karmic influences.

Page is often called "the healer of healers" because of his work helping other healers release energies they have picked up from their clients. Healers can burn out if they have not trained their bodies to work with the high levels of energy needed for healing work or how to release others' energy when sessions are through.

The structure of Heart and Soul Healing is based on nine self-empowering and ongoing principles. The first involves the use of clear light instead of white light. Many healing modalities use the imagery of white light as a general purpose healing tool. Page believes that clear light, found in the region between white light and darkness, is a more effective tool for healing and that it has also been mentioned in the *The Tibetan Book of Living and Dying* and talked about by various Buddhist masters.

The second principle concerns the nonprojection of energy, light, or love. Page believes that when someone projects energy of any kind, outside thoughts, beliefs, and emotions can contaminate that projection and cause distortions within the recipient. He suggests that healers remain in a somewhat neutral state of compassion that does not project any form of energy while doing healing work, which also makes it easier to stay centered and grounded.

The third principle involves centering and clearing the energy field, enabling the practitioner to focus more clearly on matters at hand.

Another principle is keeping one's thought processes clear while eating. Negative thoughts such as worry or anger can affect the digestive process and bring in negative energy while a person is digesting food.

Accepting responsibility for creations, thoughts, words, and deeds is another principle. Students of Heart and Soul Healing are taught to take responsibility for their thoughts and actions and to be aware of how these things can affect the healing of others. This responsibility is also considered an important step in self-healing.

Heart and Soul Healing also asks that students commit themselves to unconditional love, which involves acceptance of and compassion for others, as well as themselves, without any judgment.

The seventh principle includes techniques for staying in the moment. By letting go of the past and staying out of the future, practitioners can much more easily focus and set intentions for healing.

Principle number eight involves facing one's fears and transforming them into strengths. Students can discover their greatest strengths by confronting what scares them the most.

Integrating your own heart and soul is the last principle of Heart and Soul Healing, which students do by moving the focus of their awareness to the pineal center of their brain using techniques Page has developed.

A Heart and Soul Healing session begins with an intake interview in which the client describes her reasons for coming. The practitioner scans the client energetically and asks the client to lie down on a massage table fully clothed and often covered with a sheet. The practitioner does a more thorough scan of the person's energy field and conducts a guided meditation. From there, the practitioner proceeds to the various specific protocols needed for healing work, which she will ascertain through close work with the client. At the end of the session, the client is often given some time alone to integrate the session. The practitioner often gives the client additional resources and suggestions to help the client further integrate the healing session outside the office.

Course Descriptions

The following classes are offered by the Institute of Multidimensional Cellular Healing. Because of the high number of workshops offered, only a few are listed as examples.

▶ **Heart and Soul Course** is a nine-day intensive experiential program. It is also a training course for those interested in becoming certified Heart and Soul practitioners. Students experience hands-on sessions with volunteer clients. Please check the website www.kenpage.com for a list of requirements that need to be met before taking this course. Topics include:

- Subtle shifts in consciousness
- The student's role in the global mind of oneness
- The role of energy in the student's life
- The art of transference: healing through compassion
- Using prana/qi/chi energy for healing
- Breathwork
- Clearing energetically both internally and externally
- Demonstration of evolution as a soul
- Healing karma
- Crystal mastery
- Bioenergetic repatterning

▶ **Blended Energy™: The Healing of Heart and Soul** is an experiential workshop designed to assist in manifesting and creating a desired life. It places emphasis on personal understanding, clearing, and balancing. Topics include:

- Nervous system and spinal cord balancing
- Karma and chakra clearing

- Integrating Heart and Soul techniques with other healing modalities

▶ **Eye to Eye with God** helps students blend polarities and discover a middle path of wisdom. Students learn to:

- Access higher brain states and incorporate them into daily life
- Open hidden senses and bring these sensory abilities to conscious awareness
- Connect with Source and achieve unity consciousness

▶ **Chakras: Organs of Consciousness** explores the identity and purpose for each chakra together with the characteristics of excessive and deficient energy. Topics include:

- Locating the energy powerhouse
- Techniques for spinning, clearing, and balancing chakras
- Releasing old stored energy in the chakras
- The role each chakra holds for spiritual awareness

▶ **Dancing with Ghosts: Techniques for Spirit Releasement** addresses the angelic realm, lost souls, and discarnate and earthbound spirits. Students learn about:

- The energetic effects of carrying around past events
- Factors in soul confusion
- Freeing pieces of spirits or souls trapped in the past
- Different ways of dealing with energy imprints, soul fragments, degrees of possession, and spirit attachment
- Specific techniques to balance energy and change vibrations
- Effectively clearing themselves and helping others become energetically free and clear

▶ **Animal Healing and Clearing** offers an opportunity to assist animals by using simple techniques. Students learn:

- Empathic communication with animals
- How emotions affect animals
- How to release energetic patterns from pets and other animal friends

Continuing Education Units: Ask your instructor.

Certification: Yes.

Participants: Anyone who wants to expand his or her level of awareness.

Code of Ethics/Standards of Practice: No.

Availability: Classes are offered throughout Australia, Canada, Europe, and the United States. To find a practitioner in your area, go to www.kenpage.com.

Resources

Institute of Multidimensional Cellular Healing™, PO Box 1500, Cleveland, GA
    30528, 800-809-1290, ken@kenpage.com, www.kenpage.com

Bibliography

Page, Ken. *The Heart of Soul Healing*. Cleveland, GA: Clear Light Arts, 1999.

———. *The Way It Works*. Cleveland, GA: Clear Light Arts, 1997.

Rinpoche, Sogyal. *The Tibetan Book of Living and Dying*. New York: HarperOne,
    1994.

HOLOENERGETIC® HEALING

Leonard Laskow, MD, founder of Holoenergetic Healing, uses conscious intention, imagery, forgiveness, and love to activate and direct healing energy, which he describes as "healing with the energy of the whole." In his book *Healing with Love*, he says that in the holoenergetic healing model, "it is the intent of the observing consciousness of the healer that determines the forming perception and initiates the transformation of energy."

Dr. Laskow trained as an ob-gyn at the Stanford University Medical Center. He is a fellow of the American College of Obstetrics and served as chief of Obstetrics and Gynecology at Community Hospital in Carmel, California. He also held a postdoctoral fellowship in psychosomatic medicine and was a faculty member at the University of California–San Francisco. In 1983, he gave up his medical practice in San Francisco to study energy work and its application to the healing process. Combining his background in science and clinical practice with his studies in energy healing led to the formation of Holoenergetic Healing. He is also a founding diplomate of the board of directors for the American Board of Integrative Holistic Medicine.

It was his laboratory work documenting how energy techniques slowed the growth of tumor cells in tissue cultures and bacterial growth in test tubes that led Dr. Laskow to seriously pursue studies in energy work. He also studied how intention, imagery, and love could change the molecular configuration and properties of water. This led him to work with the physical structure of DNA to see if it could be changed using the same tactics.

Dr. Laskow's healing system uses a four-phase process. The first phase is achieving a rational understanding of the problem by discussing it verbally and deciding what needs changing or healing. The second phase is intuitive, in which the practitioner uses tools to access information at an energetic level to find where the problem resonates within the body or energy field. Third, the practitioner helps the client overcome fear or uncertainty through positive intention and a forgiveness process, thereby releasing the energy of the problem. The last phase of the healing process is about reformation, in which the client makes the conscious choice to change.

One of the tools Dr. Laskow uses for gaining information at an energetic level is called an L-rod. It is made of a thin wire bent in the shape of an L. The smaller length of the L is placed into a tube, often a straw, so that the wire can move freely while held in the hand. The longer length of the L projects from the tube and can be easily seen as it moves. The practitioner uses two rods, one in each hand, while holding the hands and arms parallel to each other just as a dowser holds rods when dowsing for water. The wires separate or cross in response to the answers provided by the client's energy field as the practitioner questions him. In this way, the practitioner gains information concerning the person's issue or energy state.

Breathwork is another important tool for healing. Dr. Laskow recommends a four-step breathing process in which the client alternately holds and releases the breath to create and release tension.

During a session, clients either sit in a chair or lie down comfortably. The practitioner notes the client's medical history and presenting issue. Once this is done, the practitioner may evaluate the client's energy centers to help clarify where the issue lies. The practitioner then places one hand on the front of the client's heart/thymus area (a little above the heart) and the other hand on the back of the client in the same area. The client is asked to perform breathing exercises until the practitioner determines the right time to release the energy pattern of the issue. At the moment of release, the practitioner removes his or her hands. The client may be asked to do a forgiveness process and/or unconditional love process to complete the healing. The last part of the healing involves a discussion with the client concerning making healthy choices and accepting the gift of unconditional love.

Course Descriptions

The following list of workshops comes from the Holoenergetic Healing website, www.laskow.net. Some classes are held at the Esalen Institute in Big Sur, California. Please check the site, as workshops are constantly being updated and revised.

▶ **Awakening through Love** is a four-day workshop that allows students to experience the unconditional love at the heart of Holoenergetic Healing. Using step-by-step processes that blend ancient wisdom with modern scientific research, students are encouraged to release the limitations that obscure their essential nature. Topics include:

- Clearing personal and ancestral conditioning and wounds that foster pain, illness, and suffering
- Quieting the mind and managing physical and emotional stress
- Awakening to the truth of who we really are
- Deepening intuitive connections with divine guidance
- Supporting the body's healing, unimpeded by mental, emotional, and energetic blocks
- Creating what is most wanted in life
- Improving decision making, personally and professionally
- Accessing loving energies that are the unifying force of healing and self-awakening

▶ **Holoenergetic Healing** addresses issues of personal history and the personality. Using expanded awareness, love, and conscious choice, students learn to transform and heal themselves and others. They go beyond relieving symptoms to find the fundamental source of distress and illness. Topics include:

- Developing and holding a coherent focus in the heart
- How to do a holoenergetic tracing to discover the source of illness, suffering, and stress
- How to energetically replace dysfunctional patterns

- The forgiveness process
- Expanding awareness of the transpersonal self
- Developing intuition and inner guidance

▶ **Opening to Oneness through Loving Presence** is a three-day workshop designed to discover one's true nature. Topics include:

- Releasing veils that obscure a person's essential nature
- Clearing personal conditioning
- Supporting the body's healing process
- Overcoming mental and emotional blocks
- Creating what is most desired in life
- Finding divine grace

· · · · · · · · · · · · · · · ·

Continuing Education Units: CEUs are available at the Esalen Institute for RNs, marriage and family therapists, and licensed clinical and social workers. Call and ask for provider information.

Certification: No for practitioners, yes for instructors.

Participants: The Holoenergetic Healing Program recommends its classes to health and healing professionals as well as individuals and groups who wish to deepen their personal development and capacity for self-healing and self-awakening.

Code of Ethics/Standards of Practice: No.

Suggested Reading
Laskow, Leonard. *Healing with Love.* San Francisco: HarperSanFrancisco, 1992.

Availability: Classes are offered in France, Spain, Switzerland, and the United States. E-mail wholeness@laskow.net to find a practitioner in your area.

Resources
· ·
Holoenergetic Healing, 2305-C Ashland St #230, Ashland, OR 97520,
541-535-0099, wholeness@laskow.net, www.laskow.net

Bibliography

Laskow, Leonard. *Healing with Love.* San Francisco: HarperSanFrancisco, 1992.

www.health-quest.ca

www.iups.edu

www.laskow.net

www.naturalhealthcentre.com

www.trsincprofessinalsuite.com

HOLOTROPIC BREATHWORK™

THE WORD "HOLOTROPIC" comes from the Greek *holos* ("whole") and *trepein* ("moving in the direction of something"). Thus the idea of Holotropic Breathwork is based on the idea of "moving toward wholeness." The techniques used in Holotropic Breathwork are based on Stanislav Grof's research into nonordinary states of consciousness (including early research into the use of psychedelic drugs to reduce the fear of death in cancer patients), anthropology, transpersonal psychology, mystical traditions, shamanism, astrology, the Tibetan Book of the Dead, and Eastern mystical practices.

Holotropic Breathwork is a pyschotherapeutic form of breathwork developed by psychiatrist Stanislav Grof, MD, PhD, and his wife, Christina Grof. Stansilav Grof organized his work into five elements: group process, deep and rapid breathing, rhythmic music, focused bodywork, and Mandala drawings. In addition to psychotherapeutic applications, Holotropic Breathwork is used as a form of self-exploration and self-development outside of a therapeutic context.

Dr. Grof was born in Prague, Czechoslovakia, and received his medical degree from the Charles University of Medicine and a PhD from the Czechoslovakian Academy of Sciences. He came to the United States in 1967 to complete a two-year fellowship at the Johns Hopkins University in Baltimore, Maryland. From 1973 to 1987, he lived as a scholar in residence at the Esalen Institute in Big Sur, California. It was there he developed Holotropic Breathwork with his wife, Christina.

Grof broke the experiences in nonordinary states of consciousness into four categories. The natural inner healing process of the client brings to consciousness an event from one or more of the four categories of experience. The first category consists of sensory experiences and motor manifestations. When beginning a breathwork session, an individual may experience heightened states of the senses, such as a stronger sense of smell, tingling skin, or even elements of synesthesia, such as hearing and feeling colors.

Biographical experiences make up the second category. The client is encouraged to allow life experiences to come to mind during a session, and if desired, to continue to work with them in a more traditional therapeutic setting at a later date. The client may also choose to relive the experience while doing breathwork and allowing his or her inner healer to release the experience once it has been healed.

The third category pertains to perinatal experiences (from conception to birth). Dr. Grof contends birth to be one of the most traumatic events in a person's life. It is the first event in life over which there is no control. The individual's experiences in the womb and during birth have a strong influence in forming psychological patterns later in life. By working with these perinatal experiences in a nonordinary state, practitioners help clients to release difficult patterns and achieve more satisfying relationships with themselves and others.

The last category concerns transpersonal experiences beyond the physical body and personal identity. It includes any experiences not found in the first three categories. Some examples of transpersonal experiences are the moment of conception, out-of-body experiences, near-death experiences, or a feeling of oneness with anything and everything.

Holotropic Breathwork sessions are usually done in a group. Participants are asked to fast or have a small, light meal before a session. Members of a group session work in pairs, alternating roles. The one who is experiencing the healing work, referred to as the "breather," lies on a mattress in a darkened room with eyes closed. The partner, referred to as the "sitter," sits nearby to help the breather with his or her experience. After an initial guided relaxation by the practitioner the breathers are requested to breath more deeply, more quickly, and in an uninterrupted way (no pause between in breath and out breath) until the breathing takes on its own rhythm.

Although the healing is an internal experience and mostly done without talking, there may be some interaction between the practitioner and individuals within the group. The practitioner may help the client bring deep-seated tensions to the surface for release. Grof believes that corrective work involving body contact and touch is more easily done in a group setting.

Evocative music, beginning with deeply rhythmic pieces, building to a peak, then quieter integrative music is played throughout the session. Sessions last from 1½ hours to 3½ hours, but can in some cases last longer, The end of the session is decided based on each participant's sense of completion. After a session each participant is invited to draw a Mandala as a nonverbal expression of the experience. After all group participants have completed their experiences (and usually after a pause), the group meets in a Sharing Circle where participants share what they feel is important about their session.

Various creative techniques such as journaling, dream work, ritual, or focused energy release work may be used to assist individuals to complete and integrate their experiences.

Participants are screened by the practitioner before a workshop for contraindications. Since the work is similar to a strenuous sport and sometimes includes tensing of muscles as traumas are released, anything that would keep a person from a strenuous sport is a possible contraindication. In addition, a history of epilepsy, hypertension, heart disease, or glaucoma can be a contraindication. In such cases the advice of one's physician should be sought. Pregnancy is also a contraindication, since reliving birth or birth-related experiences could potentially initiate a premature birth process. In addition, individuals with an acute psychiatric history should not do this work except in a setting with the support required to enable them to fully process difficult material that may come up in the session, and in the period following the session.

Course Descriptions

A student may take any of the modules in no particular order and continue at his or her own pace. Students may apply to take any of the classes even if they do not wish to certify. The optional workshops listed are examples only. The Grof Personal Training website has a list of current courses. Classes change from time to time due to instructor and student interest in various topics.

▶ **The Practice of Holotropic Breathwork, Part A:** The Facilitator Adventure is a six-day residential training module. It is one of four required for certification. Topics include:

- The healing potential of nonordinary states of consciousness from a practical and cultural perspective
- Giving workshops, including facilitator presence, creating the didactic, cartography, problematic areas, contraindications, facilitating the session, and integration
- Holotropic bodywork including its history, theory, and practice
- Hands-on work by participants
- Discussion of specific challenging situations facilitators encounter

▶ **The Practice of Holotropic Breathwork, Part B: Music and Transcendence** is a six-day residential training module and is one of the four requirements for certification work. Topics include:

- Holotropic music: its history, theory, and practice
- Detailed discussion of three-part music structure with demonstrations of specific pieces for each section
- Sound system quality and power requirements
- Holotropic group work: its history, theory, and practice
- Discussion of common group experiences and challenging situations
- Demonstration of relaxation
- Facilitator self-care
- Practical workshop information: types, venue, pricing, promotion, and so on

▶ **Abnormal Psychology and Architecture of Psychopathology,** another required module for certification work, explores the traditional understanding of various forms of psychopathology. This six-day residential module includes discussions of:

- Various phobias
- Inhibited and agitated depression
- Suicidal behavior
- Obsessive-compulsive neurosis
- Conversion hysteria
- Sexual dysfunction and deviation
- Impulsive disorders, pyschosomatic illnesses, and addictions

▶ **Spiritual Emergency: Understanding and Treatment of the Crises of Transformation** is a six-day residential module and a requirement for certification. Discussions of the concept of spiritual emergency include:

- Its manifestations and forms
- Historical and anthropological perspectives
- Treatment strategies
- Work with family and friends

Optional Modules

Optional modules change depending on the facilitators. The following list gives samples of the modules offered each year. Many modules are open to those not in the certification training and to those new to Holotropic Breathwork.

▶ **Transpersonal and Holotropic Perspectives of the Schools of Depth Psychotherapy** reviews the history of depth psychology and the lives and work of the founders of its major schools (Franz Mesmer, Sigmund Freud, Carl Gustav Jung, Wilhelm Reich, and many more). This workshop includes an astrological perspective and discusses the correlations between the lives and ideas of these pioneers and major aspects in their natal charts and important transits. Students critically examine which ideas in psychology and psychotherapy have been violated by modern consciousness research and which of them have been refuted, revised, and transcended.

▶ **The Experience of Death and Dying: Psychological, Philosophical, and Spiritual Aspects** explores observations from various areas of modern consciousness research. Thanatology, anthropological shamanic studies, psychedelic research, experiential psychotherapies, and work with people in psychospiritual crises all have important implications for understanding the psychospiritual aspects of death and dying. Focus will be on such topics as:

- The process of psychological death and rebirth
- Psychedelic therapy with terminal cancer patients
- The shamanic initiatory crisis
- Aboriginal rites of passage

- Ancient mysteries of death and rebirth
- Near-death experiences
- Survival of consciousness after death
- Instrumental transcommunication
- Karmic reincarnation
- Eschatological mythologies

▶ **The Spiritual Quest, Attachment, and Addiction** looks at psychology and spirituality as they pertain to recovery, both for individual seekers and for those who work in the treatment field. This workshop explores a continuum, from the idea of addiction as an extreme form of attachment to the more specific forms of addictions such as substance, process, and relationship. Through theory, discussion, and experiential exercises, the class covers:

- The disease paradigm of recovery
- The wellness paradigm and the transpersonal recovery center
- Implications of perinatal and transpersonal dimensions for recovery
- The twelve steps as a world yoga
- Addiction as a spiritual emergency
- Addiction as shamanic crisis
- Recovery as a mystery school
- Psychedelics and recovery
- Recovery and the feminine
- Addiction from the homeopathic perspective
- Recovery as death/rebirth
- Addiction and the global crisis

▶ **The Art of Integration in Holotropic Breathwork** explores the theme of integration from both a personal and a professional perspective. Participants learn a variety of tools useful in further exploring the themes, issues, and insights that have emerged during sessions.

▶ **The Power of Archetype, Integrating Astrology, and Holotropic Breathwork** provides an overview of the essential elements for beginning an astrological practice and shows how astrology can be especially useful with Holotropic Breathwork.

The absolute beginner to those skilled in astrology will find this class useful. Topics may include:

- How astrology influenced Grof's breathwork and how his work influenced astrology
- How to read a chart and calculate transits
- Using astrology for insight into challenging breathwork experiences
- Astrological insight into perinatal matrices
- Astrological archetypes experienced through film clips and through music
- Astrological insight into 9/11 and other moments in history
- Comparing the spiritual insights gained through astrology with other wisdom traditions

▶ **The Ringbearer and Moving Toward Wholeness: Transformation in the *Lord of the Rings* Film Trilogy** uses Peter Jackson's film adaptation of the *Lord of the Rings* and Holotropic Breathwork to create a deep personal experience of being a Ringbearer in the twenty-first century. The popularity of this movie demonstrates culture's striving toward a new world myth, as well as the yearning to discover the deeper dimensions of what it means to be human. Students explore:

- The Fellowship characters as mythic dimensions of our individual lives
- Joseph Campbell's hero's journey
- Carl Jung and the realm of the archetypes
- The reemergence of the epic soul
- Film as catharsis and spiritual path
- Death/rebirth in modern popular culture
- Holotropic practitioner as Ringbearer
- Art, ritual, dance, meditation, and role playing

· · · · · · · · · · · · · · · ·

Continuing Education Units: This varies depending upon region and the background of the instructor, so inquire with your instructor.

Certification: Certification requires 600 hours of residential training in Grof Transpersonal Training, which approves the title of Holotropic Breathwork Certified Practitioner. It takes roughly two years to complete.

Participants: Students may enroll in modules without commitment to the entire program, but a written application is required.

Code of Ethics/Standards of Practice: The Association for Holotropic Breathwork International has an ethical agreement practitioners are asked to follow. It is available online at the www.ahbi.org website.

Availability: Workshops are available in Argentina, Australia, Austria, Brazil, Canada, Czech Republic, Denmark, England, Egypt, France, Germany, Ireland, Italy, Mexico, Norway, Spain, Sweden, Switzerland, the United States, and Venezuela. For a session in your area, go to www.ahbi.org.

Resources
. . . .

Association for Holotropic Breathwork International, PO Box 400267, Cambridge, MA 02140, office phone and fax: 617-674 2474, office@ahbi.org, www.ahbi.org, www.holotropic.com

www.stanislavgrof.com

Bibliography
. . . .

Taylor, Kylea. *The Breathwork Experience: Exploration and Healing in Nonordinary States of Consciousness.* Santa Cruz, CA: Hanford Mead Publishers, 1994.

www.ahbi.org

www.breathwork.com

www.wikipedia.org

www.holotropicbreathwork.net

www.stanislavgrof.com

MATRIX ENERGETICS®

RICHARD BARTLETT, DC, ND, founder of Matrix Energetics, noticed that the techniques involved with the various forms of energetic healing seemed to work erratically. To get to the root of this, he studied over thirty healing modalities to determine which ones worked on a regular basis and why. In 1996, he practiced healing through light touch with focused intent that heals through the principles of quantum physics. Bartlett's Matrix Energetics is a healing technique that communicates at the quantum level with energy and information interacting to create reality.

According to Bartlett, everything a person believes, accepts, experiences, and internalizes forms a living matrix or grid of energy. The matrix is structured by vibrations and waveform patterns built from biological information. It provides pathways and interconnections for intercommunication throughout the body. Each person has a unique matrix that he calls the energetic signature. In order to change something within the matrix, the person must change the arrangement of thoughts and feelings through a shift in consciousness.

Through journey work and visualization, the practitioner collapses the current reality to establish a new flow of biological information. By changing the observance of the reality, attaching a new paradigm and the consciousness attached to that paradigm, physical changes can manifest in the body. Bartlett does not work on the disease, trauma, or injury, because he believes that focusing on these experiences reinforces them. Using the shamanic practices of journey work and meditation, practitioners in Matrix Energetics are taught to see the client's body as one small part of a wave front of consciousness and virtual particles. The practitioner navigates the individual's awareness into a realm where the disease or injury does not exist as a problem and begins to promote healing.

Practitioners do not run energy through their body or energy field, but rather maintain a state of possibility where the perfect outcome is able to manifest itself. According to Bartlett, people have the keys to limitless possibilities as long as they don't actually try to make anything happen. Practitioners are taught to relinquish the tendency to measure or observe with conscious limitations. Because everything is composed of quantum particles, anything is theoretically possible.

Sessions are often only a few minutes long. Clients may stand, sit, or recline on a massage table or couch. Practitioners will do what they call skimming, which involves moving their hands over the body and the energy field, looking for a spot that feels rigid. They then measure the negative energy pattern at the quantum level and get out of the way to let the positive change happen. This process may be repeated in different areas of the body, with the objective not to fix something, but to allow reality to be positively transformed.

Course Descriptions

Classes are offered throughout the United States and Canada. The classes listed below come from the Matrix Energetics website. Certified practitioners are required to attend at least one seminar or training every year. Certified practitioners who live outside North America need to make arrangements for yearly classes with Matrix Energetics.

Local and teleconference study groups are available for students who desire to become certified practitioners. Students have one year from the date of the certification course to complete the requirements for certification.

▶ **Level 1** teaches students how to use the matrix to make physical and observable changes in the human body. Students learn to move outside the concept of a problem set into a solution set. The class teaches specific techniques to use the power of active imagination, focused intent, playfulness, and gentle touch to create real-time changes in physical and emotional patterns.

The format is experiential learning with demonstrations that present new ways of thinking about matter, disease, and healing. Topics include:

- An introduction to quantum physics

- How to engage the flow of universal intelligence
- Exploring the idea and experience of cocreating inside the living matrix
- Presentation of a background understanding of cocreating in the matrix and the use of subtle energy
- A simple system of palpation
- Light measuring techniques
- Archetype technique
- Time travel technique
- Twenty-one key healing frequencies

▶ **Level 2** offers advanced techniques and examples of how to use this work. Topics include:

- Templates to streamline healing
- Advanced hands-on work using the templates
- Dr. Bartlett's thinking process in action through specific demonstrations

▶ **Level 3: Wizard Training, Treading the Inner Corridors of Power and Possibility** helps the student master Matrix Energetics techniques and consciousness expansion. Level 2 is a prerequisite. Topics include:

- The ability to successfully employ Matrix Energetics using the wave for transformation
- Accessing healing frequencies
- Ancient principles of magick
- Quantum-based consciousness
- Advanced techniques and treatment strategies
- How to take Matrix Energetics into business, finances, relationships, goals, and desires

▶ **Practitioner Certification Class** is a one-day class designed for students who want to pursue certification. Students must have completed Levels 1 and 2. Level 3 does not count toward certification. Students must also have 60 documented hours of practical experience using Matrix Energetics as a discipline. Students take a written and practical examination during this class.

Continuing Education Units: Yes. Approved by the National Certification for Therapeutic Massage and Bodywork as a provider, authorization #450193-06. The Naturopathic Board State of Washington and the Chiropractic Board State of Washington will accept credits if the individual doctor feels they are applicable to his or her practice. Outside Washington, check to see if your state board needs pre-approval.

Certification: Participants receive certificates upon completion of each course. Upon receipt of a journal documenting certified practitioner requirements, Matrix Energetics bestows the title of Matrix Energetics Certified Practitioner. Dr. Bartlett occasionally bestows the title of Master Practitioner to certified practitioners who have long been of service to the Matrix Energetics training program.

Participants: The program is open to all individuals whether they have no medical or healing background or are an experienced practitioner.

Code of Ethics/Standards of Practice: No.

Availability: Classes are currently available in Newark, NJ, Seattle, WA, and San Francisco, Los Angeles, and San Diego, CA. To find a session in your area, go to www.matrixenergetics.com.

Resources

Matrix Energetics International, 19909 Ballinger Way NE, Suite 100, Shoreline, WA 98155, 800-269-9513, info@matrixenergetics.com, www.matrixenergetics.com

Bibliography

Bartlett, Richard. *Matrix Energetics: The Science and Art of Transformation*. New York: Simon & Schuster, 2007.

www.matrixenergetics.com

www.matrixmatters.com

MELODY CRYSTAL HEALING

MELODY IS A CRYSTOLOGIST and author of the Love Is in the Earth series, a collection of six books that describe the properties of hundreds of stones and associated crystal healing techniques.

Melody has had an interest in the geological and mystical properties of stones since childhood. After the publication of her first book, she began teaching workshops, and in 1997, she began to certify instructors to teach her crystal healing work. In 2009 her certified instructors came together under the name of the Academy of Melody Crystal Healing Instructors (TAOMCHI).

According to *Merriam-Webster's Dictionary*, a crystal is defined as "a body that is formed by solidification of a chemical element, a compound, or a mixture and has a regular repeating internal arrangement of its atoms and often external plane faces." Www.wordnet.princeton.edu defines a stone as "a lump or mass of hard consolidated mineral matter." Mineral contents of the stones used for healing purposes vary. The use of a specific mineral is determined by the needs presented by the client. Wordnet also defines a gem as "a crystalline rock that can be cut up and polished for jewelry." Emeralds, diamonds, sapphires, and rubies are called precious stones. Semiprecious stones, sometimes called gemstones, are less rare but still valued for their beauty. Opal and topaz are examples of semiprecious stones.

Crystals play an active part in the field of energy medicine, used both as an ancillary tool to augment energy healing techniques and directly as a specific treatment for the energy field, chakras, meridians, and the physical, emotional, mental, and spiritual bodies. Crystals may be worn as necklaces or bracelets and carried in a pocket or in a pouch close to the body. Healers using crystals in a healing session may lay them out in a pattern on the client's body or hold a crystal in their hand while scanning the energy field around the client's body to determine the points where energy is blocked or draining away from the energy field or the physical body.

Stones may be used to aid relaxation, soothe and stimulate the energy field and the body's organs and immune system, and also enhance a user's emotions. For example, according to Melody, danalite is a comforting stone that encourages the wearer or holder of the stone to pass the burdens of the inner self and mind to the stone. Amazonite calms the nervous system and strengthens the heart. Jade aids the kidneys and the immune system.

In addition to the types of stones, the color of a particular stone or crystal is an important factor in healing. When working with chakras, healers use crystals exhibiting the same color as the chakras needing healing work, and often stimulate, balance, and open the chakras by laying stones directly on the individual in a particular pattern depending on the client's needs and each stone's healing properties.

A session usually lasts about an hour. Clients recline, fully clothed, on a massage table or couch while the practitioner plays soft music in the background. The practitioner does an intake of the client's history and the problem presented. He or she then determines which crystals and/or stones need to be placed on or around the client's body, often in intricate patterns and corresponding to the acupressure points and meridians. Often the practitioner will recommend crystals for the client to wear or carry after the session is through.

Course Descriptions

The Level I and II Melody Crystal Workshops are based on Melody's Love Is in the Earth series of books about the mineral kingdom. The workshops teach specific crystal arrays for personal healing and self-actualization drawn from sacred traditions around the world. The classes listed here are offered by the Academy of Melody Crystal Healing Instructors and are examples only. They are subject to change.

▶ **Love Is in the Earth Level I Melody Crystal Workshop** provides the foundation for understanding and accessing the energies of the mineral kingdom. Topics include:

- Self-limiting belief systems
- Chakras activation and cleansing cords and connections

- Connecting to the inner self
- Laying on of hands and stones
- Selected crystal arrays including the Gateless Gate

▶ **Love Is in the Earth Level II Melody Crystal Workshop** expands on and enhances the skills developed in Level I. Areas of focus include:

- Advanced laying on of stones
- Actualizing desires
- Past life ascension
- Intuitive healing
- Soul journeying
- Tibetan pulsing
- Group laying on of stones
- Jin Shin Jyutsu techniques

· · · · · · · · · · · · · · · · · ·

Continuing Education Units: Offered by individual instructors depending on locale.

Certification: Yes, granted by each individual Academy of Melody Crystal Healing instructor.

Participants: Classes are open to qualified candidates with instructor approval.

Code of Ethics/Standards of Practice: They have a statement of Ethical Standards that members must agree to.

Suggested Reading

Melody. *Love Is in the Earth: A Kaleidoscope of Crystals.* Wheat Ridge, CO: Earth-Love Publishing, 1995.

———. *Love Is in the Earth: Laying-on-of-Stones.* Richland, WA: Earth-Love Publishing, 1992.

Melody, with illustrations by Julianne Guilbault. *Love Is in the Earth: The Complete Crystal and Mineral Encyclopedia, The Liite Fantastic, The Last Testament.* Wheat Ridge, CO: Earth-Love Publishing, 2008.

Availability: Classes are offered throughout Australia, the United Kingdom, and the United States. To find a practitioner in your area, go to www.taomchi.com.

Resources
. . . .

The Academy of Melody Crystal Healing Instructors, www.taomchi.com

Bibliography
. . . .

Melody. *Love Is in the Earth: A Kaleidoscope of Crystals.* Wheat Ridge, CO: Earth-Love Publishing, 1995.

www.embodyforyou.com

www.mineralkingdom.com

www.mountainspringsmassage.com

www.taomchi.com

www.tddir.com

www.vhsg.com

www.whatreallyworks.co.uk

PHYSIOHELANICS™

D R. C. DIANE EALY BEGAN STUDYING ENERGY HEALING with various healers in the mid-1970s and also trained as a psychotherapist and received her doctorate in behavioral science in 1980. At that time, she felt a need for an energy modality that would integrate the physical, emotional, intellectual, and spiritual aspects of a person. At the end of the 1980s, she developed her own modality called Physiohelanics. *Physio* is the Greek word for natural and *helan* is Old English for healing.

Clients requested classes and in 2003 Ealy founded the Ealy Center for Natural Healing, LLC. Her program is the first school of energy healing to be licensed by the Arizona State Board for private postsecondary education and only one of three such programs in the United States.

Practitioners of Physiohelanics are considered facilitators of the healing process. They use techniques to restore the flow of energy to and through the physical body and the energy field that surrounds and penetrates the body. They work to bring conscious awareness to the healing process and to educate the client in methods to help continue the healing work. According to Ealy, all energy in and around the body is connected, cleared, and balanced at the heart. Ealy also believes this healing work is sacred and that practitioners are guided by the higher self of both the client and the practitioner. Healers align with what she calls the Divine Universal and Earth energy while doing a Physiohelanics treatment. Healers also learn to communicate with guides and totems present during the healing session. Totems are spirit guides in the form of animals that are said to help an individual through life, much like a guardian angel.

All work begins with the client fully clothed and lying facedown. Treatments usually last forty-five to sixty minutes. The practitioner begins the treatment by working on each of five layers in the etheric energy field surrounding the human body. Each level has distinctive energetic structures. The practitioner determines the condition of these structures and proceeds to clear and repair them. All work at this point is done off the body.

Once this stage of the treatment is complete, the practitioner will lightly lay her hands on the shoulders of the client and work down the back while running energy to clear any further blockages. Next, the client is asked to turn over and the practitioner works to clear and connect the eight major chakras and the minor chakras found at the hands, feet, and major bone joints. Once the treatment is over, the practitioner discusses any findings of interest to the client, answers questions, and perhaps teaches the client a few energy maintenance techniques.

Course Descriptions

Upon completion of requirements, a student may apply to become certified as a Physiohelanics Master Practitioner. The Master Practitioner program is designed for working adults with online classes as well as live hands-on workshops and seminars that are held in the Tucson, Arizona, area. The following course descriptions come from their website.

▶ **Applied Physiohelanics Techniques** consists of one five-day and three four-day residency seminars in Tucson. Students are expected to participate through the course of the year in the Physiohelanics web log and a monthly conference call. They are required to complete class papers and projects at the rate of one per month. During the course of the year, they must also complete and document 200 healing sessions using Physiohelanics techniques. Students learn the following:

  • The multiple energy structures within the etheric and physical bodies
  • How to locate and correct any abnormalities within the etheric and physical bodies

- How to facilitate deep levels of healing within an individual, working simultaneously with the spiritual, intellectual, emotional, and physical aspects of each client
- How to make energy-related recommendations to clients for overall improvements in health and well-being
- How to avoid going beyond their capabilities in healing others and to refer to another professional when appropriate
- In-person and distance healing

▶ **Ethics of Energy Healing** explores Physiohelanics ethical standards as well as those found in other therapeutic professions. Students learn to understand the purpose for these principles in Physiohelanics healing. Students make an agreement to abide by these ethical standards during and after training.

▶ **Channeling Energy** addresses the following:

- Channeling and directing healing energy
- Protecting oneself from the negativity of others
- Extracting blocked and negatively charged energies from a client
- Using the various colors of energy

▶ **Creating and Maintaining Case Files** teaches students how to assemble and maintain case files for each client, including the content and structure of case notes, intake, and release forms.

▶ **Fundamental Understanding of Human Anatomy** provides basic knowledge of anatomy and ready references available for working with clients.

▶ **Developing and Trusting Kinesthetic Intuition** teaches methods for continuously developing and trusting the kinesthetic intuition. Students will understand and be able to use their kinesthetic intuition during a Physiohelanics treatment.

▶ **Communication Skills** emphasizes interpersonal and intrapersonal communication skills. Students learn communication techniques such as listening skills to be applied during treatment sessions.

▶ **Working with Spirit Guides and Totems** addresses the function of spirit guides and totem animals during a Physiohelanics session, including the practitioner's and the client's. Students learn to work with their own guides.

▶ **Survey of Healing Modalities, Ancient and Modern** requires students to research at least two other healing modalities or disciplines and demonstrate a basic knowledge of other healing practices.

▶ **Fundamental Understanding of Consciousness and Quantum Physics** offers students a basic understanding of consciousness and quantum physics as they relate to energy healing. Students will be able to verbally explain the relevance of these areas to energy healing.

▶ **Building a Private Practice** teaches students the following:

- How to create appropriate marketing materials
- Setting price
- Creating an appropriate physical space for healing
- Networking with other professionals
- Getting referrals
- Bookkeeping
- Avoiding burnout

▶ **Demonstration of Excellence** requires students to demonstrate their acquired and developed Physiohelanics healing skills in a manner approved by their mentors and satisfactory to the Master Practitioner level. Students further demonstrate how the process of becoming a Master Practitioner has impacted them.

· · · · · · · · · · · · · · · ·

Continuing Education Units: No.

Certification: Granted by the Ealy Center for Natural Healing, LLC. The program consists of 400 hours, including 200 hours of practicum time.

Participants: Physiohelanics recommends their program to working adults who are able to attend classes part time with both online and on-site courses of study. Prospective students must have completed high school or the equivalent and at least 10 hours of documented experience with an energy healing modality. No credit for certification is given for other energy healing study.

Code of Ethics/Standards of Practice: Yes.

Availability: Classes are only available at the Ealy Center in Tucson. To locate a practitioner in your area, go to www.becomeahealer.com.

Resources

The Ealy Center for Natural Healing, 5210 East Pima, Suite 210, Tucson, AZ
85712, 520-270-3868, diane@cdianeealy.com, www.becomeahealer.com

Bibliography

www.becomeahealer.com

www.jewishtucson.org

www.withawhitefeather.blogspot.com

ROSALYN BRUYERE

R OSALYN BRUYERE IS ONE OF THE LEADING PIONEERS in the field of energy medicine. From 1972 to 1980, she worked with Dr. Valerie Hunt, then chair of the Department of Kinesiology at UCLA, and Emilie Conrad, a shamanic healer, to provide evidence that hands-on healing involves electrical and magnetic phenomena rather than only psychological healing.

Bruyere has the ability to see the energy field. Experiments using electromagnetic fields in a special room, called a Mu room, were performed on a number of volunteers. The Mu room is a shielded room located in the physics department at UCLA. Natural electromagnetic energy can be altered by the physicists. Bruyere was able to accurately describe changes in the energy fields of the subjects, including the chakras and the meridians flowing inside the body. Much of what she observed could be verified by instrumentation.

Since that time, Bruyere has continued to participate in a number of studies concerning the efficacy of energy healing, working with people such as Dr. Elmer Green at the Menninger Clinic as well as Dr. Fritz Popp in Kaiserslautern, Germany. Her interests have led her to study Egyptian temple symbology, sacred geometry, ancient mystery school rites, and the pre-Buddhist Tibetan Bon-Po Ways.

Bruyere has also spent many years studying with Native Americans. In her book *Wheels of Light*, she describes Hopi oral history going back fifteen thousand years containing references to the chakras, including pictures of prehistoric dolls found near Lapton, Arizona, with jewels placed in them that mark the location of chakras. These markings correspond to traditional Chinese medicine and to the early teachings of healers in India. In *Wheels of Light*, she also describes an Egyptian priest-scribe named Tehuty, more often known for his Greek name, Hermes, who lived over fifty thousand years ago and documented and described the chakra system as we know it today.

While scientific studies are important to her, she also remains committed to learning, practicing, and preserving the ancient ways of healing. She is the founder and director of the Healing Light Center Church, which provides practical tools for a spiritual life using traditions from African, Native American, and Tibetan cultures. She also founded the Crucible Program as a basis for the classes and workshops taught around the world.

Bruyere is one of the world's foremost authorities on the chakra system. The term "chakra" comes from the Hindu language and means "wheel of light." Chakras are spinning centers of energy located within the energy field. Bruyere documents seven major chakras along the spine and 122 smaller chakras located at the various bone joints. A healthy chakra spins in a clockwise circle. Unhealthy chakras may spin elliptically or move back and forth horizontally, vertically, or at an angle. Sometimes a chakra does not spin at all. By holding the hands over the chakra a healer can energize the chakra and bring it back into balance and cause it to spin in a healthy clockwise circle. The seven major chakras are balanced when all of them spin clockwise.

Sessions are usually done with the client reclining on a massage table, but may be done with the client sitting in a chair or lying on the floor. The session begins with an intake interview. Assessment of the energy field is done about five to six inches away from the body. Healing techniques involve touch. Bruyere believes that most practitioners are more likely to have an effect on the client if they touch. The practitioner moves his or her hands over the body using techniques to aid in clearing and balancing the chakras.

Course Descriptions

The Crucible Program is an international program of the seminary division of the Healing Light Center Church. Bruyere refers to it as a modern mystery school whose purpose is to train medical practitioners and others in the healing arts. The following classes are available at the time of this writing and subject to change. They are listed as examples only.

▶ **The Medicine Wheels: Sacred Spirit and Earth Science, the Human Body and Energy Spheres** is an experiential six-day workshop in which students study ancient Native American spiritual philosophy as it pertains to the human energy system. Topics include:

- Ancient Native American spiritual philosophy and earth science
- The way of the medicine wheels
- Human body/energy spheres (chakras)
- Dimensions of sacred ceremony
- Working with spirit and energy and physical presence of the great powers of our natural world
- Spirit and substance of life
- Personal energetic intimacy with the natural world
- Earth wisdom

▶ **Self-Expression and Manifestation: A Fifth Chakra Intensive** is a five-day workshop addressing the use of the fifth (throat) chakra as the bridge to the etheric realm. Topics include:

- The transformation of the pure energy of the spiritual realm into a verbal message
- The fifth chakra's ability to say the right thing at the right time
- The fifth chakra as a channel to bring the mystical into physical reality
- The perfect vibrational template
- Accessing the matrix of higher potential and abilities

▶ **Reincarnation and the Journey of the Soul** is a five-day workshop for self-understanding and spiritual growth as well as bringing past knowledge and talents into the present. Topics include:

- Reconciling the past, present, and future
- Learning to appreciate the Earth and life in a new way
- Understanding emotions and where they come from
- Exploring emotions and life histories through hands-on techniques and meditative practices

▶ **The Care and Feeding of the Brain: A Third Chakra Intensive** is a five-day intensive seminar that combines information and practical healing techniques involving the third chakra (solar plexus). Topics include:

- Alzheimer's disease, Parkinson's disease, and autism
- Microwave and other forms of radiation
- Tumors and lesions
- Growing new synapses in the brain
- Examining the brain's meaning and implications for spiritual development

▶ **Ancient Healing Techniques for the Modern Era: An Egyptian Mysteries Workshop** addresses a system of beliefs and spiritual practices going back over four thousand years. Topics include:

- Egyptian understanding of how the mind and emotions affect the disease process
- Egyptian use of sound, color, symbolism, and ceremony
- An energy-based understanding of life
- Egyptian understanding of the energy field and the chakras
- A self-initiation process

▶ **The Alchemy of Change** introduces both science and mysticism as a pattern for the modern practice of healing. Topics include:

- Definition of alchemy
- The alchemical nature of chakras
- Transformation of the self
- Mystical and practical applications of alchemy
- Seven alchemical processes that match the chakra system

· · · · · · · · · · · · · · · · ·

Continuing Education Units: Yes; the provider is the California Board of Registered Nursing, provider #06153. There is an extra fee for the CEU credit certificate.

Certification: Students are offered certificates of completion for a course at an extra fee.

Participants: Although many enter the program to study energy healing, students of widely divergent interests use the program to achieve their goals.

Code of Ethics/Standards of Practice: Yes.

Suggested Reading

Bruyere, Rosalyn. *Wheels of Light: Chakras, Auras, and the Healing Energy of the Body*. New York: Fireside Books, 1994.

Availability: Classes are held internationally. Go to www.rosalynlbruyere.org to locate a class in your area.

Resources

Healing Light Center Church, 261 East Alegria Ave #12, Sierra Madre, CA 91024, 626-306-2170, hlcc2@earthlink.net, www.rosalynlbruyere.org

Bibliography

Bruyere, Rosalyn. *Wheels of Light: Chakras, Auras, and the Healing Energy of the Body*. New York: Fireside Books, 1994.

Hunt, Valerie V. *Infinite Mind: The Science of Human Vibrations of Consciousness*. Malibu, CA: Malibu Publishing, 1989.

SANDRA INGERMAN

SANDRA INGERMAN IS A WORLD-RENOWNED PSYCHOTHERAPIST and shamanic practitioner known for her many books on spirituality and shamanism
and for bringing soul retrieval to a wide audience. Her interest in shamanic studies
led her to the Foundation for Shamanic Studies, where she served as educational
director starting in 1990 and as a member of the board of trustees from 1994 to
2001. She is a licensed marriage and family therapist, professional mental health
counselor, a board-certified expert on traumatic stress, and is certified in acute traumatic stress management. Ingerman hopes to integrate shamanic healing practices
with allopathic medicine. She envisions a time when enough people heal their toxic
thoughts, and the toxins in the environment will begin to disappear. People cannot
hope to create a positive future when they are stuck in the wounds of the past. This
is true for individuals, cultures, societies, and nations.

Ingerman began her formal education with a degree in marine biology and an
interest in reversing the pollution occurring in rivers and later with all of environmental pollution. However, her interests changed and she acquired a master's degree in counseling psychology from the California Institute for Asian Studies, which
later became the California Institute of Integral Studies. While there she took a
class on shamanic journeying.

Modern science and allopathic medicine ignore the spiritual side of the patient
presenting an illness. A shaman knows that all things are permeated by a spiritual
essence and that illness is a symptom of an imbalance or displacement of that spiritual essence. As a shamanic healer, Ingerman noticed her clients, through their
stories, expressed the feeling either that something was missing from their lives
or that they felt cut off from a connection with life. Her shamanic studies gave her

techniques to aid her in helping her clients reconnect with life and gain back what was missing.

The shamanic journey is the core technique for all shamanic work. It is a way for the shaman to access spiritual information and work with spirit guides. It is a form of meditation, usually accompanied by drumming, to help the mind reach a state of calm, enabling the journeyer to reach realities outside of normal perception.

Ingerman believes that it is who we become, not what we do, that changes the world and its environment. As people heal their inner environment, that reflects back in the outer world. She calls this work Medicine for the Earth. She has a formula for this: intention + union + love + focus + concentration + harmony + imagination = transmutation.

She sees imagination as an important part of this formula. In order to be able to create a clean environment, people must imagine the earth as wholesome and a place of beauty. By healing themselves people can feel free to imagine that world of peace and beauty. She writes about this in her book *Medicine for the Earth: How to Transform Personal and Environmental Toxins.*

While the feasibility and acceptability of shamanic treatments being used for clinical trials are often questioned, a recent study shows the efficacy of such treatments. An article in *Alternative Therapies* (Nov./Dec. 2007, vol. 13, no. 6) reports on the results of applying shamanic healing techniques for temporomandibular joint (TMJ) disorders. The study, which took place at Kaiser Permanente Medical Center in Portland, Oregon, showed a significant decrease in the pain levels of the patients receiving shamanic treatments. The most frequently used shamanic treatment in this study and in most shamanic sessions centers on a shamanic technique called soul retrieval that aims to restore spiritual wholeness to an individual. According to Ingerman, during traumatic moments a part of the soul or essence of an individual can break away from his or her core identity. The shaman does a form of meditation called journeying in which he or she goes into an altered state of consciousness and "journeys" to identify that individual's missing soul pieces. Once they have been found, a ceremony is conducted in which the essence is reconnected to the soul of the client. Later sessions may involve helping the client integrate the returned essence.

Shamanic healing works with the spiritual aspects of the client's imbalance or illness. Sessions may include journey work, ceremony, or ritual, and aim to restore a sense of wholeness to a fragmented self. The shamanic practitioner listens carefully to the client's description of the problem and then consults with spiritual guides that assist in the diagnosis and help her advise the client on the appropriate treatment.

Power animals, also known as animal spirit guides or totems, frequently show up during journey work to help the client. The practitioner will ask the client to notice if there is an animal present during the beginning of the journey process. The type of animal that appears during the meditation is a symbolic message. Each animal represents one or more character traits and is of significance to the client.

To ensure the client best responds to the treatment, the practitioner may suggest additional sessions to help the client integrate changes that have been made. Shamans are also trained to conscientiously enhance whatever allopathic health treatments the client may be working with. Shamanic treatments do not replace the need for psychological and medical treatments, and often the practitioner will refer to the client to a doctor or psychologist for treatment.

Course Descriptions

The following list of courses comes from Ingerman's website, www.sandraingerman.com. Instructors in the Sandra Ingerman program work with her for two years before teaching on their own. Because the program is constantly growing and changing, the classes are subject to change. Instructors offer several introductory and advanced lectures, small workshops, and intensives. Go to www.shamanicteachers.com for a list of what is currently available.

▶ **Medicine for the Earth Gatherings and Healing with Spiritual Light** is a five-day seminar taught in a retreat setting. The theme is based on Ingerman's book *Medicine for the Earth: How to Transform Personal and Environmental Toxins.* Experience with shamanic journeying is required before taking this class, which covers the following topics.

- Transforming personal and environmental pollution by transmuting negative beliefs, attitudes, and energy generated by emotions
- How to work in cooperation with helping spirits, spirits of the land, and internal divine nature to create healing and transmutation

- Working in cooperation with the elements: earth, water, air, wood, and fire
- Transforming and transmuting environmental and personal toxins
- Integrating spiritual work into everyday life
- Ceremonies to transmute water and other substances
- Fire ceremony to help manifest visions
- Updating healing methods for diseases caused by environmental pollution

▶ **The Shamanic Journey: The Path of Direct Revelation** is a two-day workshop in which students are introduced to core shamanism. Topics include:

- Nearly universal methods used by the shaman to enter nonordinary reality for problem solving and healing
- Shamanic journeys
- The shamanic state of consciousness
- Awakening spiritual abilities
- Connecting with nature
- Introduction to shamanic divination and healing
- Restoring spiritual power and health
- How shamanism can be applied in contemporary life to help heal the self, others, and the planet

▶ **Five-Day Soul Retrieval Training** is done in a retreat setting. The work is based on Ingerman's books *Soul Retrieval* and *Welcome Home*. The workshop is created exclusively for those who wish to add shamanic techniques to their healing practice. Previous experience with shamanic journeys, power animals, and nonordinary reality is essential for participation. Topics include:

- Exploring the experience of partial soul loss resulting from personal trauma or illness
- Tracking a soul fragment
- Returning the lost essence to the client
- Integrating soul retrieval into modern culture
- Communication skills

- Ethics of doing the work
- Life after soul retrieval
- Shamanic journeying, ritual, and ceremony

. . . .

Continuing Education Units: Some instructors may be qualified to offer CEUs. Ask your instructor.

Certification: No.

Participants: Sandra Ingerman's courses are open to students desiring to learn ancient shamanic ways and/or wanting better ways to heal themselves, others, and the environment.

Code of Ethics/Standards of Practice: Yes. Sandra Ingerman teaches ethics in every workshop and has a strong Code of Ethics.

Suggested Reading

Ingerman, Sandra. *How to Heal Toxic Thoughts: Simple Tools for Personal Transformation.* New York: Sterling, 2007.

———. *Medicine for the Earth: How to Transform Personal and Environmental Toxins.* New York: Three Rivers Press, 2001.

———. *Shamanic Journeying: A Beginner's Guide.* Boulder, CO: Sounds True, 2004.

———. *Shamanic Journeying: A Beginner's Guide,* Boulder, CO: Sounds True, 2006 (paperback).

———. *Soul Retrieval: Mending the Fragmented Self.* San Francisco, CA: HarperSanFrancisco, 1991.

Availability: Classes are offered throughout the United States, Canada, Europe, and South America. To find an instructor or a practitioner go to www.shamanic teachers.com or www.medicinefortheearth.com.

Resources
· ·

Sandra Ingerman, PO Box 4757, Santa Fe, NM 87502, info@shamanicteachers .com, www.shamanicteachers.com, www.sandraingerman.com

Bibliography
· ·

Ingerman, Sandra. *Soul Retrieval: Mending the Fragmented Self.* San Francisco: HarperSanFrancisco, 1991.

———. *Welcome Home: Following Your Soul's Journey Home.* San Francisco: HarperSanFrancisco, 1993.

www.sandraingerman.com

www.shamanicteachers.com

www.shamanicvisions.com

www.shamanism.org

VORTEXHEALING®
DIVINE ENERGY HEALING

O N NOVEMBER 26, 1994, RIC WEINMAN, founder of VortexHealing, experienced a vision in which he received information concerning a method of healing he later called VortexHealing. As a practitioner of the healing arts for fifteen
years, Weinman was open to new forms of energy healing. However, it took some
time before he was able to integrate the knowledge into his healing practice.

According to Weinman, this healing method was given as a gift to a healer in
Great Britain. In 753 BC, that healer started what became known as the Merlin lineage, named for the vibrational quality of healing energy they were able to manifest.
The term "Merlin" was a title to honor the divine being able to manifest and maintain the healing art. The Merlin of King Arthur's time was the fifth Merlin in this
line. The line died out in AD 1247 because the last Merlin did not find a qualified
pupil who could be a lineage holder to carry on the energy of the lineage.

VortexHealing is not a technique-oriented modality that is taught via a teacher-
student relationship. Rather, the student receives the healing knowledge through
what is called "direct consciousness transmission," of which there are three parts.
The first part gives the student direct access to Vortex energy and the healing realm.
The second part develops the student's energy system to become an effective vehicle
for divine consciousness and light. The third part enables the student's energy system to become a bridge between the healing realm (divine Source) and a receiver
in need of healing energy. Practitioners become links between divine light and consciousness and human consciousness. The more practitioners work with the Vortex-
Healing tools, the more they spiritually awaken, deepening the healing process both

for themselves and for their clients. VortexHealing is designed as a healing art and to create spiritual awakening. Advanced students may take classes that focus solely on different levels of spiritual awakening.

VortexHealing uses forty-nine forms of vortex light or energy. Each one is a different aspect of the light and energy of the vortex that is given in the form of a transmission to the student. The vortex itself is an interdimensional structure made from Merlin's light and energy that connects the student to the divine healing realm used in this therapy. Each vortex light has a different function and is considered a tool. These tools can be used for grounding, nurturing, releasing blockages, or for specific physical ailments. They may also enhance drug therapies to help speed up healing on a physical level.

A session can last a few minutes or an hour or more depending on the needs of the client. Usually work is done with the client reclining on a massage table, but it can be done anywhere, with the client sitting or lying down. Starting at the head of the client, the practitioner creates a healing grid through the use of invisible energy crystals. He or she then fluffs the energy field by clearing the field and raising the vibration level. Work is done both on and off the body. The procedure is multidimensional and may connect the client with his or her divine consciousness and higher purpose. Depending on the needs of the client, various vortices of light are brought into the client's energy system to do the healing work.

Course Descriptions

Seven levels of training make up the VortexHealing Institute educational program. All seven levels are listed here. The first class in each level is the prerequisite for all the other classes at that level and for the next level as well. Some classes have other prerequisites and are mentioned in the class descriptions.

All VortexHealing classes are taught by direct consciousness transmission from the divine Source of the lineage. The mind is taught to understand what is happening, but the tools of VortexHealing are not learned by the mind. They are given directly to the student's consciousness by divine consciousness. All tools, with the exception of the Unwinding the Fascia Energy technique, are expressions of divine light and consciousness. As students become more advanced, the tools they learned at the basic level will be used at a much deeper level.

VortexHealing does not have a curriculum or direct path for becoming a VortexHealing instructor. Candidates must present qualities such as maturity, spiritual development, honesty, responsibility, psychic ability, leadership skills, and the ability to organize groups. They must also demonstrate they have the ability to handle the energetic power involved in passing on the VortexHealing transmissions. Teachers are picked from the most advanced students and voted on by the faculty. Once a candidate has been accepted and agrees to become a teacher, the lineage holder will pass on the Teaching Transmission Star and the candidate is free to organize and teach VortexHealing classes.

Basic Level

▶ **Basic VortexHealing Training** is a five-day intensive seminar. Students undergo a process of light acceleration that is said to evolve the energy system and enable them to receive the Vortex Wheel. Students experience direct healing work with each other for self-healing. With the Vortex Wheel students learn to:

- Channel forty-nine different forms of vortex light
- Access the divine healing realm, called Mauma, created from the merged consciousness of seven divine beings
- Clear karma knots and corresponding issues from the karmic body
- Release emotional and mental imprinting from the emotional and mental bodies
- Energize, harmonize, and create deep healing on the physical body
- Re-create the grounding cord
- Work with both the vital and divine webs in the body and channel light through both webs simultaneously
- Do VortexHealing at a distance
- Clear physical spaces of negative energy
- Meditate to open and deepen the spiritual heart

▶ **Clearing the Kundalini Channel** is a two-day class with the focus of cleaning the Kundalini channel, especially near the base of the spine. Students work on each other. The Basic VortexHealing Training is a prerequisite. Topics include:

- Defining Kundalini energy
- Kundalini uses as a vehicle for divine energy and opening the upper chakras
- Kundalini as a core source of energy to feed and strengthen the nervous system
- Clearing the Kundalini channel

▶ **Unwinding the Fascia Energy** is a three-day class involving work with the fascia. Basic VortexHealing Training is a prerequisite. Students learn to:

- Be more comfortable and aligned with the body
- Play with the fascia and feel the energy flow through it
- Sense the body energy pathways

Magical Structures Level

▶ **Magical Structures** is a five-day intensive workshop. The Basic VortexHealing Training is a prerequisite. Topics include:

- Magical Energetic Structures made of "wizard thread"
- Vortex crystal-grid release
- Vortex meditations for karmic acceleration and evolving the energy system
- Open vortex spaces
- Merlin's global healing grid
- Energetic hookups to the vital web
- Pujas that harmonize with transiting planets and help alleviate negative astrological influences

▶ **Vortex Intensive/Karmic Acceleration** is a three-day workshop to accelerate karma and evolve the energy system. Magical Structures is a prerequisite. Students will:

- Do Vortex meditations specific for this class
- Use VortexHealing tools

- Develop awareness of the vital web
- Develop psychic awareness
- Learn to tune in to the energy systems of clients

▶ **Vortex Earthshift Intensive** is a two-day seminar that gathers Vortex students together to facilitate movements in the consciousness of the Earth and in the field of human consciousness. Magical Structures Training is a prerequisite.

▶ **Sensing: Psychic and Consciousness Development** is a one-day class designed to promote psychic and consciousness development. Magical Structures Training is a prerequisite.

Multi-Frequency Level

▶ **Multi-Frequency and Merlin's Jewel** is a six-day class that allows students to release past conditioning on deeper levels. Prerequisite: one Vortex intensive or one Vortex Earth/Shift intensive. Students will learn the following tools:

- *Multi-Frequency* contains millions of life frequencies and all the color variations of light in dense and homeopathic form.
- *Oneness Frequency* specifically breaks down the vibration of separateness in the human personality, releasing attachment and identification and thus breaking down emotional/karmic and ego positions, as well as some attachments.
- *Life Essences* are pure energetic nourishment combining the energies of crystals, herbs, colors, and vibration with the intention of nourishing different organs, systems, and conditions.
- *Merlin's Jewel* enables the student to make a kind of structure that acts as a portal to bring in energies from other places, including the angelic realm.
- *Crystal Energy* is a dense, stabilizing energy that can be channeled as crystal structures or as liquid crystal energy.
- *All Energetics* is a composite transmission that enables the channeling of Multi-Frequency, Oneness Frequency, Life Essences, Crystal Energy, and the forty-nine forms of Vortex simultaneously, with a single

intention, and with Merlin directing each energy to where it needs to go in the system, according to divine intelligence.

- *Body-Harmonic Frequency* is a special frequency akin to delta brain waves.

▶ **Genetics and Multi-Frequency Devices** is a six-day training that uses a transmission to enable the student to release personal, karmic, and ancestral imprints from the DNA. Prerequisite: Multi-Frequency Training.

▶ **Breaking Time Lines** is a four-day training that uses a transmission to enable the practitioner to temporarily put organs, chakras, meridians, and body systems into a special state. In this state, the divine can quickly empty that system of history and trauma to facilitate healing. Prerequisite: Multi-Frequency Training.

LifeForm Level

▶ **LifeForm** is a five-day training course that addresses the multi-frequency tool. Prerequisite: Multi-Frequency Training. Students will learn to:

- Channel energies and frequencies to release stuck areas in the energy system
- Work solely through consciousness
- Channel the consciousness of perfect LifeForm for the physical, etheric, emotional, mental, and spiritual body
- Channel a mixture of Hindu, Tibetan, Kabbalistic, angelic, and Thnguu mantras, Vortex mantras, and the Merlin mantra
- Express different aspects of divine consciousness through sound
- Channel LifeForm, mantra, crystal energy, Oneness Frequency, Multi-frequency, and Divine Lines all at once

▶ **InterDimensional Vortex** is a four-day seminar. Prerequisite: LifeForm Training. Students learn to use the InterDimensional Vortex as a tool for releasing conditioning. They learn to transform the energetic quality of a system as a whole or transform individual organs, glands, body systems, chakras, energetic bodies, Kundalini energy, the subtle nerve system, meridians, and more. Other transmissions include:

- InterDimensional Crystals
- Vedic Sounds
- Hebrew Letters
- InterDimensional Fields that can be used for personal situations
- Special transmissions for deepening the work of Inter-D in the thymus, brain, amygdala, and karmic body

▶ **Merlin's Puzzle: A Path of Awareness and Self-Inquiry** is a five-day training course focusing on developing the healing power of self-awareness. The class uses a teaching aid called Merlin's Puzzle, a structure of energy and consciousness manifested from the Wisdom of Merlin's Heart and placed within a crystal. Prerequisite: Multi-Frequency Training. Students will learn to:

- Understand how the mind works to create a point of view and how that point of view is, in fact, imaginary and unreal
- Recognize what is real and true and what is story or illusion
- Use the power of awareness to release personal issues or beliefs
- Use the power of awareness in conjunction with channeling
- Solve the class puzzle and know how to use it on a regular basis
- Use the power of awareness to deal with ghosts, negative psychic phenomena, and energetic manipulation
- Use the puzzles to work on awakening consciousness to its true nature, including the core veil

Omega Level

▶ **Omega** is an eight-day training course. Prerequisite: LifeForm Training. Students learn the twelve forms of unique expressions of Omega, each of which acts in a different area of the energy system and consciousness.

▶ **Karmic Body Release** focuses on the karmic body as the key in the human energy system for the conditioning that runs human consciousness. Students learn to release through seven layers of the karmic body. Prerequisite: Omega.

▶ **Advanced Sensing** is mostly about transmissions. Merlin builds on the foundation of perceptual restructuring that occurred in the Sensing class. The transmissions are the most cosmic of all the Vortex transmissions. Repeating the class deepens the transmission. Prerequisite: Omega.

▶ **The Core Veil** is a four-day training that describes Core Veil as a consciousness vehicle for maintaining the experience of a separate self. The class is made up entirely of dialogue and various kinds of meditation. Students may experience that dissolution that comes with losing the Core Veil. Prerequisite: Karmic Body.

▶ **After the Veil: Liberation and Realization** is a seven-day class designed to facilitate the continuing movement of awakening that is set in motion by the loss of the Core Veil.

Jewel Level

▶ **Jewel** is an eight-day training course that brings together all the transmissions from Merlin's Jewel, unifying them into a single transmission. Topics include:

- Fifth-dimensional level of blueprinting
- Transformation of the cellular consciousness of body organs and systems
- Reality shifting
- Ruunga divine magic
- Deepening oneness

▶ **Jewel II** is a two-day training course with Jewel as a prerequisite. Students will connect to the angelic divine web attached to their energy systems.

Multi-Dimensional Jewel Level

▶ **Multi-Dimensional Jewel and the Root of Enlightenment** is a sixteen-day training course with After the Veil and Jewel II as prerequisites. Students will:

- Work on all dimensions of creation
- Release emotional blueprints
- Release ancestral genetic emotional patterns
- Be taken to the root of enlightenment

Continuing Education Units: No.

Certification: Certificates of completion are given to all graduates of VortexHealing classes.

Participants: Classes are open to all interested adults. Teenagers and children are accepted on a case-by-case basis. Reasonable accommodation is attempted for those with disabilities.

Code of Ethics/Standards of Practice: Yes. The code of ethics can be read at www.vortexhealing.org.

Suggested Reading: Because of the nature of the direct consciousness transmissions, Weinman does not believe VortexHealing can be learned from a book.

Availability: Classes are offered in Argentina, England, Holland, Ireland, Israel, Spain, and the United States. To find a class or a practitioner in your area, go to www.vortexhealing.org.

Resources

VortexHealing Institute, PO Box 2087, South Hamilton, MA 01982, vh-info@vortexhealing.org, www.vortexhealing.com

Bibliography

www.vortexhealing.org

www.realitysandwich.com

www.oneheartshiatsu.com

www.healingarts.tribe.net

www.vortexhealing.com

ASSOCIATIONS OF INTEREST

ABC Coding Solutions
Code Development and Maintenance
Department
6121 Indian School Road NE, Suite
131
Albuquerque, NM 87110
505-875-0001 Ext. 212
CodeDevelopment@ABCcodes.com
www.abccodes.com

Academy for Guided Imagery
10780 Santa Monica Blvd.
Suite 2070
Los Angeles, CA 90025
800-726-2070
www.academyforguidedimagery.com

Acupressure Institute
1533 Shattuck Avenue
Berkeley, CA 94709
800-442-2232
510-845-1059
info@acupressure.com
www.acupressure.com

**The Alliance of International
Aromatherapists (AIA)**
9956 West Remington Place, Unit A10
Littleton, CO 80128
303-531-6377
info@alliance-aromatherapists.org
www.alliance-aromatherapists.org

**American Academy of Nurse
Practitioners**
PO Box 12846
Austin, TX 78711
512-442-6462
admin@aanp.org
www.aanp.org

**American Association of Drugless
Practitioners**
2200 Market Street, Suite 329
Galveston, TX 77550-1530
409-621-2600
join@aadp.net
www.aadp.net

**American Association of
Naturopathic Physicians**

4435 Wisconsin Avenue NW

Washington, DC 20016

202-237-8150

866-538-2267

member.services@naturopathic.org

www.naturopathic.org

**The American Association of Nurse
Anesthetists**

222 S. Prospect Avenue

Parkridge, IL 60068-4001

847-692-7050

info@aana.com

www.aana.com

**The American Association of
Acupuncture and Oriental Medicine
(AAAOM)**

PO Box 162340

Sacramento, CA 95816

916-443-4770

www.aaaomonline.org

**The American Craniosacral
Therapy Association**

11211 Prosperity Farms Road,
Suite D-325

Palm Beach Gardens, FL 33410

www.acsta.com

**The American Holistic
Health Association**

PO Box 17400

Anaheim, CA 92817

714-779-6152

mail@ahha.org

www.ahha.org

**American Holistic
Medical Association**

23366 Commerce Park, Suite 101B

Blackwood, OH 44122

216-292-6644

info@holisticmedicine.org

www.holisticmedicine.org

**American Holistic Nurses
Association (AHNA)**

323 N. San Francisco Street, Suite 201

Flagstaff, AZ 86001

800-278-2462

info@ahna.org

www.ahna.org

**American Massage
Therapy Association**

500 Davis Street, Suite 900

Evanston, IL 60201

877-905-2700

info@amtamassage.org

www.amtamassage.org

**American Medical Association
(AMA)**

515 N. State Street

Chicago, IL 60654

800-621-8335

www.ama-assn.org

American Nurses Association (ANA)

8515 Georgia Avenue, Suite 400

Silver Spring, MD 20910

301-628-5000

www.nursingworld.org

American Organization for Bodywork Therapies of Asia

1010 Haddonfield-Berlin Road, Suite 408

Voorhees, NJ 08043-3514

856-782-1616

office@aobta.org

www.aobta.org

American Physical Therapists Association (APTA)

1111 N. Fairfax Street

Alexandria, VA 22314-1488

703-684-2782

800-999-2782

www.apta.org

American Polarity Therapy Association

122 N. Elm Street, Suite 512

Greensboro, NC 27401

336-574-1121

APTAoffices@polaritytherapy.com

www.polaritytherapy.org

American Public Health Association (APHA)

800 I Street NW

Washington, DC 20001

202-777-2742

comments@apha.org

www.apha.org

American Reflexology Certification Board

PO Box 5147

Gulfport, FL 33737

info@arcb.net

www.arcb.net

American Society of Dowsers (ASD)

PO Box 24

Danville, VT 05828

802-684-3417

asd@dowsers.org

www.dowsers.org

The Association for Astrological Networking (AFAN)

8306 Wilshire Blvd., PMB 537

Beverly Hills, CA 90211

800-578-2326

info@afan.org

www.afan.org

The Association for Comprehensive Energy Psychology (ACEP)

349 W. Lancaster Avenue, Suite 101

Haverford, PA 19041

Mobile Office: 619-861-2237

acep@energypsych.org

www.energypysch.org

The Association for Research and Enlightenment (ARE)

215 67th Street

Virginia Beach, VA 23451

800-333-4499

are@edgarcayce.org

www.edgarcayce.org

The Association of Light Touch Therapists (ALTT)

22 Baldock Street

Ware, SA17 4UU

UK

(01920) 485265

info@altt.org

www.altt.org

The Association of Professional Chaplains (APC)
1701 E. Woodfield Road, Suite 400
Schaumburg, IL 60173
847-240-1014
info@professionalchaplains.org
www.professionalchaplains.org

The Association of Systematic Kinesiology (ASK)
104a Sedlescombe Road North
St. Leonards on Sea
TH37 7EN
UK
(08450) 200383
admin@systemic-kinesiology.co.uk
www.systemic-kinesiology.co.uk

The Association of Women's Health, Obstetric Neonatal Nurses
2000 L Street NW, Suite 740
Washington, DC 20036
800-673-8499
customerservice@awhonn.org
www.awhonn.org

The Australian Reiki Connection (ARC)
PO Box 113
Holmesglen, VIC 3418
Australia
1300-130-975
help@australianreikiconnection.com.au
www.australianreikiconnection.com.au

The Biodynamic Craniosacral Therapy Association of North America
150 Cross Creek Court
Chapel Hill, NC 27517
734-904-0546
info@craniosacraltherapy.org
www.craniosacraltherapy.org

British Complementary Medicine Association
PO Box 5122
Bournemouth
BH8 0WG
UK
(08453) 455977
office@bcma.co.uk
www.bcma.co.uk

The Canadian Reiki Association (CRA)
PO Box 54570
Burnaby, BC V5E 4J6
800-835-7525
reiki@reiki.ca
www.reiki.ca

China Reflexology Assoication
PO Box 2002
Beijing 100026
China
0086-65068310
crazhang@public.bta.net.ca

The Chopra Center
2013 Costa del Mar Road
Carlsbad, CA 92009
888-424-6772
www.chopra.com

Complementary Medical Association

(08451) 298434

admin@the-cma.org.uk

www.the-cma.org.uk

The Council of Australian Reiki Organizations (CARO)

PO Box 123

Oakleigh, VIC 3166

Australia

02 6297 3900

www.reikiaustralia.com.au

Healing Touch International

445 Union Blvd., Suite 105

Lakewood, CO 80228

303-989-7982

www.healingtouchinternational.org

Healing Touch Program

20822 Cactus Loop

San Antonio, TX 78258

210-497-5529

info@HTProfessionalAssociation.com

www.HTProfessionalAssociation.com

Healing Touch Worldwide Foundation

16211 Clay Road, Suite 106

PO Box 215

Houston, TX 77084-5478

218-856-8340

htwfoundation@aol.com

www.htwfoundation.org

Heart Centered Therapies Association (HCTA)

3716 274th Avenue SE

Issaquah, WA 98029

800-326-4418

www.heartcenteredtherapies.org

The Institute of Noetic Sciences (INS)

101 San Antonio Road

Petaluma, CA 94952

707-775-3500

membership@noetic.org

www.noetic.org

Institute of Core Evolution and Core Energetics Inc.

PO Box 806

Mendocina, CA 95460

707-937-1825

Info@CoreEnergeticInstitute.com

www.CoreEnergeticInstitute.com

European Trainings

0201-9589394

Info@CoreEnergeticEvolution.com

www.CoreEnergeticEvolution.com

The International Alliance of Healthcare Educators (IAHE)

11211 Prosperity Farms Road, Suite D-325

Palm Beach Gardens, FL 34410

561-622-4334

uiahe@uiahe.com

www.uiahe.com

**The International Association
for Energy Healers**
PO Box 1904
Tualatin, OR 97062
503-454-0469
info@iafeh.com
www.iafeh.com

**The International Association of
Healthcare Practitioners**
11211 Prosperity Farms Road,
Suite D-325
Palm Beach Gardens, FL 33410-3487
800-311-9204
561-622-4334
iahp@iahp.com
www.iahp.com

**The International Association of
Reiki Professionals (IARP)**
PO Box 6182
Nashua, NH 03063-6182
603-881-8838
info@iarp.org
www.iarp.org

**The International BodyTalk
Association**
2750 Stickney Point Road, Suite 203
Sarasota, FL 34231
877-519-9119
www.bodytalksystem.com

**The International BodyTalk
Foundation**
www.bodytalkfoundation.org

**The International Network of
Esoteric Healing (INEH)**
info@ineh.org
www.ineh.org

**International Institute of
Reflexology**
PO Box 12462
St. Petersburg, FL 33733
813-343-4811
iir@reflexology-usa.net
www.reflexology-usa.net

**International Research and
Educational Institute for Integrated
Medical Sciences (IREIIMS)**
Tokyo Women's Medical University
8-1 Kawada-Cho, Shinjuku-Ku
Tokyo 162-8666
Japan
03-3353-8111
ireiims@imcir.twmu.ac.jp
www.twmu.ac.jp/IREIIMS/english

**The International Society for the
Study of Subtle Energies and Energy
Medicine (ISSSEEM)**
2770 Arapaho Road, Suite 132
Lafayette, CO 80026
303-425-4625
www.issseem.org

Medscape LLC
76 Ninth Avenue, Suite 719
New York, NY 10011
212-624-3700
www.medscape.com

The Milton Foundation Inc.
3606 N. 24th Street
Phoenix, AZ 85016
602-956-0519
www.erickson-foundation.org

The National Association of Holistic Aromatherapy (NAHA)

PO Box 1868

Banner Elk, NC 28604

828-898-1965

info@naha.org

www.NAHA.org

The National Board for Certified Counselors

3 Terrace Way

Greensboro, NC 27403-3660

336-547-0607

nbcc@nbcc.org

www.nbcc.org

The National Center for Complementary and Alternative Medicine (NCCAM)

National Institutes of Health

9000 Rockville Pike

Bethesda, MD 20892

info@nccam.nih.gov

www.nccam.nih.gov

The National Center for Homeopathy

101 S. Whiting Street, Suite 16

Alexandria, VA 22304

703-548-7790

info@nationalcenterforhomeopathy.org

www.homeopathic.org

The National Certification Board for Therapeutic Massage and Bodywork (NCBTMB)

1901 S. Meyers Road, Suite 240

Oakbrook Terrace, IL 60181-5243

800-296-0664

info@ncbtmb.com

www.ncbtmb.com

The National Certification Commission for Acupuncture and Oriental Medicine (NCCAOM)

76 S. Laura Street, Suite 1290

Jacksonville, FL 32202

904-598-5001

info@nccaom.org

www.nccaom.org

The National Council for Geocosmic Research (NCGR)

531 Main Street #1612

New York, NY 10044-0114

212-838-6247

execsec@geocosmic.org

www.geocosmic.org

The National Qigong Association

PO Box 270065

St. Paul, MN 55127

888-815-1893

www.nqa.org

The Radiance Technique International Association Inc. (TRTIA)

PO Box 40570

St. Petersburg, FL 33743-0570

888-878-7733

TRTIA@aol.com

www.trtia.org

Reflexology Association of America

PO Box 714

Chepachet, RI 02814

980-234-0159

infoRAA@reflexology-usa.org

www.reflexology-USA.org

The Reiki Alliance

204 N. Chestnut Street

Kellogg, ID 83837

208-783-3535

info@reikialliance.com

www.reikialliance.com

Reiki Australia

136 Mapleton Road, Suite 16

Nambour QLD 4560

Australia

www.reikiaustralia.com.au

Repatterning Practitioners Association

10645 North Tatum Blvd.

PMB#134, Suite C200

Phoenix, AZ 85028-3053

800-685-2811

rpa@repatterning.org

www.repatterning.org

Sound Healers Association

PO Box 2240

Boulder, CO 80306

800-246-9764; 303-443-8181

info@soundhealerassociation.org

www.soundhealersassociation.org

The TMJ Association

PO Box 26770

Milwaukee, WI 53226-0770

262-432-0350

info@tmj.org

www.tmj.org

The UK Reiki Federation

PO Box 17

Andover

SP11 9WQ

UK

(01264) 791441

enquiry@reikifed.co.uk

www.reikifed.co.uk

GLOSSARY

acupoint: One of several hundred locations on the meridian system where obstructed energy flow is most likely to occur.

acupuncture: A Chinese technique for inserting and manipulating needles at specific points on the body to restore health and well-being.

acupuncture point: A point on the skin through which subtle energy from the surrounding environment is carried throughout the body via the meridians, supplying nutritive energy to the deeper organs, blood vessels, and nervous system.

adjunct therapies: A term frequently used by doctors when discussing two or more modes of treatment for the same illness or injury. For example: using surgery, antibiotics, and energy medicine to help heal a broken leg.

adrenal glands: Hormone-producing glands located above the kidneys; adrenalin is the most commonly known hormone produced in the adrenal glands.

Ajna center: Located in the middle of the forehead and known as the seat of the third eye.

Ajna chakra: Another term for the sixth chakra, commonly known as the brow chakra.

Akasha: The fifth element; a collective subtle body for humanity holding the imprint of everything each individual, group, family, race, or generation has ever known, done, or is in the process of knowing or doing.

Akashic Records: A cosmic library that holds the records of all that has ever happened.

alignment: The integration of the body's internal and external actions, supporting movement toward harmony.

allopathic: Contemporary Western medical approach that utilizes multiple modalities such as surgery and drugs simultaneously to provide multisymptom relief and treatment of illness.

alpha waves: Electrical activity in the brain during meditation or daydreaming, with the rate of vibration measured at 8 to 13 hertz.

alternative medicine: Medical modality other than traditional Western medicine. The term is losing favor and being replaced with the term "complementary medicine."

anahatha: Another name for the fourth or heart chakra (also spelled *anahata*).

anatomy: The study of the structure of living things.

Anma: A Chinese word meaning "to press and rub."

antibody: A specialized protein produced by the immune system that binds to the outer coating of foreign substances in the body. The antibody-binding process initiates various immune mechanisms for destroying or removing the offending substance. A protein molecule that is released by a plasma cell that binds specifically to an antigen to neutralize toxins, bacteria, and other invaders to the body.

antigen: A protein substance or material recognized as either self or nonself by the body's immune system; if a substance or part of a substance is foreign, the immune system recognizes it as foreign and activates the immune system; antibodies are then produced against foreign antigens.

archetypes: Primordial images held by all; predefined patterns of behavior each person is born with.

aromatherapy: The use of highly concentrated aromatic oils extracted from plants to treat illness and stress.

assessment: The process by which a practitioner discovers blockages or imbalances within an energy field or system.

astral body: The fourth level of density from the body in the human energy field, connected to the heart chakra. Supports emotional and energetic connections with an individual's loved ones; relationship interactions take place at this level. Also known as the astral layer, astral level, astral plane, and intuitive layer.

astral projection: An out-of-body experience.

atrophy: Reduction in size or wasting away of an organ or cell from lack of use or disease.

attuning: A process for entering into a relationship with another being through physical touch, such as placing one's hands on another's shoulders.

auditory sense: Listening inside yourself for clues to aid in healing.

aura: The energy field or bands of light that surround all living things and interpenetrate the physical body. The aura is made up of all the different energy layers that compose the physical, etheric, astral, mental, causal, and higher spiritual aspects of the multidimensional human form. Biophysical energy emission of the body.

aura sweeping: A general brushing down of the biofield.

auric field healing: A process used to assess and treat a health challenge or wound through the energy system.

autoimmune: An immune reaction in which the body attacks itself.

awareness: The ability to perceive a cognitive reaction to a condition or event.

axiatonal lines: Energetic lines that connect biocellular activities to higher energetic inputs and connect higher energetic informational grids to the physical body through the acupuncture meridian system.

Ayurveda: A term from ancient India referring to the science of life.

Ayurvedic medicine: A holistic healing modality from India using diet, cooking, yoga, breathwork, meditation, and herbalism to restore and maintain good health.

balance: A harmonious state in which all seven major chakras spin in equal size and speed.

base chakra: Another term for the root chakra, also referred to as the first chakra.

basic grid: A term used by Donna Eden to denote the foundation of the human energy centers resembling a steel building infrastructure.

beingness: The totality of an existing thing.

beta wave: The rate of vibration put out by the electrical activity of the brain during normal daily activity, usually from 14 to 21 hertz.

Bhakti yoga: A form of yoga based on devotion and service to another, usually done by a guru.

biocidic foods: Unnaturally processed, irradiated, or genetically modified food; also food containing chemicals or pesticides that can impair or harm one's health.

bioelectromagnetic field: The field formed around the body as a result of the electrical, chemical, magnetic, and life force energy that flows through the body.

bioenergetic philosophy: A belief system maintaining that repressed emotion, trauma, tension, and desire affects the body, mind, and spirit by creating diminished vitality and possibly disease.

bioenergotherapy: A healing technique used to send healing energy to a client using light, sound, music, color, and directed energy.

bioenergy: Any type of electrical, electromagnetic, or subtle energetic forces generated by living organisms. The biology of energy transformation and energy exchange within and between living things and their environments. In healing work, the auras, chakras, meridian systems, hara lines, and matrices that occur in living things; the universal life force believed to tie all things together.

bioengineering: The application of problem-solving principles to the fields of biology and medicine.

biofeedback: The technique of making unconscious or involuntary bodily processes perceptible to the senses in order to manipulate them by conscious mental control.

biofield: The layers of the electromagnetic field around all living things that store information; each successive layer from the body contains less dense fields. Magnetic, electromagnetic, and subtle energies generated by living cells that surround and interpenetrate the physical body.

biofield therapist: A technical term for an energy healer.

biofield therapy: A technical term for energy medicine.

biological electricity: The movement of charged ions such as sodium or potassium within a living system, such as the nervous system.

biological electronics: The flow of electrons within a living system, such as a cell.

biomagnetic: The magnetic energy generated by living cells.

biomagnetic field: The magnetic field found around the body.

biomagnetism: Magnetic fields produced by living things.

biophysics: A science that applies the theories and methods of physics to questions of biology and medicine.

bioplasma: A scientific term for the universal energy field found somewhere between matter and energy.

bioplasmic body: The form taken by a bioplasmic field such as the human energy system.

bioplasmic energy: Suggested as a fifth state of matter found in and around a living organism.

bioplasmic field: An energy field composed of ions, free protons, and electrons in and around a living organism.

biosignatures: Linear diagrams that may influence the energy and biological functions of a body organ. Precise sacred geometry energy patterns linked to different parts of the body.

bladder meridian: The seventh energy tract, which is related to foot and ankle problems and could indicate bladder difficulty.

blockage: Any force that stops the flow of energy within an energy system: field, chakra, hara line, or meridian; the interruption of the natural flow of subtle energy through the human energetic system.

body energetics: A form of massage that incorporates energy work to reduce stress and bring about relaxation and healing.

boundaries: In energy medicine, setting limits physically, mentally, emotionally, and spiritually.

Bowen technique: A series of gentle, noninvasive movements on skin or through light clothing to bring about a deep sense of overall relaxation, allowing the body to reset, balance, and heal.

breathwork: A general term describing a variety of techniques that use patterned breathing to promote healing, relaxation, and spiritual well-being.

brow chakra: An energy center found in the middle of the forehead that is said to influence the higher senses, such as intuition. Also known as the third eye chakra, the sixth chakra, and sometimes the mind center.

case history: A complete chronological list of an individual's injuries, diseases, surgeries, and emotional upsets.

causal body: The third layer of density from the body, also known as the mental layer. The subtle body that is composed of causal substance at the level where human consciousness stores all experiences gained during its many incarnations on the physical plane.

celestial body: The sixth layer of density from the body of the energy field.

cellular regeneration: Regrowth of cells in a living organism.

cellular repatterning: Changing programming in the body at the cellular level.

Celtic weave: Used by Donna Eden to describe the way the body's energies spin, spiral, curve, and twist into woven patterns.

centering: Being fully present, connected within, focused, and open to guidance. The goal in centering is for a practitioner to clear the ego in order to connect more deeply with the inner self, connect to a higher power, and be fully present and open to another. Meditation practice enhances and deepens centering.

central meridian: The starting meridian for energy flow. Its function is important in thinking and any activity that does not involve big muscles. In addition, it is affected by stress, anxiety, pain, and any other activity connected to the brain.

certification: Documentation awarded by a professional association to acknowledge that an individual has completed a prescribed program and meets a set of standards.

certified practitioner: An individual who has completed all the requirements for certification in a given therapy.

cervical center: Another name for the fifth chakra, also known as the throat chakra.

chakra: Sanskrit for spinning wheel or vortex. In energy medicine, a term for a vortex found within the energy field that allows the inflow and outflow of energy from the universal energy field. Chakras regulate, maintain, and manage the physical, emotional, mental, and spiritual aspects of our being on the physical plane and connect us to the multidimensional universe. They are often seen as dimensional portals within the subtle bodies that take in and process energy of a higher vibrational nature so that it may be properly assimilated and used to transform the physical body.

chakra assessment: Determining the health and status of a chakra.

chakra attunement: Balancing and connecting the chakras.

chakra blessing: A heart-to-heart sharing of unconditional love through the chakra system asking for divine intervention to assist in the healing process.

chakra restructuring: Using energy medicine techniques to rebuild a damaged chakra.

chakra system: A series of energy vortices found within a biofield.

channel: A person who receives messages from spiritual entities.

channeling: The process by which an individual relates information from a spiritual entity, allowing a higher level of consciousness to flow through him or her, often verbally or through automatic writing.

characterology: The science and study of a person's character.

chen: In traditional Chinese medicine, one of the five spiritual aspects of life: A feeling of strength, determination, and the ability to achieve things. A time to work.

chelate: A process used to remove an unwanted substance or congested energy from the body.

chelation: The clearing out of the energy system of energetic debris through the force of the energetic system of the healer.

chi: Chinese term for the subtle energy circulating through the meridians; also spelled *qi*.

chi gung (also known as *Qigong*): The ancient Chinese art of cultivating internal energy.

Christ consciousness center: Another term for the sixth chakra, also known as the brow chakra.

chronic pain: Ongoing pain that doesn't go away in spite of treatment.

circulation-sex meridian: The ninth energy tract, which may indicate menstrual cramps, prostate trouble, or sexual difficulty.

clairaudience: The psychic ability of hearing at higher vibrational levels.

clairsentience: The ability to hold an object or touch someone and sense the energy surrounding that object or individual.

clairvoyance: The psychic ability of seeing higher subtle energy patterns.

clairvoyant: A person who can see more than what is customary by transcending beyond the five physical senses.

clarity: The ability to clearly visualize an object or concept.

clearing: In energy medicine, the act of removing debris from the energy field.

closing: The process of returning chakras to a healthy functioning spin after a healing sequence.

closure: The completion of a treatment, relationship, or therapy.

coccygeal chakra: Another term for the root or first chakra.

code of ethics: A list of practices that guide a therapist, assuring the client of the professional way care is delivered.

cognitive therapy: The application of new ways of thinking, problem solving, and concept formation.

color healing: Using one or more specific colors to promote healing and a sense of well-being.

complementary medicine: Medical modalities that work side by side with traditional medicine to enhance healing.

conscious: Perceiving, apprehending, or noticing with a degree of controlled thought or observation.

consciousness: A quality of the mind that is aware of itself, its thoughts, and its actions.

continuing education units (CEUs): Contact hours with a modality often used to maintain certification or licensing.

continuum: Something that has no distinction of content that can be affirmed or recognized except by reference to something else.

contusion: A medical term for a bruise.

cords: Energetic connections between people, beings, or parts of ourselves that serve as negative relationship contracts; they can be carried across lifetimes.

core issues: Challenges and fears that surface repeatedly in people's lives causing numerous problems and providing opportunities for transformation.

core star: Located on the hara line either in the center of the body or, in people deep into their spiritual work, located just below the heart chakra. It sets the vibrational rate of the energy system and influences health and healing. It is the individuation of the Universal Force within us.

cosmic lattice: An energy grid formed around the earth and connected to a grid within the universe.

cosmic level: Looking at the world from a vast point of view.

cosmology: A branch of metaphysics that deals with the universe as an orderly system: a branch of astronomy that deals with the origin, structure, and space-time relationships of the universe.

criteria: Information, conditions, or rules by which a decision or judgment is made.

crown chakra: The seventh chakra of the chakra system found at the top of the head.

cupping: A method of applying acupressure by creating a vacuum next to a client's skin.

cure: The removal of a symptom of a health problem on a physical level.

dark energy: In energy medicine, energy that appears dark or threatening; in cosmology, energy causing the acceleration or expansion of the universe.

dark entities: Etheric beings that threaten or appear to threaten and instill fear.

delta waves: Electrical activity of the brain during very deep sleep and sometimes during states of deep meditation. The vibration rate of delta waves is from 0.5 to 4 hertz.

detox: The removal of a poison or toxin from the body. Short for detoxification.

devic beings: A good spirit guardian concerned with the plant, animal, and mineral kingdoms and maintaining balance in these realms and in the interaction of humans.

dharma: Purpose; the process that pulls us forward toward our future; the soul's calling; divine cosmic order.

didactic: Teaching by way of lecture.

disorder: An abnormal physical or mental condition.

dissociation: The compartmentalization of thoughts, emotions, or memories because they are too overwhelming for the conscious mind to handle.

DNA (deoxyribonucleic acid): the helical macromolecule that encodes the generic information that participates in cellular growth and development at the molecular level.

documentation: The written recording of an assessment, interventions and outcome forming a treatment.

dorsal: Pertaining to the back.

dorsal center: Another term for the fourth or heart chakra.

dream therapy: Working with a practitioner to decipher the meanings of dreams as a way to overcome fears or emotional dilemmas.

dreamtime: The alpha state of the mind where journey work, daydreaming, meditation, and so on takes place.

dreamweaving: Using conscious thought while in a dreaming state to create or manifest a desired item or way of being.

duality: In quantum physics, the ability of a photon to act as either a particle or a wave leading to the belief that all objects in the universe may exhibit properties of both waves and particles.

dyads: Working in pairs.

dynamics: Moral forces and the laws relating to them.

earthbound spirit: A discarnate being or ghost that has not yet left the earth.

ecospirituality: A holistic combining of spiritual and environmental concerns.

efficacy: The extent to which a given process contributes to the health and well-being of an individual person and the experience of life.

ego: A part of the personality structure that judges, including defensive and perceptual functions.

electromagnetic field: A field of energy formed around a wire or object when electricity passes through it.

electromagnetic spectrum: A name scientists give to types of radiation when they want to talk about them as a group.

elementals: Energy beings generally associated with plants, the natural environment, and the elements.

emotional root: A single experience that contains unresolved negative emotions (variations of sadness, fear, or anger) that have been stored in the subconscious mind.

endocrine system: Ductless glands found in the body that secrete hormones.

endorphins: Neurotransmitters made of protein that reduce pain and create a feeling of goodwill.

energetic defense system: A natural shielding or mask subconsciously created to cope with unpleasant situations.

energetic diagnosis: Identifying the presenting difficulties in the energy system of the person or animal in order to plan an intervention.

energetic disruptions: Disturbances in the energy field.

energetic reparenting: A formalized process to correct presenting energy problems from early childhood experiences.

energetic technique: Using the hands in a specific manner to bring about healing.

energy: In physics, the capacity of matter to do work as the result of its motion or its position in relation to forces acting on it.

energy blocks: Disturbances in the energy fields, chakras, or along meridians that stop energy flow.

energy centers (see also *chakra*): Cone-shaped vortices where energy exchanges between and among the layers of the energy field. They interface with the physical body through the endocrine glands and are the master switches of energy movement and disbursement throughout a living being.

energy field: The electromagnetic energy forming a biofield around all living things.

energy field drain: A technique to clear the field of debris and replace it with healing energy.

energy flow: A term used to describe the movement of energy.

energy focus: Adding energy to an area that is depleted.

energy leak: A hole in the energy field that allows the release of energy from the body and surrounding field.

energy level: One of the stable states of constant energy that surround a living organism.

energy system: In energy medicine, the auras, chakras, meridians, hara lines, and energy matrices found within a living entity.

energy system alignment: Balancing and connecting the different parts of the energy system.

energy system analysis: Methods and models for studying the human energy field.

enneagram: A personality test; also a nine-point figure.

entropy: The tendency for any organized system to break down into chaos.

epistemology: The study of the nature and grounds of knowledge with reference to its limits and validity.

esoteric: Obscure.

esoteric healing: Treatments that require a special knowledge of energy and how energy works that goes beyond the dimensions of space and time.

essential oils: Oils used for healing distilled form flowers, seeds, leaves, stems, bark, and roots of plants that carry the distinctive scent or essence of the plant.

etheric layer: The first layer of density next to the physical body in the energy field; also known as the vital layer, the etheric field, and the etheric body.

etheric template: The fifth layer of density from the body found in the energy field.

ethics: A set of moral principles or values.

etiology: The science of the causes, origins, evolution, and implications of diseases and other phenomena.

experiential: Learning by doing something personally, rather than by outside instruction.

faith: A firm belief in something for which there is no proof.

faith healing: Hands-on healing combined with prayer.

fascia: Specialized connective tissue that surrounds muscles, bones, and joints, providing support, protection, and structure to the body.

fascial system: A web of tiny fluid-filled microtubules that surround every cell of the body.

feng shui: A Chinese system using geographical, psychological, philosophical, aesthetic, and astrological concepts in relation to space and energy flow in a room or building.

field: A condition in space that has the potential of producing a force.

field theory: A theoretical framework in which the fundamental forces between elementary particles form a single network.

flower essences: Dilute extracts of various types of flowers and plants used to treat disease.

full-body technique: Uses the whole body to complete the balancing of the entire energy field.

full spectrum healing: Using color frequencies for healing.

gall bladder: A storage organ for bile until the body needs it for digestion.

gall bladder meridian: Energy tract eleven; relates to headache cases that stem from toxicity from dietary indiscretions or eating fats.

genetic trauma: Pain and suffering inherited from ancestors.

geopathic influences: Radiations coming from deep within earth that may possibly cause changes in living things. These radiations may come from underground streams, geological fault lines, radioactivity, and other disturbances underground or from manmade radiations coming from high voltage power lines, cell phones, and so on.

geopathic stress: A synoptic generic term designating the effects of geopathic influences.

gland: An organ specialized to secrete or excrete substances for use in the body.

gonads: Primary reproductive organs; the testes in a male and the ovaries in females.

governing meridian: Energy tract number two. The integrity of the spine and related impulses are connected to the operation of the governing energy tract.

grounding (a client): Facilitating clients' return to the here and now after a healing by holding their feet, saying their name, and helping them orient to place and time.

grounding (yourself): The process of bringing yourself fully within your body and thus heightening your awareness of all things physical.

guides: Teachers and mentors both physical and nonphysical that help us in the process of healing and learning.

gwasha: An alternative to acupuncture involving the scraping of the skin with a Chinese porcelain soup spoon to produce friction.

hand scan: A gentle movement of the hands over the body about six to eight inches out and with palms facing the person. The purpose is to determine differences in the energy field. The sensations during the process may be vibrating, tingling, quieting, blocking, denseness, feelings of pain, pressure, pulsation, or temperature differences.

hands-on: Light touch on the body for the purpose of healing.

hara alignment: The process of connecting the individuation point, the roots of the chakras, the soul seat, and the tan tien with Earth and the Universal Source.

hara line: A line of energy starting from far above the head passing through the point of individuation and through the crown chakra down through the body and out the root chakra into Earth. All of the major chakras have roots connecting to the hara line.

Hatha yoga: A form of yoga through the path of training the body.

healee: The person (or animal) receiving a healing treatment.

healer: A person who has developed the self in such a way as to positively influence the health journey of another person.

healing: The dynamic process of becoming whole, balanced, and in harmony with the self. The process of rejoining the visible and invisible parts of ourselves.

healing energy: Energy produced by a medical device or the human hand that stimulates the repair of living tissue.

healing sequence: A series of energetic techniques with the goal of balancing and clearing the energy field.

healing wounds: Focusing energy on areas that have been traumatized at some time during this and/or other lifetimes. The impact of the trauma is stored in the energy system.

heart center: Another term for the heart or fourth chakra.

heart-centered: Coming from the heart or the heart chakra.

heart chakra: The fourth chakra of the chakra system located level with the heart and centered in the chest.

heart meridian: Energy tract five. The heart is not only responsible for the circulation of the blood through the body, but also has an effect on the flow of the acupuncture meridians.

herbalism: A medical modality using herbs as the method of healing.

higher auditory perception: Hearing audible messages from beyond the normal hearing sense.

higher dimensional: Describing subtle energy systems that appear to be vibrating at speeds faster than light.

higher power: The name used for God, the Source, Universal Energy Field, Higher Spiritual Being, Allah, Jehovah, or other reference to a being beyond the reach of human beings.

higher self: The lucid and spiritually connected part of each person that has the ability to direct our lives.

higher sense perception: Receiving information from beyond the five senses.

holism: A theory in which nature and the universe are seen in terms of interacting wholes that are more than the sum of the individual atoms, molecules, and elementary particles.

holistic: A synergistic approach dealing with the combined physical, emotional, mental, psychological, and spiritual aspects of human health. Emphasizing the organic or functional relationship between parts and wholes.

holistic healing: Medical therapies that include the physical, emotional, mental, psychological, and spiritual aspects of health.

holistic medicine: A system of health care that fosters a cooperative relationship among all those involved, leading toward optimal attainment of the physical, mental, emotional, social, and spiritual aspects of health.

hologram: A three-dimensional picture made on a photographic film or plate without the use of a camera that consists of a pattern of interference produced by a split coherent beam of light and is illuminated with coherent light from behind for viewing.

holographic: A hypothesis that all of the information contained within a theoretical model of reality can be found in any part of the model.

holographic repatterning: Now known as Resonance Repatterning®, a comprehensive energy mastery therapy that transforms unconscious patterns of limitation, resonates with coherent alignment of energy, and expresses the power of the self in action.

holographic universe: A theory stemming from the study of black holes that suggests the universe is a gigantic hologram.

homeopathy: A medical practice using microdoses of natural substances to treat the whole person.

Hopi: A Native American people found in the southwestern region of the United States.

hormones: Steroidal or amino acid–based molecules released in the blood that act as chemical messengers to regulate specific body functions.

human energy anatomy: The structure of the human energy field and the interrelationships of the various fields.

human energy field: A complex combination of overlapping energy systems that define the unique spiritual, mental, emotional, and physical makeup of an individual.

Hun: In traditional Chinese medicine, one of the five spiritual aspects of life; a sense of destiny and purpose—a time to concentrate upon the self.

hydration: The replenishment of water and electrolytes.

hypnotherapy: A therapy using hypnosis as a healing tool to change a client's behavior, attitude, emotional well-being, perception, or memory.

I: In traditional Chinese medicine, one of the five spiritual aspects of life; a time when the other four aspects are in balance, leading to good health and happiness.

ideomotor cuing: Another term for muscle testing.

immune system: A functional system of the body whose components attack foreign substances or prevent their entry into the body.

Inca: A native people found in the western regions of South America.

incarnation: The conception and live birth of a sentient being.

indigo: A deep blue color.

indigo children: Exceptionally talented children with energy fields the color of indigo.

individuation point: Located about an arm's length above the body and the place where the soul comes into or leaves the body.

infrastructure: A set of elements that form a framework.

instinct: A natural or inherent aptitude, impulse, or capacity.

intake: The recording of information from a client about his or her condition in order to make decisions about treatment.

intake interview: The verbal asking of information regarding a client's state of health.

intention: What a person determines to accomplish or attain.

internal self: The observer within the mind that notices and evaluates a current situation.

intervention: A healing technique.

intervention techniques: In energy medicine, specific treatments, usually using hands-on, to influence the energy field in some way to promote health and healing.

interview: A formal consultation to evaluate an event or circumstance and to obtain information about that event or circumstance.

intervision: Looking between or among things and forces.

intervisory: Skills involving co-coaching, peer and self-assessment, and giving and receiving multilevel and multipositional feedback.

introject: To incorporate characteristics of a person or object into one's own psyche unconsciously.

intuition: Information received by means other than the five senses.

intuitive: A person able to perceive health issues of another person without using the five senses.

intuitive counseling: Using one's spiritual gifts to help others.

ion: An atom with a positive or negative electric charge.

iridology: The study of the iris of the eye to diagnose disease.

Jnana yoga: A form of yoga in which liberation is achieved through knowledge.

Kabbalah: Coming from Jewish heritage, it is the oldest written work of spiritual wisdom.

Kabbalist: A student of the Kabbalah.

kapha: One of the three forces in Ayurvedic medicine that is linked to the movement of all fluids in the body and to cell growth.

karma: A belief system that says whatever action we take comes back to us either in this lifetime or a later lifetime; a retributive process whereby we reexperience our mistakes or dilemmas until we get them right. The return effects of our actions. A reincarnation principle based on an energetic system of credits ands debits that allows the soul to experience a full range of perspectives on life.

karma yoga: A form of yoga that approaches liberation through right action.

Ketheric Body: Also known as the Ketheric Template, a name given to the seventh layer of the human energy field said to be the closest to universal energy.

ki: The Japanese word for qi, meaning breath of life.

kidney meridian: Energy tract eight; related to low back pain, kidney disturbances, improper blood filtration system thus affecting skin conditions.

kinesiology: The study of the principles of mechanics and anatomy in relation to human movement; also muscle testing for signs of disease or disturbances in the energy field.

kinesthetic sense: A medical term for the sense of touch.

Kirlian photography: An electrophotographic process using the corona discharge phenomenon to capture the bioenergetic processes of living systems on film.

kryon: A group of entities that channel through Lee Carroll.

Kundalini: Energy connected to a higher, spiritual energy point that can be reached through material and spiritual access points; the creative force of manifestation that assists in the alignment of the chakras and the lifting of consciousness into higher spiritual levels; the creative energy of spiritual illumination stored at the base of the spine.

Kundalini center: Another term for the first or root chakra.

large intestine meridian: Energy tract fourteen: relates to intestinal problems of constipation, spastic colon, colitis, and diarrhea; also chest soreness and breast pain with menstruation.

laying on of hands: An ancient healing technique in which the hands are placed directly on selected areas of the body and held still with intention for the highest good of the person receiving the treatment; a general term for a direct, hands-on type of healing.

left brain: Refers to the left cerebral hemisphere, which operates in analytical, logical, and linear modes of thought.

lesser chakra: One of the smaller chakras found wherever there is a bone joint.

life essence: The aspect of a person that continues to exist after physical life; also known as the soul, chi, ki, life force, life energy, and universal force.

life force: Also known as qi, mana, or prana: spiritual energy flowing through, in, and around the physical body.

light body: Another term for subtle body.

light therapy: Using sunlight or sun lamps to treat various physical and emotional disturbances and diseases.

linear: Involving a sequence of events happening in an orderly fashion, be it time, space, or frequency.

liver: A large glandular organ that produces bile to aid in the digestion of fats; maintains blood glucose levels; metabolizes proteins; stores certain vitamins and minerals; and performs synthetic reactions to chemicals, such as drugs, which yield inactive substances that are secreted by the kidneys.

liver meridian: Energy tract twelve: problems related to glaucoma and spots in front of the eyes, as well as liver functioning, including headaches.

living energy field: A field of energy flowing around and through plants, animals, and humans.

lumbar center: Another name for the solar plexus or third chakra.

luminous energy field: A matrix surrounding and inside the body that maintains the health and vibrancy of the physical body.

lung meridian: Energy tract thirteen: related to chest conditions, the diaphragm's ability to regulate breathing, and lung-related difficulties.

luo points: Specific places on the body that connect the meridians.

lymph nodes: Small organs that serve as filters found mostly under the arms or in the groin.

lymphatic system: Simply put, the garbage-collecting system of the body.

magnetobiology: The study of magnetic fields on living things.

major chakra: One of seven main energy centers found within the energy field connecting the adrenal glands with the energy system.

mana: The life force permeating the universe, highly concentrated in all living things and used in manifesting, performing miracles, and healing.

mandala: From the Sanskrit language originally meaning circle, but now used to describe a geometric pattern.

manipuraka: Another name for the third or solar plexus chakra.

mantra: A word or sound repeated during meditation to help achieve a deeper state of consciousness.

master: A person who, after a considerable amount of study and acquired skill, can teach others that skill.

material self: The part of ourselves that can be ascertained through the five senses.

mauma: Divine healing realm.

medical dowsing: Using a pendulum on the outside of the body to discover what is going on inside the body.

medical intuitive: A psychic or intuitive counselor who specializes in perceiving information concerning the human body.

medicine: The study and science dealing with the prevention, cure, or healing of a disease or injury.

meditation: A form of private devotion in which the mind concentrates on a particular practice while it frees itself from its normal thoughts.

medium: Someone who communicates with people who are no longer alive in the physical form.

mental: Concerning the intellect or the mind.

mental body: Another word for mental layer.

mental layer: The third layer out from the body of the human energy field said to govern thoughts and mental processes, self-esteem, and self-worth.

meridians: An energy transportation system consisting of fourteen pathways that carry energy into, throughout, and out of the body

merkabah: An interdimensional vehicle consisting of two equally sized, interlocking tetrahedrons with a common center, where one tetrahedron points up and the other down and used by advanced lightworkers and ascended masters to communicate or meet with beings in higher realms.

metaphysics: The more subtle philosophical sciences such as ontology, cosmology, and epistemology. Beyond the physical.

miasm: Found in an injured chakra where one of the minivortices making up a chakra protrudes above the rest; an energetic state that predisposes the organism to future illness, often due to the subtle effects of a particular toxic agent or noxious microorganism.

minor chakra: One of twenty-two smaller chakras found at the major bone joints such as hips and shoulders and also found front and back of the soles of the feet and the palms of the hands

modality: A therapeutic agency used in nontraditional or complementary medicine.

morphogenic field: A hypothetical theory proposed by biologist Rupert Sheldrake: an equivalent to an electromagnetic field that carries information only, not energy, and is available throughout time and space.

moxibustion: A special Asian herbal heat therapy used by burning mugwort at acupressure points to stimulate blood flow.

MRI (magnetic resonance imaging): A technique that uses magnetic fields and radio waves to resonantly stimulate and visualize certain molecular components of the physical body, thereby producing high resolution, cross-sectional images for study.

mu acupuncture points: Acupressure or acupuncture point on the front of the trunk of the body.

mudra: A sign made by the particular positioning of the hands and used as a tool in meditation.

muladhara: Another term for the first or root chakra.

multidimensional: Refers to the total spectrum of energies.

muscle testing: Also known as applied kinesiology: a noninvasive way of evaluating the body's imbalances and assessing its needs by applying light pressure to a muscle group such as an arm or a finger and drawing conclusions based on the amount of response and resistance from the muscle group.

nadis: Nonphysical threadlike subtle paths of energy flow from the chakras to the various regions of the body; channels of psychic energy in the subtle body.

natural healer: Someone who has recognized his or her healing abilities from birth on.

Neurolinguistic Programming (NLP): A set of techniques used for unlocking the mind and effecting positive change within an individual.

neurological integration: Visio-neuropsychological processes utilizing the psychological bond between the eyes, the brain, and the pineal gland.

neurology: The science and study of the nervous system.

neurotransmitters: Chemicals in the body that provide communication of information between cells.

Newtonian physics: A theoretical treatise that assumes a direct connection between cause and effect.

noninvasive: A medical procedure that does not manipulate, penetrate, or break the skin or enter a body cavity.

nonlinear: Chaotic; not in a straight line; not equal to the sum of its components.

oncology: The study of tumors.

ontology: The study of being and existence.

opening: The process of spinning open all of the chakras in preparation for further intervention work.

optimum health: To be in good health on all levels—physically, emotionally, mentally, psychologically, socially, and spiritually.

organ: A part of the body that performs a specific function such as the heart or liver.

orgonomic therapy: Working with a therapist to understand how survival styles from early childhood become defensive characteristics of the personality.

osteopathy: A system of medical practice based on a theory that diseases are due chiefly to loss of structural integrity, which can be restored by manipulation of the parts supplemented by use of therapeutic measures such as medicine or surgery.

pain release: Draining off excess energy causing pain through the use of the hands and then replacing it with healing energy.

palpation: A method of feeling with the hands of a part of the body to examine for size, consistency, texture, location, swelling, tenderness, and/or firmness.

palpitation: Awareness of the beating of the heart.

pancreas: A glandular organ most widely known for the production of insulin.

paranormal: A term used to describe psychic phenomena beyond the five physical senses.

paraphysical: Nonphysical or subtle energetic phenomena.

parapsychology: A field of study concerning the investigation of evidence for telepathy, clairvoyance, and psychokinesis.

past life: Having another living experience before being born into this lifetime.

past life healing: By way of hypnosis or trance going back into a previous life and experiencing a healing treatment.

past life trauma: Some form of pain or grievance carried forward from a past life into the current one.

pathognomy: The science and study of passions and emotions.

penduling: The use of a dangling object as a visible indicator for assessment and evaluation of the energy field and the chakras and to determine energetic interventions.

pendulum: A dangling object used in energy work to determine energy flow.

PET (positron emission tomography): An imaging device that uses particles emitted by radioactive analogues of naturally occurring biological chemicals to visualize ongoing brain processes.

phrenology: A theoretical treatise that character and personality traits can be determined from studying the bumps and shape of the head.

physical: Of or relating to the body.

physical body: In biology, a living being made up of organs and tissues.

physical plane: The visible reality of space, time, energy, and matter as perceived by the five senses.

physics: The science of energy and matter and their interactions.

physiognomy: A theory based on the interpretation of a person's outer appearance, primarily the face, that may give insights as to that person's character or personality.

physiology: The study of the functions and activities of living things and the physical and chemical phenomena involved.

physiophilosophy: The study of natural, effortless reality and human nature.

pineal gland: A part of the epithalamus located in the lower center of the brain that secretes melatonin and seems to be involved with the sleep/wake cycle and some aspects of mood.

pitta: One of the three forces in Ayurvedic medicine having to do with the digestive system and all biochemical processes.

pituitary gland: Also called hypophysis; a small endocrine gland that secretes hormones regulating homeostasis and stimulating other endocrine glands.

pneumaplasm: From the Greek words *pneuma* meaning air or spirit, and *plasma*, relating to form or substance. Pneumaplasm describes the substance that forms the connection between the invisible world of spirit and the visible world of form.

po: In traditional Chinese medicine one of the five spiritual aspects of life: a sense of social belonging and interaction—a time for others.

point of individuation: A spot about eighteen to twenty-four inches above the head, where universal energy and the individual person connect.

post-traumatic stress disorder (PTSD): A psychological response to a severe, and often prolonged, traumatic experience such as war or sexual abuse.

practitioner: In energy medicine a person trained in a specific form of healing.

prana: Subtle energy thought to be taken in during breathing; the breath of life; the moving force of the universe.

pranayama: A yogic practice of controlling or exercising the breath for purification and spiritual illumination.

process-oriented psychology: Theory and practice of a broad range of psychotherapeutic, personal growth, and group therapy applications.

protecting: The process of clearing, repairing, and/or erecting energetic boundaries to keep the healer or a client energetically safe.

protocol: In energy medicine, a special set of interventions or techniques used for healing.

psyche: The total being.

psychokinesis: The movement of objects by the mind without use of any physical means; also known as telekinesis.

psychological reversal: Where the client subconsciously sabotages him- or herself, preventing a treatment from working.

psychology: The science of mind and behavior.

psychometry: Energy analysis of objects and symbols.

psychoneuroimmunology: Medical term for the study of the interaction between the mind, body, and immune system in health and illness.

psychopomp: A person who helps souls make their transition to the next world.

psychopomp work: Addressing a deceased spirit or the suffering of the dying.

psychosocial: Relating social conditions to mental health.

psychosomatic: Symptoms that have no known physical or organic cause.

psychospiritual: Adding a spiritual content to the science and study of the phenomena of consciousness, mind, and behavior.

psychotherapy: The treatment of mental or emotional disorders or of related illness by psychological means.

psychotoxic intrusions: In energy medicine, an unwanted energetic contamination.

psychotoxic trauma: In energetic medicine, an unwanted energetic contamination that causes pain, suffering, or grief.

puja: Showing reverence to God or a divine aspect through meditation, invocations, prayers, or rituals; a blessing.

putative: That which has yet to be measured.

qi: Life energy that flows through the meridians; also spelled *chi* or *ki*.

quantum: The smallest basic unit of matter or energy.

quantum mechanics: A general mathematical theory dealing with the interactions of matter and radiation in terms of observable quantities.

quantum physics: A branch of physics that studies energetic characteristics of matter at the subatomic level.

radiatory healing: An energy healing technique in which the healer's own mirroring chakra sends healing energy to a defective chakra of a client to repair the structure, energy pattern, and/or energy flow.

radiesthesia: The science of a person's sensitivity to vibrations or energy to obtain information not available to the five physical senses.

radionics: A branch of esoteric science that seeks to psychically diagnose energy imbalances in the human multidimensional system using instrumentation at a distance from the patient.

rays: Waves of energy that are universal in nature, providing a connection to spiritual beings or entities.

reflexognosy: A therapy whose scope of practice is the legs and feet, including an assessment of the way the client walks.

reflexology: The application of pressure, stretch, and movement of the feet, hands, and ears to affect corresponding parts of the body.

regressional therapy: Using hypnosis to regress the client to the point in time in question.

Reichian segmental theory: A study of how tensions in different parts of the body affect each other and affect particular feelings or emotions.

Reichian therapy: Works to verbally and biophysically alter the cellular memory bank of the body and change patterns that manifest as personality disfunctions.

reincarnation: A philosophy of the soul having multiple lives in order to achieve a higher level of integrative and spiritual maturation.

remote healing: A form of energy healing in which the healer and the patient are not at the same location.

remote viewing: Another term for clairvoyance—the ability to psychically perceive visual information about targets separated from the subject by either distance or appropriate shielding.

resonance: The frequency at which an object most naturally vibrates.

right brain: The right cerebral hemisphere associated with spatial, intuitive, artistic, symbolic, and nonlinear thought.

Rolfing: A hands-on manipulation that works on the connective tissue to release, realign, and balance the whole body.

root chakra: The chakra at the base of the spine.

ruah: The Hebrew word for breath or spirit.

sacral center: Another term for the second or sacral chakra.

sacral chakra: The second chakra in the chakra system, found halfway between the navel and the pubic bone.

Sacred Contract™: The agreement the spirit makes before taking human form.

sacred sounding: Toning, a form of sound healing.

sahasrara: Another term for the crown or seventh chakra.

sahasrara center: The center of connection with the wisdom and oneness of the universe.

sapience: The ability of an organism or entity to act with judgment.

scanning: A term used to indicate viewing a body part such as the aura, chakras, or the physical self and noting any indicators of energy imbalance.

Schutzhund: Attack dog training—very regimented and disciplined.

science: Accumulated knowledge systematized and formulated with reference to the discovery of general truths or the operation of general laws pertaining to the physical world.

scientific method: A body of techniques for investigating phenomena and acquiring new knowledge, as well as for correcting and integrating previous knowledge; based on gathering observable, empirical, and measurable evidence subject to specific principles of reasoning.

scientific observation: Perceptions made under carefully specified and controlled circumstances.

sealing: The closing of traumatized areas that have resulted from an injury, surgery, cut, or leak in the energy field.

sedation: The use of herbs, acupressure, or acupuncture to slow down the flow of energy through the body.

self-healing: When an individual performs techniques and exercises to bring about balance, harmony, and good health.

seminar: A form of academic instruction, either at a university or offered by a commercial or professional organization.

sentient: Being conscious of self.

shaman: Any medicine person from an Earth-based spiritual belief system.

shamanic healing: Treatments performed by a shaman using herbs, prayers, and/or energy medicine techniques.

shamanism: A belief system that the physical world is just one of many planes in a multidimensional universe.

shapeshifting: The ability to change physical form or shape.

Sheldrake's morphic resonance: The tendency of things to follow patterns in the laws of nature.

shen: In traditional Chinese medicine, one of the five spiritual aspects of life; a feeling of joy; a time to be happy, relaxed, and free of worry.

Shen Tao: A Chinese philosopher who influenced both Taoism and Legalism.

small intestine meridian: Energy tract 6. Its function is related to digestion, intestinal colic, and other digestive problems.

smudging: A Native American purification technique using burning sage or other appropriate herbs to clear away unwanted energies in a space or energy field; often used before a sacred ceremony or to clear a room for healing work.

solar plexus center: Another term for the solar plexus or third chakra.

solar plexus chakra: The third chakra of the chakra system found just below the sternum.

Somatoform disorder (also known as Briquet's syndrome): Physical symptoms present as if they are a part of a general medical condition, but there is no disease, mental disorder, or substance to substantiate the symptoms.

Sotai: Japanese corrective exercises.

soul retrieval: The recovery of parts of a person's essence that he or she left or lost somewhere or that were stolen or borrowed by somebody else.

soul seat: The energetic place of the heart's desire for this lifetime; located behind the sternum and just above the heart.

soul wound: Shamanic term for damage to the soul due to severe trauma.

sound healing: Using sounds, tones, or music as a form of treatment for various physical, emotional, and spiritual disturbances.

space–time continuum: In physics, any mathematical model that combines space and time into a single construct.

sphenobasilar junction: The meeting of the sphenoid bone to the basilar process of the occipital bone.

spirit: An incorporeal, nonquantifiable energy present in all living things.

spirit guides: Beings from the other side of the veil that have had human form at one time and serve as teachers or messengers to humans in the process of healing or learning.

spiritual: Having to do with things of the spirit, higher self, soul, universal intelligence, divine spirit, and so on.

spiritual art: Drawing and interpreting energy.

spiritual beings: Entities without physical form.

spiritual body: Composed of the four upper layers of the human energy field having to do with higher sense perceptions and with relationships to each other and to universal intelligence.

spiritual distortion: A subtle variation in the energy field caused by guilt, shame, anger, etc.

spiritual healing: A nonreligious therapy that acknowledges we are spiritual beings living in a spiritual universe and that healing comes from a divine source.

spiritual plane: An aspect of reality that cannot be perceived by the five physical senses.

spiritual self: That part of ourselves that cannot be ascertained through the five senses.

spiritualism: A belief system that postulates spirits living on a higher plane can be contacted during a trancelike state and then offer advice on both current and future problems.

spirituality: A belief system that focuses on matters of the spirit without controlling dogmas.

spleen: The largest lymphatic organ providing a site for lymphocyte proliferation, immune surveillance, and response and blood cleansing functions.

spleen meridian: The fourth energy tract used in all forceful arm movements that is related to the pancreas. It is often an indicator for allergies and intolerance for sugar, caffeine, or tobacco.

splenic chakra: Another term for the second or sacral chakra.

SQUID (superconducting quantum interference device): A device used to measure the electromagnetic fields around the body.

standards of care: Authoritative statements describing the specific treatments of various illnesses and surgical procedures.

standards of practice: Authoritative statements that describe the responsibilities, values, and priorities of members of a professional organization.

stillpoint: In meditation: that point in stillness and silence from which consciousness arises

stomach meridian: The third energy tract that is connected to the stomach and registers pain and stress. It includes allergy problems and dietary intakes.

strange flows: Pathways of energy through the body.

stress: Physical, emotional, or mental tension resulting from factors that tend to alter an existing equilibrium.

subconscious: That part of the personality that dwells below the surface of waking consciousness and controls automatic human functions. It subliminally records all information taken in by the senses.

subtle body: Referring to any of the subtle energy systems that exist in the higher frequency octaves beyond the physical.

subtle energies: The minute, ongoing interrelationships between subatomic particles. Energy that exists outside the normal space-time frame.

SUD (subjective units of distress or disturbance): A psychological term for rating an emotional disturbance on a scale of one to ten.

superconscious: That part of the higher soul structure that is usually unconscious but accessible to the personality and contains higher wisdom.

supernatural: Of or relating to the existence outside of physical reality, miracles, and divine powers.

Svadisthana: Another term for the second or sacral chakra.

sweatlodge: The location of a Celtic or Native American purification ceremony using heat.

symbology: The science of finding meaning through symbols or other signs.

symptom: Evidence of disease or physical disturbance.

synchronicity: Meaningful coincidences; events that seemingly have no causal relationship, yet are related.

syndrome: A group of signs and syndromes that occur together and characterize a particular abnormality.

systematic kinesiology: A specific pattern of identifying imbalances a person has by monitoring the ability to hold his or muscles against light pressure.

Tai Chi: Chinese for the path of life energy; a series of movements to build and circulate energy throughout the body.

tan tien: The center of power in the body; located two to three inches below the navel.

technique: A basic set of movements used in healing work.

tetany: Muscle tension or cramps, often found in the hands and fingers of the body, one of the causes of which is congested energy unable to move from the area of tension and pain.

thanatology: The science and study of death, specifically among humans.

theory of relativity: A theory postulated by Albert Einstein that states the relationship of energy to matter as energy equals mass times the speed of light squared ($E = mc^2$).

therapist: A person trained in methods of treatment and rehabilitation other than the use of drugs or surgery.

therapy: Treatment of a physical, emotional, mental, or spiritual disorder.

theta waves: Electrical activity of the brain during sleep, meditation, hypnosis, or trance. The vibration rate is from 4 to 7 hertz.

third eye: The ability to see visions, energy fields, spiritual beings, and so on using the sixth (brow) chakra or higher sense perception.

third eye center: Another term for the sixth or brow chakra.

thought fields: Theoretically, thought, when properly directed and energized by concentration and intention, creates a field of energy.

thought form: A manifestation of a strong thought or emotion as an actual energetic structure within an individual's auric field.

thousand-petaled lotus: Another term for the crown or seventh chakra.

throat center: Another term for the throat or fifth chakra.

throat chakra: The fifth chakra of the chakra system found over the throat.

thymus: A gland that helps to regulate the immune response.

thyroid: A gland that regulates the body's metabolic rate.

tonification: Enhancing and rejuvenating techniques for strengthening the body.

tonification points: Specific places on the arms, legs, hands, and feet that when stimulated will increase the qi flow within the meridians.

toning: The use of sound, voice, and music for the benefit of physical, emotional, and spiritual health.

totem: An entity, often an animal, that watches over a tribe or group of people; individual totems are usually animals and function as spirit guides.

transcendence: The rising above or beyond the universe or material existence.

transcendent: Beyond the limits of ordinary existence.

transducer: A device that converts one kind of energy into another.

transformation: An act, process, or instance of change.

transmutation: The altering of the nature of a substance, species, or form into another.

transpersonal psychology: Addresses the spiritual needs and aspirations of humans as well as the behavioral.

trauma: An injury to the physical, emotional, mental, or spiritual body.

treatment: The techniques or actions used to help heal an injury or disease.

triadic: In energy medicine, working in threes (two healers and a client) with the intention of healing.

trigger points: Major acupressure points along the meridian system used by acupuncturists for clearing blocked energy.

triple warmer: The meridian that governs the body's fight/flight/freeze response.

triple warmer meridian: Energy tract 10: Thyroid conditions, digestive disturbances, weight changes and crying for no reason are indicators of problems in this meridian.

TMJ: Temporomandibular joint, where the upper and lower jaw connect.

tui na: A form of Chinese manipulative therapy where the practitioner may brush, knead, roll, press, or rub areas between each of the joints to treat acute and chronic musculoskeletal conditions.

unconscious: The part of the mind that does not ordinarily enter the individual's awareness and that is manifested by overt behavior.

universal calibration lattice: An electromagnetic structure composed of fibers of light and energy that surrounds each person.

universal energy: Theory that there is only one single source that creates and contains everything in all realities, time, space, levels of existence, this universe, and parallel universes and multiple dimensions.

universal energy field: A field that surrounds and interpenetrates all living and nonliving things and has an organizing effect on matter and builds form.

universal energy source: A secular description of God.

vata: One of the three forces in Ayurvedic medicine that controls the nervous system.

veda: The most ancient and sacred literature of the Hindus.

veil: The unseen partition between the known, material world as perceived by the five senses and the unknown spiritual world.

vibrational: Subtle or electromagnetic energy in varying frequencies and amplitudes.

vibrational level: A specific frequency range.

vibrational medicine: A healing philosophy that aims to treat the whole person by delivering measured quanta of frequency-specific energy to the human multidimensional system seeking to heal the physical body by integrating and balancing the higher energetic systems that create the physical/cellular patterns of manifestation.

visshudha: Another name for the fifth or throat chakra (also spelled vishuddha).

visualization: Creating a picture in your mind and giving it energy.

vital energy: Another term for life force, prana, qi, mana.

vital layer: Another term for the etheric field or first layer of the energy field.

wellness: A state of balanced health, happiness, vitality, and wholeness in which a person functions at an optimal level of integration between the elements of body, mind, and spirit.

will: In energetic medicine, power of choice coupled with desire and intention.

willpower: The capacity to control oneself.

wisdom chakra: Another name for the seventh or "crown" chakra.

yang: Chinese for the active, masculine, light, and logical aspect of creation.

yantra yoga: A form of yoga based on meditation of visual symbols.

yin: Chinese for the receptive, feminine, intuitive, and dark side of creation.

yoga: Vedic knowledge for attaining union with the transcendent. A practice of stretching and poses to achieve better health and higher consciousness.

yuga: One of four stages of a Hindu world cycle: *satya yuga, natya yuga, treta yuga,* and *dvapara yuga.*

yuga cycles: According to Hindu tradition, the world goes through a continuous cycle of four ages involving changes that society goes through as a whole.

zang-fu theory: A concept within traditional Chinese medicine that describes the functions of the organs of the body and the interactions that occur between them.

zero point energy: In physics, the lowest possible energy that a quantum system can have that cannot be removed from the system; the energy that remains when all other energy is removed from a system.

zero point field: The lowest energy state of a field; its ground state.

LEGALITIES

The legal basis for energy medicine disciplines is the same for manual (use of hand or body) and biofield interventions and is inherent under the auspices of the professional preparation of the practitioner of each discipline. A professional practice is one in which money changes hands or there is a trade for services. Privately working on friends and family, with no money involved, does not constitute a professional practice and, with the exception of Italy, there are no laws regulating such work. Many practitioners enter this field with a basic education in a healing profession like nursing, medicine, chiropractic, psychotherapy, social work, occupational therapy, physical therapy, or massage therapy. These professions require a license or are regulated by individual state licensing boards within a specific country.

Most states in the United States have created laws on how nonhealthcare professionals may legally practice. Other countries have developed their own laws. Each person wishing to develop an energy medicine practice must investigate the legalities of a practice for his or her specific locality. There are some surprises in some of the laws. Be sure to check your area.

Certification is not a license. Certification shows competency in a given discipline or modality. A license comes from a governing body. In the United States any laws concerning energy medicine come under the guidance of the various state massage boards.

Please note that during the time it took to write this book, several agencies changed their contact information. I found two ways to get the information I needed. If you know the name of the agency (such as the Oregon Board of Massage), you can search for the name directly online (using a search engine such as Google.com). If not, search for the name of the state legislature or country and type in massage or energy healing in the search box of the Web page; you will find the statutes that cover the laws in your area.

Laws across the United States

States without a Massage Law
Alaska, California, Idaho, Indiana, Kansas, Michigan, Minnesota, Oklahoma, Vermont, Wyoming

States with a Massage Law
Alabama, Arizona, Arkansas, Colorado, Connecticut, Delaware, Florida, Georgia, Hawaii, Illinois, Iowa, Kentucky, Louisiana, Maine, Maryland, Massachusetts, Mississippi, Missouri, Montana, Nebraska, Nevada, New Hampshire, New Jersey, New Mexico, New York, North Carolina, North Dakota, Ohio, Oregon, Pennsylvania, Rhode Island, South Carolina, South Dakota, Tennessee, Texas, Utah, Virginia, Washington, West Virginia, Wisconsin; also the District of Columbia

States Exempting Reflexology from Massage Law
Arizona, Georgia, Illinois, Iowa, Kentucky, Maine, Maryland, Massachusetts, Missouri, Nevada, New Jersey, New Mexico, North Carolina, North Dakota, Oregon, Tennessee, Texas, Washington, Wisconsin; also the District of Columbia

States with Reflexology Law
North Dakota (licensing law), Tennessee (registration law); in Missouri and Louisiana reflexology is included in the cosmetology law.

States with a Health Freedom Law with possible exemptions
(yet to be challenged in the courts)
California, Idaho, Minnesota, Rhode Island

United States

Alabama Massage Therapy Board

610 S. McDonough Street
Montgomery, AL 36104
324-269-9990
massagetherapy@warrenandco.com
www.almtbd.state.al.us

Alabama Board of Massage Therapy Administrative Code Chapter 532-x-1-.02 h) defines "massage therapy" as the profession in which the practitioner applies massage techniques and related touch therapies with the intention of positively affecting the health and well- being of the client.

Alaska

No licensing requirements at the time of this writing for reflexology or energy medicine.

As of January 1, 2010, the state of Alaska does not regulate massage therapy. However, regulation of massage therapy may occur at the local level. Please verify with your local health or licensing board regarding certification.

Arizona State Board of Massage Therapy

1400 W. Washington Street, Suite 300
Phoenix, AZ 85007
602-542-8604
info@massageboard.az.gov
www.massageboard.az.gov

Arizona State Legislature Formal Document 32-4201 Definitions 4. defines "massage therapy" as: (a) The manual application of compression, stretch, vibration, or mobilization of the organs and tissues beneath the dermis, including the components of the musculoskeletal system, peripheral vessels of the circulatory system and fascia, when applied primarily to parts of the body other than the hands, feet, and head; (b) The manual application of compression, stretch, vibration, or mobilization using the forearms, elbows, knees, or feet or handheld mechanical or electrical devices; or (c) Any combination of range of motion, directed, assisted, or passive movements of the joints.

Arkansas State Board of Massage Therapy

PO Box 20739
Hot Springs, AR 71903
501-520-0555
info@ArkansasMassageTherapy.com
www.arkansasmassagetherapy.com

Arkansas defines "massage therapy" as to engage in the practice of any of the following procedures: A) All massage therapy techniques and procedures, either hands-on or with mechanical devices; G) Any hands-on bodywork techniques and procedures rising to the level of the techniques and procedures intended to be regulated under this chapter and not covered under specific licensing laws of other boards.

California Massage Therapy Council

916-669-5336
camtc@amgroup.us
www.camtc.org

Licensing for massage therapists is by county. Check at a local county courthouse for laws on reflexology and energy medicine.

Colorado Department of Regulatory Agencies

1560 Broadway, Suite 1350
Denver, CO 80202
303-894-7800
www.dora.state.co.us/massage-therapists/licensure

According to S.B.08-219. The Massage Therapy Practice Act defines "massage" or "massage therapy" as "a system of structured touch, palpation, or movement of the soft tissue of another person's body in order to enhance or restore the general health and well-being of the recipient." Massage therapists must submit a thumbprint when registering for a license in massage therapy.

12-35.5-110. Scope of Article—exclusions—authority for clinical setting (1) Nothing in this article shall be construed to prohibit or require a massage therapy registration for any of the following: (c) (iii) Practices using touch to affect the human energy system, such as Reiki, shiatsu, and Asian or polarity bodywork therapy.

Connecticut Massage Therapy Licensure

Department of Public Health and Addiction Service
150 Washington Street
Hartford, CT 06106
860-509-7603
oplc.dph@po.state.ct.us
www.dph.state.ct.us

Massage and acupuncture therapists must be licensed. No mention of reflexology or energy medicine. Under Connecticut General Statutes Sec. 20-206a. Definitions:

d) "Massage therapy" means the systematic and scientific manipulation and treatment of the soft tissues of the body, by use of pressure, friction, stroking, percussion, kneading, vibration by manual or mechanical means, range of motion, and nonspecific stretching. Massage therapy may include the use of oil, ice, hot and cold packs, tub, shower, steam, dry heat, or cabinet baths, for the purpose of, but not limited to, maintaining good health and establishing and maintaining good physical and mental condition. Massage therapy does not encompass diagnosis, the prescribing of drugs or medicines, spinal or other joint manipulations, nor any service or procedure for which a license to practice medicine, chiropractic, naturopathy, physical therapy, or podiatry is required by law.

Delaware Board of Massage and Bodywork

Cannon Building, Suite 203
861 Silver Lake Blvd.
Dover, DE 19904
302-744-4500
customerservice.dpr@state.de.us
www.dpr.delaware.gov/boards/massagebodyworks/

The Delaware Board of Massage and Bodywork Statutory Authority: 24 Del.C. Section 5305(1) 24 DE Admin. Code 5305(1)

4 The "practice of massage and bodywork" includes, but is not limited to, the following modalities: Acupressure, Chair Massage, Craniosacral Therapy, Deep Tissue Massage Therapy, Healing Touch, Joint Mobilization, Lymph Drainage Therapy, Manual Lymphatic Drainage, Massage Therapy, Myofascial Release Therapy, Neuromuscular Therapy, Orthobionomy, Process Acupressure, Reflexology, Rolfing, Shiatsu, Swedish Massage Therapy, Trager, Visceral Manipulation

5 The practice of the following modalities does not constitute the "practice of massage and bodywork": Alexander Technique, Aroma therapy, Feldenkrais, Hellerwork, Polarity Therapy, Reiki, Shamanic Techniques, Therapeutic Touch

Note: Some massage therapists refer to Healing Touch as a form of massage having nothing to do with the energy medicine modality Healing Touch. I was unable to locate anyone in the Delaware office who knew the difference.

District of Columbia Board of Massage Therapy

Department of Health
825 North Capitol Street NE
Washington, DC 20002
202-442-5955
doh@dc.gov
www.doh.dc.gov

Title 17 District of Columbia Municipal Regulations for Massage Therapy 7599 Definitions:

Massage techniques—any touching or pressure with the intent of providing healing or therapeutic benefits through soft tissue manipulation. Massage techniques include, but are not limited to, Rolfing, Neuromuscular Therapy, Shiatsu or acupressure, Trigger Point massage, Trager, Tui na, Reflexology, Thai massage, deep tissue massage, Myofascial Release, Lymphatic Drainage, Craniosacral, Polarity, Reiki, Swedish Massage, and Therapeutic Touch. Massage techniques may be performed in any postural position including seated massage and techniques performed on clothed clients.

Florida Board of Massage Therapy

Florida Department of Health
Medical Quality Assurance
4052 Bald Cypress Way BIN#C06
Tallahassee, FL 32399
850-245-4161
MQA_MassageTherapy@doh.state.fl.us
www.doh.state.fl.us/mqa/massage

The 2007 Florida Statues Title XXXII, Chapter 480.033 3)

"Massage" means the manipulation of the soft tissues of the human body with the hand, foot, arm, or elbow, whether or not such manipulation is aided by hydrotherapy, including colonic irrigation, or thermal therapy; any electrical or mechanical device; or the application to the human body of a chemical or herbal preparation.

Georgia Board of Massage Therapy

237 Coliseum Drive
Macon, GA 31217
478-207-2440
www.sos.state.ga.us

Requirements change from county to county. The Georgia Massage Therapy Practice Act, 43-24A-3. Definitions:

(8) "Massage therapy" means the application of a system of structured touch, pressure, movement, and holding to the soft tissue of the body in which the primary intent is to enhance or restore health and well-being. The term includes complementary methods, including without limitation the external application of water, superficial heat, superficial cold, lubricants, salt scrubs, or other topical preparations and the use of commercially available electromechanical devices which do not require the use of transcutaneous electrodes and which mimic or enhance the actions possible by the hands; the term also includes determining whether massage therapy is appropriate or contraindicated, or whether referral to another health care provider is appropriate. Massage therapy shall not include the use of ultrasound, fluidotherapy, laser, and other methods of deep thermal modalities.

43-24a-19. Exceptions (8) A person who uses touch to affect the energy systems, polarity, acupoints, or Qi meridians, also known as channels of energy, of the human body while engaged within the scope of practice of a profession with established standards and ethics, provided that his or her services are not designated or implied to be massage or massage therapy.

Hawaii State Board of Massage Therapy

Department of Commerce and Consumer Affairs
PO Box 3469
1010 Richards Street
Honolulu, HI 96801
808-586-3000
massage@dcca.hawaii.gov
www.hawaii.gov/dcca/areas/pvl/boards/massage

Hawaii Revised Statues Chapter 452-1. Definitions:

"Massage," "massage therapy," and "Hawaiian massage" commonly known as lomi-lomi, means any method of treatment of the superficial soft parts of the body, consisting of rubbing, stroking, tapotement, pressing, shaking, or kneading with the hands, feet, elbow, or arms, and whether or not aided by any mechanical or electrical apparatus, appliances, or supplementary aids such as rubbing alcohol, liniments, antiseptics, oils, powder, creams, lotions, ointments, or other similar preparations commonly used in this practice. Any mechanical or electrical apparatus used as described in this chapter shall be approved by the United States Food and Drug Administration.

I contacted an executive officer of the Hawaii State Board of Massage Therapy. I was told there is no license required for energy healing if there is no touching involved. A massage license is required for practitioners of reflexology.

Idaho Legislative Services Office

PO Box 83720
Boise, ID 83720
208-334-2475
www.legislature.idaho.gov/idstat/title54

At the time of this writing there are no license requirements. However, legislation is pending with Senate Bill no. 1418, which states the following:

54-4903 Exemptions

(g) The practice of techniques that are specifically intended to affect only the human energy field including, but not limited to, polarity therapy.

Illinois Department of Financial and Professional Regulations

320 West Washington Street, 3rd floor
Springfield, IL 62786
217-782-8556
www.idfpr.com/dpr/who/masst.asp

Illinois Compiled Statutes Professions and Occupations (225 ILCS 57) Massage licensing Act. 225 ILCS 57/10 Sec. 10 Definitions:

"Massage" or "massage therapy" means a system of structured palpation or movement of the soft tissue of the body. The system may include, but is not limited to, techniques such as effleurage or stroking and gliding, petrissage or kneading, tapotement or percussion, friction, vibration, compression, and stretching activities as they pertain to massage therapy. These techniques may be applied by a licensed massage therapist with or without the aid of lubricants, salt or herbal preparations, hydromassage, thermal massage, or a massage device that mimics or enhances the actions possible by human hands. The purpose of the practice of massage, as licensed under this Act, is to enhance the general health and well-being of the mind and body of the recipient. "Massage" does not include the diagnosis of a specific pathology. "Massage" does not include those acts of physical therapy or therapeutic or corrective measures that are outside the scope of massage therapy practice as defined in this Section.

(225 ILCS 57/25) Section 25 Exemptions:

(e) Nothing in this Act prohibits practitioners that do not involve intentional soft tissue manipulation, including but not limited to Alexander Technique, Feldenkrais, Reiki, and Therapeutic Touch, from practicing.

(f) Practitioners of certain service-marked bodywork approaches that do involve intentional soft tissue manipulation, including but not limited to Rolfing, Trager Approach, Polarity Therapy, and Orthobionomy, are exempt from this Act if they are approved by their governing body based on a minimum level of training, demonstration of competency, and adherence to ethical standards.

(g) Practitioners of Asian bodywork approaches are exempt from this Act if they are members of the American Organization of Bodywork Therapies of Asia as certified practitioners or if they are approved by an Asian bodywork organization based on a minimum level of training, demonstration of competency, and adherence to ethical standards set by their governing body.

(h) Practitioners of other forms of bodywork who restrict manipulation of soft tissue to the feet, hands, and ears, and who do not have the client disrobe, such as reflexology, are exempt from this Act.

Indiana Professional Licensing Agency

Attn: State Board of Massage Therapy
402 W. Washington Street, Room W072
Indianapolis, IN 46204
317-234-2051
Pla6@pla.IN.gov
www.in.gov/pla

Senate Enrolled Act No. 320 (IC 25-21.8-2-4) Chapter 1. Definitions:

Sec. 4. "Massage therapy":

(1) means the application of massage techniques on the human body;

(2) includes:

(A) the use of touch, pressure, percussion, kneading, movement, positioning, nonspecific stretching, stretching within the normal anatomical range of movement, and holding, with or without the use of massage devices that mimic or enhance manual measures; and

(B) the external application of heat, cold, water, ice, stones, lubricants, abrasives, and topical preparations that are not classified as prescription drugs; and

(3) does not include:

(A) spinal manipulation; and

(B) diagnosis or prescribing drugs for which a license is required.

Iowa Board of Massage Therapy Examiners

Department of Public Health
Lucas State Office Bldg., 5th floor
321 E. 12th Street
Des Moines, IA 50319
515-281-6959
www.idph.state.ia.us/licensure

Iowa Bureau of Professional Licensure, Iowa Code Chapter 152C Massage Therapy

152c.1 Definitions:

3. *"Massage therapy"* means performance for compensation of massage, myotherapy, massotherapy, bodywork, bodywork therapy, or therapeutic massage including hydrotherapy, superficial hot and cold applications, vibration and topical applications, or other therapy which involves manipulation of the muscle and connective tissue of the body, excluding osseous tissue, to treat the muscle tonus system for the purpose of enhancing health, muscle relaxation, increasing range of motion, reducing stress, relieving pain, or improving circulation.

4. *"Reflexology"* means manipulation of the soft tissues of the human body which is restricted to the hands, feet, or ears, performed by persons who do not hold themselves out to be massage therapists or to be performing massage therapy.

152c.9 Exemptions:

5. Persons practicing reflexology.

6. Persons engaged within the scope of practice of a profession with established standards and ethics utilizing touch, words, and directed movement to deepen awareness of existing patterns of movement in the body as well as to suggest new possibilities of movement, provided that the practices performed or services rendered are not designated or implied to be massage therapy. Such practices include,

but are not limited to, the Feldenkrais method, the Trager approach, and mind-body centering.

7. Persons engaged within the scope of practice of a profession with established standards and ethics in which touch is limited to that which is essential for palpitation and affectation of the human energy system, provided that the practices performed or services rendered are not designated or implied to be massage therapy.

Kansas Department of Health and Environment

1000 SW Jackson
Topeka, KS 66612
785-296-1500
info@kdhe.state.ks.gov
www.kdheks.gov

No laws at the time of this writing.

Kentucky Board of Licensure for Massage Therapy

PO Box 1360
Frankfort, KY 40602
502--696-4961
kelliee.hale@ky.gov
www.finance.ky.gov/ourcabinet/caboff/OAS/op/massth

Kentucky Revised Statutes 309.350 Definitions for KRS 309.350 to 309.364.

(3) "Feldenkrais Method" means a system of somatic education in which touch and words are used to eliminate faulty habits, learn new patterns of self-organization and action, and improve a person's own functional movement patterns. The method is based on principles of physics, biomechanics and an understanding of, or learning about, human development. The practice is federally trademarked and requires permission from the Feldenkrais Guild to use the term and methodology;

(5) "Polarity therapy" means diverse applications affecting the human energy system.

These applications include energetic approaches to somatic contact, verbal facilitation, nutrition, exercise, and health education. Polarity therapy does not make medical claims, diagnose physical ailments, or allow prescription of medications. Standards for schools, education, and practice, the administration of a code of ethics, and a registration process are provided by the American Polarity Therapy Association;

(6) "Practice of massage therapy" means the application, by a massage therapist licensed by the board, of a system of structured touch, pressure, movement, and holding to the soft tissues of the human body with the intent to enhance or restore the health and well-being of the client. The practice includes the external application of water, heat, cold, lubricants, salt scrubs, or other topical preparations; use of electromechanical devices that mimic or enhance the actions of the hands; and determination of whether massage therapy is appropriate or contraindicated, or whether referral to another health care practitioner is appropriate;

309.352 Scope of KRS 309.350 to 309.364. KRS 309.350 to 309.364 shall not preclude:

(4) Persons who restrict manipulation of the soft tissues of the human body to the hands, feet, or ears, and do not hold themselves out to be massage therapists;

(5) Persons who use procedures within the scope of practice of their profession, which has established standards and ethics, provided that their services use touch, words, and directed movement to deepen awareness of existing patterns of movement in the body as well as to suggest new possibilities of movement while engaged, but who are not designated or implied to administer massage or to be massage therapists. These practices include, but are not limited to, the Feldenkrais Method and the Trager Approach;

(6) Persons engaged within the scope of practice of a profession with established standards and ethics in which touch is limited to what is essential for palpation and affecting of the human energy system, provided that their services are not designated or implied to be massage or massage therapy. These practices include but are not limited to polarity therapy.

Louisiana Board of Massage Therapy

12022 Plank Road
Baton Rouge, LA 70811
225-771-4090
admin@lsbmt.org
www.lsbmt.org

Louisiana Revised Statutes, Title 46. Professional and Occupational Standards, Part LV. Massage Therapists, Chapter 3. Definitions, Section301. Definitions:

Massage Therapy means the manipulation of soft tissue for the purpose of maintaining good health and establishing and maintaining good physical condition. The term shall include effleurage (stroking), petrissage (kneading), tapotement (percussion), compression, vibration, friction, active/passive range of motion, shiatsu and accupressure, either by hand, forearm, elbow, foot, or with mechanical appliances, for the purpose of body massage. Massage therapy may include the use of lubricants such as salts, powders, liquids, creams (with the exception of prescriptive or medicinal creams), heat lamps, whirlpool, hot and cold packs, salt glows, or steam cabinet baths. It shall not include electrotherapy, laser therapy, microwave therapy, colonic therapy, injection therapy, or manipulation of the joints. Equivalent terms for massage therapy are massage, therapeutic massage, massage technology, shiatsu, bodywork, or any derivation of those terms. As used in these rules, the terms "therapy" and "therapeutic" shall not include diagnosis, treatment of illness or disease, or any service or procedure for which a license to practice medicine, chiropractic, physical therapy, or podiatry is required by law.

Reflexology the manipulation of the superficial tissues of the feet and hands, based on the theory that manipulation of body reflex areas or zones can affect other body functions which the board recognizes as being encompassed within the definition of Massage Therapy.

Maine Massage Therapy

Department of Professional and Financial Regulation
Office of Licensing and Regulation
35 State House Station
Augusta, ME 94333

207-624-8624

massagetherapy@maine.gov

www.maine.gov/pfr/professionallicensing/professions/massage/purpose.htm

Maine Revised Statutes, Title 32: Professions and Occupations, Chapter 127: Massage Therapists Heading: RR1991, c. 2, Section 124 (cor), Section 14301. Definitions:

4. Massage therapy. "Massage therapy" means a scientific or skillful manipulation of soft tissue for therapeutic or remedial purposes, specifically for improving muscle tone and circulation and promoting health and physical well-being. The term includes, but is not limited to, manual and mechanical procedures for the purpose of treating soft tissue only, the use of supplementary aids such as rubbing alcohol, liniments, oils, antiseptics, powders, herbal preparations, creams or lotions, procedures such as oil rubs, salt glows and hot or cold packs or other similar procedures or preparations commonly used in this practice. This term specifically excludes manipulation of the spine or articulations and excludes sexual contact as defined in Title 17-A, section 251, subsection 1, paragraph D.

Section 14307. Exemptions to registration or certification

2. Other exemptions. This chapter does not apply to the activities and services of individuals who practice other forms of tissue work exclusive of massage therapy, such as rolfing, Trager, reflexology, Shiatsu, Reiki, and polarity, if those practitioners do not use the title "massage therapist" or "massage practitioner," unless they choose to meet the requirements of this chapter.

Maryland Massage Therapy Advisory Committee

Board of Chiropractic Examiners
4201 Patterson Avenue, 5th floor
Baltimore, MD 21215
410-764-4726
Kelter@dhmh.state.md.us
www.mdmassage.org

Title 10, Department of Health and Mental Wellness, Subtitle 43, Board of Chiropractic Examiners

Authority: Health Occupations Article, Sections 3-5A-01, 3-5A-02, 3-5A-05, 3-5A-06, 3-5A-07, 3-5A-09, and 3-5A-12, Annotated Code of Maryland

Chapter 17 General Regulations for Massage Therapy

(7) Massage Therapy.

(a) "Massage therapy" means the use of manual techniques on soft tissues of the human body including effleurage (stroking), petrissage (kneading), tapotement (tapping), stretching, compression, vibration, and friction.

(b) "Massage therapy" includes massage, myotherapy, and synonyms or derivatives of these terms, with or without the aid of:

(i) Cold packs;

(ii) Nonlegend topical applications; or

(iii) Heat limited to hot packs and heating pads.

(c) "Massage therapy" does not include the:

(i) Diagnosis or treatment of illness, disease, or injury;

(ii) Adjustment, manipulation, or mobilization of any of the articulations of the osseous structures of the body or spine; or

(iii) Laying on of hands, consisting of pressure or movement, with the exception of such techniques described in Section B(7)(a) of this regulation on a fully clothed individual to specifically affect the electromagnetic energy or energetic field of the human body.

Massachusetts Board of Registration of Massage Therapy

Division of Professional Licensure
239 Causeway Street
Boston, MA 02114
617-727-3074
consumer@state.ma.us
www.mass.gov/dpl

Board of Registration of Massage Therapy: Rules and Regulations Governing Massage Therapists, 269 CMR 1.00 - 7.00

269 CMR 2.00: Definitions:

Massage: The systematic treatment of the soft tissues of the body by use of pressure, friction, stroking, percussion, kneading, vibration by manual or mechanical means, range of motion for purposes of demonstrating muscle excursion or muscle flexibility and nonspecific stretching. Massage therapy may include the use of oil, ice, hot and cold packs, tub, shower, steam, dry heat or cabinet baths, in which the primary intent is to enhance or restore the health and well-being of the client. Massage therapy shall not include diagnoses, the prescribing of drugs or medicines, spinal or other joint manipulations, or any services or procedures for which a license to practice medicine, chiropractic, occupational therapy, physical therapy, or podiatry is required by law. For purposes of these regulations, the use of the term "Massage" shall also mean the term "Massage therapy."

Michigan Board of Massage

At the time of this writing the massage board has not yet been formulated. It was approved by the Michigan State Legislature House Bill 5651 on January 9, 2009.

January 2011 is the goal for the board to begin the application and licensure process.

bhpinfo@michigan.gov

www.legislature.mi.gov/documents/2007

www.massage-exam.com/michigan-massage.php

Michigan House Bill 5651 Complete to 3-3-08

Licensure. Only a person licensed under the bill could engage in the practice of massage therapy. However, a license would not be needed by a person engaging in the use of touch, words, or directed movement to deepen awareness of patterns or movement in the body so long as those services are not designated or implied to be massage or massage therapy. These practices include the Feldenkrais Method or the Trager Approach.

(These terms are defined in the bill.)

The bill would also exempt the affectation of the human energy system or acupoints or meridians of the human body while engaged within the scope of practice of a profession with established standards and ethics and as long as those services are not designated or implied to be massage or massage therapy. These practices include Polarity or Polarity Therapy, Polarity Therapy Bodywork, Reflexology, Rolf Structural Integration, Reiki, and Shiatsu.

Minnesota

No massage board or regulations at the time of this writing.

The Minnesota chapter of the American Massage Therapy Association, www.amtamn.org, can answer questions.

2007 Minnesota Statutes 146A.01 DEFINITIONS.

Subd. 4. **Complementary and alternative health care practices.** (a) "Complementary and alternative health care practices" means the broad domain of complementary and alternative healing methods and treatments, including but not limited to: (1) acupressure; (2) anthroposophy; (3) aroma therapy; (4) ayurveda; (5) cranial sacral therapy; (6) culturally traditional healing practices; (7) detoxification practices and therapies; (8) energetic healing; (9) polarity therapy; (10) folk practices; (11) healing practices utilizing food, food supplements, nutrients, and the physical forces of heat, cold, water, touch, and light; (12) Gerson therapy and colostrum therapy; (13) healing touch; (14) herbology or herbalism; (15) homeopathy; (16) nondiagnostic iridology; (17) bodywork, massage, and massage therapy; (18) meditation; (19) mind-body healing practices; (20) naturopathy; (21) noninvasive instrumentalities; and (22) traditional Oriental practices, such as Qi Gong energy healing.

Subd. 6. **Unlicensed complementary and alternative health care practitioner.** (a)

"Unlicensed complementary and alternative health care practitioner" means a person who:

1) either:

(i) is not licensed or registered by a health-related licensing board or the commissioner of health; or

(ii) is licensed or registered by the commissioner of health or a health-related licensing board other than the Board of Medical Practice, the Board of Dentistry, the Board of Chiropractic Examiners, or the Board of Podiatric Medicine, but does not hold oneself out to the public as being licensed or registered by the commissioner or a health-related licensing board when engaging in complementary and alternative health care;

(2) has not had a license or registration issued by a health-related licensing board or the commissioner of health revoked or has not been disciplined in any manner at any time in the past, unless the right to engage in complementary and alternative health care practices has been established by order of the commissioner of health;

(3) is engaging in complementary and alternative health care practices; and

(4) is providing complementary and alternative health care services for remuneration or is holding oneself out to the public as a practitioner of complementary and alternative health care practices.

(b) A health care practitioner licensed or registered by the commissioner or a health-related licensing board, who engages in complementary and alternative health care while practicing under the practitioner's license or registration, shall be regulated by and be under the jurisdiction of the applicable health-related licensing board with regard to the complementary and alternative health care practices.

Mississippi State Board of Massage Therapy

PO Box 20
Morton, MS 39117
601-732-6038
director@msbmt.state.ms.us
www.msbmt.state.ms.us

Mississippi Code Title 73: Professions and Vocations, Chapter 67: Professional Massage Therapists Section 73-67-7. Definitions [Repealed effective July 1, 2008]:

(g) "Massage" means touch, stroking, kneading, stretching, friction, percussion and vibration, and includes holding, positioning, causing movement of the soft tissues and applying manual touch and pressure to the body (excluding an osseous tissue manipulation or adjustment). "Therapy" means action aimed at achieving or increasing health and wellness. "Massage therapy" means the profession in which the practitioner applies massage techniques with the intent of positively affecting the health and well-being of the client, and may adjunctively (i) apply allied modalities, heat, cold, water and topical preparations not classified as prescription drugs, (ii) use hand held tools such as electric hand massagers used adjunctively to the application of hand massage or devices designed as t-bars or knobbies, and (iii) instruct self-care and stress management. "Manual" means by use of hand or body.

Reflexology is part of the basic required massage therapy curriculum. The Modern Institute of Reflexology may issue certificates in the absence of state regulation. We do not have sub-specialty certifications in Mississippi, therefore you must attend all of the required education to practice any modality of massage therapy. You must be registered by the MSBMT to practice reflexology.

No one may perform and charge individually for a massage or any technique that moves soft tissue unless they are registered as a massage therapist with the State Board or otherwise licensed and authorized by law. Energy healing, if hands do not touch the body to the extent that tissue is moved, is not regulated by this board.

Missouri State Board of Therapeutic Massage

Division of Professional Registration
3605 Missouri Blvd.
PO Box 1335
Jefferson City, MO 65102
573-522-6277
massagether@pr.mo.gov
www.pr.mo.gov/massage.asp

Missouri Revised Statutes Chapter 324, Occupations and Professions General Provisions

Section *324.240* August 28, 2007 Definitions.

324.240. As used in sections 324.240 to 324.275, the following terms shall mean:

7) "Massage therapy," a health care profession which involves the treatment of the body's tonus system through the scientific or skillful touching, rubbing, pressing or other movements of the soft tissues of the body with the hands, forearms, elbows, or feet, or with the aid of mechanical apparatus, for relaxation, therapeutic, remedial or health maintenance purposes to enhance the mental and physical well-being of the client, but does not include the prescription of medication, spinal or joint manipulation, the diagnosis of illness or disease, or any service or procedure for which a license to practice medicine, chiropractic, physical therapy, or podiatry is required by law, or to those occupations defined in chapter 329, RSMo;

Missouri Revised Statutes, Chapter 324, Occupations and Professions General Provisions

Section *324.265*

7. The following practitioners are exempt from the provisions of this section upon filing written proof with the board that they meet one or more of the following:

(1) Persons who act under a Missouri state license, registration, or certification and perform soft tissue manipulation within their scope of practice;

(2) Persons who restrict their manipulation of the soft tissues of the human body to the hands, feet or ears;

(3) Persons who use touch and words to deepen awareness of existing patterns of movement in the human body as well as to suggest new possibilities of movement;

(4) Persons who manipulate the human body above the neck, below the elbow, and below the knee and do not disrobe the client in performing such manipulation.

Montana Board of Massage Therapy

301 South Park Avenue, 4th floor
PO Box 200513
Helena, MT 59620-0513
406-841-2380
dlibsdlmt@mt.gov

(4) (a) (i) "Massage therapy" when provided by a massage therapist means the application of a system of structured touch, pressure, positioning, or holding to soft tissues of the body, Swedish massage, effleurage, petrissage, tapotement, percussion, friction, vibration, compression, passive and active stretching or movement within the normal anatomical range of motion, the external application of water, heat, cold, lubricants, salts, skin brushing, or other topical preparations not classified as prescription drugs, providing information for self-care stress management, and the determination of whether massage is contraindicated and whether referral to another health care practitioner is recommended.

(ii) The techniques described in subsection (4)(a)(i) must be applied by the massage therapist through the use of hands, forearms, elbows, knees, or feet or through the use of hand-held tools that mimic or support the action of the hands and are primarily intended to enhance or restore health and well-being by promoting pain relief, stress reduction, and relaxation.

Exempt practices under . . . subsection (5)(a)(i) include but are not limited to the Feldenkrais method of somatic education, the Trager approach to movement education, and body-mind centering.

(ii) touch to affect the human energy systems, energy meridians, or energy fields. Exempted practices under this subsection (5)(a)(ii) include but are not limited to polarity bodywork therapy, Asian bodywork therapy, acupressure, jin shin do, qigong, reiki, shiatsu, and tui na.

(iv) touch to affect the reflex areas located in the hands, feet, and outer ears. Exempt practices under this subsection (5)(a)(iv) include but are not limited to reflexology.

Nebraska Massage Therapy Board

Health and Human Services

Regulation and Licensures—Credentialing Division

PO Box 94986

Lincoln, NE 68509

402-471-2117

Rita.warson@dhhs.ne.gov

www.hhs.state.ne.us/crl/mhcs/mass/massage

Nebraska Statutes Relating to Massage Therapy

71-1,278. Terms, defined; department; powers. (1) For purposes of sections 71-1,278 to 71-1,282, unless the context otherwise requires:

(c) Massage therapy shall mean the physical, mechanical, or electrical manipulation of soft tissue for the therapeutic purposes of enhancing muscle relaxation, reducing stress, improving circulation, or instilling a greater sense of well-being and may include the use of oil, salt glows, heat lamps, and hydrotherapy.

Nevada Board of Massage Therapy

1755 E. Plumb Lane, Suite 252

Reno, NV 89502

775-688-1888

nvmassagebd@state.nv.us

www.massagetherapy.nv.gov

CHAPTER 640C - MASSAGE THERAPISTS

NRS 640C.060 "Massage therapy" defined.

1. "Massage therapy" means the application of a system of pressure to the muscular structure and soft tissues of the human body for therapeutic purposes, including, without limitation:

(a) Effleurage;

(b) Petrissage;

(c) Tapotement;

(d) Compressions;

(e) Vibration;

(f) Friction; and

(g) Movements applied manually with or without superficial heat, cold, water or lubricants for the purpose of maintaining good health and establishing and maintaining good physical condition.

2. The term does not include:

(a) Diagnosis, adjustment, mobilization or manipulation of any articulations of the body or spine; or

(b) Reflexology.

New Hampshire Office of Program Support, Licensing and Regulation Services

Board of Massage Therapy
129 Pleasant Street
Concord, NH 03301
603-271-0853
www.dhhs.state.nh.us/DHHS/LRS/ELIGIBILITY/massage-license

New Hampshire Statutes: TITLE XXX: OCCUPATIONS AND PROFESSIONS, CHAPTER 328-B, MASSAGE THERAPISTS AND MASSAGE ESTABLISHMENTS

Section 328-B:2

328-B:2 Definitions.—In this chapter:

VI. "Massage" means the application of a system of structured touch which includes holding, pressure, positioning, or causing movement, by manual means, for the purpose of promoting, maintaining, and restoring the health and well-being of the client. Massage is designed to promote general relaxation, improve movement, relieve somatic and muscular pain or dysfunction, stress and muscle tension, and provide for general health enhancement, personal growth, and the organization, balance, and integration of the body.

Statutory Authority: RSA 328-B:4

PART He-P 901 DEFINITIONS

He-P 901.02 "Allied body worker techniques" means techniques that enhance therapeutic effects on the body, which may be used in conjunction with massage therapy.

He-P 901.16 "Massage" means massage as defined in RSA 328-B:2, VI, excluding therapies where there is no soft tissue manipulation.

New Jersey Board of Massage, Bodywork, and Therapy Examining Committee

Division of Consumer Affairs
124 Halsey Street
Newark, NJ 07102
973-504-6430
Theresa.McFadden@lps.state.nj.us
www.state.nj.us/lps/ca/massage

January 13, 2008, new laws were passed. The paperwork is not yet complete at the time of this writing.

New Mexico Massage Therapy Board

2550 Cerrilos Road
Santa Fe, NM 87505
505-476-4870
Massage.board@state.nm.us
www.rld.state.nm.us/massage/index.html

TITLE 16: Occupational and professional Licensing, Chapter 7 - Massage Therapists, Part 1: General Provisions, 16.7.1.7 Definitions:

E. "Massage therapy" means the assessment and treatment of soft tissues and their dysfunctions for therapeutic purposes primarily for comfort and relief of pain. It is a health care service that includes gliding, kneading, percussion, compression, vibration, friction, nerve strokes, stretching the tissue and exercising the range of motion, and may include the use of oils, salt glows, hot or cold packs or hydrotherapy.

Synonymous terms for massage therapy include massage, therapeutic massage, body massage, myomassage, body work, body rub or any derivation of those terms. Massage therapy is the deformation of soft tissues from more than one anatomical point by manual or mechanical means to accomplish homeostasis and/or pain relief in the tissues being deformed, as defined in the Massage Therapy Practice Act, NMSA 1978, Section 61-12C-3.E.

L. "Related hands-on modalities" means manual therapies, not directly defined as massage therapy.

Until May 23, 2005, Title 16, Chapter 7, Part 1 of the Massage Therapy regulations stated the practice of massage therapy applied to shiatsu, tui na, and rolfing and that the practice of massage therapy DOES NOT apply to the practice of: Craniosacral, Feldenkrais, Polarity Therapy, Reiki, Foot and Hand Reflexology (without the use of creams, oils, or mechanical tools), and Trager. These regulations were eliminated in May 2005 and negotiations are still going on as to how to address these modalities.

At the time of this writing, the New Mexico Massage Therapy Board is waiting for an updated copy of the Massage Therapy Practice Act.

New York Board of Massage Therapy

Office of the Professions
Division of Professional Licensing Services
89 Washington Avenue
Albany, NY 12234
518-474-3817
msthbd@mail.nysed.gov
www.op.nysed.gov/mtlic

Office of the Professions: Article 155 Massage Therapy

Section 7801. Definition of practice of massage therapy.

The practice of the profession of massage therapy is defined as engaging in applying a scientific system of activity to the muscular structure of the human body by means of stroking, kneading, tapping and vibrating with the hands or vibrators for the purpose of improving muscle tone and circulation.

North Carolina Board of Massage and Bodywork Therapy

PO Box 2539
Raleigh, NC 27602
919-546-0050
admin@bmbt.org
www.bmbt.org

North Carolina General Statutes: Article 36 Section 90-622. Definitions:

Massage and Bodywork Therapy Practice

(3) Massage and bodywork therapy. Systems of activity applied to the soft tissues of the human body for therapeutic, educational, or relaxation purposes. The application may include:

a. Pressure, friction, stroking, rocking, kneading, percussion, or passive or active stretching within the normal anatomical range of movement.

Section 90-624. Exemptions:

(6) The practice of movement educators such as dance therapists or teachers, yoga teachers, personal trainers, martial arts instructors, movement repatterning practitioners, and

(7) The practice of techniques that are specifically intended to affect the human energy field.

Revised 2007 North Carolina Administrative Code, Title 21 Occupational Licensing Boards: Chapter 30 Board of Massage and Bodywork Therapy

Amendments

.0203 Exemptions from Licensure

(a) Persons who are utilizing certain therapeutic techniques may claim exemption from licensure pursuant to G.S. 90-624 (6) or (7) only by meeting one of the following criteria:

(1) Such persons are practicing techniques that are defined by national organizations that meet the criteria for exemption set forth in either G.S. 90-624 (6) or (7); or

(2) Such persons are practicing techniques that do not involve any contact with the body of the client; or

(3) Such persons are practicing techniques that involve resting the hands on the surface of the client's body without delivering pressure to or manipulation of the soft tissues.

(b) Persons who are utilizing exempt techniques along with techniques that are not exempt and constitute the practice of massage or bodywork therapy, as defined in G.S. 90-622(3), are not considered to be exempt and will be required to be licensed.

c) Pursuant to G.S. 90-623, such exempted practitioners may not hold themselves out to be a massage and bodywork therapist; they may not utilize or promote themselves or their services using such terms as "massage, massage therapy, bodywork, bodywork therapy," or any other derivative term that implies a soft tissue technique or method.

North Dakota State Board of Massage

PO Box 218
Beach, ND 58621
701-872-4895
k_wojahn@yahoo.com
www.ndboardofmassage.com

State Statute ND Century Code

Chapter 43-25: Massage Therapists

43-25-02. Definitions :

2. "Massage" means the scientific and systematic manipulation of the soft tissues of the human body through any manual or mechanical means, including superficial hot and cold applications, hydrotherapy, reflexology, and the use of salts or lubricants. "Massage" does not include diagnosing or treating diseases, manipulating the spine or other joints, or prescribing or administering vitamins.

The following is an excerpt of a letter from the ND Attorney General found on the web site of the North Dakota Board of Massage under ND Laws Governing Massage Therapists State Statute - ND Century Code 43-25-01 through 43-25-19

It is the opinion of the State Attorney General, Wayne, Stenehjem, "...that a nurse may only engage in massage if the massage is performed in the bona fide practice of nursing, which would require the nurse to make an evaluation of the client's health needs and be performed in connection with a health care regimen prescribed by a health care practitioner. It is my further opinion that when a nurse is working in a massage establishment, spa or similar business rather than a medical or health-care setting, the nurse represents to the public that he or she is engaged in the practice of massage. In that situation, a nurse may not take advantage of the exemption from massage licensure and must be a licensed massage therapist or the nurse will have violated N.D.C.C. ch. 43–25."

Ohio State Medical Board

Massage Licensing Division
30 E. Broad Street, 3rd floor
Columbus, OH 43215-6127
614-466-3934
www.med.ohio.gov/mt_about_massage_therapy_htm

Ohio is the only state in which massage therapy is considered a limited branch of medicine. The Medical Board licenses massage therapists and regulates massage therapy schools and practitioners through its standing committee on the Limited Branches and Alternative Medicine with the assistance of the Massage Therapy Advisory Committee.

The State Medical Board of Ohio Governing Statutes

Ohio Revised Code Chapter 4731-1 Limited Practitioners

4731-1-05 Scope of practice: massage therapy.

(A) Massage therapy is limited to the treatment of disorders of the human body by the manipulation of soft tissue through the systematic external application of massage techniques including touch, stroking, friction, vibration, percussion, kneading, stretching, compression, and passive joint movements within the normal physiologic range of motion; and adjunctive thereto, the external application of water, heat, cold, topical preparations, and mechanical devices.

Oklahoma

No laws at the time of this writing.

Oregon Board of Massage

748 Hawthorne Avenue NE
Salem, OR 97301
503-365-8657
Patty@oregonmassage.org
www.oregonmassage.org

Oregon Board of Massage Therapists

Oregon Revised Statutes (ORS) Chapter 687

5) "Massage" or "massage therapy" means the use on the human body of pressure, friction, stroking, tapping or kneading, vibration, or stretching by manual or mechanical means or gymnastics, with or without appliances such as vibrators, infrared heat, sun lamps, and external baths, and with or without lubricants such as salts, powders, liquids, or creams for the purpose of, but not limited to, maintaining good health and establishing and maintaining good physical condition.

Pennsylvania

Bureau of Professional and Occupational Affairs
PO Box 2649
Harrisburg, PA 17105
717-787-8503
www.dos.state.pa.us

Act 118, Section 3 definitions : "Massage therapy." The application of a system of structured touch, pressure, movement, holding and treatment of the soft tissue manifestations of the human body in which the primary intent is to enhance the health and well-being of the client without limitation, except as provided in this act.

"Section 14. Other professions. Nothing in this act shall be construed as preventing, restricting, or requiring licensure of any of the following activities":

"(6) The practice of an individual who uses touch to affect the energy systems, acupoints, qi meridians or channels of energy of the human body while engaged within the scope of practice of a profession with established standards and ethics."

Rhode Island Department of Health

Division of Professional Regulation
3 Capitol Hill, Room 410
Providence, RI 02908
401-222-2827
www.health.ri.gov/hsr/professions/massage

Rhode Island Department of Health: Rules and Regulations for Licensing Massage Therapists, Masseurs and Masseuses

Section 1.0 Definitions

1.9 "The practice of massage" shall be defined as engaging in applying a scientific system of activity to the muscular structure of the human body by means of stroking, kneading, tapping and vibrating with the hands or vibrators for the purpose of improving muscle tone and circulation.

South Carolina Division of Professionals

110 Center View
PO Box 11329
Columbia, SC 29210
803-896-4501
jonese@mail.llr.state.sc.us
www.llr.state.sc.us/POL/massagetherapy

South Carolina Code of Laws Title 40 - Professions and Occupations

CHAPTER 30.

MASSAGE/BODYWORK PRACTICE ACT

SECTION 40-30-30. Definitions :

S.C. Code of Laws Title 40 Chapter 30: Massage/bodywork Practice Act

8) "Massage/bodywork therapy" means the application of a system of structured touch of the superficial tissues of the human body with the hand, foot, arm, or elbow whether or not the structured touch is aided by hydrotherapy, thermal therapy, a massage device, human hands, or the application to the human body of an herbal preparation.

South Carolina Massage/Bodywork Therapy

INTERPRETATIONS OF THE MASSAGE PRACTICE ACT

C. In addition to the definitions provided in Section 40-1-20, as used in this chapter, unless the context indicates otherwise:

4. ...It is further defined by pressure, friction, stroking, rocking, kneading, percussion, or passive active stretching within the normal anatomical range of movement. Complementary methods including the external application of water, thermal therapy, hydrotherapy, lubricants, and other topical preparations, including but not limited to herbal remedies, body wraps, and salt scrubs.

D. Exemptions from Licensure

The Department considers exempt those persons engaging in a profession with established standards and ethics in which touch is limited to that which is essential for affecting the human energy system, provided that their services are not within the scope of practice of massage/bodywork therapy as defined. Further, their services cannot be designated or implied to be massage or massage/bodywork therapy as defined.

South Dakota Board of Massage Therapy

PO Box 1062
Sioux Falls, SD 57101-1062
605-271-7103
sdmtb.msp@midconetwork.com
www.state.sd.us/doh/massage

South Dakota Codified Laws Chapter 36-35:Massage Therapists

36-35-1. Definitions. Terms in this chapter mean:

(2) "Massage," the systematic mobilization of the soft tissues of the body through the application of hands or devices for the purposes of therapy, relaxation, or education through means which include:

(a) Pressure, friction, stroking, rocking, kneading, percussion, compression, or stretching;

(b) External application of water, heat, cold, lubricants, or other topical agents; or

(c) The use of devices that mimic or enhance actions done by hands;

Tennessee Massage Licensure Board

Cordell Hull Building, 1st floor
227 French Landing, Suite 300
Nashville, TN 37243
615-532-3202
800-778-4123
www.Tennessee.gov/health/Boards/Massage/index

Tennessee Annotated Codes: TENNESSEE MASSAGE LICENSURE BOARD

CHAPTER 0870-1 GENERAL RULES GOVERNING LICENSED MASSAGE THERAPISTS AND ESTABLISHMENTS

0870-1-.01 DEFINITIONS. As used in these rules, the following terms and acronyms shall have the following meaning ascribed to them:

(14) Massage/bodywork/somatic—The manipulation of the soft tissues of the body with the intention of positively affecting the health and wellbeing of the client.

Texas Department of State Health Services

Massage Therapy Licensing Program
1100 W. 49th Street
Austin TX 78756
massage@dshs.state.tx.us
www.dshs.state.tx.us/massage/default

Texas Administrative Code, Title 25 Health Services, Part 1: Department of State Health Services; Chapter 141: Massage Therapists; Subchapter A: The Department Rule Section 141.1. Definition:

(11) Massage therapy—The manipulation of soft tissue by hand or through a mechanical or electrical apparatus for the purpose of body massage. The term includes effleurage (stroking), petrissage (kneading), tapotement (percussion), compression, vibration, friction, nerve strokes, and Swedish gymnastics. Massage therapy may include the use of oil, lubricant, salt glows, heat lamps, hot and cold packs, or tub, shower, jacuzzi, sauna, steam or cabinet baths. Equivalent terms for massage therapy are massage, therapeutic massage, massage technology, myo-therapy, body massage, body rub, or any derivation of those terms. Massage therapy is a health care service when the massage is for therapeutic purposes. The terms "therapy" and "therapeutic" do not include diagnosis, the treatment of illness or disease, or any service or procedure for which a license to practice medicine, chiropractic, physical therapy, or podiatry is required by law. Massage therapy does not constitute the practice of chiropractic.

Utah Division of Occupational and Professional Licensing

Board of Massage Therapy
160 E. 300 South
Salt Lake City, UT 84111
801-530-6628
www.dopl.utah.gov/licensing/massage

MASSAGE THERAPY PRACTICE ACT

Part 1 - General Provisions

58-47b-102. Definitions:

(6) "Practice of massage therapy" means:

(a) the examination, assessment, and evaluation of the soft tissue structures of the body for the

purpose of devising a treatment plan to promote homeostasis;

(b) the systematic manual or mechanical manipulation of the soft tissue of the body for the

therapeutic purpose of:

(i) promoting the health and well-being of a client;

(ii) enhancing the circulation of the blood and lymph;

(iii) relaxing and lengthening muscles;

(iv) relieving pain;

(v) restoring metabolic balance; and

(vi) achieving homeostasis;

(c) the use of the hands or a mechanical or electrical apparatus in connection with this Subsection

(6);

(d) the use of rehabilitative procedures involving the soft tissue of the body;

(e) range of motion or movements without spinal adjustment as set forth in Section 58-73-102;

(f) oil rubs, heat lamps, salt glows, hot and cold packs, or tub, shower, steam, and cabinet baths;

(g) manual traction and stretching exercise;

(h) correction of muscular distortion by treatment of the soft tissues of the body;

(i) counseling, education, and other advisory services to reduce the incidence and severity of

physical disability, movement dysfunction, and pain;

(j) similar or related activities and modality techniques; and

(k) the practice described in this Subsection (6) on an animal to the extent permitted by:

(i) Subsection 58-28-307(12);

(ii) the provisions of this chapter; and

(iii) division rule.

(7) "Soft tissue" means the muscles and related connective tissue.

Vermont

As of January 1, 2007, the state of Vermont does not regulate massage therapy. However, regulation of massage therapy may occur at the local level. Please verify with your local health or licensing board regarding certification.

Virginia Board of Nursing

Department of Health Professions
9960 Mayland Drive, Suite 300
Henrico, VA 23233
804-367-4400
nursebd@dhpvirginia.gov
www.dhp.state.va.us

Regulations Governing the Certification of Massage Therapists, Virginia Board of Nursing, Title of Regulations: 18 VAC 90-50-10 et seq. Statutory Authority: Sections 54.1-2400 and Chapter 30 of Title 54.1 of the *Code of Virginia*

Revised Date: March 22, 2006 Part I. General Provisions.

18VAC90-50-10. Definitions :

"Massage therapy" means the treatment of soft tissues for therapeutic purposes by the application of massage and bodywork techniques based on the manipulation or application of pressure to the muscular structure or soft tissues of the human body. The terms "massage therapy" and "therapeutic massage" do not include the diagnosis or treatment of illness or disease or any service or procedure for which a license to practice medicine, nursing, chiropractic therapy, physical therapy, occupational therapy, acupuncture, or podiatry is required by law.

Washington State Department of Health

Massage Therapy Program
PO Box 47867
Olympia, WA 98504
360-236-4700
Hpqa.csc@doh.wa.gov
www.doh.wa.gov/massage/default

Revised Code of Washington

RCWs > Title 18 > Chapter 18.108 > Section 18.108.010

RCW 18.108.010 Definitions:

(2) "Massage" and "massage therapy" mean a health care service involving the external manipulation or pressure of soft tissue for therapeutic purposes. Massage therapy includes techniques such as tapping, compressions, friction, Swedish gymnastics or movements, gliding, kneading, shaking, and fascial or connective tissue stretching, with or without the aids of superficial heat, cold, water, lubricants, or salts. Massage therapy does not include diagnosis or attempts to adjust or manipulate any articulations of the body or spine or mobilization of these articulations by the use of a thrusting force, nor does it include genital manipulation.

State of West Virginia Massage Therapy Licensure Board

179 Summers Street, Suite 711
Charleston, WV 25301
304-558-1060
linda_lyter@verizon.net
www.wvmassage.org

State Laws

ARTICLE 37, MASSAGE THERAPISTS.

Section 30-37-2. Definitions:

c) "Massage therapy" means a health care service which is a scientific and skillful manipulation of soft tissue for therapeutic or remedial purposes, specifically for improving muscle tone, circulation, promoting health and physical well-being. Massage therapy includes massage, myotherapy, massotherapy, bodywork, bodywork therapy, or therapeutic massage including hydrotherapy, superficial hot and cold applications, vibration and topical applications or other therapies which involve manipulation of the muscle and connective tissue of the body, for the purpose of enhancing health, reducing stress, improving circulation, aiding muscle relaxation, increasing range of motion, or relieving neuromuscular pain. Massage therapy does not include diagnosis or service which requires a license to practice medicine or surgery, osteopathic medicine, chiropractic, or podiatry, and does not include service performed by nurses, occupational therapists, or physical therapists who act under their own professional license, certificate, or registration.

Wisconsin Department of Regulation and Licensing

Massage Therapy Board
1400 E. Washington Avenue
Madison, WI 53703
877-617-1565
DRLBoards@wisconsin.gov
www.dri.wi.gov

State of Wisconsin Department of Regulation & Licensing

Massage Therapist or Bodyworker

Administrative Code (Code Book)

A massage therapist or bodyworker is a person who engages in the science and healing art that uses manual actions to palpate and manipulate the soft tissue of the human body and includes determining whether massage therapy or bodywork is appropriate or contraindicated, or whether referral to another health care practitioner is appropriate.

Massage therapy or bodywork does not include making a medical diagnosis or instructing in or prescribing rehabilitative strengthening or conditioning exercises that are within the practice of physical therapy. An individual may practice massage therapy or bodywork without obtaining certification, but may not use certain titles without obtaining certification.

Wyoming

There are no licensing requirements for energy medicine at the time of this writing.

Massage licensing requirements vary depending upon location.

Australia

. . . .

Australian Capital Territory Department of Health

GPO Box 825

Canberra City ACT 2601

Australia

HealthACT@act.gov.au

www.health.act.gov.au

New South Wales Health

73 Miller Street

North Sydney NSW 2060

Australia

02 9391 9000

nswhealth@doh.health.nsw.gov.au

www.health.nsw.gov.au

Northern Territories Department of Health and Community Services

PO Box 40596

Casuarina NT 0811

Australia

08 8999 2400

Healthprofessions.ths@nt.gov.au

www.nt.gov.au/health/contact

Queensland
Office of Health Practitioner Registration Boards

GPO Box 2438

Brisbane QLD 4001

07 3225 2523

Australia

generalenquiries@healthregboards.qld.gov.au

www.healthregboards.qld.gov.au

South Australia Department of Health

PO Box 287

Rundle Mall

Adelaide SA 5000

Australia

(+61 8) 8226 6000

dhce@health.sa.gov.au

www.health.sa.gov.au

Tasmania
Department of Health and Human Services

GPO Box 125

Hobart TAS 7001

Australia

03 6233 3185

www.dhhs.tas.gov.au

Western Australia Department of Health

PO Box 8172

Perth Business Center

Perth WA 6849

Australia

(+61 8) 9222 4222

PRContact@health.wa.gov.au

www.health.wa.gov.au

Canada

Canadian Examining Board of Health Care Practitioners, Inc

658 Danforth Avenue, Suite 204

Toronto ON M4J 5B9

Canada

416-466-9755

Celebinc@rogers.com

www.canadianexaminingboard.com

Each municipality writes its own by-laws. Usually each energy medicine discipline or energy modality has a member on the board writing the by-law. For many areas, the energy medicine discipline must get approval from the Canadian Examining Board before it can be accepted by a local government. Without that recognition and acceptance, it may be very difficult to get a license to practice.

Canadian Massage Therapist Alliance
365 Bloor Street E., Suite 1807
Toronto ON M4W 3L4
Canada
416-968-2149
www.cmta.ca

Massage Therapist Association of Saskatchewan
PO Box 7841
Saskatoon SK S7K 4R5
306-384-7077
www.saskmassagetherapy.com

Massage Therapists' Association of British Columbia
Suite 180 Airport Square
1200 – W. 73rd Avenue
Vancouver BC V6P 6G5
Canada
888-413-4467
www.massagetherapy.bc.ca

Massage Therapists' Association of Nova Scotia
PO Box 9410, station A
Halifax NS B3K 5S3
Canada
902-429-2190
www.mtans.com

Massage Therapy Association of Alberta
Box 24031 RPO Plaza Center
Red Deer AB T4N 6X6
Canada
888-848-6822
info@mtaalberta.com
www.mtaalberta.com

Massage Therapy Association of Manitoba
611-428 Portage Avenue
Winnipeg MB R3C 0B2
Canada
204-927-7979
info@mtam.mb.ca
www.mtam.mb.ca

New Brunswick Massotherapy Association
PO Box 21009
Fredericton NB E3B 7A3
Canada
506-465-0003
www.nbma-amnb.ca

Newfoundland and Labrador Massage Therapists' Association
PO Box 23212 Churchill Square
St. John's NL A1B 4J9
Canada
709-747-7767
nlmta@nlmta.ca
www.nlmta.ca

Ontario Massage Therapist Association
2943 B Bloor Street W.
Etobicoke, ON M8X 1B3
Canada
800-668-2022
info@omta.com
www.omta.com

Prince Edward Island Massage Therapy Association
PO Box 1882
Charlottetown PE C1A 7N5
Canada
866-566-1955
president@peimta.com
www.peimta.com

Germany

Bundesministerium für Gesundheit
Minister of Health
11055 Berlin
+49 18 88 441-0
info@bmg.bund.de
www.bmg.bund.de

Energy medicine practitioners must take a special exam from a state-licensed school that provides them with a certificate showing they have studied foot reflex, back massage, Dorn and Breuss, and energy therapy. With that they can open a private practice anywhere.

India

Department of Ayuveda, Yoga & Naturopathy, Unani, Siddha, and Homeopathy
Ministry of Health & Family Welfare, Government of India
Red Cross Building, Red Cross Road
New Delhi India 110001
www.indiamedicine.nic.in

Republic of Ireland

Irish Department of Health
Customer Service Unit
Hawkins House
Dublin 2 Ireland
+353 1 635 3000
info@health.gov.ie
www.dohc.ie/public/customer_service

Ireland does not require licensing of energy healers at the time of this writing.

Italy

Ministero della Salute
Ministry of Health
Lungotevere Ripo 1
00153 Roma
06.5994.1
www.ministerosalute.it

Japan

Ministry of Health, Labor and Welfare
1-2-2 Kasumigaseki Chiyoda
Tokyo 100-8916 Japan
03-5253-1111
admin@mhlw.go.jp
www.mhlw.go.jp

New Zealand

Ministry of Health
Box 5013
Wellington
New Zealand
+64 04 496 2000
emailmoh@moh.govt.nz
www.moh.govt.nz

South Africa

South Africa Department of Health
bhengu@health.gov.za
www.doh.gov.za

United Kingdom

· ·

At the time of this writing there were no licensing requirements for energy healers in any of the United Kingdom countries.

British Department of Health

Richmond House

79 Whitehall

London SW1A 2NS

UK

(02072) 104850

Dhmail@dh.gsi.gov.uk

www.dh.gov.uk

Northern Ireland Department of Health, Social Services and Public Safety

Castle Buildings

Stormont Estates

Belfast BT4 3SJ

Northern Ireland

(92890) 765602

communitypharmacy@dhsspsni.gov.uk

www.dhsspsni.gov.uk

Scottish Executive Health Department

Health Department

St. Andrew's House

Regent Road

Edinburgh

EH1 3DG

UK

www.sehd.scot.nhs.uk

Welsh Health and Social Care Department

Cathays Park (1)

Cardiff

CF10 3NQ

(02920) 68 1239

health.enquiries@wales.gsi.gov.uk

www.wales.gov.uk

Linnie may be contacted through the

International Association for Energy Healers

PO Box 1904

Tualatin, OR 97062

linnie@iafeh.com

www.iafeh.com